Librarianship and
Information Work Worldwide
1995

Librarianship and Information Work Worldwide 1995

General Editor
Maurice Line

Editors
Graham Mackenzie
John Feather

London • Melbourne • Munich • New Jersey

© 1996 Bowker-Saur, a division of Reed Elsevier (UK) Ltd
All rights reserved. No part of this publication may be reproduced or transmitted in any form or by any means (including photocopying and recording) without the written permission of the copyright holder except in accordance with the provisions of the Copyright, Designs and Patents Act 1988 or under the terms of a licence issued by the Copyright Licensing Agency, 90 Tottenham Court Road, London W1P 9HE. The written permission of the copyright holder must also be obtained before any part of this publication is stored in a retrieval system of any nature. Applications for the copyright holder's written permission to reproduce, transmit or store in a retrieval system any part of this publication should be addressed to the publisher.

Warning: The doing of any unauthorized act in relation to a copyright work may result in both a civil claim for damages and criminal prosecution.

Published by Bowker-Saur
Maypole House, Maypole Road
East Grinstead, West Sussex RH19 1HU, UK
Tel: +44 (0) 1342 330100 Fax: +44 (0) 1342 330191
E-mail: lis@bowker-saur.co.uk
Internet Website: http://www.bowker-saur.co.uk/service/

Bowker-Saur is part of REED REFERENCE PUBLISHING

ISBN 1-85739-112-8

Cover design by John Cole
Typeset by The Castlefield Press, Kettering, Northants
Printed on acid-free paper
Printed and bound in Great Britain by Bell & Bain Ltd, Glasgow

Contents

Foreword		xv
1.	Library and information services in context *William Y. Arms*	1
2.	National libraries *Eric Wainwright and Viola Bátonyi*	15
3.	Public libraries *Bob Usherwood*	77
4.	Academic libraries *Janet Wilkinson*	99
5.	Parliamentary libraries *Ernst Kohl*	133
6.	Bibliographic control and access *Giles Martin*	157
7.	Libraries in Western Europe: a bird's-eye view *Giuseppe Vitiello*	187
8.	Librarianship and information work in Central and Eastern Europe *Péter Szántó and Tibor Futala*	203
9.	Librarianship and information work in Southeast Asia *Mark Hepworth and Michael Cheng*	233
10.	Document supply *Peter Johan Lor*	259
11.	Information technology *Alan Poulter*	299
12.	Management *Patricia Layzell Ward*	321
Epilogue *Graham Mackenzie*		349
Subject Index		353
Author Index		359

About the editors

Maurice B. Line is a consultant specializing in strategic planning, staff development and the management of change. He retired in 1988 as Director-General, Science Technology and Industry, of the British Library. Before that he worked in five university libraries. He is a Professor Associate at Sheffield University. He has honorary doctorates from Heriot-Watt and Southampton Universities, and a fellowship from Birmingham Polytechnic. He was President of the UK Library Association in 1990, and was awarded the IFLA Medal in the same year. He has travelled widely on professional work. He edits *Alexandria* and has written over ten books and 300 articles and papers, covering a wide variety of topics from bibliometrics to library management; translations have appeared in 19 languages.

Graham Mackenzie read Classics at Glasgow. He was the founding Librarian at the University of Lancaster in 1963, establishing its Library Research Unit in 1967, and he was Librarian of the University of St Andrews from 1976 until he retired in 1989. A member of the Editorial Board of the *Journal of Documentation* since 1965, he has published widely, and retains a long-standing interest in consultancy work.

John Feather is Professor of Information and Library Studies, and Dean of the School of Education and Humanities, at Loughborough University of Technology. He has experience in both publishing and librarianship, and has travelled extensively throughout the world as a consultant and teacher. His recent publications include *Preservation and the management of library collections* (1991) and *The information society* (1994), as well as many journal articles. He has wide-ranging interests in the library and information field, and in education and training for information work.

About the contributors

William Yeo Arms is a member of the Corporation for National Research Initiatives (CNRI). He is responsible for advanced work in library systems including fundamental architectural developments and electronic copyright management systems for the Library of Congress. He has degrees from Oxford University, the London School of Economics, the University of Sussex and Dartmouth College, and he has been a pioneer in applying advanced computing to academic and scholary activities, notably educational computing, computer networking and digital libraries. He has been a constant advisor to major libraries about computing and has had consulting assignments to The British Library and the J. Paul Getty Trust.

Viola Bátonyi is Head of the Public Relations and Cultural Affairs Office of the National Széchényi Library, Budapest, Hungary. He graduated from the School of Library Science, Eötvös Loránd University, Budapest, and studied two semesters at Kent University, Ohio, USA, on a Fulbright Scholarship. He is International Secretary of the Association of Hungarian Librarians, and a member of the Round Table for the Management of Library Associations (IFLA RIMLA).

Michael Cheng completed his studies in Library Science at the University of British Columbia after obtaining a science degree from the University of Singapore. He was Head of the Medical Library at the National University of Singapore before his present appointment as Deputy Librarian. He has served in the Library Association of Singapore in various capacities including Vice-President, and Chairman of the Publications Committee. He is currently the editor of the association's two journals, *Singapore Libraries* (an annual) and *Singapore Libraries Bulletin* (a quarterly), and is the editor of *Directory of Libraries in Singapore*.

Tibor Futala is the retired director of the Hungarian Central Technical Library, Budapest, and is currently engaged in minority research. He graduated from the

Eötvös Loránd University, faculty of Library Science and Hungarian Language, in 1953 and acquired his professional experience at the Central Library of the Kossuth Lajos University, Debrecen, and then at the National Széchényi Library, Budapest, mainly in the field of processing and bibliography. From 1962 he worked for the Ministry of Education, Department of Libraries, and in 1979 he was nominated Director of the Hungarian Central Technical Library from where he retired in 1989. His studies and articles on varying subjects number more than 200, and in addition to Hungarian special journals, he has published in Serbian, Slovakian and Russian periodicals.

Mark Hepworth qualified initially in Social Anthropology and African History at the School of Oriental and African Studies, London. After a number of different occupations, including starting a second-hand and antiquarian book business, he took his MSc in Information Studies at Sheffield University. Thereafter, he worked in electronic publishing, namely customer support and, later, in strategic planning and product development. He now holds an appointment as a Senior Lecturer in Information Studies at the Nanyang Technological University, Singapore.

Ernst Kohl was the Chairman of the IFLA Section of Parliamentary Libraries from 1989 to 1993, and Vice-Chairman of the Parliamentary Libraries Working Group of the European Centre for Parliamentary Research and Documentation from 1989 to 1993. After graduating in African history at the University of Kiel, he became a professional librarian at the Bavarian State Library. After two years as lecturer a the Bavarian Civil Service College, he was appointed project manager of the Library Network of the Supreme Federal Authorities in Bonn in 1980. Having been head of the German Bundestag Library from 1986 to 1990, he is now in charge of the Bundestag's Administrative Library.

Peter Johan Lor held positions in academic and research libraries and taught in university departments of library and information science before becoming Director of the State Library, Pretoria, South Africa, in 1992. Many of his publications are concerned with interlending, resource sharing and access to information resources in Southern Africa. He holds a DPhil degree from the University of Pretoria.

Giles Martin has been a cataloguer at the University of Newcastle, Australia, since 1975. He is currently in charge of the Quality Control Section, and is responsible for authority control, cataloguing policy and training of cataloguers. In 1993 he was appointed as the first Australian member of the Dewey Decimal Classification Editorial Policy Committee.

Alan Poulter is lecturer in the Department of Information and Library Studies at Loughborough University of Technology. He has been a cataloguer with The British

Library, Deputy Systems Manager at the Science Museum Library in London and a Senior Lecturer at Leeds Metropolitan University. He teaches and researches widely on advanced information technology applications, notably multimedia, hypermedia, Internet and virtual reality.

Péter Szántó holds Master's degrees in Applied and Mathematical Linguistics and in Russian Language and Literature from the Eötvös Loránd University, Hungary, and in Library Science from the Kent State University, USA. He has been the Director of the Hungarian Technical Library, part of the National Technical Information Centre and Library (OMIKK), Budapest, since 1989. Previous posts include Head of the Department for Coordination and International Affairs at OMIKK from 1976–1988, and as a System Analyst at a computer centre from 1970–1976. He represents OMIKK in IFLA, in UNIDO/INTIB, is a member of FID/II and is editor-in-chief of the scientific and technical information periodical, *Tudományos és Müszaki Tájékoztatás*.

Bob Usherwood is a Senior Lecturer at Sheffield University's Department of Information Studies. Before joining the Department he was Chief Librarian in the London Borough of Lambeth. He has also worked for Devon County Libraries, the London Boroughs of Havering and Sutton, and the Polytechnic of North London. He obtained his Doctorate researching the role of elected members in the operation of public library services. He was Chairperson of the Library Association's Working Party on Ethics which led to the LA adopting a Code of Professional Conduct in 1983. He was presented with an Honorary Fellowship of the Library Association in 1992 and made a Fellow of the Institute of Information Scientists in 1993. He is also a member of the ASLIB consultancy appointed by the then Heritage Minister, Peter Brooke, to review the public library service in Great Britain. His publications include *The visible library* (1981), *The public library as public knowledge* (1989) and *Public library politics* (1993).

Giuseppe Vitiello is in charge of the 'Books, reading, translation and archives' programme of the Council of Europe. He has worked previously for the National Library of Florence, where he was Assistant to the Director and Head of the R&D Department. From 1989 to 1991 he worked for DG XIII – European Commission as expert for the Libraries Programme. He has published extensively on topics such as national libraries, bibliographic services, legal deposit and comparative librarianship.

Eric Wainwright is Deputy Director-General at the National Library of Australia in Canberra. After graduating from Cambridge University and the College of Librarianship in Wales, he worked in a number of universities in the UK and Australia including his previous position as University Librarian at the University of Adelaide.

About the contributors xi

Patricia Layzell Ward was appointed as Professor and Head of the Department of Information and Library Studies at the University of Wales at Aberystwyth in 1994, having enjoyed 11 years in a similar post at Curtin University of Technology, Perth, Western Australia. Previous posts include Director of the Centre for Library and Information Management at Loughborough University of Technology, teaching and research at several UK universities, and experience of professional practice in special libraries, information services and public libraries. She is a Fellow of the Institute of Management and of the Library Association, and holds a Master's and Doctoral degree from University College London.

Janet Wilkinson was appointed Sub-Librarian for Management and External Services at the British Library of Political and Economic Science at the London School of Economics in 1993. Since graduating in history from the University of Newcastle-upon-Tyne, she has worked at the College of St. Paul and St. Mary and Cambridgeshire College of Arts and Technology, before becoming Business School Librarian in 1988, then Sub-Librarian for Academic Services at the University of Hertfordshire in 1990. She became Secretary of the University, College and Research Section of the Library Association in 1995 and has published in the areas of fund-raising and income generation.

Editorial advisory board

A O Banjo
Director, Library and Documentation Services, Nigerian Institute of International Affairs, Kofo Abayomi Road, Victoria Island, GPO Box 1727, Lagos, Nigeria

Melvyn Barnes
Director of Libraries and Art Galleries, Corporation of London, Guildhall Library, Aldermanbury, London EC2P 2EJ, UK

Dr Virginia Betancourt Valverde
Director, Biblioteca Nacional de Venezuela, Biblioteca Nacional M-392, Jet Cargo International, PO Box 020010, Miami FL 33102-0010, USA. E-mail: vbetanc@dino.conicit.ve

Brett Butler
Director of Development, Memex Research Institute, California State University, 101 Shell Road, #S-44, Watsonville CA 95076, USA

Hilmi Celik
Director, Library and Documentation Centre, Grand National Assembly of Turkey, Kütüphane Müdürü, Ankara, Turkey

Marc Chauveinc
Inspection Générale des Bibliothèques, Ministère de l'Enseignement Supérieur et de la Recherche, 3-5 Boulevard Pasteur, 75015 Paris, France

Katarzyna Diehl
Biblioteka Narodowa, Al. Niepodlegosci 213, 00-973 Warszawa, Poland

Dr Richard Dougherty
President, Dougherty and Associates, PO Box 8330, Ann Arbor MI 48107, USA. E-mail: 72263.1222@CompuServe.com

Dr Miriam Drake
Director, Price Gilbert Memorial Library, Georgia Institute of Technology, Atlanta GA 30332, USA

Peter Durey
Librarian, University of Auckland, Private Bag, Auckland, New Zealand. E-mail: pb.durey@auckland.ac.nz

Dr Rudolf Frankenberger
Bibliothekar, Universitätsbibliothek, Universitätsstraße 22, 8900 Augsburg, Germany

Mariam Abdul Kadir
Director General, National Library of Malaysia, 232 Jalan Tun Razak, 50572 Kuala Lumpur, Malaysia

Professor Michael Koenig
Dean, Graduate School of Library and Information Science, Rosary College, River Forest IL 60305, USA

Stanley Made
Librarian, University of Zimbabwe, PO Box MP 45, Mt Pleasant, Harare, Zimbabwe

Professor Tamiko Matsumura
University of Library and Information Science, 2 Kasuga 1-chome, Tsukuba-shi, Ibaraki-ken 305, Japan

Vinyet Panyella
Manager, Biblioteca de Catalunya, Hospital 56, 08001 Barcelona, Catalonia, Spain

Stephan Roman
Assistant Director, Libraries, Books and Information Division, British Council, Medlock Street, Manchester M15 4AA, UK

Ursula Schadlich
Coordinadora de Biblioteca, Biblioteca Nacional de Chile, Av. Libertador B. O'Higgins 651, Santiago de Chile 1400, Chile

Piet Schoots
Former Director, Rotterdam City Library, Vijverlaan 508, 2925 VL, Krimpen a/d Ijssel, Netherlands

Dr Marianne Scott
National Librarian, National Library of Canada, 395 Wellington Street, Ottawa K1A 0N4, Canada. E-mail: mfs@nlo.nlc-bnc.ca

Péter Szántó
Director, Hungarian Central Technical Library, Budapest VIII, Muzeum U. 17, H-1428 Budapest, Pf.2, Hungary

Colin Steele
University Librarian, Australian National University, Canberra ACT 0200, Australia. E-mail: c.steele@info.anu.edu.au

Dr John Willemse
Chief Director, Dept of Library Services, University of South Africa, PO Box 392, Pretoria, South Africa. E-mail: willej@alpha.unisa.ac.za

Ms Hellevi Yrjölä
Chief Librarian, Central Statistical Office of Finland, PO Box 504, Annakatu 44, SF-00101 Helsinki, Finland

Foreword

This is the fifth volume of *Librarianship and Information Work Worldwide* to make its appearance. We hope it is now well on the way to becoming a permanent feature of the literature of librarianship and information work. It is evident from the comments that we have received, as well as from the reviews that have appeared, that *LIWW* fulfils a real need.

It may be useful at this stage to remind readers of the nature and purpose of *LIWW*. It aims to give a picture of what is happening in librarianship and information work all over the world. This is a very ambitious aim, which we recognize can never be fully met. We do not even try to meet it in every volume, since every topic cannot possibly be included; rather, we hope that volumes of *LIWW* over a period of five or six years should give fair coverage of events, developments and trends. Authors are asked to cover not only printed literature (though this will be their main source) but to supplement this as far as they can by unpublished material, electronic bulletins and news, personal knowledge and contacts with others, especially the members of our Editorial Advisory Board. It will be evident that membership of this is not ornamental, as with most journals, but that some work is expected of them – and this is an appropriate place to thank members warmly for their contribution to making *LIWW* a success.

We have pursued a policy of having some regular chapters, for example on different types of library, mixed with chapters on a variety of subjects, which change from year to year. Authors of these latter chapters are asked to cover the last two or three years, rather than just the previous year, to provide more complete coverage. We intend to continue this practice, enabling us to keep up with changing interests and topics, and readers are invited to make suggestions for topics that might be dealt with in future volumes. More recently, we have included chapters on different regions of the world, which are of interest in themselves and may also do something to improve coverage of less developed countries.

One of the two main – almost the only – criticisms made by reviewers of the first two or three volumes of *LIWW* is that most contributors came from the UK. Readers will, I hope, have noticed that we have managed to achieve a wider distribution of authors for this and the previous volume. We hope to maintain this, but it would be very helpful if we could have suggestions for potential authors – or, better still, if potential authors would volunteer themselves. Writing reviews is hard work, as many authors have commented, but they have also said how much they learn in the process.

The other subject of criticism, the relatively poor coverage of less developed countries, proves more intractable. Even if we had more contributors from the Third World, and even if they had access to current published literature, it is very unlikely that they could cover developments much beyond their own countries. The literature they publish is, with some exceptions such as India and Nigeria, relatively small, and information would have to be gained by other means such as personal contact and correspondence. Practical suggestions as to how we could achieve better coverage would be very welcome. (It is worth noting that some European Union countries such as Italy and Greece are also very poorly represented).

One review criticized *LIWW* for the inconsistent lengths of the chapters and reference lists. Authors are given a good deal of freedom, within broad limits, and they are also encouraged to give a personal slant to their writing, so that their chapters are not mere recitations of references, a practice we intend to continue. But in any case, a Procrustean bed would be totally inappropriate; there is far more literature on some subjects than on others, and some topics demand much fuller treatment.

Two reviewers commented critically on the absence of a chapter on special libraries in the last volume. This is partly because of the policy stated in the previous paragraph, but the main reason is that 'special libraries' constitute a very heterogeneous category, and we decided it made little sense to try to cover them all in one chapter. This year we have a chapter on one type of 'special library' – parliamentary libraries. We hope to cover other types in subsequent years.

Finally, the publishers have decided to produce *LIWW* in a cheaper, but still durable, format, in the belief that it should reach a larger number of libraries and individuals. This is a hope that we the editors of course wholeheartedly share.

Maurice B. Line
September 1995

Library and information services in context

1

William Y. Arms

Introduction

A year dominated by computing

Every year, *Library and Information Work Worldwide* has an introductory chapter. It provides a context for the rest of the volume, as seen from one writer's perspective. This year, the introduction concentrates almost exclusively on technology and its impact on libraries. Changes induced by computers and communications networks are having an enormous impact on libraries, publishers and information services. During 1993 and 1994, the pace of change accelerated; the next few years look to be hectic.

Before discussing some highlights of the year, it is interesting to look briefly at the long-term context. When computing first began to have an impact on libraries, about 25 years ago, several barriers reduced its effectiveness. These included the high cost of computers, the difficulty of using them, the lack of networks, and the problem that all library information was on paper not in digital formats. For example, in the early 1970s, a systems study for computing in the British Library devoted considerable attention to low-cost ways of storing catalogue data (Department of Education and Science, 1972). Not surprisingly, the earliest online library systems were in fields where either the quantity of data stored was small or the value of efficient searching was very high. These systems included online catalogues such as OCLC, retrieval systems such as the Lockheed system, which became Dialog, and legal information, notably Lexis. In each case, the information was simple text, with minimal formatting and no pictures.

Twenty-five years have steadily eroded these technical barriers. The price of disc stores has fallen by 30% annually, so that storing information on computer is becoming cheaper than storing paper in a library. Personal computers, with their large displays and modern user interfaces, are much easier to use than their predecessors. High-speed networks now link many scholars and professionals around the world (though universal access remains a distant dream). Much of this technology is still rough and ready, and it is unlikely that computers will ever match the convenience of books for general reading, but low-cost computing has stimulated an explosion of online information services. Some of these have already become an integral part of research and scholarship.

The World Wide Web and Mosaic

Recent developments

The most important development in libraries for many years has been the emergence of the World Wide Web as an international source of online information. Despite lacking key features that will be in a full electronic library, the Web appears to be the basis for the online library of the future.

The World Wide Web was developed by Tim Berners-Lee and colleagues at CERN in Geneva. They have published articles about their work (Berners-Lee *et al.*, 1992), but the best reference to the Web is a pointer to online information (CERN, 1995). The Web has been in existence for several years, but lacked a really good user interface. In 1993, Marc Andreessen, Eric Bina and colleagues at the National Center for Supercomputing Applications at the University of Illinois introduced Mosaic, a superb user interface for the Web. There are published descriptions of Mosaic, but the authoritative information is online (National Center, 1994).

In essence, the World Wide Web is very simple. Organizations and individuals from around the world mount collections of information on their own computers, attached to the Internet. Anybody who has a personal computer connected to the Internet can use Mosaic to read this information. The Web provides three main building blocks to organize and retrieve these collections. The first is a universal resource locator (URL), which identifies how to retrieve information from any computer on the Internet. The second is a hypertext mark-up language (HTML) to embed links in a document which refer to other documents or elements of documents, such as images. The third is a simple hypertext transfer protocol (HTTP), which is used to get a file from another computer. One of Mosaic's strengths is that, in addition to these three building blocks, it supports older methods of retrieving information across the Internet. It also provides ways to display various formats, notably colour images. Using these simple tools, the World Wide Web has become a vast collection of publicly accessible information.

The dominant question facing academic libraries and information services today is how the dynamic growth of the Web and other online services fits with existing library services. Publishers are striving for ways to generate revenue from this new world, while protecting intellectual property. Computer scientists are doing research to overcome technical limitations of the present system. Lawyers are searching for a new legal framework. Meanwhile, individual authors and readers frequently mount their own information on the Web, bypassing traditional publishing. Some of these themes are discussed later in this chapter.

Online collections for library research

People who are unfamiliar with the online collections often make derogatory statements about the information on the Internet. The two most common complaints are that the information is of poor quality and that it is impossible to find it. A few years ago, both complaints were true, but the situation has changed dramatically.

As an example, consider the field of librarianship and library research. Several well managed collections provide current information on library issues. They include the Bulletin Board for Libraries (BUBL) at the University of Bath in England (Bulletin, 1995) and the collection operated by the Coalition for Networked Information (1995) in the USA. These collections are open to the whole world. In recent years, computer scientists have become important contributors to library research and much new material is being published online in collections of computer science reports. One of the most important of these is the archive of the Internet Engineering Task Force (IETF) (Internet, 1995). The IETF is the protocol engineering and development arm of the Internet and provides extensive information online. Most of the material is not available in print. Two important technical collections, which are maintained online, are the World Wide Web Consortium at MIT (World Wide Web Consortium, 1995) and the National Center for Supercomputing Applications at the University of Illinois.

Since much of the material in these online collections is not available in print, any active researcher in librarianship and information services must expect to use them. This does not mean that conventional libraries are unimportant, but their use has changed. Many researchers use libraries for works of reference, background information and historical archives. Secondary information services, particularly those that are online, are of great importance. However, for current information and active research, the Internet with its online collections has become the working library.

References to the literature of librarianship and information services

Every year, the introductory chapter to *Library and Information Work Worldwide* contains numerous references to the recent literature of the field. In the past, most of these references have been to articles in library journals and associated publications. This year, many of the references are to material that has not yet been published formally and exists only in online collections. This creates a problem, since, as yet, there is no good way to cite online information.

What reference should an author provide to online material? At present, the custom is to use the World Wide Web's URLs. This introduction follows the same convention. Where there are good printed references, they are given, but in many cases the best reference is a URL and that is the citation given. However, URLs are ugly to look at and cannot be depended on for the long term, since they specify where an item is physically stored, which can change without notice. How to refer to online information is an active topic of research; hopefully, it will be resolved during 1995.

Libraries and change

Change and people

Authors, readers, libraries, publishers and information services are adopting new technology with remarkable speed. However, change brings problems, some of them potentially serious. The central issue for libraries today is how to respond to technical change. Inevitably, the pace of change has differed widely among organizations and disciplines. Some corporate libraries, notably those of leading drug companies, are already spending more than half their acquisition budgets on electronic materials and services. At the other extreme, for the foreseeable future, the great humanities libraries will revolve around their collections of printed material.

Most people have no wish to spend time learning new ways of carrying out their daily work, unless they see great benefits. Yet people who do not make the effort to understand the new technology can get badly left behind. This is sometimes called the generation gap, but the name is a misnomer, since people of all ages can be receptive to new ideas. It is a challenge to libraries. Every library is likely to have some patrons who wish to use the most technically advanced systems (even when not appropriate) and other patrons who demand traditional services (even when the new ones are superior).

The education of librarians is a related challenge. The changes in libraries and information services demand new skills from everybody involved. Already, mid-career librarians are finding that their opportunities are limited unless they are familiar with computing. When senior people do not use or understand the new methods, key decisions are being made by people who lack the necessary background. This is more than an issue of retraining. Training is important, but only replaces one set of static skills with another. Modern librarians must develop awareness of the changes that are happening around them, inquisitiveness to discover new ideas and organizational flexibility.

The intellectual excitement that technology brings to libraries is a great opportunity for a new generation of library schools. In the past, library schools have never had the academic prestige of other professional schools, such as law, medicine, engineering and business. They have often been small, with underfunded research programmes. Digital libraries provide an opportunity for library schools to carry out difficult and visible research. Unfortunately, as yet, while universities are responsible for much of the research that is reshaping libraries, most is happening outside the library schools.

Universities in the USA have responded to this opportunity in various ways. The most disappointing was Columbia University, which simply closed down its library school. The University of California at Berkeley is much more exciting. In 1993, the university came close to following Columbia and closing its library school. However, after a considerable outcry, the university accepted the recommendations of a university-wide committee (University of California, 1993). This committee recommended a rejuvenated school, with a heavy emphasis on advanced research and a new professional Master's programme. In looking to the new world of librarianship, the committee explicitly rejected the traditional library curriculum. Their report states: 'The degree to be awarded by this program will be substantially different from the current MLIS degree, reflecting the broader mission of the new School'. The university then set out to recruit an outstanding candidate to be dean of the new school.

While the library profession is adapting to the new technology, the intellectual excitement is bringing new talent into the field. Traditionally, some heads of major research libraries are distinguished scholars, rather than librarians. We are now seeing an influx of talent into libraries at all levels. For example, in 1992, the library school at the University of Michigan appointed Dan Atkins, a computer scientist and engineer, as dean. Under his leadership, the school is melding the traditional approach of a strong library school with the research methodology and broad fund-raising of big science.

Library buildings

While digital libraries and information services are the focus of research and development around the world, for many libraries the biggest problem is the perennial lack of space. For example, in December 1993, the Funding Councils for higher education in the UK released a report on university libraries, known as the Follett Report (Joint, 1993). This report covers essentially all university libraries in Britain. In terms of money, the biggest recommendation from the Follett Committee was the need for a major building programme. This need is especially acute in Britain, because the numbers of students at most universities have grown sharply and much of the space is required to provide study space on campus.

The problem is to know what will make a good library building in future years. A recent British government report on the new British Library building in St. Pancras shows the problems that happen without good planning (House of Commons, 1994). Library buildings typically last at least 50 years, but nobody can anticipate what an academic library will look like even a few years from now. Therefore the emphasis in new library buildings is on flexibility. Since modern library buildings must anticipate communication needs that are only glimpsed today, general purpose network wiring and generous electrical supplies must be led to all spaces. Yet the same structures must be suitable for traditional stacks.

Two recently completed buildings are the new libraries at the University of Tilburg in the Netherlands and at Indiana University-Purdue University at Indianapolis in the USA (Burrow and Lewis, 1994). The philosophies behind these two buildings are remarkably similar. Both continue the traditional role of a library as providing stacks for printed materials, places for faculty and students to study, and offices for staff. Both take an integrated approach to computing. They provide large numbers of personal computers, specially configured to give access to applications and sources of information.

This approach of providing a standard computing environment for all patrons in a library has considerable advantages for training and support. The disadvantage is that patrons are likely to find different computing tools in the library from those in the rest of their work. The plans for rebuilding the Harvard Law Library are based on a very different concept. The plans make no assumptions about the types of computing that patrons will prefer. They assume that patrons will bring their own computers; the library will provide electrical power and communication jacks in all study areas.

Intellectual preservation of information

The preservation and conservation of electronic materials constitute a fascinating new area. Research libraries have traditionally kept their collections for ever. Despite the deprivations of theft, acidic paper and catastrophes, both natural and man-made, printed materials have survived fairly well in libraries. The potential for long-term preservation of electronic materials is even better, but achieving this potential is not easy. Partly, the problems are technical. There is no value in a library storing electronic media if 20 years later all devices that read that medium have disappeared. Partly, the problems are organizational. If a library relies on access from a commercial supplier, such as Lexis, what happens if that supplier withdraws the material from its service? Worse still, what happens if the supplier goes bankrupt?

Over the past year, great progress has been made in understanding these problems of intellectual preservation of information. An excellent overview is a report written for the (US) Commission on Preservation and Access (Graham, 1994). This report stresses the challenges in preserving the intellectual content of material over time while the technology it is stored on changes. The paper has a simple description of digital signatures, which ensure that an item has not been altered, and digital time stamps, which put a secure date on an item. One of the first places seeking to implement these ideas is the Library of Congress. The library has been working with Robert Kahn and others to develop a secure repository for the legal deposit of copyrighted information. Another study, led by Bearman (1994), looks at digital information from the viewpoint of those who need secure long-term evidence, such as archives, accounting records, prior art for patents and so forth.

Less technically advanced communities

This chapter has concentrated on the most technically advanced communities, notably in the USA and Europe. Libraries serve an enormous variety of communities across the world. Some find technology accessible and attractive, but others find it a barrier.

One problem is access. The supply of books and journals to developing countries has long been a problem, but no special equipment or training is needed to use those printed materials that can be obtained. Online information requires computers and networks. Most scholars in western universities and research organizations have access to such facilities. For them, the emergence of the Internet as a working library is breaking down barriers by making the working literature available to everybody. Unhappily, not everybody belongs to one of these fortunate organizations. Even in Europe and the USA, the networks do not yet reach all independent scholars and the broad array of people who depend on public libraries.

In other parts of the world, the situation is much worse. Many countries of the world have no network, or have a network that is confined to the fortunate few. However, although personal computers are often expensive, they are widely available. Many of the information sources that are online become available later on CD-ROMs. Many libraries in remote parts of the world find that it is easier to build up collections of material on CD-ROM than to acquire traditional printed journals.

The humanities

Humanities scholars form another community that at times has seen computing as an unwelcome distraction. The raw material of the humanities is printed material or physical artefacts, and most humanities scholars have more interest in books than in technology. Since the driving force in electronic libraries and information services has come from the scientific and technical fields, quite basic needs of other disciplines, such as character sets beyond English, have often been ignored. The humanities have been in danger of being left behind, but a new generation of humanities scholars is embracing computing and fortunately they have friends. In the USA, the Getty Art History Information Program, the Coalition for Networked Information and the American Council of Learned Societies have launched a national initiative to ensure that the humanities and arts have their proper place on the networks (Getty, 1994).

Publishers and information services

Motivation

Most of the development of online collections has been independent of established publishers. Much of the impetus came from scholars distributing their own work directly. While commercial publishing on CD-ROM has developed into an important part of the industry, little regularly published material has been distributed online. Publishers could not make a business case for online publishing and feared that, if materials were available online, sales of the same materials in print would suffer. Experience to date suggests that such substitution is small scale, if it occurs at all (Arms, 1993). The big substitution is happening at a macro level. During the past decade, libraries expanded their purchases of online information services, CD-ROMs and other forms of electronic information much more rapidly than their print budgets. Print publications are competing for a declining portion of essentially static – in some cases declining – library budgets.

Today, almost every academic publisher has some experiment in online information. As is well known, journal publishing is in the grip of a price spiral with flat or declining circulation. In the past decade, publishers have used new technology to reduce production costs, thus mitigating some of the problems of declining circulation, but these savings are becoming exhausted. They realize that, if they want their business to grow or even sustain its current level, they need to have products for the expanding online market. Electronic information is seen as a promising growth market.

An example – the Association for Computing Machinery

The Association for Computing Machinery (ACM) provides a good example of a progressive publisher, which is one of the pioneers in moving from print-based to electronic publishing. Traditionally, the definitive version of a journal has been a printed volume. Today, the same text can have many forms and formats: paper, CD-ROM, online text, hypertext, and so on. Producing these versions is simplified if the production of the journal uses a structured mark-up language, such as SGML. A pioneer application in using SGML in this way was the new *Oxford English Dictionary* (Painter, 1988). In 1993, the ACM made a technical commitment that its future production process would use a computer system that creates a computer database of journal articles, conference proceedings, magazines and newsletters, all marked up in SGML.

One use of this database is as a source for printed publications. It can also be used for document delivery. However, the plan is much more progressive. The ACM envisages a day when members will retrieve articles directly from the online database, sometimes reading them on the screen of a computer, sometimes downloading them to a local printer. Libraries will be able to license parts of the database or take out a general subscription for their patrons. ACM plans to make the material available online soon, probably during 1996.

ACM has confronted the problem of building a business model for this online database that will create revenue to cover the various costs, but not restrain authors and readers unduly. It has recently published an interim copyright policy, which tries to balance the interest of the authors against the needs for the association to generate revenue from its publications. The fact that ACM first published the new policy on its World Wide Web server is a sign of the times (ACM, 1994).

The policy retains the traditional copyright transfer from author to publisher and affirms that ACM can use material in any format or way that it wishes. At the same time, however, it allows authors very great flexibility. The most controversial aspect of the policy is to allow authors to continue to mount their materials on private servers, both before and after publication. In fast-moving fields, such as those covered by ACM journals, preprints have always been important. Recently, these preprints have been replaced by online collections of technical reports and preprints, freely available over the network. These are maintained privately or by departments. Since they are important to ACM members, ACM does not want to remove them, yet the association does not want private online collections to destroy the journal market.

A second example – Elsevier Science

Academic publishing is an unusual business. It includes companies who are in business to make money and not-for-profit organizations whose underlying mission (at least in theory) is charitable, educational, or the support of an academic discipline.

Whereas ACM is a scholarly society and aims to put the interests of its members above potential profits from publishing, Elsevier Science is a major commercial company. In the last few years, it has taken over Pergamon, merged with Reed Publishing and, in 1994, reached agreement to pay $1.5 billion for the online services Lexis and Nexis. Its editorial staff are as committed to scholarship as editors everywhere, but its shareholders expect profits.

Technically, Elsevier is following a track that is very similar to ACM's. It too is converting its production to the creation of a database of information, marked up in SGML. This will be used to print conventional journals, for document delivery and for potential online services. Elsevier is running a number of pilots to experiment with various business models. The TULIP project is one large pilot, where nine university libraries have mounted images of 42 journals in material sciences (Hunter and Zijlstra, 1994). Elsevier has announced that, in 1995, all 1,100 of its journals will be available in TULIP format. A second pilot is with OCLC. Beginning in January 1995, *Immunology Today*, one of Elsevier's 'Trends' journals (monthly magazine-like review journals), is available through OCLC's

Guidon software. This is part of the small but growing package of online journals that OCLC offers. As yet, Elsevier is concentrating on experimental services and has not announced any business plan that will use its full database to provide electronic services.

Many librarians fear the economic power of the commercial publishers, yet these developments are crucial. Elsevier and other publishers have to develop electronic services that the academic community wants and can afford, yet generate revenues that will satisfy its shareholders. If they succeed, conventional journal publishing will move smoothly into the electronic world. If they cannot find the right business model, we can anticipate turmoil.

Research and development

Library research

Today's online libraries are built on flimsy foundations. Much research and development are still needed. In developing the World Wide Web, the Internet community has been amazingly successful in building public online services, but bypassed many of the tough questions. As a result, the Web, as it exists at present, lacks some very important aspects of libraries and traditional information services. These difficulties are the subject of vigorous research being carried out in the USA and around the world.

During the past decade, the mainstream of library development has been for libraries to mount databases on central computers and provide a search interface for patrons to search the databases, display and print the materials. At present, most of the databases are of secondary information, such as online catalogues, or reference materials, such as dictionaries and bibliographies. As well as individual libraries, the bibliographic utilities such as OCLC, RLG and Pica have been active in developing such services.

In the past five years, several library projects have gone beyond secondary information to mount collections of journal articles online for their patrons. These projects include Mercury at Carnegie Mellon University (Arms *et al.*, 1992), Core at Cornell University led by Lesk (1994) of Bellcore, and Elsevier's TULIP project. These projects have slowly wrestled with tough problems of authentication, markup languages, scanning, protocols for search and retrieval, user interfaces, and database maintenance. They have also developed distributed computing methods that allow teams of computers to replace the mainframes of the past. One theme of current library research is how to merge these techniques into the dynamic world of the World Wide Web.

Copyright and business issues with electronic information

The key challenge in creating a true worldwide digital library is to establish an economic, legal and social framework for online information where the information has value. Across the world, people are working at making the networks suitable for services that wish to charge for information or control access. This goes far beyond technology. New laws may be needed. Certainly, new contracts are needed and new business practices.

The first step has been an analysis of copyright laws. In the USA, the national Information Infrastructure Task Force issued a working paper on this topic (National Telecommunications, 1994). The bulk of this paper is a survey of existing law, both in the USA and elsewhere. The final section suggests modifications to copyright law. This final section has been widely criticized as not giving sufficient weight to the interests of the users of information. However, the basic conclusion appears to be gaining acceptance: that existing copyright law can be adapted to the new world, but will need clarification and other detailed changes.

Another step is copyright registration, creating a definitive version of an electronic work and placing it in a repository. This highly technical subject has been the subject of a joint project by the Library of Congress and the Corporation for National Research Initiatives (Corporation, 1995).

A third topic where rapid progress is being made is billing for information delivered over the networks. A good example of work in this field is the NetBill project led by Marvin Sirbu at Carnegie Mellon University (Sirbu and Tygar, 1995). This is building an Internet billing service that will be secure, have very low transactions costs, and allow small organizations to set up network services without the complexity of developing private billing services. In many ways, NetBill aims to be the Internet's counterpart to credit cards.

A final area of research is rights management. The assumption is that many of the objects on the networks will be compound documents assembled from components with different rights holders. The challenge of rights management is to know what rights are involved in any object and to track the usage.

National initiatives

The development of online collections and electronic libraries is a worldwide phenomenon, but each country has its own style and is handling the change slightly differently. Not surprisingly, much of the energy and noise is coming out of the USA. The European Union is stressing collaboration. Individual countries, such as Britain and the Netherlands, have more centralized programmes.

In Britain, the Follett Report has already been mentioned. The report's underlying assumption is that university libraries will have to support indefinitely both traditional printed materials and new forms of electronic information. It recommended a major programme to fund technology in libraries. The government moved rapidly and allocated £20 million for the programme, which is now called FIGIT (Follett Implementation Group on Information Technology). It is instructive to see how the programme envisages this money being spent. The basic building block is a national network funded from other sources. The new initiatives being supported are: electronic document delivery, digitization and distribution of out-of-copyright journals, refereed electronic journals and other electronic texts, online bibliographic databases and retrospective conversion of catalogues, awareness and training.

The NSF/ARPA/NASA digital libraries initiative

In the USA, little money for education or libraries comes directly from the federal government, but government agencies sponsor huge amounts of university research. During 1994, three of these agencies announced funding for large-scale projects in digital libraries. The agencies are the National Science Foundation (NSF), the Department of Defense's Advanced Research Projects Agency (ARPA) and the National Aeronautics and Space Administration (NASA). Each of these agencies has a different mission. The NSF funds basic scientific research, but has occasional projects to support the implementation of services that are important to science. ARPA funds fundamental research in many areas of computing; for example, today's Internet is a direct descendant of work supported by ARPA more than 20 years ago. Sponsored research is not the primary mission of NASA.

Funding for each project was over one million dollars per year for four years. Awards were made to six groups, led by Carnegie Mellon University, Stanford University, University of California at Berkeley, University of California at Santa Barbara, University of Illinois and the University of Michigan (National Science Foundation, 1995). Each group has many industrial and academic partners and is committed to creating a large library test-bed that can be used for further research. If previous history is any guide, the research carried out by these six projects will have enormous impact on the shape of electronic information in the USA.

Conclusion

As recently as two years ago, it was a fair criticism that despite all the efforts to develop electronic libraries, very little use was made of them. In the past two years, the whole world of libraries and information services has changed dramatically.

Traditionalists may regret that modern researchers are as likely to be found searching online collections as exploring published literature in the stacks, but such nostalgia is unwarranted. Online collections are beginning to provide a range of accessible information which previously was available only to those who were privileged to work in a major research library. These are exciting times. We are fortunate to be part of them.

References

ACM (1994) Publications Board. *Interim copyright policies.* World Wide Web: http://info.acm.org/pubs/copyright_policy.txt.
Arms, W. Y. *et al.* (1992) The design of the Mercury Electronic Library. *Educom Review,* **27**(6), 38–41.
Arms, W. Y. (1993) Experience in collection development for an electronic library. In: H-P. Geh *et al.* (eds) *Knowledge for Europe: librarians and publishers working together.* München: K.G. Saur, pp. 144–157.
Bearman, D. (1994) Strategies for cultural heritage information standards in a networked world. *Archives and Museum Informatics,* **8**(2), 93–106.
Berners-Lee, T. J. *et al.* (1992) World-Wide Web: the information universe. *Electronic Networking: Research, Applications and Policy,* **2**(1), 52–58.
Bulletin (1995) Board for Libraries [Home page]. World Wide Web: http://ukoln.bath.ac.uk/BUBL/home.html.
Burrow, D. and Lewis, D. (1994) *Indiana University-Purdue University at Indianapolis.* [Paper presented at the Educom Conference, San Antonio, Texas].
CERN (1995) *The World Wide Web.* World Wide Web: http://info.cern.ch/hypertext/WWW/TheProject.html.
Coalition for Networked Information (1995) [Home page]. World Wide Web: http://www.cni.org/home.html.Follett (1993)
Corporation (1995) for National Research Initiatives. *Computer science technical reports.* World Wide Web: http://WWW.CNRI.Reston.VA.US/home/cstr.html.
Department of Education and Science (1972) *The scope for automatic data processing in the British Library.* London: HMSO.
Getty (1994) Art History Information Program *et al. Humanities and arts on the information highway: a profile.* Los Angeles, CA: J. Paul Getty Trust.
Graham, P. S. (1994) *Intellectual preservation: electronic preservation of the third kind.* Washington, DC: Commission for Preservation and Access.
House of Commons (1994), National Heritage Committee. *Fifth report. The British Library.* London: HMSO.
Hunter, K. and Zijlstra, J. (1994) TULIP – The University Licensing Project. *Journal of Interlibrary Loan, Document Delivery and Information,* **4**(3/4), 19–22.
Internet (1995) Engineering Task Force. *Welcome to the Internet Engineering Task Force!* World Wide Web: http://www.ietf.cnri.reston.va.us/home.html.
Joint (1993) Funding Councils' Libraries Review Group [Chair: Sir Brian Follett]. Bristol: HEFCE.
Lesk, M. E. (1994) Electronic chemical journals. *Analytical Chemistry,* **66**(14), 744–756.

National Center (1994) for Supercomputing Applications. *The Mosaic project.* World Wide Web: http://www.ncsa.uiuc.edu/SDG/Software/Mosaic/Docs/help-about.html.

National Science Foundation (1995) [Home page]. World Wide Web: http://www.nsf.gov.

National Telecommunications (1994) and Information Administration. Information Infrastructure Task Force. *A preliminary draft of the Report of the Working Group on Intellectual Property Rights.* World Wide Web: http://ntiaunix1.ntia.doc.gov:70/0/papers/documents/ipwg_draft.txt

Painter, J.D. (1988) Marking up the dictionary (the *Oxford English Dictionary*). *Information Media and Technology,* **21**(2), 72–74.

Sirbu, M. and Tygar, J.D. (1995) NetBill: an electronic commerce system optimized for network delivered services. In: *Proceedings of the IEEE Computer Conference, March 1995.* New York: IEEE.

University of California at Berkeley (1993) Planning Group. *Proposal for a School of Information Management and Systems Information.* Berkeley, CA: The University.

World Wide Web Consortium (1995) [Home page]. http://www.w3.org.

National libraries 2

Eric Wainwright
and Viola Bátonyi

Introduction

This chapter, dealing with national libraries in 1993 and 1994, is the work of two authors based on different sides of the world: one from Hungary and the other from Australia. National libraries, or at least libraries performing national functions, exist in most countries of the world. Inevitably, this selection of material is limited to that which authors have been able to peruse in languages with which they have some familiarity or have been able to obtain assistance in translation. These are severe limitations. Relevant material from smaller national libraries is often not available, as it does not appear in the mainstream journal literature; if it exists at all, it is in the form of short items in national newspapers, as annual reports or internal working documents. The authors were greatly assisted by the annual exhaustive reviews of the literature in the journal *Alexandria* (De Beer and Hendrikz, 1993 and 1994). The number of countries covered by our review was also broadened by two major collections of work on national libraries – the massive proceedings of the International Conference on National Libraries held in Taipei, Taiwan, in April 1993 (International, 1993a), and the thematic issue (April-June 1993) on national libraries in the journal *Documentation et Bibliothèques*. Nevertheless, for the reasons quoted above, the review overall tends to mirror the Eurocentric inclination of previous years, leavened this year by some greater emphasis on the Asia/Australasia/Pacific regions.

In passing, we note that the 1994 review may well be the last in which it would be wise to rely only on printed sources. As discussed later, many of the national libraries in countries with an advanced level of computing and networking now have information servers, usually based on the World Wide Web, which contain the latest information relating to their collections and services. While some of this information is available in printed sources such as annual reports, newsletters and guides, increasingly the servers include internal working documents, press releases, organizational information and information for the public which is not generally accessible in any other way, and is adding significantly to our knowledge of the institutions concerned.

While we have tried to assess all the available literature that we consider essential to an understanding of the trends in national libraries in the mid-1990s, it has been impossible to cover all areas and functions, and we have tried to provide emphases which differ from those expressed in the chapters of this publication for 1993 and 1992.

One of the themes given special attention is the strengthening of national identity: the national library as the memory of the nation and the way it fulfils this function. This is an especially important question in the newly established states of Eastern Europe (Kovač, 1994). Cooperation spanning frontiers and the free flow of information through networks form another line that can be clearly traced. National libraries are often the largest in the country as regards their holdings and services. They have played, and in places are still playing, a special historical role. Following the political changes in the countries of Central and Eastern Europe, national libraries have made every effort to have legislation passed ensuring their central position and providing financial guarantees. However, if they are now unable to keep pace with the developments generated by computerization, their opportunities to join in the global networks as equal partners will steadily decrease. While the developed countries are already replacing their computer systems with even more advanced ones, these countries of Eastern Europe, like so many throughout Africa, Asia, the Pacific and Latin America, are still struggling to set up their first systems, even though they attempt to draw on every possible source of assistance.

While effective networking seems the key to the successful national library of the future, financial constraints may well mean that the gap between the rich and poor nations will increase rather than diminish. National libraries in the developed countries can play a strong role in ensuring the necessary flow of aid, through training and equipment, to enable their counterparts in the developing world to play a full part in improving education and information flow in their own countries.

The role of national libraries

The roles of national libraries have been a regular theme of authors over recent years, as summarized in the previous chapters on national libraries in this publication by Line (1992) and Antonsson (1993a), and in the regular reviews of national libraries around the world in the journal *Alexandria*, most recently by De Beer and Hendrikz (1993, 1994). It is difficult to imagine that much new can be said, but once again this review has unearthed a continuing literature on the topic, as evidenced by articles by Bolos (1993), Brault (1993), Line (1993a), Nielsen (1993) and Wan (1993).

New perspectives on national libraries are currently derived from a consideration of the effects of changing political structures of nations, particularly in Eastern Europe; the effects of technology and in particular the growth of new information formats, electronic materials and networking; reconceptualization of the national library as part of a country's broader cultural institutions, and the abandonment of the goals of universality of collecting – for many countries, even for their own country's publications. Line (1993a) continued to be a perceptive commentator on the role of national libraries, and noted that:

> there has been a general shift towards services rather than collections as such, for it is by the services they give that most libraries will be judged in future: collections will still be important, but mainly as a basis for services.

In this environment, Line predicated that:

> national libraries are under a much more serious threat than other libraries; because they have no clear and established body of users, no institution to serve . . . to put it crudely, national libraries have no 'supporters' club . . . several lists of functions of national libraries have been posited, but whichever one is examined, it is apparent that there is not a single function that cannot be performed by other bodies.

Line argued, convincingly in our view, for a radical re-examination of roles by every national library '. . . to determine the most appropriate body or bodies in the country to carry out each function.

'What should the national library be like?', asked one author (Borodin, 1994), in listing the functions and rights of a Russian national library. As a consequence of the recent political changes and the disintegration of a few European states, this question arises again and again. The changing technological environment and the shrinking funds available also force the same question. Studies dealing with the existence and future of the national libraries attempt to analyse and predict the effect of two trends. One of these is the political changes mentioned above, principally in Eastern Europe, and the aspirations for independence of a few nations with a rich cultural tradition within larger states which now have their own centrifugal tendencies. The other is the effect of the achievements of computerization and other technological developments on the collections, services and conservation of holdings. It may therefore reasonably be concluded that the development and continued existence of national libraries will depend very much on political, economic and technological developments which, over the long term, have an inexorable effect on the national library as an institution, regardless of the pattern in which it is currently organized in any particular country, and regardless of its particular origins (Wainwright, 1993a, 1993b).

In connection with the collapse of the nation state, Line (1993b) cited conclusions drawn from political analyses and relates them to the development of the national libraries. Nation states have to face three trends: transnationalism, regionalism and tribalism. What could this mean for the national libraries? Technological developments, ever more extensive networking and dwindling funds act in the direction of greater cooperation at both international and regional level. The virtual library has already been the subject of a number of international events (European Library Automation Group, 1993). At the same time, the national libraries of the new, or rather of the 'old new', states arising in Eastern Europe are making great efforts, partly through legislation, to re-regulate and strengthen their status. All this can be seen in the details of new legislation, since, in the last two years, library Acts in general, or national library Acts in particular, have played an outstanding role – for example, in the Baltic countries, as well as in countries that were previous independent but under Soviet political influence. National libraries have always been a symbol of nationalism (Line, 1993b). Tribalism can lead to such extreme events as the complete destruction of the Bosnian national library in Sarajevo, but another, positive, example of historical development is the development and progress of the Catalonian national library in recent years.

In seeking the place of the national libraries in the next century, Brault (1993) approached the question less from the angle of social development than on the collection and the question of content:

> Let us accept first of all the hypothesis of the viability of the national library. The attitude of the human being in face of documentary heritage throws light on the level of his cultural evolution. But it is not reasonable to think that he will reject this heritage, that he will adopt a negative view of it, that he will neglect or even abandon it. Why would he not consider it as a step towards a constantly active evolution, as a witness to the past he has left behind and an encouragement for the future offered to him and which will be what he makes of it. It is even predictable that he will make of it what the stimulus of the society of which he is a member suggests to him.

In Brault's opinion, the collections of the future are more likely to be called national multimediathèques or mediathèques. One of the questions to be decided will be how and in what form libraries are to preserve the national output of documents, to what extent this is to be done in the original format or in terms of its content.

> Everything is contained in the enormous mandate of national libraries, exhaustive acquisition of the national documentary collection, conservation, the inventory of the national bibliography which serves for dissemination both within the national territory and in all the countries participating in the programme proposed by the international bodies. National libraries of the future will live and develop to the extent that they show themselves to be indispensable in their respective countries and in the international network, to the extent that they

fulfil the mandate given by their respective government, a mandate based on the model proposed by UNESCO.

Brault continued:

> What will the national library of the future be? It will be the national institution which will continue to show that it is an essential element in the cultural development of a state. Open to the boldest technologies and even participating in their progress, welcoming all documents that bear a message whatever its support, it will be located in a dynamic context rejecting all sterilizing stasis. Only those national libraries will survive which have refused to mummify themselves, or which at least will have rapidly loosened their bindings.

It is not only political and economic changes and the great variety of documents, or rather information carriers, to be preserved that could oblige national libraries to rethink their role and tasks. A significant influence is also the development of information technology. A new vision of the future needs to be developed: a future built on a national information infrastructure that will improve the ways national libraries serve the public. This has to be done in an active and aggressive way: in other words, those national institutions which are in a monopoly position – where they have no real rivals in the country – must strive to make their valuable collections available globally through networks, not only in the form of bibliographic information, but also as full content. National libraries, because of their unique collections, have a special responsibility to participate in the research and development needed to enable us to finally go beyond bibliographic information supply (Wuest, 1993).

This research was already under way in 1990, when a study was conducted within the framework of the Universal Availability of Publications Programme, and with the support of UNESCO, on the role of the national libraries in the new information environment. The findings of the study were summed up by Cornish (1992). It found clearly observable characteristic trends in the automation of catalogues, the general introduction of online remote access, participation in broader networks and the production of ever larger numbers of CD-ROMs, above all to ensure broad access to the national bibliographies.

Roberts (1993) examined national libraries in the light of these influences from the human angle; that is, from the viewpoint of the experts who accept the challenge to create and use the new technologies. Despite the fact that they essentially preserve historical and conservation traditions, staff in national institutions must also adopt new training in the future and synthesize the traditional historical studies with modern information science.

The quasi-national role played by many libraries in universities and other research institutions has often been overlooked in the past, particularly where these roles are performed outside any nationally agreed cooperative scheme. Any library, in theory, may play such a role – it simply has to be recognized by a reasonable number of people nationally as providing the strongest collections and/or services covering a particular subject area. This may be very narrow, as in the case of the Sinological Institute at Leiden University in the Netherlands (Wu, 1993), or as broad as the Canada Institute for Scientific and Technical Information (CISTI). Often, these quasi-national libraries exist because of accidents of history, but sometimes they have been established quite purposefully as a reaction to perceived failure by a country's *de jure* national library to provide effective services, commonly in areas such as science and technology.

Regardless of the origin of the present patterns of 'national' libraries in various countries, there seems to be a greater realization that, with financial resources stretched in most public institutions, there is a necessity for all institutions which play a national role to collaborate effectively. Pressure for this is perhaps likely to be strongest in those countries where there is no *de jure* national library. One outstanding case in the developed world has been the USA, where the Library of Congress has long played a *de facto* national library role, but sometimes in relative isolation from other institutions. Some of its potential role as coordinator has therefore been in the hands of a separate body, the National Commission on Libraries and Information Science, but this has been significantly under-resourced (Farrell, 1993). It is interesting that, with such long established arrangements for the US Library of Congress and the National Diet Library in Japan to act as *de facto* national libraries while also serving their legislatures, there should be current calls (Ishizuka, 1993; M.G. Mason, 1993) for making both libraries true national libraries by law, to minimize conflict between their national obligations and their services to the legislatures. In the USA, such a call has existed in one form or another for around 100 years (Bowker, 1993). Nevertheless, the Library of Congress seems clearly geared towards high levels of collaboration, such as in collecting with the National Library of Medicine, in preservation (Librarian, 1994) and with a range of bodies in cataloguing and bibliographic data activities (Fialkoff, 1993): for example, with major universities under the National Cooperative Cataloguing (NACO) programme, and with OCLC for copy cataloguing purposes. In Norway, where the University of Oslo Library has played the *de facto* role of national library for decades, the decision to establish a separate national library has now been made, and the division of collecting responsibilities between the new library and its former host have yet to be fully determined (Eide, 1993).

Both chaos and order can be important for any development. These features characterize the present situation of Austrian libraries. A new university law was introduced in 1993 which repealed the previous ones and had a few paragraphs concerned with libraries. These prescribed that the universities be economic in their use of resources, but the growing number of information resources, and the increased need for expenditure on acquisitions, require greater cooperation, sharing of resources and standardization. It is therefore important that the university libraries build up cooperation with other libraries, especially with the national library. Cooperation had already started in the late 1970s, but the new law provides for the national library to extend and build up new central services. The following central services already existed in the national library: training, coordination of the Austrian research libraries' computer networks, a periodicals database, union catalogues and restoration workshops. In the future, the following areas will also be coordinated by the national library: retrospective conversion, research on valuable collections, rare book restoration, the establishment of a body to improve automation standards and re-establishment of an Institute for Library and Information Science (Marte, 1994).

Articles by Barua (1992; 1993) and Tyagi (1993) outlined attempts in India to improve coordination of the activities of the National Library, the National Science Library, the National Medical Library, the Library of the Indian Agricultural Research Institute (the *de facto* national library for agriculture) and the National Social Science Documentation Centre Library. India presents a good example of the difficulties of coordination in a country where the government gives no mandate for leadership of such a coordinating process. Launo (1993) has described the network of national resource libraries in Finland, formed in support of industrial information needs, illustrating the benefits of government recognition and assistance to the national roles performed by many libraries. In many countries, formal recognition of quasi-national roles in terms of legislation and funding assistance has long been recognized – for example, in Sweden, where the Royal Library's Office for National Planning and Coordination (BIBSAM) plays a strong role in support of Swedish research libraries generally, with funding provided through the Ministry of Education (Nilsson, 1994).

Etheredge (1994) has suggested that with the growth of universal networking the opportunity now exists for a new approach to national library provision, based on a distributed system of institutions, each responsible for designated subject areas and strongly networked together. Debate on this issue is likely to be provoked in future by the emerging prototypes of the global distributed library, such as the 'virtual library' established by CERN in Switzerland, linking electronic material through hypertexed images. Green (1994) has proposed the development of global subject information networks (SINs!), and these worldwide arrangements, such as the European Molecular Biology Network, are emerging with a speed which seems sure to challenge the roles of any national institution concerned with library and information services.

It is clear that international networking is having a significant effect on the thinking of national libraries in those countries which are already heavily networked. Griffiths (1993) has argued that the key roles now for a national library are ensuring the development of national network infrastructure suitable for library purposes, coordination of an online Conspectus database which enables cooperative collection development, a flexible index to the national union catalogue which integrates not only the records in a central national database, but also those in the distributed online catalogues of libraries throughout the country, and the development of 'metadata' standards providing description of documents which enable them to be retrieved efficiently through distributed databases and networks. Matheson (1993), from the National Library of Scotland, and Cornish (1993), from the British Library, largely concur, stressing networking as the key activity for national libraries in facilitating national access to documents.

In countries where the national library has no legislative mandate to provide financial support for institutions playing national roles, support has to be achieved through leadership by the national library (or some other body accepted as having the authority) in organizing activities which lead to more effective national coordination of services. New Zealand and Australia provide two interesting examples of national library organization of processes and events leading to greater collaboration. The National Library of New Zealand (1993b), in conjunction with the New Zealand Library and Information Association (1994), has been developing between 1991 and 1994 the 'N-Strategy', a comprehensive programme of collaborative action for the development of library and information services in New Zealand. This has involved a coordinated process of regional and national meetings and workshops, culminating in an agreed action plan (Kirkus-Lamont, 1993). One interesting feature of the New Zealand process has been the extent to which it has been sponsored by two large communications companies operating in the country – both subsidiaries of US businesses. In Australia, the National Library's whole strategy for development (National Library of Australia, 1994) is based on its conceptualization of a 'distributed national collection', in which the publicly accessible resources of libraries throughout the country (including the national library itself) are coordinated in a way that will allow them to be accessible to users as easily as if they were a single national resource (Crook, 1993; Henty, 1993). Australia has been developing this concept, which began with the Australian Libraries Summit of 1988, through a series of focused initiatives, such as its 'Towards Federation 2001: Linking Australians and their Heritage' conference, which concentrated on the coordination of materials relating to Australia and Australians (Wainwright, 1993c), and the development of cooperative cataloguing arrangements between the national library, state and university libraries (Cooperative, 1994).

Canada is another country in which the national library has attempted to develop a 'whole of country' strategy in relation to resource sharing and access to collections. Following an original strategy developed internally by the National Library (Resource Sharing Strategy Team, 1989) during 1994, a much more broadly based working group to review and update the Canadian Information Resource Sharing Strategy was established. The group produced a draft discussion paper (National Library of Canada, 1994), which provided a comprehensive set of recommendations covering interlending and document delivery, coordinated collection development, resource sharing databases and cooperative cataloguing. This delineated the role of the National Library of Canada *vis-à-vis* other institutions. A more detailed study of interlibrary document delivery (Beaumont and Lunau, 1994) has set out the requirements for collaboration between the National Library of Canada and CISTI.

National libraries have traditionally been the centre for cataloguing of a nation's publications, and it is unsurprising that, with the high cost of such processing, they are seeking collaborative means of sharing the burden more broadly. International exchange of cataloguing records through the MARC format is longstanding. National library networks such as PICA in the Netherlands, the Australian Bibliographic Network and the New Zealand Bibliographic Network have harnessed savings in this area for more than a decade, but we are now seeing more national libraries establishing formal arrangements within their countries for shared cataloguing of national publications. Apart from the examples referred to above, Britain has also been experimenting with shared cataloguing arrangements between the British Library and the other 'copyright libraries' which have legal deposit arrangements (Bourne, 1993b; Copyright Libraries, 1993). It is noteworthy that a survey of national library agencies by the Conference of Directors of National Libraries (1994b) Task Force on Issues Relating to Bibliographic Records revealed that in a majority of countries there is more than one agency responsible for bibliographic control of the national publishing output. Bourne (1993a) has gone so far as to question the whole existence of national bibliographies in an internationally networked world; he sees increased collaboration in the future between national libraries and the book trade. Britain has gone a long way in this area, with contractual arrangements between the British Library and the book trade, and the establishment of a formal Book Industry Communications group between the British Library and the booksellers', publishers' and library associations to progress collaborative matters generally (BIC, 1993).

Given the variety of reassessment of national library roles, and with the various models for national services now available, it is perhaps not surprising that there is a move in some developing countries to question the traditional models of the national library, which have usually been handed down by former colonial powers (as one small example, Anyanwu (1994) has pointed out the inadequacy of colonial-based classification schemes for government publications in relation to Nigeria). In the Pacific region, where there are cultural, geographical and logistic issues quite foreign to Europe and North America, there has been investigation of a number of alternative models. Simmons (1993) outlined three models, all of which currently exist in the region:

1) the combined national archives/national library model, as in Tuvalu and Kiribati;
2) the national library commission model, which exists in Papua New Guinea, albeit alongside a national library;
3) the national library dependency model, in which a poorer developing country can have a number of functions carried out by a more developed country – suggested for Niue and Tuvalu in association with New Zealand.

E.B. Williams (1993), on the other hand, has advocated a specific model which combines in one national cultural and educational centre the functions of a library, museum and archives, in which there is a significant emphasis on capture of the oral tradition and functions relating to reading, literacy and the promotion of local writing. Writing of New Zealand, with its present emphasis on bicultural development, A.E. Smith (1993) also stressed the national library's role in the progress and vibrancy of national cultures, and local and national publishing. Both Wali (1993), writing from Nigeria, and E.B. Williams (1993), from Fiji, questioned whether the developing countries need a national library so much as a clear national policy on library services, in which various functions may be carried out by existing institutions, thus reducing the financial burdens of overall provision – very much as Line suggested has often happened (see above). Lee (1993) confirmed the difficulties faced by traditional national libraries in developing countries in relation to funding, trained staff, a non-reading tradition in the community, lack of adequate buildings, custodial attitudes and the absence of networking infrastructure – all of which tend to confirm the necessity to look at new models in these countries.

It may well be that the development of more effective models in some rapidly developing countries may result in pointers also for libraries in the developed countries. As Chan (1993) has pointed out:

> users acknowledge their debt to these great national libraries [speaking of the Library of Congress and the British Library] for their preservation of human knowledge and the generous services they have provided. However, one may wonder how long their traditional role [of worldwide collecting] can last.

It may be argued that it would be a better long-term investment for major national libraries spending heavily on acquisitions from developing countries rather to divert these funds to building the capacity of the national libraries in those countries to collect and organize their own national heritage, and then to make networked access available to other countries.

Legislation

The literature on legislation can be divided into two main groups. One consists of commentary on Acts passed or to be introduced in the near future, defining the legal status and functions of libraries in the country as a whole, or national libraries in particular – either as a section in a general library Act or as a separate law. This has been given priority mainly in the former Eastern European socialist countries after the political changes, because of the weakening of the former centralized system, but there are also Western European national libraries which have obtained their legal status through recent regulations or laws, or are expecting to obtain it soon (Spain, Switzerland, the Netherlands). The other major legislative group is aimed at a modern regulation of legal deposit.

The adoption of library legislation or an Act dealing specifically with the national library is often related to the changed political situation. In those countries which have recently become independent, such an Act has generally been passed at parliamentary level (Estonia, Lithuania, Russia). A law regulating the operation of national institutions also came into force in Bulgaria in 1994. Besides defining the functions of organizations, this can also offer guarantees as to their existence. In Poland, the Czech Republic, Hungary and Slovakia, drafts of library laws are being debated, in some cases very actively. In Hungary, for example, the debate over a library Act dragged on for over a year, greatly diminishing its chances of coming before parliament, although a new legal deposit Act has now been put on the agenda. The reason for this is that in a decentralized system there are far fewer areas of library affairs that can be regulated by legislative means, and, where such situations exist, the direction of autonomous or semi-autonomous institutions can only be in the form of recommendations. However, if the old legislation is not changed, the national document output will not find its way into libraries with a long-term organization and preservation capability.

A similar debate took place in the Czech Republic, over the provision of an Act whereby the right of access to published documents and the information derived from them was to be declared as part of basic human rights. The Act is not designed to undertake more than the legal regulation of public library affairs, a principle that was quite difficult to assert in face of the proponents of a 'uniform library system' embracing all libraries: even international recommendations on this topic did not easily persuade opponents for a long time (Pilar, 1992). Under the Acts passed in Estonia and Lithuania, the national libraries also perform functions of parliamentary libraries (Bulavas, 1993; Eenmaa, 1993).

A regulation governing library affairs as a whole is also being drafted in Russia (Proekt, 1992b). However, a decision was adopted on the Russian State Library (formerly the Lenin State Library), under Presidential decree no. 38 of 1992 and the 1993 resolution of the Council of Ministers. This latter contains basic regulations for the State Library, which stress its independence of political parties, social movements and religions. The state ensures and protects the lasting survival of the library's stock, its unity and indivisiblity, and its inalienability. The Russian central state budget guarantees the operation of the library, but it also allows financial support from other sources. In addition to Russian literature and Russia-related literature published abroad, the State Library's field of collection also includes literature on the former Soviet Union and Soviet affairs (Polozenie, 1993). Similarly, a Presidential decree regulates the tasks of the national library in St Petersburg (the Russian *National* Library, previously the Saltykov-Shchedrin Library, now serving the State of Russia, while the Russian *State* Library serves the CIS), which is principally the library of Russian patriotic (Russica) material and also has an important collection of early material (Zaitsev, 1993).

The National Library in St Petersburg will celebrate its 200th anniversary in 1995. The holdings of the library are more than 31 million units, and contain the oldest text written in Russian and one of the largest incunabula collections in Europe (Zaitsev, 1993). This library has a long history of restricted access to its collection (restricted for political reasons, according to a 'temporary' censorship regulation). The collection was opened to the public after 1917 for a short while, and then a small part again in the 1960s. Finally, most of the collection was opened for public access between 1987 and 1990. There are still documents under restriction and the librarians are hoping to solve this problem through a law on mass communication (Varlamova, 1993).

A law has also been drafted on the so-called 'all-Russian' national libraries. This would regulate not only the national libraries having full rights, but also what are known as the 'paranational libraries', which are specialized libraries with national competence in agriculture, technical subjects, etc. (Proekt, 1992a). Another approach has been recommended by Borodin (1994). According to this, there are two possible solutions for legislation: either a few large libraries would be given full or partial national library status (as is the case at present for the Russian State Library in Moscow and the Russian National Library in St Petersburg), or a consortium would be formed from the currently operating large libraries under a common name, the Russian National Library. Within this consortium, each library would preserve its autonomy, but would also be given new rights.

In Switzerland, reorganization of the national institutions at government level and later also within the institutions themselves resulted in a new act, under which the national library plays a new role in the library system of the confederation. The National Library of the future is envisaged as an information centre for Switzerland's documentary heritage (i.e. Helvetica). Furthermore, it will serve as a national and international centre for all information held in Switzerland. Those using its services will include other institutions (libraries, multimedia libraries, archives, etc.) as well as scientific researchers and the general public. A total revision of the 1911 law was recently submitted by the government to Parliament (Jauslin, 1992).

Legal deposit legislation

The history and purpose of legal deposit copies, and the most significant elements of current legislation, have been summarized by Fournier (1993). In his view, the potential elements of legal regulations are the following:

- the publisher and/or the printing house is obliged to provide copies;
- publications may be subject to selection according to their cultural value,

and it may also be an aim to collect national literature published abroad (patriotica);
- types of documents and regulations relating to edition;
- both traditional print documents and electronic media;
- the number of copies deposited;
- protection of deposited items through copyright;
- free or fee-based provision of legal deposit copies.

Having analysed the French example, he provides a general framework for revision of legal deposit legislation.

In his overview of legislation relating to legal deposit, Vitiello (1993) called attention to two trends: the so-called 'legalistic' and the 'functional' approach. He summarized his conclusions as follows:

> It is a question of priorities and of cost benefit policies . . . Librarians working in depository libraries should therefore take into account both contemporary and historical needs in the framework of their national library and information systems; for legal deposit purposes, the present is not simply the past of the future.

The issue of legal deposit in relation to electronic materials has been under investigation since 1992 by the CDNL Working Group on Legal Deposit and Electronic Publishing, which presented a report to the CDNL meeting in Havana in 1994 (Conference of Directors of National Libraries, 1994c). The paper encourages enactment of legislation on legal deposit of non-print publications, and work in Europe is being furthered by the CoBRA (Computerized Bibliographic Record Actions) Forum of the Conference of European National Librarians, with the aim of developing a paper to be put to the European Commission (CoBRA, 1994). These groups are building on the work done by the Norwegian Department of Culture in relation to the development of the Norwegian law of legal deposit (Fagerli, 1993).

Among legal deposit regulations also providing for modern information formats, a Norwegian Act which came into force in 1990 is of exceptional significance (Dahlø, 1992). According to this Act, all documents containing generally available information must be submitted to the national library:

- documents of paper or a paper-like medium, microforms, photographs;
- sound recordings, films, videograms, electronic data processing (EDP) documents, and combinations of these types of documents;
- documentary recordings of broadcast material.

Deposit provisions which exclude audiovisual materials continue to be a problem in many countries, as commented upon in relation to the USA (Young, 1994) and more generally by Pinion (1993). That there should be some confusion and difficulty in this area is not surprising. Often, there have been institutions separate from the national libraries which have either legal or *de facto* national responsibilities for collection and preservation of formats other than print; in areas such as film and audio-recordings, these may be longstanding. It is understandable that, with the increasing range of audiovisual and electronic materials, and their greater role as information sources, national libraries should seek to broaden their deposit provisions. However, in practice, they often have neither the facilities nor staff skills able to handle these formats successfully.

Experience with the new French law of June 1992 has been outlined by Chevallier (1993), where the aims of legislation are said to be to:

- to gather and preserve documents;
- to compose and circulate national bibliographies;
- to allow consultation of documents.

The French law introduces the new notion of consultation of documents which is more restrictive than communication to the public, in order to strike a balance between the conflicting interests of copyright owners and researchers. In France, legal deposit rights and responsibilities are now shared between the Bibliothèque Nationale de France, the National Centre for the Cinema and the National Institute for Audio Visual Production.

The National Library of Spain also recently put revision of the legal deposit law on its agenda. Here too, among the reasons was the lack of nationally centralized collection and preservation of material stored on electronic media and of radio and TV programmes, and the desire to create responsibilities in which bibliographic control would be decentralized.

In Sweden, regulation applying to the legal deposit of micro and electronic documents came into force in 1994.

In the former Socialist countries, legal deposit regulation is becoming increasingly urgent, since publishers or printing houses operating under privatized conditions are not providing their publications in the required number of copies. This had not been a problem in the previous centralized economic system. In Hungary, for example, printing houses were required to provide sixteen deposit copies for the national library, which used them not only for its collections but also for international exchange and to enlarge the holdings of university and research libraries. There is now a need to regulate the number of copies received, to give printing houses and publishers an incentive to deposit, and to define the range of information formats to be supplied to the library (Ershova, 1994; Poprády, 1994a).

According to Cornish (1992) the role and functions of legal deposit legislation need to be reviewed, and he listed the factors which justify this:

- comprehensiveness;
- exclusion of undesirable materials and definition of what needs to be preserved;
- amendment of the scope;

- specification of which institution is to receive the deposit copies.

If new deposit copy regulations gradually come into force and the holdings of the national libraries are enriched by multimedia and by electronic databases and software, the question then arises of whether the libraries have the technological infrastructure for conservation and access. In turn, networked public and research access raises a need for a new approach to copyright legislation.

Organization and management

In the last two years, a number of general articles on the activities of national libraries have appeared in the journal *Alexandria*, making it clear that some institutions have recently undergone substantial organizational change. The reasons may be of a political or economic nature, or automation may require a new style or organizational structure. In some cases, the appointment of a new director to head a library may also result in significant changes; for example, the new director-general of the Austrian National Library has set up a new development programme for the library, which includes organizational change, a programme for building restoration, and a new public relations area. Of course, all of these factors may play a role simultaneously.

Two important studies published on the reorganization of the Danish Royal Library analysed the main elements in the organizational change, not only from the professional viewpoint but also from the angle of applied sociology (Krarup, 1993a). Economic pressures, that is, the requirement for cost-effective operation, as well as the decentralization of functions, call for the establishment of coordination and planning at a national level. This was the reason for setting up the National Library Authority in Denmark, which previously exercised oversight over academic and research libraries, and also an advisory body under the Ministry of Cultural Affairs. In 1990, it was merged with the Directorate of Public Libraries and formed a new body, the Danish National Library Authority, headed by the National Librarian (who is not the same person as the Royal Librarian, and in fact has no direct responsibility for managing any specific library). This single responsiblity can facilitate cooperation, planning and the formulation and implementation of national information policy. The Royal Library, which is officially recognized as the national library, serves also as the humanities library of the University of Copenhagen. A modernization project has been under way from the late 1980s in the library and this has also affected the university library function, physical planning and internal modernization. In the latter case, on the basis of a detailed study, new work flows have been introduced. It is envisaged that a strategic plan will also be produced as a result of the modernization project. The quantitative methods applied in measuring the library's performance have drawn the attention of several other libraries (Larsen, 1992; Rugaas, 1993).

In Norway, the Ministry of Cultural Affairs was responsible for deciding to develop the new national library, established in 1993 from institutions which were separated from the Oslo University library, together with the Mo i Rana branch set up in northern Norway in 1989. The National Office for Research and Special Libraries (Riksbibliotektjenesten) planned the creation of the independent national library (Dahlø, 1992).

Severe financial cuts made at the end of the 1980s are described as the cause of a drastic reorganization of the Dutch national library (Van Drimmelen and Van Trier, 1994). The continuing development of the national infrastructure, the spread of information technology and its influence on the organization and its services also played a role. Here too, the aim has been to achieve efficiency with a smaller staff and, for this reason, certain work processes have been merged. In addition to the internal causes, there were also external, political causes, namely the library's growing autonomy. This was officially obtained in 1993 when the independent position of the Koninklijke Bibliotheek was legally established, with a new organizational structure. The elaboration of a new strategic plan began here also in 1994, and a new management information system has been developed.

In Switzerland too, ministerial reorganizations and financial and organizational problems were the cause of the 'urgently needed reorganization' of the national library (Jauslin, 1992). The reorganization project, launched in 1990 under the name of RAMSES, placed special emphasis on improving library services and installing modern equipment and automation, areas in which the library was regarded as lagging. It is hoped that the development and changes will be promoted by a new national library Act now being drafted.

In 1990–1991, staff of the Spanish National Library also made a comprehensive organizational and functional analysis, with the aim of reducing administration costs and in view of an anticipated law to make the library an autonomous body. The study comprised an analysis of the purposes of the library, a detailed flow chart of processes and the implementation of a self-assessment system. A new Act came into force in 1991, and this further influenced the organization, especially in the areas of top management and the library's advisory body (Girón, 1994). The Biblioteca de Catalunya, now recognized as the Catalonian National Library, also reported on organizational changes for the reasons similar to those outlined above (Panyella, 1993).

In the countries of Eastern Europe too, there have been substantial changes in the organization of the national libraries, although there is as yet little public information available on this. The main cause of the changes is the termination or restriction of earlier centralized functions that have lost their rationale. The addition of new functions, such as the parliamentary services mentioned earlier, and the attachment of bibliographic centres to national libraries (ISSN, ISBN), have also led to change. In Hungary, the Director General published in a professional journal the text of his application for the post, thus giving wide publicity to the priorities and tasks he wished to realize during his tenure (Poprady, 1994b). There is a clear tendency toward greater delegation of responsibilities and an effort to achieve a more decentralized, democratic style of management.

As generalist organizations, collecting materials in a wide range of formats, national libraries have a weakness in providing subject assistance to users with specialized needs. In a very large institution, there may be sufficient staff resources for there to be many subject specialists, but this is rare in smaller and medium-sized libraries. In some countries, specialized national services are often performed by institutions other than national libraries, as with CISTI in Canada, INIST in France, and the networks of libraries performing national functions in Finland, Germany, India, Sweden and the USA. One initial reaction to this problem was reported from the US National Agricultural Library (in itself a response to a specialized national requirement), with its establishment of a number of subject 'information centres' within the library, such as the Aquaculture Information Centre, with staff dedicated to serving a particular user group (McVey and Hanfman, 1993). As national libraries move from being collectors of material to facilitators of access to materials in electronic form wherever located, they may have to consider more carefully how to structure staff in ways that meet defined user needs. For national libraries, this is difficult, compared with libraries serving specific clienteles, for, as the above quotation from Line (1993a) pointed out, national libraries generally have no defined clientele. National libraries may therefore be forced in future to undertake much more rigorous definition of the client groups they principally aim to serve, and then organize their resources to service those groups most effectively.

Strategic planning

The growth of strategic planning processes in national libraries has been evident since the mid-1980s. It is clearly part of the regular management processes for many libraries, as indicated by Jauslin and Bauermeister's survey (1993) of 25 European national libraries, which revealed that fourteen currently had strategic plans and another six expected to have such plans fairly shortly. The survey was interesting in drawing out some major themes effecting European national planning:

1) Legal deposit legislation: modifications were under way in Finland, France, Germany, Ireland, Italy, Norway, Portugal, Sweden, Switzerland and the Vatican.
2) New and extended buildings: completed in the Netherlands and Portugal, and either in advanced planning or under way in Denmark, Finland, Germany, Hungary, Luxembourg, Sweden, Switzerland and the UK.

3) Retrospective conversion of bibliographic data: programmes were under way in Czechoslovakia, Denmark, Finland, France, Germany, Hungary, Ireland, the Netherlands, Portugal, Sweden, Switzerland and the Vatican.
4) International collaboration and preservation: particularly participation in the European register of microform masters, and the establishment of mass deacidification facilities.
5) Research: a stress on the need for greater amounts of research.

Major new strategic plans were produced in 1993/94 by the national libraries of Australia (Giese, 1993b; National Library of Australia, 1994), the Netherlands (Van Drimmelen and Van Trier, 1994), New Zealand (National Library of New Zealand, 1994), the UK (Bradbury, 1993; British Library, 1993) and the USA (Librarian, 1993); and these are discussed further below. However, while each plan reflects the particular situation of each institution, it is noteworthy how much stress is given in those plans to the opportunities created by the growth of electronic materials and networks to improve access to national library collections, and particularly to unique 'heritage' materials which are currently confined to in-house use. All five libraries foresee significant changes in the methods of collection access by the year 2000.

With so much formal planning now taking place, it is salutary to remind ourselves that national libraries may also be heavily influenced by the work of individuals, as evidenced by the impact on the National Library of Australia of its long-serving head, Harold White, over the years 1923 to 1970 (*Australian*, 1993).

Building planning

As national libraries adapt in response to the greatly increased volume of publication, the variety of formats, and the growth of electronic information access to users both within and external to their buildings, space planning for national library services has become an essential part of overall strategic planning. It is not surprising that many libraries have been engaged in the construction and planning of new buildings, extensions and renovations to existing facilities, and separate storage areas.

Apart from the extensive literature on the massive projects of the new British Library and the Bibliothèque Nationale de France, significant new buildings are described in Denmark (Krarup, 1993b; Rugaas, 1993), Germany (Lehmann, 1993), Norway (Hot, 1993) and Wales (National Library of Wales, 1993). Major remodelling exercises have been reported from the National Library of Australia (Giese, 1993a), at the Library of Congress (National, 1993a) and in both major buildings of the South African Library (On, 1993; Further, 1994). The

Japanese National Diet Library's new building contains eight underground storage floors specially designed to stabilize temperature and humidity (Kenjo, 1993).

Though few publications have been found on planning, building and refurbishing projects of national libraries in Europe (except for the Bibliothèque Nationale de France and the British Library), unpublished reports presented at the Conference of European National Libraries show that a number of other projects have completed or will be completed in the near future. In Tallinn, the new building of the Estonian National Library, the largest library building in the Baltic States and Scandinavia, was opened in 1994. Besides performing national library functions, it serves the Parliament as well. There are conference centre facilities, an open air theatre, exhibition halls and restaurants for the public. The building was designed to be a modern information centre and a public centre of the city under the same roof. The new building of the Polish National Library (some parts of the institution have moved in already) is hoped to be finished by 1995. The new building of the Russian National Library in St Petersburg is expected to be inaugurated by 1995, but there have been delays in the completion of the different phases (Zaitsev, 1993). Extension and remodelling of buildings have been completed in Spain and Bulgaria, and a new depository library is under construction in the Czech Republic. Austria opened a large underground storage facility in 1993 and, in Sweden, a similar stack will be built with the refurbishing of the existing building by 1996. Similar underground stack construction is current at the Swiss National Library. Ten years after the move into its impressive and reconstructed Palace building, the Hungarian National Library is also running out of space, and it is planning an underground stack built into the castle hill. Latvia has also completed the design stage of a new building.

In spite of the wealth of descriptive material, very little has been published on the complexities of design now faced by those planning national library buildings. Just what balance of collection storage space, reader space and staff spaces is required in future? What is the impact of multimedia formats? How do we best provide for online access in the building? How will remote access capabilities impact on public demand on buildings? Should we be planning for the use of wireless rather than wired buildings? How do we make such large buildings, with special temperature and humidity stability requirements, energy-efficient? There is a dearth of analytical material available and, if it exists in the internal reports and planning documents of some institutions, there is a strong need for that material to be made more widely available through the published literature.

Funding and charges

In recent years, many national libraries have experienced reductions in the purchasing powers of the budgets that they receive from their governments. Few national libraries at present have substantial sources of funds other than government grants, with the exception of the British Library (where the Document Supply Centre recovers 60% of its spend, and the BL as a whole earns 30% of its budget and, to a lesser extent, the National Library of Australia, which earns over 20% of its funds, mainly through sales of network services and document supply. In this situation, many libraries have examined whether services should be cut or charges introduced. Both paths present difficulties and can lead to significant public reaction, as the Library of Congress discussions in 1993 illustrate, when the Librarian of Congress proposed to introduce a range of public charges (Berry, 1993; Nelson, 1993). In the event, the Library of Congress took the politically more acceptable step of suspending interlibrary loans to foreign libraries (LC, 1993). The Library of Congress, on the other hand, has been highly successful in raising over US$10 million towards the building of its 'National Digital Library' (LC, 1994). Similarly, the British Library was successful (T. Mason, 1993) in obtaining sponsorship of £1 million from a computer equipment company towards its automation programme in the new library building.

Recognizing the difficulty, the Bibliothèque Nationale de France has been developing, ahead of the opening of the new building, principles for charging for services, distinguishing between free general public access, charges for access to research reading rooms, copying charges and commercial services (Massuard, 1993).

In the area of copyright, the increasing transmission of electronic copies over networks, and the growth of commercial document suppliers such as UnCover, have highlighted the problem of determining copyright fees on international copying. After long negotiation, the British Library agreed to pay royalty charges to publishers on photocopies sent to the USA (British, 1993b), even though photocopies supplied under the fair dealing legislation in the UK, as in many other countries, attract no such royalty charges. This problem is likely to become increasingly difficult in the years ahead.

In an extensive survey of Eastern European national libraries, Lehmann (1994) has noted the potential role that the libraries have in contributing to the wider changes those countries are experiencing. However, he also noted the restrictions caused by the critical budget situations faced by many institutions, compounded by reductions in the effectiveness of deposit provisions, and inadequate physical conditions. The restricted funds are creating problems in two areas particularly: in acquisitions, where in some libraries without foreign funds it is impossible to subscribe to journals or to buy books, and in computer systems development. The only national library in Eastern Europe which reports a substantial income (close to 10%) generated from the sale of publications, training programmes and services is Slovenia (CENL, unpublished reports).

International cooperation

Cooperation among national libraries – whether in the form of general 'twinning' arrangements, or for specific projects, as direct bilateral agreements or within geographical regions – has been given increasing emphasis in recent years. The reasons for these efforts can be traced back mainly to economic factors, such as libraries on a more developed level helping those less developed, and the sharing of resources for processing the outputs of particular cultural or language areas, making them accessible to others.

Cooperation between individual national libraries has been longstanding, but, until recently, relatively limited in the areas covered. International resource sharing has principally been concentrated on interlending and the sharing of bibliographic records. While the International Federation for Library Associations (IFLA) forms have been a standard, the volume of international lending has been relatively low, with the major exception of the British Library's Document Supply Centre, which has a worldwide supply role, and to a lesser extent the traffic between the USA and Canada. Greater facilitation of international interlending has been discussed for many years within IFLA. With the support of the Conference of Directors of National Libraries, the IFLA Offices for UAP and International Lending are piloting an international voucher scheme aimed at overcoming the problems that some countries have in making international payments (*IFLA*, 1994b). Advanced information technologies are now playing a decisive role in shaping cooperation programmes.

MARC records have been exchanged on tape between national libraries for more than 20 years. However, with the continuing reduction in communication costs, particularly over the Internet, and advances in record handling procedures, it has now become feasible for records to be directly downloaded from one library to another. As experience between the National Library of Australia and Library of Congress has shown (using the Internet FTP file-transfer protocol), this significantly reduces the costs of record exchange and the delays in records being available in each country.

The growth of the Internet seems sure to spur an increasing range of collaborative activities between national libraries, with the realization that the full benefits of internationally networked access can be achieved only through the much greater harmonization of standards for communication, electronic storage, information retrieval, interlending and catalogue practices.

One significant project, running since 1990, has been aimed at harmonizing access to European national bibliographies, involving the national libraries of Denmark, France, Germany, Italy (Florence), the Netherlands, Portugal and the UK, under the aegis of the European National Libraries Cooperative Project on CD-ROM and with European Commission funding support. The key aims of the project were to:

1) promote better and easier access to European national bibliographies;
2) promote economies in library cataloguing through an improved interchange of national bibliographic records;
3) develop shared approaches to strategies, applications and formats for bibliographic data on CD-ROM.

The first part of the project has been concluded and its results can be summed up as follows:

- specification of a retrieval interface;
- a pilot UNIMARC CD-ROM product;
- MARC to UNIMARC conversion procedures;
- a multilingual interface.

One important outcome is that a close connection has been established between the producers and publishers of national bibliographies and the results are now being spread to other countries. The project is also said to have had significant side-effects, in bringing together staff from many libraries in a way that is likely to lead to more productive future working relationships and other collaborative projects. The project will continue in the direction of further broader cooperation in technical matters, standardization and content. An important feature is that the products will also be accessible through the Internet (Salomonsen, 1993; R. Smith, 1993, 1994).

Another multinational project is being conducted through the Conference of Directors of National Libraries (1994a) – that of online access to the catalogues of national libraries. The project currently involves eight European national libraries, plus the National Library of Canada and Library of Congress, and is expected to be extended to the national libraries of Australia and New Zealand in 1995. The aim is to achieve interoperation through the use of Z39.50/ISO storage and retrieval protocols, and to reduce problems of different MARC formats and character sets. Related to this aim are moves to further harmonize various cataloguing-related practices. The Royal Library in the Netherlands is leading a cooperative project with the British, German and Portuguese national libraries to develop a generic MARC converter (*User*, 1994), while the Library of Congress, the British Library and the National Library of Canada have held a series of meetings aimed at establishing a single Anglo-American authority file and investigating the feasibility of a common MARC format for the three countries (Anglo-American, 1994). Within the aegis of the Conference of European National Libraries the Computerized Bibliographic Record Actions group (CoBRA) of national libraries from Britain, Finland, France, Germany, Ireland, the Netherlands, Portugal and Switzerland, with EU funding, currently has projects aimed at facilitating the exchange of bibliographic information between national libraries, publishers and booksellers, to study how European libraries can move to the use of UNICODE, to investigate the feasibility of UNIMARC becoming the standard format for a multinational European bibliographic database, and to test the networking of EU national name authority files (CoBRA, 1994; Lang, 1994). European and North American national libraries were also heavily represented at the UBCIM/UNIMARC seminar held in Lithuania in June 1994 (Report, 1994). Several European national libraries were also collaborating in extending coverage of 'grey' literature through the SIGLE project (Wood and Smith, 1993).

1994 also saw the establishment of the Consortium of European Research Libraries, on which many European national libraries are represented (Consortium, 1994). Meanwhile, a wide range of collaborative activities between the national libraries of the UK and the Republic of Ireland was outlined by McGowan (1993). In an even more ambitious project under the auspices of UNESCO, the Conference of Directors of National Libraries (CDNL) is collaborating in the 'memory of the world' programme to develop a plan for the protection of significant endangered manuscripts and archives around the world, with a major international conference planned for Oslo in 1996 (Arnoult, 1993).

In an analysis of the impact of the political changes in Eastern Europe, Lehmann (1994) pointed out that the disintegration of the old system will have lasting consequences for the more advanced countries of Western Europe too, including the areas of culture and libraries. It is essential to develop a cooperative cultural dialogue so that the differences arising from the political separation of the past can be bridged:

> As cultural memories, the (national libraries) provide a sense of identity through the existing literary potential; they are important providers in services and assistance in scholarship and research and are the same time focal points in international relations and multipliers in the complex of national libraries.

Lehmann's survey of the problems of the national libraries of Eastern and Central Europe (for example their very limited funds for acquisition, the problems of physical storage, the underdeveloped state of services, not meeting international standards) shows that these are all potential areas for cooperation. A start has already been made, with the exchange of experts, further training and book donation programmes. The greatest demand exists for the latter, together with the facilitation of interlibrary lending, and the assistance of experts in automation. Results have already been achieved in some areas and direct contacts have been formed, but a solution for the long term would be greatly assisted if a medium-term strategy could be elaborated with the effective participation of the Council of Europe and the European Union. The importance of international exchange programmes is also stressed by the Czech authors, Balik and Knoll (1993).

The range of collaborative activities undertaken by some national libraries is quite staggering; for example, the 1993/94 annual report of the British Library (British Library, 1994b) reveals its staff representation on 72 international organizations, as well as 165 bodies in the UK itself. It is clear that the number of international organizations involving national libraries has been increasing in number and in scale of activity. The longstanding work of IFLA's Section of National Libraries is being increasingly complemented by that of the CDNL, as both organizations have become stronger (Rugaas, 1994), and the two bodies have a number of cooperative activities, such as the scheme for international interlibrary loan forms referred to above. Rugaas notes that with

> organization, leadership and management, and information policies high on the present and future agenda of national libraries, it should be possible to find a number of interesting joint venture projects for the two organizations also in the future.

It needs to be remembered also how much IFLA work as a whole has been underpinned by individual national libraries, such as the hosting of the UBCIM core programme (News, 1994) by the Deutsche Bibliothek, the programme for UAP and the office for International Lending by the British Library (IFLA, 1994b), the Universal Data Transfer programme at the National Library of Canada (Forget and Beriault, 1993) and the various Preservation and Access programme centres based at national libraries in Australia, Japan, the USA and Venezuela.

Regional groupings of national libraries are becoming stronger also. ABINIA, the association of 21 national libraries from the Iberian Peninsula and Latin America, which was set up in 1992, is active on projects relating to a union catalogue of 16th to 18th century publications and associated conversion and microfilming projects (Betancourt Valverde, 1994; Caro, 1994). In Asia, the sixteen-member Conference of Directors of National Libraries in Asia and Oceania held its fifth conference in Kuala Lumpur (Kadir, 1994a) and is planning a sixth conference in Bangkok in 1996. A sub-group of the conference has formed the National Libraries Group – South East Asia (NLG-SEA), covering Singapore, Thailand, the Philippines, Indonesia, Malaysia, Cambodia and Vietnam (Kadir, 1994b), and has formulated the following objectives:

1) To formalize, sustain and strengthen cooperation among national libraries in South East Asia;
2) To initiate linkages for the implementation of mutually beneficial projects;
3) To serve as a forum to discuss common problems and share expertise.

In Africa, the Conference of National Libraries of Southern Africa, founded originally in 1986, has been active in focusing on the resources needed for a better future for library services in Southern Africa (Du Prez, 1993).

Munasque (1993) has reported on library activities within the Association of South East Asian Nations (ASEAN) Committee on Culture and Information, involving exchanges of librarians, networking and document supply, while Sexton (1993) discusses the international collaborative efforts between the National Library of Vietnam, the National Library of Australia and other libraries in the development of a worldwide union catalogue of material originating in Vietnam.

The National Diet Library in Japan was active throughout 1993 and 1994 in the areas of international exchange of publications (International, 1993b), in its annual international symposium on preservation (Fourth, 1994), its international training programme for librarians abroad, linking the national libraries of Korea, China, Australia, Thailand, Singapore and Malaysia (Training, 1994), and in bilateral cooperation with the Russian State Library (Iwasawa, 1993; Third, 1994) and the National Library of China (*National Library of China*, 1994). A perhaps surprising amount of collaboration was reported between the National Central Library of Taiwan and the National Library of China and other Chinese institutions (Professional, 1993; Seminar, 1994), while substantial collaboration took place between the National Libraries of Australia and New Zealand, particularly on a joint networked services redevelopment (Scott, 1994) under the two libraries, Closer Information Relations programme (Closer, 1994). The National Library of Australia is increasingly involved in collaboration with national libraries in the Asia/Pacific region and, as well as projects with Vietnam and New Zealand, is active in a range of aid activities in Cambodia, Laos, Nepal, Burma and several Pacific nations (Horton, 1994).

The assistance provided by many national libraries of the developed countries continues. The programme for the revival of the National and University Library of Bosnia and Herzegovina in Sarajevo needs special mention. In August 1992, the library was destroyed – the fire, ignited by grenades, completely demolished the historical building and most of its collection of 1.5–2 million volumes. This collection had contained very valuable sections of incunabula and manuscripts. A unique collection of Bosniaca and Bosnian serial publications dating from the middle of the 19th century was consumed in the flames. In 1994, UNESCO, in conjunction with other agencies, launched an international assistance programme by setting up an expert commission of representatives of several national libraries. The objective of the programme is the full restoration of the National and University Library. This library and its former collections reflected the multicultural, multi-ethnic and multi-religious character of Bosnia and Herzegovina. The programme also allows for cultural, educational and scientific exchanges between Sarajevo and the international community. Short- and medium-term objectives have been set. The international expert commission met twice in 1994 and discussed possible areas of support with the representatives of the national library and the cultural authorities of Sarajevo. The most significant results have been:

- a UNESCO mission to Sarajevo with a library consultant, who prepared a study on the present situation and proposals for action;
- a meeting in Prague to support the rebuilding of the Bosniaca collection;
- donation of equipment, CD-ROMs and documents.

Several associated national assistance programmes have been initiated in Italy, the UK, the USA and Slovenia (Mowat, 1994; UNESCO General Information

Programme, 1994).

Another major aid programme has been for the redevelopment of the Russian State Library. The Government of the Russian Federation and UNESCO signed a Memorandum of Understanding in 1992, which included the preparation of a programme and fund-raising activities for the modernization of the library. An expert from the Bibliothèque Nationale de France prepared a report on the overall situation of the library and made recommendations for a modernization programme. The following areas were examined with the assistance of the senior staff of the library and leading figures of Russian cultural and political life: status and administration, buildings and equipment, constitution and conservation of the holdings, public services and communication. Each area showed serious problems; for example, the building was in danger because of the underground railway line underneath, the collections housing potential was very limited, acquisitions had declined and the computerization project had stalled. The report emphasized a need for an international assistance programme in order to safeguard this unique intellectual treasure of Russian and world culture.

UNESCO, with the assistance of the Conference of Directors of National Libraries, set up an International Commission of Experts in 1993. In January 1994, when the first meeting took place in Moscow, a preliminary plan was developed consisting of four major projects:

- modernization of management and operations;
- development of collections and operations;
- development of products and services;
- restoration and reconstruction of the buildings.

A second meeting, hosted by the British Library, finalized the programme and developed an action plan (CDNL, 1994; *Russian*, 1994). A number of institutions and organizations have expressed their interest in the work undertaken by the Commission, including the Danish Royal Library, the American Association of Research Libraries, the Soros Foundation in New York and a number of private enterprises. The European Commission (DG XIII) offered financial assistance to commence automation, and several fellowships, consultancy and management courses have been funded by the British Council, the Open Society Institute and the Library of Congress. The Bibliothèque Nationale de France is giving assistance to the restoration plans for the building. The Commission's involvement in this work had the overall positive impact of bringing the Russian State Library to the attention of Russian national authorities and the Russian public in general.

The Swedish Royal Library has a substantial assistance programme to the Nicaraguan national library (Antonsson and Pelling, 1994). The British Library has been active in Romania (British Library, 1994b) and both the US National Library of Medicine (Lacroix, 1993) and the National Agricultural Library (André and Pisa, 1994) are involved in an ongoing programme of assistance to many countries, as is the National Library of Australia through its Regional Cooperation

Programme to many poorer countries in the Asia-Pacific region (Nugent, 1994).

One may wonder whether this plethora of cooperative activity always results in discernible benefits. As Line (1994) has cautioned, cooperation rarely saves money, although it may often lead to better use of existing resources, and it can also inhibit initiative and retard progress in individual libraries. Line's useful summary (1994) of the potential for cooperation between national libraries points out that collaboration is often primarily a means of assisting institutions in poorer countries to have access to the skills and facilities of the more developed institutions. He sees the priorities as being retrospective conversion, joining appropriate networks and sharing of conservation facilities. Acquiring and preserving documents represents a difficulty not only for countries at an economic disadvantage but also for others that have suffered natural catastrophes. In Line's opinion, there is a need to elaborate an overall programme in which the developed countries provide assistance for the national institutions in need of it in the areas of acquisition, conservation and bibliographic control.

Automation

The literature on automation in national libraries reveals the very considerable disparities of technological sophistication between different countries. In the most developed countries, what might be described as the 'basic housekeeping' automation of acquisitions, cataloguing, loans, etc. has largely been completed, although often conversion of the card and printed catalogues into electronic form is some way from completion. Several libraries are into their second, third or even fourth generation of computer systems. In the most advanced libraries, 1993–1994 has seen significant reaction to the growth of the Internet. A number of libraries have seized the potential of the Internet technologies, particularly that of the World Wide Web, to establish online 'information servers' of a wide range of information about the libraries' collections and services, including catalogues, guides and internal working documents. These include the national libraries of Australia (whose Internet address is www.nla.gov.au), Canada (gopher.nlc-bnc.ca), the Netherlands (www.konbib.nl), Norway (mack.nbr.no), Switzerland (www.snl.ch) and the Library of Congress (lcweb.loc.gov). See, for example, the discussion of the Library of Congress' Web services (Notess, 1993; *Electronic*, 1994). Internet access also enables the libraries' staff to participate in discussion groups linking professionals in similar areas across the world, and may be expected to provide significant assistance to those libraries in establishing 'world best practice' in each institution.

Networking

A second and related area of automation in those countries is networking in relation to document supply. Use of the Internet as an access mechanism is commonplace in countries such as Australia, New Zealand, Canada, the USA and the Netherlands. The British Library Document Supply Centre's request processes are now almost entirely automated (Braid, 1993a and 1993b), and the centre has made many recent advances through the development of its Inside Information and Inside Conferences databases (Everest, 1994) and its Electronic Table of Contents service (Wood, 1993). The British Library has further extended its techniques of document supply in the patents area with the installation of one of the world's largest CD-ROM jukebox systems (Blake, 1993). With the advent of commercial document suppliers, the British Library has been quick to link its services to those of the commercial sector, such as UnCover, Ebsco, Faxon and Swets, realizing the advantages of reaching extra markets worldwide, and the National Library of Australia has recently followed with a link to UnCover (UnCover, 1994). In the USA, the National Library of Medicine (NLM) has long been a leader in automated document supply, and has been steadily integrating its bibliographic services such as Medline and its Grateful Med CD-ROM with its document supply services such as Docline and Loansome Doc (Dorsch and Landwirth, 1993; Lacroix, 1994; Lovas, 1994). Internet access to all NLM automated services is in place (Chiang, 1994), but the library has also realized the importance of extending Internet access to health services professionals in rural and remote areas, with the introduction of an Internet linkage grants programme (Corn and Johnson, 1994). As national libraries themselves gain Internet access, and potentially the capability to provide online services cheaply to homes and businesses, they will have to develop strategies which will assist their potential client communities to gain network access. Canada, for example, has announced that all schools and libraries will be connected to the Canadian part of the Internet by 1998, and the USA has a similar objective for the year 2000.

Digitization

Another major area of development in the more advanced national libraries is the digitization of collections. In the USA, the Library of Congress has ambitious plans to work with other major institutions to establish a 'National Digital Library' of electronic materials, and, with the assistance of substantial private sponsorship, so far totalling over US$13m, plans to digitize five million images by the year 2000 (LC, 1994). The Library of Congress programme builds on experience gained through its five year old 'American Memory' project (Hagenbruch, 1994) of digitizing over 200,000 items from its book, photograph and sound recording collections. In the establishment of the Bibliothèque Nationale de France, there are ambitious plans to digitize several hundred thousand items before it opens. Under its Initiatives for Access programme (Initiatives, 1994), the British Library has been experimenting with a range of digitization projects, including the Electronic Beowulf, Treasures of the British Library, digitization of popular microfilm, image digitization for document supply, and the Patent Express jukebox service.

Major work is also being carried out in the Spanish National Library. In 1993, the library reformulated its policy on the reproduction of holdings: reprography, document access, information access and bibliographic control are all linked through the library's ARIADNE database. The library sees digitization as improving preservation, access, speed in the retrieval of information, the possibility of online and remote transmission, and enabling a very high storage capacity at reasonable cost. Since the best means of physical preservation of many non-traditional information formats is still uncertain, the possibility of further copying the content is being provided through digitization. The library is combining this method with microfilming, by transferring frequently used documents to microfilm; filming is also being carried out for the preservation of holdings. Existing microfilms or original documents are being digitized for the sake of rapid access.

Few libraries have gone as far as the US National Agricultural Library, which announced (André and Pisa, 1994; National Agricultural Library, 1994) that, as from the beginning of 1995, its 'preferred medium' for the supply of information would be electronic, and that, following its Electronic Information Initiative (Ditzler *et al.*, 1993) which commenced in late 1992, it was now fully committed to the goal of an electronic library. Such a goal might be achieved for a library specializing in science, technology and medicine within a reasonable number of years, but would seem a long way off in national libraries with major printed collections in the humanities and social sciences. Nevertheless, the rapidly increasing amount of information being produced in electronic form, the declining costs of digitizing and electronically storing existing printed materials, and the increased effective bandwidth of national and global networks, mean that for the first time very substantial storage and supply of text, visual and audio material has become feasible. There are a large number of problems to be overcome before national libraries can provide the same level of service in relation to electronic materials as they have traditionally provided for print. Many national libraries have been leaders in national networking of services (such as the national libraries of New Zealand, Australia and Singapore and CISTI in Canada), in electronic document supply (such as the British Library, where most requests are now handled electronically) and in the development of standards for electronic transmission, such as the Library of Congress with the MARC formats and the National Library of Canada in the development of the ISO search and retrieval protocols (Tallin, 1993; Turner, 1993). However, libraries are now having to wrestle with the difficulties of accessing electronic journals, and linking cataloguing records to sources of online information on the Internet, as well as the library locations of printed documents traditional to union catalogues. The techniques enabling users to find electronic information through the Internet are in the early stage of development, but projects such as CATRIONA (Cataloguing and Retrieval of Information over Networks Applications) funded by the British Library, and the cataloguing of Internet resources projects at OCLC and the Royal Library of the Netherlands (Van der Werf, 1994; Goossens, 1995), may well point the way to viable solutions. In the meantime, few national libraries have the staff with the skills necessary for dealing with all the implications of electronic publication.

CD-ROM publishing

While digitization is being seen in some countries as a means for online access, it has been given a significant boost by the widespread availability of CD-ROM drives attached to personal computers, and the greater storage capacity of CD-ROMs – enabling them to be a viable storage mechanism for both text and images. With the costs dropping quickly, CD-ROMs present a real possibility for many poorer national libraries to extend access to their unique collections.

Most of the exhibitors at the 1994 London Online Conference offered CD-ROM products. This medium now represents an increasing part of the publishing activity of national libraries (European Library Automation Group, 1994). The reasons can be summed up in the following advantages:

- low production costs;
- easy distribution;
- updatable;
- able to store a very large quantity of data;
- readily accessible for users.

Two main groups of products can be distinguished as regards CD-ROM bibliographic developments:

1) the national bibliographies, or other national data (e.g. union catalogues);
2) processing and publication of older valuable materials in bibliographic or digitized form.

(Examples here are the CD-ROM of Czech manuscripts and incunabula published with the support of the UNESCO Memory of the World programme (Arnoult, 1993), and the ADMYTE project of the Ibero-American countries which aims to publish the manuscripts and texts needed for the study of Spanish literature and culture (Agenjo and Hernández, 1994.)

Many further examples could be given from Western Europe, and the use of CD-ROM is spreading throughout the world, with CD-ROM databases in the Russian State Library (Shraiberg and Zaluzhshaya, 1994), and with Singapore launching its national bibliography on CD-ROM (Boudville, 1994).

General developments

In spite of the rapid advances in networking and digitization, for many national libraries in the former Socialist countries the first stages of automation are only now in train. Only with the financial assistance of various foundations such as Mellon and Soros have some of the libraries been able to make progress in the purchase and installation of integrated systems. It is likely that the further expansion, development and operation of these systems will have to depend on the programmes for information infrastructure that the countries themselves are able to ensure in future. Individual countries are at very different levels of development. In Hungary, the National Library is basing its current development on DOBIS and, apart from local online public access catalogue (OPAC) access, is now able to offer access through X25 and the Internet. In the Czech Republic and Slovakia, a consortium of two national and two university libraries has established the CASLIN (Czech and Slovak Library Information Network) project under a foundation arrangement, and has selected the ALEPH Ex-Libris system as the core software. Acquisition and cataloguing modules have now been tested, using the UNIMARC format for description. The service is planned to be available online and through the Internet (Czech, 1993; Svoboda, 1993, 1994).

Several countries are in the preliminary phases of selecting or implementing integrated systems (European Library Automation Group, 1993, 1994): Bulgaria, through its NALIM project, Estonia, which is trialling the Finnish KIRI system, and Latvia, which is installing the VTLS system with the financial assistance of the Swedish royal family. In Poland, automation has been developed primarily using local software and personal computers, and the resulting databases are being continuously expanded and are purchasable from the national library (Sadowska, 1994). However, an integrated system for national library automation has not yet been chosen. At the Russian State Library, modernization projects include the automation of the library (see below), while the Russian National Library in St Petersburg reports that the development of the main information system is delayed because of the lack of financial sources and expertise (Zaitsev, 1993). There are, however, several relatively small projects designed to solve particular tasks, including the incunabula catalogue project which uses the CDS/ISIS/M software. It is planned to extend this database to the whole collection, and to continue the work with books of the 16th century (Gorfunkel et al., 1993). In some Western European countries also, automation is still in its early stages, as evidenced by the installation of CDS/ISIS system at the National Library of Greece (Bokos, 1993), the VUBIS system at the Royal Library in Belgium, the URICA system at the National Library of Wales (Jeremiah, 1993), and the evaluation process at the National Library of Switzerland, discussed by Wuest and Osswald (1994). Apart from the British Library and the Bibliothèque Nationale de France, where new automated systems are being installed as part of the new buildings, major system redevelopments were also reported from Canada (Williamson, 1993) and Australasia, where the National Libraries of Australia and New Zealand are collaborating in replacing their bibliographic systems in networked services with the latest database technologies based on parallel processing (State, 1995).

Multiple scripts

One area of automation that has caused all libraries some difficulties has been the handling of languages which use scripts other than the extended Roman alphabet. Advances in this area have been fuelled by the rapid technological advances in Asian countries, which is leading to a need for all computers to be able to handle scripts such as Chinese, Japanese, Korean and Arabic. As the countries of Eastern Europe start to use more computers, a similar need has risen in relation to the languages based on the Cyrillic character set. For some years, a dedicated group has been evolving the UNICODE, as a means of encoding all scripts in an internationally standardized way. However, few automated library systems have been able to handle UNICODE, although the US bibliographic utilities OCLC and RLIN have offered a range of script capabilities for some years. Several automated system vendors are now offering multi-script capability to some extent, and it may be expected that any national library which chooses to invest in such systems as Innovative Interfaces, URICA and VTLS will have multi-script capability in the near future. In the meantime, in-house developments have been reported for the new British Library (Butcher, 1993a), covering scripts other than Chinese, Japanese, Korean and Arabic; from the National Library of Canada (Ballance, 1993), where sixteen character sets are handled as part of the library's Multilingual Biblioservice; and by the National Library of China (Cheng, 1993) in the development of a CNMARC-based system. In Australia, a collaborative approach between the national library and eight universities is leading to a nationally shared system for handling Chinese, Japanese and Korean scripts, based on software supplied by Innovative Interfaces and the Institute of Systems Science in Singapore (Landmark, 1994; Layland, 1994).

Special materials

While many libraries have now automated the handling of their 'mainstream' materials, i.e. books and journals, the full automation of access to specialized formats such as maps, photographs and manuscripts remains a significant task. In general, approaches to these formats have been collaborative, recognizing the need for national standardization and the difficulties of integrating access through library catalogues. In the USA, the work of the Research Libraries Group in adopting the MARC/AMC (Archival and Manuscripts Control) standards has been instrumental in providing access to a wide range of archival materials throughout North America, but this sensible approach remains to be followed in other countries. Maps are a particularly difficult format in which to meet user needs, and the initiative of the IFLA Section of Geographical and Map Libraries and the LIBER Groupe de Cartothécaires in holding a conference on conversion of map catalogues, in August 1993, was welcome in providing much better information on current approaches in Denmark, France, Portugal, Spain and the UK (Map, 1993). The approach of the National Library of Wales was also described by Fleet (1994).

Retrospective conversion of records

In almost all national libraries, the massive task of retrospective conversion of older printed and card catalogues remains to be completed. Several projects were reported.

In Belgium, the so-called MORE (MARC Optical Recognition) project aims at retroconversion of the Belgian National Bibliography to UNIMARC format, through development of software for optical character and structure recognition. This is a joint French-Belgian project which was being tested in 1993. The Czech Republic and Slovakia have set up workshops to undertake manual retroconversion by typing the data into the newly installed automated system (ALEPH), while in Croatia original catalogue cards of old, rare books are being converted into the library's own database CROLIST in UNIMARC format, as a pilot project. Austria, Switzerland, Sweden and Germany are contracting out their retroconversions to SAZTEC (a company based in the UK which specializes in retroconversion). Austria is in a test phase (European Library Automation Group, 1993 and 1994).

Services to people with disabilities

Several national libraries have services aimed at improving access to libraries by people with disabilities. Improvements in service through the use of new technologies are now possible; for example, through software which enables printed materials and Braille to be 'read' aloud by a computer, for blind people, and also allows typing input to be 'heard' as it is typed. Progress with new technologies was reported from the National Library Service for the Blind and Physically Handicapped at the Library of Congress (McNulty, 1993), the National Library of Canada (Bays, 1994) and the Library Cooperative Office for the Blind at the National Diet Library in Japan (Miyashiro, 1993). As the issues of equity of access to all government services become more prominent in many countries, it may be expected that national libraries will have to offer a range of specialized equipment to assist users with impaired sight and other physical disabilities. As national library services become more networked, similar problems will have to be faced at the community level, either through public libraries or other local public access points.

The British Library

The new British Library building at St Pancras continued to receive much debate throughout 1993 and 1994, to the extent that Day (1994) has written a whole book on the history and development of the project from its origins in 1975 through to 1994. There remains a strong lobby of users committed to the retention of the old Round Reading Room in the British Museum building, after the move of most services to St Pancras (British Library Regular Readers Group, 1994). Some of this criticism derives from a mere nostalgia, but critics have made much of the fact that the new building will provide only a very small increase in the number of seats for readers, and will run out of shelving space within three years of its opening. In late 1994, the National Heritage Committee (NHC) report on the British Library also recommended retention of the Round Reading Room and the vacant land adjacent to the new building for further expansion (BL, 1994). The issue is difficult, as retention of services and stock on the British Museum site would impact adversely both on costs and service delivery, as compared with a single technologically supported operation in the new building. This part of the NHC report was rejected by the Minister; the present position is therefore that the Round Reading Room would belong to the Museum.

There seems little doubt that, for a variety of reasons, some of which are in dispute, including alleged corruption (Overspend, 1994), the new building's rising costs have forced compromises in size and design which will prevent it from fulfilling all the original hopes of its proponents. Nevertheless, library staff generally remain convinced of the significant advantages to be gained when the new building is eventually occupied (Lang, 1993). As Phillips (1993) has noted, the new building will provide significantly improved services to support the increasingly interdisciplinary nature of researchers' interests and needs. The rising costs and increasing delays in the project (which meant that, by early 1995, the announced opening date had slipped to late 1996) have been frustrating for staff and enabled critics of the project to prosper. The project has suffered two major blows, with the discovery of both substandard shelving and faulty electrical wiring, which required massive programmes of work to replace them (Mishaps,1994).

As with the Bibliothèque Nationale de France, moving collections from sites all over the city to the new library is a massive logistical task, which has been in planning for some years, and has required the development of an automated 'book move computer system' to manage the project (Greenwood and Shawyer, 1993).

The new building will incorporate some of the most modern technologies for transport of material from shelves to reading rooms. The library has also undertaken a major redevelopment of its automated system; a new multi-script online catalogue is already in place, which will be linked to a Reader Admission System using personalized magnetic cards, and an automated book request system integrated with the British Library Document Supply Centre in northern England (Butcher, 1993b and 1994).

With the new building taking so much of the attention of senior management, it is a tribute to the British Library that it built on its pioneering efforts in strategic planning to produce a major new plan (British Library, 1993) for developments up to the year 2000, and also to sponsor a strategic planning course for the wider library management in the UK (Malley, 1993). The new plan gives high priority to obtaining funding for the collections, including securing greater sponsorship, making users aware of services, improving service delivery through exploitation of electronic information and networking, collaborating with the book trade and other national libraries in Europe and the USA, and preservation of the collections (Ede, 1993; Ladizesky, 1993; Vickers, 1993). The plan has generally been well received by the library profession in the UK, although there has been some criticism of the change in collecting emphases for the library to be 'comprehensive for [UK] material of research interests, but increasingly selective for ephemeral material and for popular low use reprints' (Vickers, 1993). Several articles (e.g. British, 1993a; Craig, 1993) have noted the potential problems of resourcing, and the uncertainty as to priorities if the funds sought are not achieved. The plan is interesting in its willingness to state 'service delivery targets' for the year 2000, for example:

1) deliver six million items annually to users in their homes, their workplaces or their libraries;

2) satisfy 95% of valid requests from British Library's stock or via back-up libraries;
3) remotely deliver 25% of documents immediately, a further 35% of documents within two hours and a further 20% within 24 hours;
4) enable readers to have access to all new acquisitions within ten working days of their being received by the library, eliminating cataloguing backlogs by 1997 and processing backlogs by 1998;
5) waiting times within reading rooms for online catalogue terminals no longer than two minutes.

It will be interesting to see whether these aims are achieved, as they are consistent with the British Library's response to the wider UK government's 'Citizen's Charter' objectives, which has led the library to publish a code of service (British Library, 1994a; Code, 1994) detailing expectations library users may have of each service.

The British Library has been, for many years, a world leader in the breadth and depth of its applied research programmes, which has been documented by Meadows (1994). In two issues of its *Research Bulletin*, the British Library Research and Development Department (1994) reveals a very large number of projects supported by the library, through an annual budget of around £1.5 million. While some of the work is directed specifically at UK needs, the British Library-sponsored work continues to be useful to libraries worldwide, as many of the results are transferable to other countries.

Bibliothèque Nationale de France

Work on the new building of the French national library, which has aroused so much debate and criticism, appears to be progressing according to plan. The building is to be commissioned in 1995 and moving in will begin at once. The official opening of the library is planned for the end of 1996.

The official name of the establishment, Bibliothèque Nationale de France, is supplemented with a phrase intended to indicate its ambitious scale: 'bibliothèque de toutes les recherches', that is, its collection aspires to cover the literature of all fields of learning, reviving the encyclopedic traditions that were interrupted in the 19th century (Jamet, 1993). In its aspirations, the collections and services of the British Library also serve as a model. The services are divided into two major units, according to the depth of service provided: la bibliothèque de recherche spécialisée (the specialized research library for researchers) and la bibliothèque publique de recherche (the public research library for general enquirers and university students). These two units alone will have the capacity to serve close to 8,000 visitors a day. The departments of the specialized research library will be:

bibliographic services, services by subject discipline, audio and video collections, multimedia collections, old and rare books, and the history of printing and the book collection. The collections available to the wider general public will also have similar services, although naturally in reference rather than research depth. The library will offer exhibitions, lectures and other events for those who come to the building only as visitors.

The printed works of the present Bibliothèque Nationale (BN) and the copyright audiovisual material of the Phonothèque Nationale will be brought together. The latter institution was set up in 1938 and has more than one million items: its collection is expected to grow even further with the addition of radio and TV programmes when the new deposit copy regulations come into force. Part of the sound archive will be copied or digitized. This collection will also be organized for use by scientific researchers or by the general public. A national union catalogue of audiovisual materials is also planned (Wellhoff, 1993). The six special collections remaining in the old building, together with other historical collections, will form a national library of the arts, with educational and research facilities. According to the present plans, this will mean provision of a union catalogue and a common acquisitions policy, and will not involve the incorporation of art history collections at present belonging to other institutions (Melot, 1993). A number of articles have already dealt with details of the move, the highly expansionary holdings policy begun in the interest of serving the new functions, the extension of the deposit copy obligations, the creation of the new collections, building the databases, retrospective conversion, and the services based on the fully automated catalogues. The *Bulletin des Bibliothèques de France* devoted an entire issue (3/1993) to the library. Moving the printed materials, the periodicals and the sound archives involves the preliminary checking of ten million documents and their arrangement in the existing stores (Pasquignon, 1993; Sanson, 1993).

The effort to achieve greater comprehensiveness in foreign literature and the humanities represents a major change in acquisitions policy, and supports the two-level research services mentioned above. Even greater emphasis will be placed on the acquisition of patriotica and national literature. Special committees have already been set up, with the participation of experts, to detail the acquisitions programme, and it is aimed to coordinate collections with the universities and research institutes (Simon, 1993). On both the research level and the general information level, there will be direct public access to close to 400,000 volumes. Six million entries have recently been loaded into the BN computer catalogue system (BN-OPALE). The aim is for the entire stock to be accessible and available on request through the terminals of a new system to be set up to cover all types of document. Work is still being carried out on checking and correcting the converted data, and ways are being sought to give readers access to the documents required despite their different former processing methods (Duchemin, 1994). Outstanding works of French literature and the national heritage will also be stored and accessible in digitized form (Beaudiquez, 1993; Boudet, 1993). According to present plans, the automated catalogue system being built will also serve as the union catalogue for a number of major university and public libraries – that is, it will be the centre of a national bibliographic network (Richard, 1993).

It is interesting that two national libraries in Europe, outstanding in their physical dimensions and their use of the achievements of the modern information technology, should be approaching completion on the two sides of the Channel; in the two countries that were linked only a few months ago by the Chunnel, another project that was marked by debates and doubts. Debates have surrounded the glass towers of the Bibliothèque Nationale de France, which have been questioned from the point of view of the protection of the holdings, and design faults that have also marked the construction of the British Library, as well as the enormous escalation of costs. Kessler (1994) has provided an interesting history of criticism of the project, noting it as an example of the Parisian centralist planning endemic to France and of the high-technology 'dirigisme' of successive French governments and presidents.

In a few years time, when we evaluate and analyse the operation of these massive libraries, when they are full of documents, terminals and users, will we be able to say that at the end of the 20th century they represent the realization of a new concept in the history of national libraries, with their electronic databases incorporating the latest in modern technology, their services, and their openness to the public, or will they represent the last of the monumental structures of national cultural policy dreams?

National libraries in Asia and the Pacific Region

It is at least as hard to make generalizations about national libraries in Asia and the Pacific region as it is for those in greater Europe – indeed, the range of country sizes, populations, technological levels and financial resources is considerably greater than in Europe or the Americas. For this reason, few generalizations are submitted, other than that for readers located in Europe or North America. They may be surprised by the technological sophistication of libraries in some countries in the region; and the speed of advance in some libraries in parts of Asia is quite startling.

Throughout this region, various aid programmes are active under the auspices of the World Bank, UNESCO, IFLA and individual programmes of countries such as Australia, Canada, France, Japan, New Zealand and the USA. The British Council has also been active in assisting a number of countries with former British connections, and the French influence also remains clear in the Francophone countries of the region.

South East Asia

National libraries in South East Asia vary very considerably. In some countries, such as Burma, Cambodia and Laos, the libraries are barely recovering from the effects of long civil wars and authoritarian regimes; while at the other extreme is Singapore, which has advance plans for a fully automated 'Library of the Future' with a strong role in national education (*Library*, 1994). More commonly, libraries in the region are in the early stages of automation development and are struggling to play a lead role in developing the library services of their countries as a whole, as in Indonesia, Malaysia, the Philippines, Thailand and Vietnam.

Cambodia
The national library in Cambodia is still recovering from the excesses of the Khmer Rouge regime in the 1970s, when the library was closed, staff were deported and collections were dispersed (Vroomans and Stiller, 1993). With the aid of many countries, much has been done to help, but the library remains critically short of funds, in inadequate physical conditions, and with few skilled staff (Jarvis, 1993). With the current assistance from France, it is hoped that the library building will be fully restored and be equipped with some facilities for preservation, microfilming and binding (IFLA, 1994a).

Indonesia
The National Library of Indonesia has steadily strengthened its role, particularly since the opening of its new building in 1989 (Hariyadi and Gani, 1993). It is gradually acquiring skilled staff, is building collections that are stored in adequate conditions and has a modest programme of automation using personal and minicomputers. During 1992 and 1993, the library signed a memorandum of understanding with four government departments, the Open University of Indonesia and the National Institute of Administration, aimed at a more coordinated approach to national library development and the development of skills in library and information science (Memorandum, 1994). It now has a role in organizing 26 regional libraries throughout Indonesia and in the development of staff throughout the country (Hardjoprakoso, 1993). Recently, its role and functions have been strengthened under an agreement with one of the parliamentary House of Representatives commissions (Hearing, 1994).

Laos
As in Cambodia, the National Library of Laos is in early stages of recovery, but somewhat more advanced. Through the IFLA Preservation and Access (PAC) programme and French government assistance, the restoration of the national library building is complete, the old collections have been cleaned and classified, and a staff training programme is established (IFLA, 1994a). Like many national libraries in Asia, the library has a strong role in improving libraries in the country;

with the aid of the IFLA Advancement of Librarianship in the Third World (ALP) programme, UNICEF and the Japan Sotushu Relief Committee, and in conjunction with Thailand, it has been conducting a Books for Young People project for delivery of books to schools in rural areas (Halfway, 1993).

Malaysia
Malaysia opened its new National Library building in December 1994, and this is expected to act as a catalyst for the further development of services in the country. However, no details were available by the end of the year.

Singapore
In Singapore, the situation is in significant contrast. The national government of Singapore has ambitious plans under its 'Intelligent Island' strategy to make Singapore the information and communications hub of Asia, and is rapidly transforming its communications and computing facilities throughout government, private business and the community. Already, the National Library has online remote access to its catalogue and some other information sources, providing also some transaction capabilities such as online reservations. By the end of the 1990s, the ordinary citizen in Singapore is likely to have greater access to network facilities than anywhere in the world. The National Library, while at present still in outdated central facilities, seems likely to share in this rapid development, following the government's acceptance of the report of the Library 2000 Review Committee (*Library*, 1994). The report sees the vision of its library of the future as 'to continuously expand the nation's capacity to learn through a national network of libraries and information resource centres providing services and learning opportunities to support the advancement of Singapore' and sees a strong role for the National Library in a future knowledge-driven society. The library already has advanced facilities in some of the public libraries for which it is responsible, including home delivery facilities and prototype multimedia information kiosks (Singapore National Library, 1993), and the Singapore government has a highly developed Internet Web server capability. The library is likely to be an interesting model for study in the years ahead.

Thailand
The National Library of Thailand has long played a strong collaborative role in South East Asia, providing a centre for, or with strong involvement in, the IFLA Asia and Oceania Regional Office, the International Serials Data Service for South East Asia, the NLDC for South East Asia, various ASEAN programmes, the ASTINFO and APINESS programmes, and various activities such as the UNESCO PGI Document Supply Centre for the Asia Pacific Region (Abraham, 1992). Within the country itself, the library, founded in 1905 as the result of the amalgamation of three royal libraries, has seventeen branches and has a strong role in the promotion of literacy and reading throughout Thailand, including coordination

of the THAI-NATIS network of information centres, which is currently based on a Dynix system at the library (Wattananustit, 1993).

Vietnam

In contrast to the rest of the Indo-China peninsula, Vietnam's economy is relatively strong and rapidly expanding. This is evident in recent progress in the National Library of Vietnam, where use of technology is increasing rapidly, though the library remains relatively underdeveloped by Western standards (Jarvis, 1993).

South Asia

South Asia has been regarded as something of a backwater for library development in the past, and it remains true that libraries are badly developed generally in countries such as Bangladesh, Bhutan, Nepal (which are heavily dependent on external aid) and to a lesser extent in Pakistan and Sri Lanka. Nevertheless, progress has been made in the region, and the rapid economic advances in India are enabling it to upgrade library services in concert.

India

National library services in India have suffered from the lack of coordination of institutions serving national functions (Barua, 1992, 1993). While the National Library of India has existed under this name since 1948 (though for much longer as an institution), the National Science Library, the National Medical Library, the *de facto* national library for agriculture – the Indian Council of Agricultural Research Library – and the National Social Science Documentation Centre Library all play national roles. In 1985, a Commission on National Policy on Library and Information Systems made several recommendations aimed at coordinating activities more effectively. However, these recommendations have not been acted upon, and the National Library of India operates somewhat in isolation, with a strong emphasis on public library services to the city of Calcutta. A recent examination of the 1985 recommendations by the Ministry of Culture is hoped to result in change.

The Maldives

The Maldives present an example similar to many Pacific Island nations: a national library striving to provide a basic service to a small population scattered over a number of islands. Services are based on small 'atoll libraries', and Habeeb (1993) laments that, in so small a nation, the lack of cooperation between the library and the Ministry of Education remains a barrier to progress.

Pakistan

In August 1993, the National Library of Pakistan opened its new building. While it is relatively conservative in scope and functions, Akhtar (1994) reports that the opening by the Prime Minister is seen as a sign of potential progress in national library services. Pakistan remains, however, relatively underdeveloped in library services generally.

North East Asia

The countries of North East Asia are, by and large, relatively modern economies, led by Japan, which has one of the world's highest gross national products per capita. Throughout North East Asia, the pace of economic advance is very fast, with real growth rates of between 6% and 10% being sustained over many years. As these countries move from being simply sources of cheap labour to competition in highly technological goods, as with Singapore, they have realized the value of information support, and this is leading to considerable expansion of library services.

China

Since the opening of its large new building in 1987, the National Library of China has been developing fast. It now has a substantial automation programme and has developed the Chinese MARC format, a Chinese name authority file and Chinese subject indexing thesaurus to underpin its integrated systems development (National Library of China, 1994). Chinese MARC records are available to other libraries on floppy discs, and the library is working with OCLC to mount its 1911–1949 bibliographic records on the OCLC database (Tang, 1994). The library has a number of CD-ROM products under development, both bibliographic and full text, and, with its recent connection to the Internet, it is working with the library of the Australian National University to provide access to the contents of a range of Chinese language serials.

Hong Kong

There is no national library in Hong Kong, and such an institution seems unlikely, with the incorporation of the British colony into China when the existing lease terminates in 1997. Nevertheless, Hong Kong has a highly developed economy, as one of the communication hubs of Asia and with the second highest per capita currency resources in the world, and its library services are generally sophisticated, with a high degree of automation and skilled staff. National library functions are spread over four legal deposit institutions: the University of Hong Kong, the Chinese University of Hong Kong, the Urban Council Public Libraries and the Regional Council Public Libraries. The government's Book Registration Office performs the national bibliographic function. Other functions regarded primarily as national are performed by the Chinese University of Hong Kong, which indexes Hong Kong periodicals, the Hong Kong Catholic Social Council Office, which indexes Hong Kong newspapers, and the joint University and Polytechnic Computer Centre, which hosts the major library catalogues on its

HARNET network and a cooperative MARC database of materials in Western languages (Lee and Kan, 1993).

Korea
Developments in Korean libraries have recently been outlined in a book by Lee and Um (1994), which outlines the history of the two major libraries performing national functions in Korea: the National Central Library and the National Assembly Library. The National Central Library concentrates on the national literature and has the usual range of deposit, national bibliography and preservation functions, while the National Assembly Library has been responsible for the acquisition and control of foreign literatures. While the two libraries are funded by different ministries, there is a reasonable degree of collaboration. With the significant improvement in the Korean financial and political positions in recent years, both libraries have increasingly sophisticated automation systems, although neither is yet attached to the Korean section of the Internet.

Taiwan
Library and information services have recently been given a greater emphasis under the Taiwanese government's latest long-term plans, and it seems likely that the National Central Library will continue its rapid development (Tseng, 1993a). Taiwan has the world's largest foreign currency reserves, and the National Central Library has benefited from the government's need to reduce these levels; in particular, through its sponsorship of the large 'International Conference on National Libraries' in April 1993, which brought together librarians from 26 countries, and through the library's regular presence at book fairs and conferences around the world. The National Central Library is well described in the various conference papers as a library with a strong programme of automation and networking (including skills in the standards area), publications and exhibitions. Regardless of the future relationship of Taiwan to mainland China (a relationship which is quickly improving behind the scenes), the library sees itself as a world class centre for Sinological research, based on a strong existing rare book collection (Liu, 1993; Tseng, 1993a, 1993b).

The South Pacific

The South Pacific islands of Micronesia, Melanesia and Polynesia include 25 countries and territories, of which 22 are included within the South Pacific Commission. Apart from Papua New Guinea, the total population amounts to less than 1.5 million, spread over a region three times the size of mainland China, with hundreds of islands. Only fourteen of the countries have any form of library service and only five have national libraries – Kiribati, Papua New Guinea, Solomon Islands, Tuvalu and the Cook Islands – with only Fiji, the Solomon Islands and Vanuatu having legal deposit legislation. Some of the problems for national libraries in the region have been discussed above by Simmons (1993), who also gives an overview of the present development of national library services throughout the area. She notes the emphasis needed for a national library in the region to be involved in the wider education and cultural environment, in support of literacy programmes and capture of the oral tradition of the region. Climatic conditions have also required a focus on preservation, and microfilming programmes exist in the Cook Islands, Fiji, Kiribati, Niue and Vanuatu.

With such a small population scattered across so many countries, it is interesting to note the role of the University of the South Pacific Library, which in many ways plays a supranational role in the region because of the centrality of the university to higher education and its relatively greater resources. The university has operated a Pacific Information Network since 1982, and has played a leading role in the establishment of library and information services in the region (Simmons, 1993). Nevertheless, the provision of skilled staff on the ground in each country is not one that can easily be solved, no matter how strong a central supporting resource exists, and training is a significant problem throughout the region.

Fiji

While Fiji has the largest population of the South Pacific island states, it has no national library as such, although the Library Services of Fiji, under the aegis of the Ministry of Education, provide a range of public library facilities through fixed and mobile libraries, and services to government departments. The service is not comprehensive, however, and remains badly under-resourced (Tuimoala, 1993). While there are current proposals for a genuine national library by the end of the 1990s, it remains unlikely without substantial foreign aid for both its establishment and operation (Simmons, 1993).

Solomon Islands

P. Williams (1993) reports on development of the national library of the Solomon Islands since its foundation in 1979. It is salutary for richer nations to note that its book budget comprised only US$4,000 in 1990, and it remains heavily dependent on aid. The Legal Deposit Act is widely ignored; the library has considerable difficulties in obtaining training for staff and has the extra complexity of dealing with the many languages of the nation. There is a system of ten community libraries in the Islands, with advice provided by the national library, but no coordination of library services nationally.

These brief descriptions illustrate the significant difficulties of developing national library services in very small nations. While each of the countries probably receives library-related aid from one developed country or another, or from an international organization, this aid is usually provided for reasons of national advantage; aid programmes remain uncoordinated and achieve less than they might. A more coordinated international programme would undoubtedly achieve greater results, but the *realpolitik* of the situation suggests regrettably that this is unlikely in the near future. In the meantime, the aid efforts of major national libraries in the region – Australia, Japan and New Zealand – remain important, if not over-generous.

Australia and New Zealand
Along with the National Diet Library in Japan and the National Library of Singapore, the National Libraries of Australia and New Zealand remain by far the most developed in the Asia Pacific region, and have a technological capability on a par with the most developed libraries in North America and Europe. They both operate out of relatively new buildings, have integrated materials processing systems for acquisitions, cataloguing and retrieval, and have largely completed retrospective conversion of their bibliographic records (National, 1993b). Both libraries have operated major bibliographic utility services – the New Zealand Bibliographic Network and the Australian Bibliographic Network – from the early 1980s; these have as strong a national coverage of the library resources of their countries as anywhere in the world. Both libraries have had well developed strategic and corporate planning processes for some years (National Library of New Zealand, 1993a, 1994; National Library of Australia, 1994). There are differences in the organizational structure of the two libraries. This is partly because of the greater involvement of the National Library of New Zealand in school and public library development, whereas, in Australia, as a federal state, these functions are carried out at state level, but also because of the National Library of New Zealand's heavy commitment to the project management approach. The New Zealand government has one of the most developed systems of government departmental accountability in the world, and the national librarian is personally responsible for the fact that the library meets its 'key results areas' each year. It is an interesting perspective on the library's perceptions under this system, that its latest Strategic Plan states that:

> . . . the national library's sole direct client is the government. The library will provide policy advice as a basis for government decisions about information and library issues and will develop a role as a second opinion provider of advice on information and culture, relative to other government departments (National Library of New Zealand, 1994).

With the degree of commonality of the two library situations, the similarity of the countries' historical backgrounds and the free movement of labour between them, it is not surprising that there should be a high level of cooperation, as noted in several places above.

National libraries in Africa

It has generally been difficult to obtain information on national library developments in Africa, with the exception of South Africa. As with Asia, there is a wide range of situations in the different countries. The difference is that very few African countries enjoy a strong rate of economic advance; the poverty of most countries, and therefore of their national libraries, may continue for many years. Brief descriptions of the current situation in Togo (Mamah, 1993) and Tunisia (Attia, 1993) are provided in the thematic issue on national libraries in *Documentation et Bibliothèques*.

South Africa

With the re-entry of South Africa into the international community, South African librarians are participating more strongly in international organizations, particularly IFLA, and Westra and Wali (1993) have outlined the national library situations in southern and eastern Africa. South Africa has two major libraries performing national functions: the South African Library, founded in 1818, and the State Library, founded in 1887. The South African Library acts as the national reference and preservation library, with legal deposit provisions. The State Library, as well as having legal deposit and an extensive collection of South African materials, has purchased from overseas to supplement the book stock of the country's libraries generally (although recently much less because of funding restrictions) and has an extended role in the production of the national bibliography and union catalogue functions.

Each of the ten 'homelands' of the old apartheid system also had a 'national' library, and cooperation between all these libraries and with the national libraries of neighbouring states such as Botswana took place under the mechanism of the Conference of National Librarians of Southern Africa.

While still considerably wealthier than most countries of Africa, South Africa has experienced a considerable depression, caused by international sanctions over many years, and its national libraries have been hit with substantial reductions in funding, from which they have not yet begun to emerge. As with national libraries in more advanced countries, the response has been to seek extra funding through the sale of products and services, particularly through joint ventures, and through the improved efficiencies of automation. The national libraries' shortages of funds have prevented extensive retrospective conversion of records for older South African materials, but both libraries are relatively advanced in automation and are active particularly in the national bibliographic network SABINET. Strategic planning exercises conducted by both libraries over 1992/93 (State, 1993) have to some extent focused the position of each library within the South African library system, but there remains a degree of duplication of functions (Westra and Lor, 1993). The libraries' role within the broader South African education system has been explored as part of the national educational policy investigation, and Lor (1993) predicted that 'the report will rank as a major formative event for the development of South African librarianship'. The implementation remains to be seen – the transition required for South African librarianship in the post-apartheid era will probably be long and difficult (State Library, 1993; Nassimbeni, 1994); however, the ANp has ambitious plans for libraries, which include the merging of the two national libraries with some other organizations. These plans have been strongly opposed and perhaps will not be implemented in their fullest form; nevertheless, some closer coordination seems likely.

Zimbabwe

The most recent annual report of the National Free Library of Zimbabwe (1993) illustrates the typical situation of a national library in a middle-level country of Africa today. The annual report is a long description of the difficulties faced by the library in its lack of access to foreign currency, reductions in its book budget, serial cancellations, staff turnover and reductions in opening hours. The library purchased only 717 books in the year 1992–1993, and reports the resumption of copying services as a success. Nevertheless, in its wider role, the library was successful during the year in extending public access to libraries through the establishment of ten new community libraries in the country, and this perhaps illustrates the different priorities that national libraries must have in developing countries.

Other national libraries

There has been a significant number of articles published in 1993/94 which contain simply descriptions of the history and present state of national libraries in particular countries. Other than those referred to above, because there is a dearth of material in English relating to some of these libraries, we have included articles in the bibliography giving introductions to the national libraries of Belgium (Cockshaw, 1993), Canada (M. Scott, 1993), Quebec (Sauvageau, 1993), Russia (Filippov, 1993), Saudi Arabia (Sa'ati, 1993), Spain (Montero, 1993) and Sweden (Antonsson, 1993b).

Conclusion

To us, it seems that national libraries are at various points of transition. In Central and Eastern Europe, many libraries are in the throes of the difficult move, experienced by all institutions in those countries, to a completely changed economic and political system. The greater freedom of movement of library personnel and the improved flow of professional information generally seem likely to assist those libraries over the next decade to acquire the skills and information technologies needed to begin to upgrade their services to levels approaching those of Western Europe and North America. Yet whether the wider economic problems that so many of the countries face can be overcome to enable national libraries to invest in those skills and equipment remains to be seen.

The ability of all national libraries to link to the global networks seems a critical issue. On the one hand, the growth of the Internet is presenting a considerable challenge to the national libraries of the advanced countries. To what extent should national libraries move from largely collecting institutions to facilitators of access to the collections of their countries as a whole and to the increasing amount of electronic material held on the networks? To what extent does it make sense for national libraries to acquire in printed form from other countries materials which are available online on demand? Can national libraries make the necessary transitions in a way that preserves the best of the existing services, while capturing the opportunities of the new?

On the other hand, the communication links that the Internet offers seem also to provide great opportunities for national libraries to gain access to the best practices of their colleagues throughout the world. Through both electronic mail and discussion groups, staff can talk over issues with colleagues, while the growth of national library gophers and Web servers containing details of library plans and activities enables one library's successes (and occasional failures!) to be shared, analysed and put in practice by another at a far more rapid rate. We await with some anticipation reviews of this process in the years to come.

References

Abraham, A. (1992). The National Library of Thailand. Library profile. *Asian Libraries*, 2(1), 80–88.

Agenjo, X. and Hernández, F. (1994) Digitization of library materials in the National Library. *LIBER Quarterly*, 4(2), 144–153.

Akhtar, A. H. (1994) The National Library of Pakistan inaugurated by the Prime Minister. *CDNLAO Newsletter*,(21), 6–9.

André, P.Q.J. and Pisa, M.G. (1994) Managing national resources in a time of change: the

National Agricultural Library perspective. *Library Management,* **15**(17), 16–22.
Anglo-American (1994) cooperation . *Select:* [British Library] *National Bibliographic Service Newsletter,* (13), 11–12.
Antonsson, B. (1993a) National libraries. In: *Librarianship and information work worldwide 1993: an annual survey.* London: Bowker-Saur, pp. 57–80.
Antonsson, B. (1993b) The role and function of the Royal Library – National Library of Sweden. In: *Proceedings of the International conference on national libraries – towards the 21st century, Taipei, 20–24 April 1993.* Taipei: National Central Library, pp. 267–280.
Antonsson, B. and Pelling, B-M. (1994) *The cooperation project between the Royal Library – National Library of Sweden and the Biblioteca Nacional Rubén Darío, Nicaragua.* [Paper presented to IFLA Conference Standing Committee Open Forum, Havana, August 1994.]
Anyanwu, V. (1994) Toward a national classification scheme for Nigerian official publications. *Journal of Government Information,* **21**(2), 129–138.
Arnoult, J-M. (1993) *Memory of the world programme: suggested guidelines for the protection of endangered manuscripts and archives.* Paris: UNESCO General Information Programme and UNISIST. (PGI-93/WS/14).
Attia, R. (1993) La Bibliothèque Nationale de Tunisie. *Documentation et Bibliothèques,* **39**(2), 79–82.
Australian (1993) *Academic and Research Libraries* (Special issue: Sir Harold White, 1905–1992), **24**(3), 149–230.
Balik, V. and Knoll A. (1993) The role of the international exchange of publications in the National Library in Prague. *Resource Sharing and Information Networks,* **8**(2), 57–64.
Ballance, V. (1993) Using the Windows GUI to create a multilingual, multiscript database on MINISIS. *Library Software Review,* **12**(3), 24–29.
Barua, B.P. (1992) The national library system. In: *National policy on library and information system and services for India: perspectives and projections.* Bombay: Popular Prakashan, pp. 41–60.
Barua, B.P. (1993) National Library of India : past, present and future. In: *Proceedings of the International conference on national libraries – towards the 21st century, Taipei, 20–24 April 1993.* Taipei: National Central Library, pp. 427–439.
Bays, D. (1994) Equalizing opportunity for students with disabilities: the role of the National Library of Canada and Canadian university libraries. *National Library News,* **26**(12), 6–7.
Beaudiquez, M. (1993) Le chantier conversion retrospective de la Bibliothèque Nationale. *Bulletin des Bibliothèques de France,* **38**(3), 8–19.
Beaumont, J. and Lunau, C. (1994) Document supply: a challenge for Canadian libraries. *Interlending and Document Supply,* **22**(3), 15–21.
Berry, J. N. (1993) Why adopt Reagan/Bush solutions in the Clinton era? Don't sell the Library of Congress. *Library Journal,* **118**(5), 6.
Betancourt Valverde, V. (1994) ABINIA's report to the 20th meeting of the Conference of Directors of National Libraries, Barcelona 1993. *IFLA Section of National Libraries Newsletter,* (1), 34–36.
BIC (1993) – the story so far. *Bookseller,* (4552), 44–46.
BL (1994) to keep Round Reading Room? *Library Association Record,* **96**(8), 401.
Blake, P. (1993) British Library's Patent Express adds jukebox system. *Information Today,* **10**(7), 36–37.

Bokos, G. (1993) UNIMARC, CDS/ISIS and conversion of records in the National Library of Greece. *Program,* (27), 135–148.

Bolos, A.M. (1993) Role and functions of national libraries. In: *Proceedings of the International conference on national libraries – towards the 21st century, Taipei, 20–24 April 1993.* Taipei: National Central Library, pp. 497–515.

Borodin, O. R. (1994) Kakoj dolžna byt 'nacional'naâ biblioteka? *Nauchnye i Tekhnicheskie Biblioteki,* (4), 7–10.

Boudet, I. (1993) Project d'enrichissement pour le catalogue de la Bibliothèque de France. *Bulletin des Bibliothèques de France,* **38**(3), 50–52.

Boudville, V. (1994) Singapore National Library produces its first CD-ROM. *CDNLAO Newsletter,* (21), 3.

Bourne, R. (1993a) National bibliographies do they have a future? *Alexandria,* **5**(2), 99–110.

Bourne, R. (1993b) Shared cataloguing: the way forward. *New Library World,* **94**(1107), 25–26.

Bowker, R. R. (1993) A Congressional or a National Library? *Library Journal,* **118**(17), 86–87.

Bradbury, D. (1993) British Library Document Supply Centre strategy: the next ten years. Interlending and Document Supply, **21**(3), 7–11.

Braid, J.A. (1993a) Electronic document delivery: a reality at last? *Aslib Proceedings,* **45**(6), 161–166.

Braid, J.A. (1993b) Electronic document delivery: the dawn of a new age. In: *Proceedings of the 7th Annual Computers in Libraries Conference, London, February 1993.* Westport, CT: Meckler, pp.155–159.

Brault, J-R. (1993) La Bibliothèque nationale de l'avenir: quelques réflexions impertinentes. *Documentation et Bibliothèques,* **39**(2), 101–104.

British (1993a) Library sees the electronic future. *Library Association Record,* **95**(7), 390.

British (1993b) Library to pay copyright fees on all photocopies sent to USA. *British Library News,* (180), 1.

British Library (1993) *For scholarship, research and innovation: strategic objectives for the year 2000.* London: British Library.

British Library (1994a) *Code of service.* London: BL.

British Library (1994b). *Twenty-first annual report 1993–94.* London: BL.

British Library Regular Readers' Group (1994). *The great British Library disaster.* 2nd rev. ed. London: BLRRG.

British Library Research and Development Department (1994). *Research Bulletin,* (10), 1–27; (9), 1–22.

Bulavas, V. (1993) The Lithuanian library network. *LIBER Quarterly,* **3**(3), 258–274.

Butcher, R. (1993a) Multi-lingual OPAC developments in the British Library. *Program,* **27**(2), 165–171.

Butcher, R. (1993b) An overview of British library automation at St. Pancras. *Program,* **27**(3), 281–292.

Butcher, R. (1994) The British Library online catalogue. *Managing Information,* **1**(2), 41–43.

Caro, C. (1994) ABINIA: a project for cooperation between libraries in Latin America. *IFLA Journal,* **20**(4), 441–448.

CDNL (1994) and Unesco support rehabilitation of the Russian State Library. *IFLA Journal,* **20**(1), 86.

Chan, Y-S. (1993) The role and function of national libraries. In: *Proceedings of the International conference on national libraries towards the 21st century, Taipei, 20–24 April 1993*. Taipei: National Central Library, pp. 281–293.

Cheng, Z. (1993) The development of Chinese bibliographical automation in China. *Committee on East Asian Libraries Bulletin*, (99), 24–31.

Chevallier, A. (1993) Cultural heritage and legal deposit: the new French law (20 June 1992). In: *Proceedings of the International conference on national libraries - towards the 21st century, Taipei, 20–24 April 1993*. Taipei: National Central Library, pp. 188–209.

Chiang, D. (1994) Reaching NLM through the Internet. *Medical Reference Services Quarterly*, **13**(1), 83–92.

Closer (1994) information relations. *National Library of Australia Gateways*, (12), 1.

CoBRA (1994) initiates electronic media study. *Select:* [British Library] *National Bibliographic Service Newsletter*, (14), 8.

Cockshaw, P. (1993) The tasks and role of national libraries: the case of Belgium. In: *Proceedings of the International conference on national libraries towards the 21st century, Taipei, 20–24 April 1993*. Taipei: National Central Library, pp. 613–619.

Code (1994) of service. *Select:* [British Library] *National Bibliographic Service Newsletter*, (12), 7.

Conference of Directors of National Libraries (1994a) *Access to electronic catalogues of national libraries: progress report*. (CDNL Report 1994/6). [Paper presented to Conference of Directors of National Libraries, Havana, 25 August 1994.]

Conference of Directors of National Libraries (1994b) Task Force on Issues Relating to Bibliographic Records. *Comparative study of the role of national bibliographic agencies in achieving bibliographic control of their national publishing output. Final report on stage one.* Canberra: National Library of Australia, p. 13.

Conference of Directors of National Libraries (1994c) *Working Group on Legal Deposit and Electronic Publishing*. (CDNL Report 1994/4) [Paper presented at the Conference of Directors of National Libraries, Havana, 25 August 1994.]

Consortium (1994) of European Research Libraries. *British Library News*, (188), 1.

Cooperative (1994) cataloguing scheme. National Library of Australia *Gateways*, (12), 8.

Copyright Libraries (1993) Shared Cataloguing Project Steering Group. *Shared cataloguing: report to the principals of the six copyright libraries*. London: British Library National Bibliographic Service.

Corn, M. and Johnson, F.E. (1994) Connecting the health sciences community to the Internet: the NLM/NSF grant program. *Bulletin of the Medical Library Association*, **82**(4), 392–396.

Cornish, G. (1992) The changing role of the national library in the new information environment. *Alexandria*, **4**(2), 125–142.

Cornish, G. (1993) Au centre ou à la peripherie? Aperçu international du rôle des bibliothèques nationales dans les réseaux de documentation. *Documentation et Bibliothèques*, **39**(2), 53–57.

Craig, J. (1993) UBIS response to British Library Strategic Plan. *UBIS News*, (2), 5–6.

Crook, A. (1993) The distributed national collection: an overview. *Australian Library Journal*, **42**(1), 3–12.

Czech (1993) and Slovak libraries to be modernized. *ACCIS Newsletter*, **11**(1), 3.

Dahlø, R. (1992) Norwegian research and special libraries. *LIBER Quarterly*, **4**(2), 385–400.

Day, A. (1994) *The new British Library*. London: Library Association Publishing.
De Beer, J. and Hendrikz, F. (1993) National libraries around the world 1991–92: a review of the literature. *Alexandria*, 5(1), 3–39.
De Beer, J. and Hendrikz, F. (1994) National libraries around the world 1992–93: a review of the literature. *Alexandria*, 6(1), 3–49.
Ditzler, C. *et al.* (1993) *The Electronic Information Initiative. Phase 1 final report. A key success factor in the NAL strategic plan.* Beltsville, MD: National Agricultural Library.
Dorsch, J. L. and Landwirth, T. K. (1993) Rural GRATEFUL MED outreach: project results, impact, and future needs. *Bulletin of the Medical Library Association*, 81(4), 377–382.
Du Prez, I. (1993) A short introduction to the Conference of National Librarians of Southern Africa. *IFLA Section of National Libraries Newsletter*, (1), 21–22.
Duchemin, P-Y. (1994) The retrospective conversion of the catalogues in the Département des Cartes et Plans of the Bibliothèque Nationale. *Inspel*, 28(1), 80–99.
Ede, S. (1993) Strategic planning for the millennium: a national library perspective. *Information Services and Use*, 13(1), 25–34.
Eenmaa, I. (1993) *Serving the parliamentarians by serving the nation: the establishment of parliamentary library and information services by national libraries in Baltic States.* [Paper presented at the 59th IFLA General Conference, Barcelona (061-PAR-E).]
Eide, E. (1993) The development of a national library that has not been established. In: *Proceedings of the International conference on national libraries – towards the 21st century, Taipei, 20–24 April 1993.* Taipei: National Central Library, pp. 211–216.
Electronic (1994) access: Dr. Billington testifies on role of libraries. *Library of Congress Information Bulletin*, 53(10), 16 May, 187, 206–207.
Ershova, T. V. (1994) *The new economic situation and its impact on the acquisition policy and methods in Russian libraries.* [Paper presented at the 60th IFLA General Conference, Havana (85-ACQUIS-3-E).]
Etheredge, L.S. (1994) National knowledge strategies and the library of the future. *FID News Bulletin*, 44(7/8), 142–145.
European Library Automation Group (1993) *The virtual library: 17th Library system seminar, European Library Automation Group.* Graz: Universitätsbibliothek.
European Library Automation Group (1994) *Library services in an electronic environment: 18th Library system seminar, European Library Automation Group.* Budapest: Orszàgos Szèchènyi Könyvtár.
Everest, A. (1994) Inside Information on CD-ROM. *Managing Information*, 1(2), 52–53.
Fagerli, H. M. (1993) Legal deposit of electronic documents. In: *The effects of digitisation on library and information services: proceedings of a conference organised by NORDINFO and the British Library, Edinburgh, 17–20 September 1992.* London: British Library Research and Development Department, pp. 75–79.
Farrell, J.M. (1993) National libraries: the role of the US National Commission on Libraries and Information Science in national library and information services policy development. In: *Proceedings of the International conference on national libraries – towards the 21st centry, Taipei, 20–24 April 1993.* Taipei: National Central Library, pp. 573–584.
Fialkoff, F. (1993) We've been LC-centric too long: LC has a new attitude of cooperation with the library community. *Library Journal*, (118), 108.
Filippov, I.S. (1993) Russian State Library: development strategy towards the 21st century. In: *Proceedings of the International conference on national libraries – towards the 21st century,*

Taipei, 20–24 April 1993. Taipei: National Central Library, pp. 185–186.

Fleet, C. (1994) Comparing automated map catalogue systems: a pilot study based on the National Library of Wales. *Program*, **28**(3), 223–237.

Forget, L. and Beriault, J-E. (1993) Open Systems Interconnection (OSI) and achievements at the National Library of Canada. *Documentation et Bibliothèques*, **39**(1), 25–29.

Fournier, C. (1993) Le dépôt légal. *Documentation et Bibliothèques*, **39**(20), 95–99.

Fourth (1994) Annual Symposium on Preservation. *National Diet Library Newsletter*, (92), 9.

Further (1994) building works. *News from the South African Library*, **8**(3), 2.

Gespräch, (1994) Das. *Mitteilungen der VÖB*, **47**(2), 21–25.

Giese, D. (1993a) The ground floor in focus: redesigning the National Library. *National Library of Australia News*, **3**(8), 4–6.

Giese, D. (1993b) Looking towards the future: a new Strategic Plan for the National Library. *National Library of Australia News*, **4**(3), 3–5.

Girón, A. (1994) The Biblioteca Nacional of Spain. *Alexandria*, **6**(2), 91–105.

Goossens, P. (1995) ELAG 94: report of the library systems seminar on library services in an electronic environment. *Program*, **29**(1), 63–67.

Gorfunkel, A. *et al.* (1993) Machine-readable incunabula catalogue of the Russian national library. *International Cataloguing and Bibliographic Control*, **22**(1), 10–12.

Green, D. (1994) Network publishing and the World Wide Web. *AARNet Newsletter*, **2**(7), 7–9.

Greenwood, D. and Shawyer, J. (1993) Moving the British Library – the book control system. *Aslib Information*, **21**(1), 28–31.

Griffiths, J-M. (1993) Information access in the emerging global network. In: *Proceedings of the International conference on national libraries – towards the 21st century, Taipei, 20–24 April 1993*. Taipei: National Central Library, pp. 667–691.

Habeeb, H.H. (1993) Maldives' libraries towards the year 2000: vision and reality. *CDNLAO Newsletter*, (18), 3–5.

Hagenbruch, H. (1994) American Memory – history meets the age of technology. *Library Software Review*, **13**(1), 35–38.

Halfway (1993) along the Thai-Laos Project on Books for Young People: IFLA-ALP Project 52, 1991–1993. *IFLA Regional Section for Asia and Oceania Newsletter*, **5**(1), 18–19.

Hardjoprakoso, M. (1993) Strengthening professionalism to support library systems and services. In: *Proceedings of the International conference on national libraries – towards the 21st century, Taipei, 20–24 April 1993*. Taipei: National Central Library, pp. 293–302.

Hariyadi, U. and Gani, F. (1993) Library profile. The National Library of Indonesia. *Asian Libraries*, **3**(2), 7–12.

Hearing (1994) between the National Library of Indonesia and Commission IX House of Representatives. *IFLA Regional Section for Asia and Oceania Newsletter*, **6**(2), 4–5.

Henty, M. (1993) Resource sharing among Australian libraries: a distributed national collection. *Library Acquisitions: Practice and Theory*, **17**, 311–317.

Horton, W. (1994) *The cooperation between the National Library of Australia and the South East Asian and Pacific regions.* [Paper presented to IFLA Conference Standing Committee Open Forum, Havana, August 1994.]

Hot (1993) news from national libraries. *IFLA Section of National Libraries Newsletter*, (1), 24–26.

IFLA (1994a) PAC news from Laos. *IFLA Regional Section for Asia and Oceania Newsletter*, 6(2), 6.
IFLA (1994b) Voucher scheme to simplify payment for international interlibrary transactions: progress report to July 1994. Boston Spa: IFLA Offices for UAP and International Lending.
Initiatives (1994) for Access. *Document Supply News*, (42), 2.
International (1993a) conference on National Libraries, Taipei, 20–24 April 1993. *Proceedings: towards the 21st century*. Taipei: National Central Library.
International (1993b) cooperation activities of the National Diet Library: review of international exchange of publications. *National Diet Library Newsletter*, (90), 1–3.
Ishizuka, E. (1993) A problem that faces the National Diet Library [in Japanese]. *Toshokan-Kai*, **45**(1), 26–32.
Iwasawa, S. (1993) Participating in the Second Russo-Japanese National Library Seminar [in Japanese]. *Toshokan Zasshi*, **87**(5), 304–305.
Jamet, D. (1993) La Bibliothèque de France, bibliothèque de toutes les recherches *Documentation et Bibliothèques*, **39**(2), 59–64.
Jarvis, H. (1993) Restoring the bibliographic heritage of Vietnam and Cambodia. *International Cataloguing and Bibliographic Control*, **22**(3), 42–45
Jauslin, J. F. (1992) The Swiss National Library. *Alexandria*, **4**(3), 187–195.
Jauslin, J.-F. and Bauermeister, O. (1993) Survey of the strategic plans of Europe's national libraries. *IFLA Section of National Libraries Newsletter*, (1), 12–18.
Jeremiah, D. (1993) Investing your own reality: open systems at the National Library of Wales. *Aslib Information*, **21**(4), 161–162.
Kadir, M. A. (1994a) 5th Conference of Directors of National Libraries of Asia and Oceania (CDNLAO). *IFLA Section of National Libraries Newsletter*, (1), 27–32.
Kadir, M.A. (1994b) National Libraries Group – Southeast Asia (NLG-SEA). *IFLA Section of National Libraries Newsletter*, (1), 32–34.
Kenjo, T. (1993) Ideal environment for preservation: underground stacks of the National Diet Library [in Japanese]. *Biblos (Japan)*, **44**(6), 12–16.
Kessler, J. (1994) The Bibliothèque Nationale de France project: access or expediency? *Journal of Librarianship and Information Science*, **26**(3), 121–133.
Kirkus-Lamont, J. (1993) The N strategy. *Wilson Library Bulletin*, **67**(8), 52–54.
Kovač, M. A. (1994) Ozivotvorena Matica Slovenska a geolovakistika. *Knizice a Informacie*, **26**(1), 1–3.
Krarup, K. (1993a) The process of modernization and organizational change. *Nordinfo*, **16**(4), 12–24.
Krarup, K. (1993b) The Royal Library, Copenhagen – architectural competition 1993. *LIBER Quarterly*, **3**(4), 347–353.
Lacroix, E-M. (1993) The international role of the National Library of Medicine. *Bibliotheca Medica Canadiana*, **14**(3), 123–132.
Lacroix, E-M. (1994) System for automated interlibrary loan. *Bulletin of the Medical Library Association*, **82**(2), 171–175.
Ladizesky, K. (1993) The British Library's strategic objectives for the year 2000. *Focus on International and Comparative Librarianship*, **24**(2), 65–67.
Landmark (1994) decisions made by CJK Steering Committee. *National Library of Australia Gateways*, (9), 1.
Lang, B. (1993) La British Library à St. Pancras. *Documentation et Bibliothèques*, **39**(2), 65–68.

Lang, B. (1994) The exchange of bibliographic data across Europe. *Select:* [British Library] *National Bibliographic Service Newsletter,* (14), 10–12.
Larsen, S. (1992) The reorganization of national library functions in Denmark. *Alexandria,* 4(2), 113–122.
Launo, R. (1993) National resources libraries policy – industrial information sources. In: *Proceedings of the International conference on national libraries - towards the 21st century, Taipei, 20–24 April 1993.* Taipei: National Central Library, pp. 13–21.
Layland, P. (1994) The CJK Project. *National Library of Australia News,* 4(10), 9–11.
LC (1993) suspends interlibrary loan to foreign libraries. *Library of Congress Information Bulletin,* (52), 183.
LC (1994) announces major donations for National Digital Library. *Advanced Technology Libraries,* 23(11), 1–2.
Lee, C.C. (1993) Functions and problems of national libraries in developing countries. In: *Proceedings of the International conference on national libraries – towards the 21st century, Taipei, 20–24 April 1993.* Taipei: National Central Library, pp. 1039–1056.
Lee, C-F. and Kan, L-B. (1993) Services to the community in a metropolis without a central library: the Hong Kong experience. In: *Proceedings of the International conference on national libraries – towards the 21st century, Taipei, 20–24 April 1993.* Taipei: National Central Library, pp. 1019–1037.
Lee, P. and Um, Y.A. (1994) *Libraries and librarianship in Korea.* Westport, CT: Greenwood Press, pp. 15–32.
Lehmann, K-D. (1993) Die Deutsche Bibliothek: Germany's National Library and National Bibliographic Agency. *Alexandria,* 5(3), 161–174.
Lehmann, K-D. (1994) National libraries in Eastern Europe – a period of transition. *Alexandria,* 6(2), 107–113.
Librarian (1993) of Congress presents Strategic Plan to Congress. *IRLA Newsletter,* pp. 4–5.
Librarian (1994) appoints Film Preservation Task Forces to assist planning national program. *Library of Congress Information Bulletin,* 53(4), 63–64.
Library (1993) of Congress suspends ILL to foreign libraries. *American Libraries,* (24), 469.
Library (1994) *2000: investing in a learning nation. Report of the Library 2000 Review Committee.* Singapore: SNP Publishers.
Line, M. B. (1992) National libraries. In: *Librarianship and information work worldwide 1992: an annual survey.* London. Bowker-Saur, pp. 51–70.
Line, M.B. (1993a) The changing role of national libraries. In: *Proceedings of the International conference on national libraries – towards the 21st century, Taipei, 20–24 April 1993.* Taipei: National Central Library, pp. 87–104.
Line, M.B. (1993b) National libraries and the decline of the nation state (Editorial). *Alexandria,* 5(2), 95–98. [A fuller version of this paper appears as 'The new tribalism: its implications for libraries all over the world'. *Logos,* 5(1), 1994, 6–12.]
Line, M. B. (1994) The scope for cooperation between national libraries: some ideas and observations. *IFLA Section of National Libraries Newsletter,* (1), 13–23.
Liu, E.F. (1993) A review of the functions of the National Central Library. In: *Proceedings of the International conference on national libraries – towards the 21st century, Taipei, 20–24 April 1993.* Taipei: National Central Library, pp. 391–404.
Lor, P. (1993) Library and information services: report of the NEPI Library and Information

Services Research Group Review. *Innovation*, (6), 47–53.
Lovas, I. (1994) A look at LOANSOME DOC service. *Bulletin of the Medical Library Association*, **82**(2), 176–180.
McGowan, I.D. (1993) *National library cooperation in the United Kingdom and the Republic of Ireland.* [Paper presented to the IFLA Conference Workshop on Cooperation, Networking and Resource-sharing between National Libraries, Barcelona, August 1993.]
McNulty, T. (1993) EASI access to library technology. *Library Hi Tech News*, (104), 23–25.
McVey, E. M. and Hanfman, D. T. (1993) National evaluation of user profiles in aquaculture. *Journal of Agricultural and Food Information*, **1**(2), 107–124.
Malley, I. (1993) Preparing for the top: the British Library's policy-making and strategic management course. *Librarian Career Development*, **1**(2), 25–27.
Mamah, Z. (1993) Coup d'oeil sur la Bibliothèque Nationale du Togo. *Documentation et Bibliothèques*, **39**(2), 75–77.
Map (1993) retroconversions issue. *LIBER Quarterly*, **3**(1).
Marte, H. (1994) Die Auswirkungen des UOG 1993 auf die ÖNB. *Mitteilungen der Vereinigung Österreichischer Bibliothekarinnen and Bibliothekare*, **47**(1), 32–38.
Mason, M. G. (1993) More than a library for Congress: making the nation's library. *Library Journal*, **118**(18), 40–43.
Mason, T. (1993) Boost for BL as Digital donate £1m for equipment. *Library Association Record*, **95**, 320–321.
Massuard, A. (1993) Principles for charging at the Bibliothèque de France. *UC&R Newsletter*, (38), 16–17.
Matheson, A. (1993) The role of the national library. In: *Proceedings of the UK Office for Library Networking Conference, April 2–5, 1992*, ed. J.W.T. Smith. Westport, CT: Meckler, 1993, pp. 178–185.
Meadows, A. J. (1994) *Innovation in information: twenty years of the British Library Research and Development Department.* East Grinstead: Bowker-Saur. (British Library Research Series).
Melot, M. (1993) The national library of arts project in Paris. *Art Libraries Journal*, **18**(4), 4–10.
Memorandum (1994) of understanding between the National Library of Indonesia and several departments and non-departmental government institutions. *IFLA Regional Section for Asia and Oceania Newsletter*, **5**(2), 3.
Mishaps (1994) spark doubts at BL deadline (defective wiring and sprinkler systems installed). *Library Association Record*, vol. **96**(2), 64–65.
Miyashiro, N. (1993) Guide to the Library Cooperative Office for the Blind, National Diet Library [in Japanese]. *Semnon Toshokan*, (146), 34–37.
Montero, C.L. (1993) Roles and functions of national libraries today: the National Library of Spain. In: *Proceedings of the International conference on national libraries – towards the 21st century, Taipei, 20–24 April 1993.* Taipei: National Central Library, pp. 585–602.
Mowat, I. (1994) *The revival of the National and University Library of Bosnia and Herzegovina in Sarajevo. A study of options and proposals.* Paris: UNESCO.
Munasque, N.V. (1993) National libraries cooperation through networking, resource sharing and interchange of materials, the ASEAN National Libraries model. In: *Proceedings of the International conference on national libraries – towards the 21st century, Taipei, 20–24 April 1993.* Taipei: National Central Library, pp. 967–978.

Nassimbeni, M. (1994) Constructing national library and information policy options for South Africa within the framework of educational transformation. *Journal of Librarianship and Information Science,* **26**(3), September, 149–155.

National (1993a) Library Service spruces up: renovation celebrates services and efficiency. *Library of Congress Information Bulletin,* **53**(2), 14 January 1994, 31–32.

National (1993b) Library's retrospective conversion – finished at last. *National Library of Australia Gateways,* (2), 1–2.

National (1994) Diet Library sends a delegation to China for the 13th Mutual Visit Program. *National Diet Library Newsletter,* (92), 7–8.

National Agricultural Library (1994) *Annual report for 1993.* Beltsville, MD: NAL.

National Free Library of Zimbabwe (1993) *Annual report of the Chairman of the Council of the National Library and Documentation Service for the year ended June 1993.* Bulawayo: NFLZ.

National Library of Australia (1994) *Service to the nation: access to the globe. Strategic plan 1993–98.* Canberra: NLA.

National Library of Canada (1994) Working Group to Review and Update the Canadian Information Resource Sharing Strategy. *Discussion document: a Canadian information resource sharing strategy.* Ottawa: National Library of Canada.

National Library of China (1994). Beijing: NLC.

National Library of New Zealand (1993a) *Corporate plan 1993/94.* Wellington: NLNZ.

National Library of New Zealand (1993b) *The N strategy: recommendations for actions for prosperity.* Wellington: National Library of New Zealand and New Zealand Library and Information Association.

National Library of New Zealand (1994) *Strategic directions: linking the peoples of New Zealand with information.* Wellington: NLNZ.

National Library of Wales (1993). *Annual report 1992–93.* Aberystwyth: NLW.

Nelson, M. (1993) The Library of Congress: an important stop on the information highway. *Information Today,* **10**(4), 68–70.

New Zealand Library and Information Association (1994) *The N strategy: update for the NZLIA/ALIA Joint Conference.* Wellington: NZLIA.

News (1994) from the IFLA UBCIM Core Programme. *IFLA Journal,* **20**(4), 509–511.

Nielsen, E. K. (1993) Stagnation or change: on the crisis and rebirth of national libraries worldwide. An optimist's view. In: *Proceedings of the International conference on national libraries – towards the 21st century, Taipei, 20–24 April 1993.* Taipei: National Central Library, pp. 253–265.

Nilsson, K. (1994) BIBSAM and its role in coordination and support of Swedish research libraries. *Alexandria,* **6**(1), 63–71.

Notess, G. R. (1993) LC's debut on the Internet. *Database,* **16**(5), 84–87.

Nugent, A. (1994) The Regional Cooperation Program. *National Library of Australia News,* **4**(4), 9–12.

On (1993) the move. *News from the South African Library,* **8**(2), 1.

Overspend (1994) on an overdue project. *Library Association Record,* **96**(8), 401–402.

Panyella, V. (1993) The Biblioteca de Catalunya – National Library of Catalonia. *Alexandria,* **5**(2), 127–142.

Pasquignon, A. (1993) Le récolement à mi-parcours. *Bulletin des Bibliothèques de France,* **38**(3), 20–25.

Phillips, A. (1993) Leaving the reading room: some personal reflections from within the

British Library. *Alexandria*, **5**(3), 201–213.
Pilar, J. (1992) Pokus o nacrt obsahu knihovnickiho zakona. *Kinžnice a Informace*, **24**(8–9), 392–401.
Pinion, C. F. (1992) Our audiovisual heritage: a national and international challenge. *Alexandria,* **4**(3), 155–170. [Reprinted in *Audiovisual Librarian*, **19**(3), 1993, 205–219.]
Položenie (1993) o Rossijskoj gosudarstvennoj biblioteke. *Bibliotekovedenia*, (5–6), 3–10.
Poprády, G. (1994a) Az Országos Széchényi Könyvtár és a köteles példány kérdése. *Könyv, Könyvtár, Könyvtáros,* (5–6), 8–12.
Poprády, G. (1994b) Az Országos Széchényi Könyvtár főigazgatói állásának elnyerése esetén megvalositandó szakmai koncepció. *Könyvtári Figyelő*, **40**(3), 351–358.
Proekt (1992a) zakona Rossijskoj Federacii o obserossijskih nacional'nych bibliotekah. *Naučhnye i tekhničeskie biblioteki*, (9), 7–14.
Proekt (1992b) zakona Rossijkskoj Federacii o bibliotečnom dele. *Naučnye i Tekhničeskij Biblioteki*, (8), 5–25.
Professional (1993) exchanges with mainland China. *National Central Library Newsletter*, **25**(3), 5–6.
Report (1994) of the UBCIM/UNIMARC Seminar held in Vilnius, Lithuania, 2–4 June 1994. *IFLA Journal*, **20**(4), 518–520.
Resource Sharing Strategy Team (1989) *Canadian resource sharing: a proposed strategy and plan*. Ottawa: National Library of Canada.
Richard, M. (1993) Le programme de numerisation de la Bibliothèque de France. *Bulletin des Bibliothèques de France*, **38**(3), 53–63.
Roberts, B. (1993) Librarians in the new Europe. Training and education needs of librarians working in national libraries. *Education for Information,* **11**(4), 283–288.
Rugaas, B. (1993) Changing for the future – the Royal Library in Copenhagen in transition. *Alexandria*, **5**(2), 143–147.
Rugaas, B. (1994) Past, present and future relations between the IFLA Section of National Libraries and the Conference of Directors of National Libraries. *IFLA Journal*, **20**(2), 141–144.
Russian (1994) *State Library: a giant in transition. Programme for the modernization of the Russian State Library*. Paris: UNESCO.
Sa'ati, Y. M. (1993) King Fahd National Library: background, aspects and prospects. In: *Proceedings of the International conference on national libraries – towards the 21st century, Taipei, 20–24 April 1993*. Taipei: National Central Library, pp. 441–464.
Sadowska, J. (1994) Serwisy bibliograficzne Biblioteki Narodowej na nosnikach komputerowych. *Bibliotekarž*, (1), 11–13.
Salomonsen, A. (1993) The European National Libraries Cooperative Project on CD-ROM: results, experiences and perspectives. *Alexandria*, **5**(3), 193–200.
Sanson, J. (1993) From the Bibliothèque Nationale to the Bibliothèque de France: moving ten million volumes. In: *Proceedings of the International conference on national libraries – towards the 21st century, Taipei, 20–24 April 1993*. Taipei: National Central Library, pp. 175–183.
Sauvageau, P. (1993) État de la Bibliothèque Nationale du Québec. *Documentation et Bibliothèques*, **39**(2), 89–93.
Scott, M. (1993) Le rôle de la Bibliothèque Nationale du Canada. *Documentation et Bibliothèques*, **39**(2), 83–87.
Scott, P. (1994) *The Australian and New Zealand national libraries' joint information technology*

project and its wider ramifications. [Paper presented to the IFLA Conference Standing Committee Open Forum, Havana, August 1994.]

Seminar (1994) on cross-strait publishing. *National Central Library Newsletter (Taiwan),* **26**(1), 2–4.

Sexton, M. (1993) International meeting on the Vietnamese union catalogue. *CDNLAO Newsletter,* (19), 1.

Shraiberg, Y. and Zaluzhshaya, M. (1994) Creation of problem-oriented and CD-ROM databases and user's service in the Russian National Public Library for Science and Technology. *FID News Bulletin,* **44**(2), 28–32.

Simmons, D. (1993) Changing course: alternative models for Pacific Island national libraries. In: *Proceedings of the International conference on national libraries – towards the 21st century, Taipei, 20–24 April 1993.* Taipei: National Central Library, pp. 323–359.

Simon, N. (1993) Chantier et politique d'acquisition de la Bibliothèque Nationale. *Bulletin des Bibliothèques de France,* **38**(3), 26–39.

Singapore National Library (1993) *Report for the period April 1992 - March 1993.* Singapore: SNL.

Smith, A. E. (1993) National identity and international knowledge: the library's bridging role. *Resource Sharing and Information Networks,* **8**(2), 27–36.

Smith, R. (1993) National libraries project on CD-ROM. *Select:* [British Library] *National Bibliographic Service Newsletter,* (11), 79.

Smith, R. (1994) National bibliographies on CD-ROM: development of a common approach. *International Cataloging and Bibliographic Control,* **23**(1), 1518.

State (1993) Library gears up for 2000. *Informat,* **9**(2), 1.

State (1995) of the art technology for NDIS. *National Library of Australia Gateways,* (13), 1–2.

State Library. (1993) *Annual report 1993.* Pretoria, South Africa: SL.

Svoboda, M. (1993) Automation in Czech libraries – how to proceed. *LIBER Quarterly,* **3**(3), 235–255.

Svoboda, M. (1994) *CASLIN – a project for library co-operation.* [Paper presented at the 1994 Prague Book Fair and Library Forum.]

Tallin, P. (1993) The ILL Protocol Implementation Program: update. *National Library News (Canada),* **25**(2), 5.

Tang, S. (1994) The present and future development of the National Library of China. *Focus on International and Comparative Librarianship,* **25**(2), 73–78.

Third (1994) Japan-Russia Bilateral Seminar and Lecture Meeting . *National Diet Library Newsletter,* (92), 2–6.

Training (1994) program for librarians abroad by the NDL. *National Diet Library Newsletter,* (92), 10–11.

Tseng, C-C. (1993a) The National Central Library and its future development. In: *Proceedings of the International conference on national libraries – towards the 21st century, Taipei, 20–24 April 1993.* Taipei: National Central Library, pp. 23–36.

Tseng, C-C. (1993b) The role and functions of a national library in the age of information. *National Central Library Newsletter (Taiwan),* **25**(2), 3–5.

Tuimoala, S. (1993) Prospects of establishing the National Library of Fiji: towards the twenty-first century. In: *Proceedings of the International conference on national libraries – towards the 21st century, Taipei, 20–24 April 1993.* Taipei: National Central Library, pp. 129–151.

Turner, F. (1993) Search and Retrieve Protocol Implementation Project. *National Library News (Canada)*, **25**(2), 5–6.

Tyagi, K.G. (1993) National subject libraries in India. In: *Proceedings of the International conference on national libraries – towards the 21st century, Taipei, 20–24 April 1993*. Taipei: National Central Library, pp. 531–553.

UnCover (1994) Australia service launched. *National Library of Australia Gateways*, (10), 1, 11.

UNESCO General Information Programme (1994) *Meeting of the Expert Group on the Reconstruction of Bosniaca, National Library, Prague, 25–26 November 1994*.

User (1994) *controlled generic MARC convertor (USEMARCON). Factsheet*. The Hague: Koninklijke Bibliotheek.

Van der Werf, T. (1994) *Cataloguing the Internet*. [Paper presented to the 18th European Library Automation Group Meeting, Budapest, 27–29 April 1994.]

Van Drimmelen, W. and Van Trier, G. (1994) The Koninklijke Bibliotheek: National Library of the Netherlands. *Alexandria*, **6**(1), 53–62.

Varlamova, S. F. (1993) Spechran RNB prosloe i nastoasee. *Bibliotekovedenia*, (2), 72–82.

Vickers, S.C.J. (1993) For scholarship, research and innovation: the British Library's strategic objectives for the year 2000. In: *Proceedings of the International conference on national libraries – towards the 21st century, Taipei, 20–24 April 1993*. Taipei: National Central Library, pp. 231–251.

Vitiello, G. (1993) Legal deposit throughout the European Community: results of an inquiry. *Alexandria*, **5**(1), 41–52.

Vroomans, M. and Stiller, L. (1993) Pol Pot attempted to erase our memory: reconstruction of the National Library of Cambodia is largely a question of passing on skills. *Bibliotheek en Samenleving*, **21**(9), 308–310.

Wainwright, E. (1993a) The national library in an electronic age: dinosaur or catalyst? In: *Proceedings of the International conference on national libraries – towards the 21st century, Taipei, 20–24 April 1993*. Taipei: National Central Library, pp. 375–390.

Wainwright, E. (1993b) The National Library in an electronic age: dinosaur or catalyst? *Alexandria*, **5**(2), 111–118.

Wainwright, E. (1993c) Towards Federation 2001: an overview from a national library perspective. *Australian Library Review*, **10**(4), November, 404–415.

Wali, A.M.H. (1993) The role and functions of national libraries: the Nigerian experience. In: *Proceedings of the International conference on national libraries – towards the 21st century, Taipei, 20–24 April 1993*. Taipei: National Central Library, pp. 405–425.

Wan, W. (1993) The functions of the national library: an examination of the conceptual national library in the information-oriented society. In: *Proceedings of the International conference on national libraries – towards the 21st century, Taipei, 20–24 April 1993*. Taipei: National Central Library, pp. 303–321.

Wattananusit, P. (1993) Role and functions of the National Library of Thailand. In: *Proceedings of the International conference on national libraries – towards the 21st century, Taipei, 20–24 April 1993*. Taipei: National Central Library, pp. 465–495.

Wellhoff, M-C. (1993) The audiovisual department of the Bibliothèque de France. *Audiovisual Librarian*, **19**(2), 116–120.

Westra, P.E. and Lor, P.J. (1993) The national libraries of South Africa: functions, problems and challenges. In: *Proceedings of the International conference on national libraries – towards*

the 21st century, Taipei, 20–24 April 1993. Taipei: National Central Library, pp. 993–1017.
Westra, P. E. and Wali, M. H. (1993) *The present situation of national libraries in southern and eastern Africa.* [Paper presented to the IFLA Conference Standing Committee Open Forum, Barcelona, August 1993.]
Williams, E. B. (1993) The new national library: some considerations for developing countries. In: *Proceedings of the International conference on national libraries – towards the 21st century, Taipei, 20–24 April 1993*. Taipei: National Central Library, pp. 517–529.
Williams, P. (1993) Libraries in the Solomon Islands. *Focus on International and Comparative Librarianship*, **24**(2), 59–65.
Williamson, N.J. (1993) The National Library of Canada: technology towards the 21st century. In: *Proceedings of the International conference on national libraries – towards the 21st century, Taipei, 20–24 April 1993*. Taipei: National Central Library, pp. 721–735.
Wood, D. N. (1993) Recent developments at BLDSC. *Serials*, **6**(1), 21–26.
Wood, D. N. and Smith, A. W. (1993) SIGLE: a model for international cooperation. *Interlending and Document Supply*, **21**(1), 18–22.
Wu, J.Y-T. (1993) National function, university setting: the library of the Sinological Institute, Leiden University. In: *Proceedings of the International conference on national libraries – towards the 21st century, Taipei, 20–24 April 1993*. Taipei: National Central Library, pp. 603–611.
Wuest, R. (1993) From national libraries to the global village library: networks offer new opportunities for traditional institutions. *IFLA Journal*, **19**(4), 385–390.
Wuest, R. and Osswald, A. (1994) Interaction between the consultant and client: a two-sided view from the national library of Switzerland. *Information Services and Use*, **14**(1), 51–57.
Young, W.L. (1994) Access to government audiovisual materials. *Audiovisual Librarian*, **20**(3), 202–209.
Zaitsev, V. N. (1993) La bibliothèque nationale de Russie à la veille de son bicentenaire. *Documentation et Bibliothèques*, **39**(2), 69–74.

Public libraries 3

Bob Usherwood

One of Britain's most respected newspapers recently reported on 'a bitter behind-the-scenes battle between the advocates of the well-funded free public library service and the proponents of market forces' (Hughill, 1995). The newspaper referred to the situation in the UK, but in the last year there have been similar battles across the world as public librarians and library legislators have sought to predict the future of the service.

The idea of market forces was reflected, one hopes ironically, in the title of Australia's first national conference for public libraries. With the theme of 'Public libraries: trading in futures', it aimed to bring together decision-makers in Australia's public libraries to explore the future and develop a shared vision for the service (Bundy, 1994; Savige, 1994). Similarly, in America, the PLA, at its fifth national conference, set out to 'face the future with new ideas' (Flagg, 1994).

In Britain, the Department of National Heritage (DNH) established a major review to assess the scope and value of public libraries in England and Wales. Described as the most important investigation since the McColvin study of 1942, it attracted considerable professional and public interest. The draft report (Aslib, 1994), summarized by Myers (1994), provoked a great deal of comment in the professional and national press (Hyperfutures, 1994; Largest, 1994), including an editorial and a full page of features in *The Times* (Alderson,1994; Preston, 1994). The final report (Aslib, 1995) was significantly revised following further research and wide consultation. It is being considered by the DNH as this chapter is being prepared. Capital Planning Information Ltd organized a seminar in light of the draft report and also published the proceedings of an earlier event on the future of public libraries (Ashcroft, 1994).

In Canada, the Minister of Education and Human Resources for Prince Edward Island established a working group to study the public library service in the province. In addition, a Public Library Review Committee was set up in Alberta, while in the previous year both New Brunswick and Manitoba established groups to look at the future of public libraries. On the other side of the world, *Granthama* devoted two special issues to the future development of public libraries in a comprehensive report on the All India Public Library conference (All, 1994), and Yamaguchi (1993) surveyed the problems and perspectives in Japanese public libraries. In Saudi Arabia, where successive development plans have played a prominent part in the development of libraries, the current Five Year Development Plan 1990–95 focused attention on the expansion of public libraries and the quality of library services in the community (Abbas, 1994).

The future of librarianship was also the theme of the Second International Budapest Symposium organized by the Hogeschool van Amsterdam (Verwer *et al.*, 1994). At this gathering, the changing face of public libraries was examined in papers by Audunson (1994a), who compared the change process in three metropolitan libraries; Emerek (1994), who considered their changing purpose and roles; Usherwood (1994a), who wondered if librarianship was a profession in retreat, and Vestheim (1994), who described public libraries as 'cultural institutions on the crossroads between purposive and humanistic rationality'.

At the international level, the final version of the revised UNESCO Public Library Manifesto was agreed at the UNESCO PGI meeting held in Paris during November. Earlier in the year, those attending the IFLA Conference in Havana heard two papers (Abid, 1994; Niegaard, 1994) which indicated some differences in emphasis as to the precise way forward. However, agreement was eventually reached between IFLA and UNESCO and the final version of the text encourages national and local governments to support and engage in the development of public libraries. It also sets out 'key missions which relate to information, literacy, education and culture'. It reaffirms that the public library 'shall in principle be free of charge' and includes guidance on the operation and management of the service. The full English text has already been published (UNESCO, 1995) and the French text is also complete. Translation into other UNESCO languages is under way at the time of writing. UNESCO's General Information Programme and the Bibliothèque Publique d'Information at the Georges Pompidou Centre had earlier organized a conference which enabled the Central and Eastern European countries and the countries of Western Europe to exchange views on the role of the library in the community (*Bibliothèques*, 1994).

Users

During the year, the views of different communities were obtained through a number of studies that examined public opinion on public library services. Users were a major focus of the DNH review (Aslib, 1995). As part of this study, 922 people were interviewed in their homes and 3,600 people were surveyed by post.

In addition, the research team received in the region of 3,000 comments as a result of a poster campaign and a leaflet distributed by the Library Association. The data show that about 60% of the population uses public libraries at some time and that the service is used by all sections of the community, although not equally by all. England's (1994) study of the reading habits and attitudes of public library users in Great Britain also demonstrated that the public library serves a wide cross-section of the community. A poll commissioned by the Library Association for the 1993 British National Library Week also found that libraries have a large influence on the population overall and that they are important to all age and social groups (Daines, 1994b; Positive, 1994)).

Similar results were reported by Scheppke (1994) in an analysis of an American National Household Education survey, which included data showing 'who's using the public library'. The question of why adults use the public library was considered by Marchant (1994) in an interesting piece of research that looked at the motivation of the people who use public library services. Further evidence was provided by Waters (1994) in a paper discussing the way that public libraries changed people's lives.

Other surveys sought to examine the use made by specific groups of the population. In Scotland, the Community Services Group of the Library Association published the proceedings of a conference concerned with minority ethnic communities in that country (*Every,* 1994) and a report on the needs of elderly people (*Into,* 1994). The needs of adult independent learners were investigated in a research project funded by the European Commission's Action Plan for Libraries (*Needs,* 1994). A report from New Zealand suggested 'that the Maori people are the most disenfranchised when it comes to library and information services' (Baron, 1994).

Papers in the *African Journal of Library Archives and Information* reflected the needs of other groups of users. Leach and Verbeek (1993) considered the reading habits of adults in anglophone sub-Saharan Africa, and Moahi and Monau (1993) discussed the needs of disabled persons in Botswana. Also writing from an African perspective, Raseroka (1994) reported that African public libraries are mainly used by schoolchildren and youths. Fourie and Kruger (1994) supported this view in their paper on the use of South African libraries by secondary school pupils. The importance of libraries to young people was also reflected in a fascinating multinational study of the 'reading habits of children and youth' by Kolodziejska and Luckham (1994). This noted that 'one of the common features almost in all countries is [the] high percentage of public library use by children'. One of the highest levels of use was found to be in the Netherlands, where 63% of young people use libraries. In Britain, a report found a wide disparity in services for children, resulting in a 'failure to accord proper priority to children and their needs' (Hughill, 1995).

In Africa, in particular, attempts are being made to reach potential users in rural and village communities. Services to rural areas were the subject of a pan-

African seminar held in Gaborone in June 1994, under the auspices of IFLA with the support of UNESCO. In Malawi, the basic aim of 'the Rural Library Service [is] to deal with the new literates so that they maintain, reinforce, and consolidate the acquired skills lest they relapse into illiteracy' (Shongwe, 1994).

Political and social change

As Plaister (1994) noted in the previous volume, there have been profound political, economic and social changes in many parts of the world. Nowhere is this more true than in the former Soviet bloc where it is claimed that 'public libraries can now work freely without fear of ideological censorship' (Smita, 1994). Thus, in Lithuania 'a lot of work is already done to deideologize library activities and to consolidate in them the principles of democracy. This work must guarantee the right of all Lithuanian citizens to use information stored in libraries.'(Gudauskas, 1994). Lithuanian libraries were also the subject of a paper (Skuodyte, 1994) given at the 14th Anglo-Scandinavian Public Libraries Conference. Also included at that conference were contributions outlining the position in Latvia (Smita, 1994), and Estonia (Valm, 1994). where public library collections have been enriched by book donations from Finland, Sweden, Norway, Germany and England.

In other parts of the old Soviet world, such as Hungary, changes in the political system have brought about threats to the accustomed level of provision (Papp, 1993). Likewise, Maj (1993), in providing an overview of the position in Poland, warns that 'the losses and the difficulties of the period of change to a new model of public librarianship may be painful'. Public libraries in Poland have also been affected by restructuring. There are many fewer than before, although there is some hope that 'this quantitative regression may be compensated for by automation, and changes in organization' (Czajka, 1993?). A more positive development is reported from Szeczcin, where a business information service is being based on the public library. This service is modelled on the service provided by Dorset County Library in England.

Taylor (1994), following a visit to Albania, reported on a land of literate people without access to library shelves. He observed that 'many librarians are acutely conscious that closed access systems are not what their communities require'. Guilhaud (1993) reported that libraries in Erfurt were also facing the challenge of doing more with less, staffing levels having been cut by 40%.

In Britain, Pateman (1994) reminded readers of *the Library Association Record* not to forget the achievements of the former Communist states. The message was repeated by Hildenbrand (1994), who, in summarizing contributions at the IFLA conference, concluded that 'socialist nations had been generous in support of libraries . . . and the collapse of socialism has had a major and generally not beneficial impact on libraries in those countries'. Gunton (1994), however, took Pateman to task and provided a rather different view based on his experience of libraries in communist Yugoslavia.

The destruction of libraries in the former Yugoslavia has been seen on television screens around the world. These reports have tended to concentrate on the fate of the National and University Library in Sarajevo, but the devastation has been widespread throughout Croatia and Bosnia-Herzegovina. As Davis (1994) reports, 'in Croatia alone over 200 libraries have been either put out of action or reduced to rubble . . . [and] attacks on libraries in both countries have been conducted specifically to destroy any evidence of religious beliefs, linguistic differences, and ethnic origins'. Library authorities in the West have offered some help to the area. The City of Vienna, for example, donated a mobile library to the town of Vinkovici, where the library had been completely destroyed.

The traumas suffered by the countries of the former Eastern bloc have also had adverse effects elsewhere. This was all too clear to those librarians who visited Cuba for the 1994 IFLA Conference. There public libraries, despite the enthusiasm of the local librarians, are suffering as a result of the break-up of the Soviet Union and the American blockade. Minns (1994), describing a public library in Havana, observes that: 'A measure of the poor state of library finances was the fundraising table at the entrance where fruit juice, chocolate biscuits, postcards and keyrings were being sold in an amateurish way for hard currency'. The American blockade angered many visitors to the IFLA Conference; one manifestation of this was a motion passed at the Library Association's Annual General Meeting which 'recognising the damage caused to Cuban libraries by the illegal US blockade and the collapse of the USSR, called upon the Association to provide support and help for Cuban colleagues via its international committee'.

A brighter picture resulting from social and political change is provided by September (1993), reviewing developments in South Africa. He suggests that the public library should provide community information that is relevant and supportive of the new democratic process. Increasingly in South Africa, public libraries are seen as promoting social development (Pienaar, 1994). Although progress has not been entirely smooth, as Woolfrey and Omar (1993) reveal in their study of public libraries in Cape Town, the degree of change in the country can be seen in the professional discussion of the issues facing the 'post-apartheid librarian'. Thus, *Artes Natales,* the journal of the Kwa Zulu-Natal Library Service, now carries articles dealing with the question of racist texts and encourages librarians to 'help the children of this country, regardless of race, sex or creed, enjoy both literature and each other's company' (Pallet, 1994). Nuhu (1994) provided a commentary on pre-colonial and post-colonial public libraries in his paper on librarianship in Northern Nigeria.

Venezuela too has undergone a social transformation in the last fifteen years and Zapata (1994, personal communication) suggests that 'the work being carried out by the National System of Public Libraries has helped to guarantee the democratic access to knowledge and information'. Public library initiatives are being oriented towards the expansion of mobile services to meet the needs of those living in poor urban areas as well as in rural areas where it is difficult to establish services.

Although quite different in kind from those experienced in the more volatile parts of the world, the changes brought about by the growing European Union have also impacted on public libraries. The European Commission is using public libraries to disseminate information about the EU. A relay network is to be established involving public library authorities. Library authorities that are members of the relay will receive a free copy of basic texts, discounts on priced publications and EU databases, a supply of promotional leaflets and training in the use of EU material. The relay authorities bear the cost of staff overheads, are expected to establish links with other 'sectorally established links' such as Business Links, and make use of a corporate logo. So far, about 80 British library authorities have joined the relay. The August issue of the *Library Association Record* contained two papers giving details of the British experience (Dolan, 1994; Gallimore and Connor, 1994). There were plans to develop the project and a meeting was held early in 1995 with a view to extending the relay to the rest of the EU, Central and Eastern Europe.

Finance and funding

In most parts of the world, finance continues to be an issue of importance. In China, for instance, while the Chinese government has increased its investment in public libraries, there is still a serious budget shortage (Chu, 1994). The Chinese profession is split between those who believe the government should assume the total responsibility for library services and those who believe the public library must learn 'to walk with two legs'. The latter policy has resulted in some libraries 'changing unspacious floors into hotels or restaurants for rent'. In Britain, 'the crisis in local government funding has reached dangerous new heights' (*Services*, 1995) and libraries are threatened with closure and staff redundancies.

The question of charging is raising its unwelcome head in many countries. It is interesting to note that charging users is largely resisted by the public and professionals in the West, whereas some, but not all, of those in the former Eastern bloc are more ready to accept it. There, the introduction of fees is sometimes perceived as part of a move away from 'a so-called achievement of socialism . . . that services were free of charge' (Papp, 1993). However, many in the West argue against throwing out the public library baby with the Communist bath water. Strong resistance comes from Scandinavia, where the free-of-charge principle is central to most Nordic legislation' (Nilsson, 1994). It is also confidently predicted that the DNH Public Library Review (Aslib, 1995) will argue against any attempts to introduce new charges for library services in England and Wales.

In Australia, the extra fiscal burden on local authorities has prompted calls for users to pay and a professional debate about 'core' and 'value-added' services. These issues have not been resolved, but user fees are unlikely to be accepted anywhere in Australia, for a condition of the state subsidy is the retention of a free service. Booker (1993) provides a useful resumé of the debate, while Stephens and Hallam (1994) explain how the State Library of Queensland has expanded its revenue base by raising a percentage of funding from non-government sources.

In some provinces of Canada, British Columbia for example, the library legislation also forbids charging for basic services, but other provinces have allowed public libraries to charge fees for public library cards. The two largest libraries in Alberta, Edmonton and Calgary, have instituted an annual fee for a library card and many smaller libraries have followed suit. It thus appears that Canada will be a patchwork of charges, depending on the party politics of the provincial government and the economy of the province (Curry, 1994, personal communication).

Buildings and service points

Despite the financial problems experienced in many parts of the world, there has been some investment in new library buildings. In Australia, it is reported that most states and territories have seen considerable building activity – often, replacement buildings or major extensions to existing facilities (Bundy, 1994, personal communication). The Federal Government's Better Cities Funding has financed 30 such projects in Victoria. In Canada, a new $60m library is due to open in Vancouver in 1995. It will be the largest in the country at 35,000 square meters and is said to bear a striking resemblance to the Coliseum in Rome. In Great Britain, two public library buildings, one in Croydon and one in Essex, received RIBA (Royal Institute of British Architects) regional awards for architecture.

In America, 108 new public library buildings were completed between July 1993 and June 1994 (Fox and Nelson, 1994). A new library is due to open in Denver in March 1995 and, in the words of the librarian (Ashton, quoted in Fialkoff, 1994), they have 'had the good fortune to be able to open a new library with staffing and a budget that makes sense'.

The destruction of a library building was major news in Great Britain. The fire that destroyed Norwich Central Library was 'of major national, if not international significance' (Fire, 1994). It is thought that the failure in an electric cabling conduit was the cause of this disaster. The forces of nature were responsible for destruction elsewhere. The Los Angeles earthquake damaged 23 of the city's 64 public libraries, and 39 of the county's 87 branches also sustained damaged. In Papua New Guinea, a volcano totally destroyed Rabaal Public Library.

National and local legislation

The extent of public library legislation varies throughout the world. It is well established in some parts of the world and non-existent in others; in Australia, according to Catlin (1994), it is being redefined. The new Danish Public Library Act came into force on 1 January 1994, but Sweden is celebrating '30 years without library legislation' (Thomas, 1994). 'Celebrating' may not be quite the right word because there is some feeling that the country 'has come to [a] point when legislation is necessary to protect the public libraries and certain basic principles of the library service'. Sweden is alone among the Nordic countries in not having legislation. Useful reviews of the current situation in that part of the world were published in a special issue of the *Scandinavian Public Library Quarterly* (1994) and a paper by Granheim (1994).

In Great Britain, there has been no specific library legislation since the Public Libraries and Museums Act 1964, but, as Hicks (1994) has noted, since 1979 there have been 168 Acts of Parliament that have affected local government. Public libraries have frequently been influenced by these. Parker (1994) provided a review of an important piece of legislation in his briefing on Public Lending Right (PLR). This explained the operation of PLR in the UK and also considered moves within the European Union to harmonize intellectual property right provision.

In October 1994, the Secretary of State for National Heritage announced that the British Government would be proceeding with the establishment of the Library and Information Commission. The Commission's first Chairman, Matthew Evans of Faber and Faber, was appointed in January 1995 and at the same time it was announced that the existing Library and Information Services Council (England) would be wound up. The Minister has established a new advisory council to give advice on his responsibilities under the terms of the Public Libraries and Museums Act 1964 and in particular on public libraries in England.

In other parts of the world, the progress towards library legislation has been somewhat slower. In Swaziland, for example, draft legislation to establish the National Library Service and a monitoring or controlling board has been on the file since the inauguration of the service. Unfortunately, as Fakudze (1994) reports, it remains in a draft form. In Latvia, the legislative Bill dealing with libraries has been tabled in Parliament (Smita, 1994). In discussing recent developments in Slovakia, Klinec (1994) argued that it is up to library authorities at national and local level to adopt strategies, pass laws and regulations and, above all, provide funds.

In a number of countries, there have been proposals to change the shape of local government. These were of major concern to public library managers and legislators. In Great Britain, the proposed reorganization of local government in England provoked a debate about the best size for a public library authority. Research carried out by Midwinter and McVicar (1993; 1994) tended to suggest that larger authorities produced economies of scale. The Library Association (1994), while not averse to change, also concluded that the larger county authorities provided a cost-effective service. It mounted a campaign that received the support of notable people from literature, the arts and entertainment (Cleese *et al.*, 1994). A librarian, Hopkins (1994), argued that the local government review was political and had nothing to do with good management. She was particularly concerned about the implications for central support services and the library supply industry. There were some early indications that there would be 'good news for a number of county library services' (Daines, 1994a), but the final result was put into further doubt when 'the Environment Secretary . . . effectively sacked the . . . chairman of the Local Government Commission' (Simmons, 1995).

Local government restructuring also occurred in several parts of Australia, particularly in the State of Victoria. In Canada, the Province of British Columbia (1994) introduced new legislation which meant that new libraries will be set up as either municipal libraries or regional library districts, and managed by boards appointed by local government. An administrative reorganization was also promised in Holland. This led the Mayor of Alkmaar to argue that libraries must maintain close links with local government (Pop, 1994).

Politicians and the public library

Pop was just one of a number of politicians to concern themselves with library services. In Britain, Heinitz (1993) gave a politician's perspective on the public library review and the British government's moves towards compulsory tendering in library services. In addition, a former Conservative, Muffett (1993), looked critically at Conservative education policy and asked 'if . . . Margaret [Thatcher] wanted fees at opt out schools. How far is that from 30p a day to take a book out of a public library?'. Two local politicians, Hall and Richards (1994), described their experience as joint chair of Kent's Arts, Libraries and Sports Committee.

In America, the effect on public libraries of Newt Gingrich's rise to power is yet to be felt. However, his recent promise to 'zero out' government funding for public broadcasting does not bode well for those who believe in public information services. Furthermore, his ideas on free enterprise and reading, as expressed at the 1991 White House Conference on Library and Information Services (Donaldson, 1991), and recently repeated before a bewildered audience in a poor Washington neighbourhood (Carlin, 1995), suggest that the future might be a little difficult in a country which appears to have inherited 'Reagan's . . . brand of Me first conservatism and stuck with it' (Freedland, 1995).

Politics was one of the major themes of the Anglo-Scandinavian Public Libraries Conference. There, contributions considered library management in relation to the political level (Munkøe,1994) and the 'paradoxical relationship' between public library management and politics, Audunson (1994b) asking 'how can we prove to be politically relevant?'. At the same meeting, Usherwood (1994c) discussed library management from the perspective of local politicians. In America, Turock (1994), in making the case for federal support of libraries, argued that 'the issues that decide the fate of libraries will be resolved in the political arena. Librarians and library supporters must organize to be seen, heard and cause action in that arena'. She then went on to advise how librarians might get a bigger piece of the pie. In a similar vein Raseroka (1994) believes that the crucial question for public librarians in Africa is how to justify themselves to governments.

The importance of national and international politics was examined by Bouri (1994), in her analysis of the current state of decline of public libraries in Egypt. She argues that this 'cannot merely be perceived as a state of *scarcity* of various socio-economic factors, but as a consequence of government choices and policies precipitated by a shift in national development priorities'. She fears that this pattern might be followed in other parts of the less developed world.

The relationships between politicians, in the widest sense, and library professionals were also debated in the literature. In Canada, Mittermeyer (1994b) discussed the power game between the public library boards of trustees and the committees of city hall and, in a later paper (Mittermeyer, 1994a), public libraries without autonomous boards. Another Canadian writer (Curry, 1994) examined the chief officer/councillor relationship in British public libraries, while Usherwood (1994b) looked at the national and local political influences on public library services.

Public library management

Political issues were linked to management in Cottam's (1994) examination of the roles, functions and activities of directors of large libraries. The role of senior managers in the German context was discussed by Eichert (1994). Generally, management issues formed an increasingly large part of the professional agenda.

In particular, various approaches to quality management were discussed by librarians in many parts of the world, although, surprisingly, given the history of the quality movement, not in Japan, where 'measurement for the quality of services is not developed' (Oda, 1993). In other places, new literature on the subject seemed to appear almost daily (Milner *et al.*, 1994). *New Library World* (Strategies, 1994) produced a special issue on strategies for service quality, and the June issue of the *Library Association Record* (Quality, 1994) contained a special feature on the topic, including arguments in favour of the controversial BS 5750 (Brophy, 1994), the needs of users (Clayton, 1994) and 'taking a stand on good standard policy' (Watt, 1994).

Standards of service and its evaluation continued to be topics provoking considerable discussion. Two publications from Van House and Childers (1993a; 1993b) dealt with the issue of public library effectiveness. Both provided useful data for librarians wanting to justify the service to the public and politicians. Their work has strongly influenced research in New Zealand which attempts to place performance measurement in a social and political context (Calvert, 1994). Performance measures have also been the subject of some discussion in Germany (Schulte-Nolke, 1993; Kommission, 1994). In Britain, the Library Association established a working party and funded a research project at the University of Sheffield to develop standards to support *A charter for public libraries*. The consultants' recommendations were accepted by the Association in February 1995 (Stroud and Usherwood, 1994).

As indicated elsewhere in this chapter, there is a widespread concern that the value of libraries is not fully recognized. Over the years, a number of writers expressed the view that librarians must do more to market and promote their services, but it appears from the literature that there is still considerable room for improvement. In a study of the marketing strategies of public libraries and leisure services, Kinnell and MacDougall (1994) revealed the ignorance of marketing among many librarians. This view was supported by the findings of the DNH review. An Australian paper (Marks, 1994) also argued that an increasingly sophisticated understanding of the complex forces involved is needed to contribute to a model of public sector marketing more practicable for library application. On the other hand, the London Library Week was considered a most successful promotional activity and the Library Campaign was featured in several British television programmes.

Another aspect of what has been termed the 'new managerialism' is the tendency for public libraries to contract out services. In some places, this has been made compulsory. In Melbourne, for example, the adoption of CCT (compulsory competitive tendering) has led to one outer metropolitan authority contracting out its total library service. In New Zealand, national and local governments have adopted the purchaser-provider model, and this is to be found in some public libraries.

In Britain, the Department of National Heritage appointed KPMG and CPI to investigate the extent to which contracting out library service would be both feasible and desirable. Part of their study has involved a number of pilot projects, including the contracting out of two branch libraries in the London Borough of Brent (Casale, 1994; Verstraete, 1994). A less reverential view of the process was presented by Walker (1994). The draft report of the consultants (KPMG/CPI, 1994) did not make any firm recommendations, but emphasized that 'customer reaction as to how the service is provided (either internally or externally) is a very important factor'. The data from the draft report on the Public Library Review (Aslib, 1994) show quite clearly that the majority of both internal and external customers do not want business interests to operate libraries. The government has stated that the contracting out study will be informed by the findings of the Public Library Review; it remains to be seen if it will enforce contracting out against the wishes of the public, professionals and most local politicians. Press reports, at the time of writing, suggest that 'management consultants from KPMG conclude that "there is no overwhelming case for compulsory contracting out"'(Brooks, 1995).

A mixture of the new managerialism and political imperatives has led to the commercialization of library services in countries as far apart as the USA and China. In an analysis of democratic ideals and the American public library, Hafner and Folker (1993) state that 'in their conscious attempts to copy and compete with the mass communications industry for customers ... librarians are promoting the very conformity and sameness that they, as symbols of our highest political ideals, should be fighting against'. In very much the same tone, Chu (1994) reports that some of the public libraries in China 'ignore their fundamental aims while excessively concentrating on economic income alone'. The partnership between a Canadian provincial library and Kentucky Fried Chicken is perhaps an example of the kind of commercialism that gives cause for concern.

The relationship between management and the high ideals of the library profession was explored in Gertzog and Beckermann's (1994) extensive study of the administration of the public library. The tension between the traditional and commercial culture in Polish libraries was examined by Kolodziejska (1994), in her paper to the IFLA Conference. In this, she asked 'whether under the new cultural situation there will be a place for the public library'.

Technology

Technology is part of a new culture; while public libraries are taking advantage of the new information and communications systems, their use is very uneven across the world and indeed within some countries. In Australia, for example, Bundy (1994, personal communication) reports that the application of information technology (IT) and telecommunications is weakest in small rural libraries, while some of the states, such as New South Wales and South Australia, have recognized the potential of the public library as an access point to the global information resource. Some public libraries have also incorporated federally funded telecottages.

In Canada, public libraries are taking a leading role in trying to give the public free access to the Internet. Several major city libraries now give their users Freenet access, and many more are scheduled to do so in 1995 (Curry, 1994, personal communication). In Norway, public libraries are taking the path towards using the Internet (Bringedal, 1994). Elsewhere in Scandinavia, the Danish government appointed a two-member committee on the information society by the year 2000 (Denmark, 1994). The final report includes a substantial chapter on libraries as part of an overall strategy 'which will tie public institutions and companies together by means of modern information technology and create new possibilities for citizens'. Helsinki Public Library's Internet entry declares itself to be the first public library on the Net; overall, the functioning of the library network in Finland is expected to improve substantially in the near future. This improvement will be achieved by introducing the common data register, MANDA, and giving public libraries access to the database, LINDA, which is maintained by university libraries (Kekki, 1994, personal communication).

In the USA the National Commission on Libraries and Information Science advised policy makers and librarians on public libraries and the Internet (McClure et al. 1994). In the USA about 20% of public libraries are already connected to the Internet, and this was reflected in a large number of papers and reports. Kinder (1994), for example, edited a practically oriented collection on the impact of the Internet on reference services. Public library oriented Freenets are used by a wide range of social groups. In Seattle, for instance, a group of homeless men 'discovered the Internet . . . and are now considered to be the in-house experts on the information highway' (Jordan, 1994). Maryland opened its first cyber-library by allowing its citizens a free connection to the Internet. This project, known as Sailor, uses the resources of public, school and academic libraries throughout the state. It has provoked a great deal of discussion, not the least of which is on the Net itself. To quote Powledge (1994): 'Sailor simply fuses Internet customers with an equally vigorous but much older tradition of free information – that of the public library'.

The draft report of the Public Library Review (Aslib, 1994) suggested that British public libraries enhance their services by providing access to the 'information highway'. At the moment, 'access to the Internet . . . is spreading slowly to public libraries' (Batt, 1994a). There are already major projects in Croydon and Solihull, and Manchester Metropolitan University has been awarded a grant by the DNH to identify the use of IT by public libraries in England and Wales. In November 1994, the UK Government Centre for Information Systems held a conference on the opportunities for the use of information superhighways within public services. This identified a need to exploit links between central and local government departments and agencies, public library services, medical centres, schools and colleges. At the end of 1994 the fifth edition of Batt's (1994b) *Information technology in public libraries* provided a comprehensive picture of developments in Britain.

In Russia, the Ministry of Culture convened a conference on 'The Establishment of Information Library Networks as Ways to an Information Society' which, according to Kuzmin (1994), achieved spectacular results. The first stage of Project LIBNET will set up a Moscow library computer network that will unite the six largest Russian libraries.

Public library research and development

Many of the major events of the year have, as indicated above, been based on research; it is slowly being recognized that research is essential if the public library service is to grow and develop. In Australia, the Cultural Ministers' Council, which consists of State and Federal Ministers, has committed $70,000 per annum for three years to national public library research. Across the Tasman Sea, Baron (1994) called for a research agenda specifically related to the library and information needs of the Maori community. McDonald (1993) had already provided strong arguments for additional research in this area.

As indicated earlier, much research has been centred on users. In Britain, attempts were made by CIPFA to establish a national standard for a public library user survey (Fuegi, 1994). CIPFA's Committee on Public Library Statistics produced a draft report (Committee, 1994) and a guidance manual. In addition, IPF Ltd is developing an advisory service. Subscribers to the service 'will be able to develop a range of other products and services related to the undertaking of surveys'. In another paper, Rowley (1994) suggested a 'walk-through audit' for monitoring users' experience. The importance of 'understanding what users encounter as they move through the complex, multidimensional, and dynamic experience of information seeking' was emphasized by Westbrook (1994) in her review of qualitative research methods.

In the UK, the last awards were made under the Public Library Development Incentive Scheme. A successor scheme for 1995–96 was announced by Peter Brooke, the Secretary of State for National Heritage at that time. This will be used 'to fund new projects . . . specifically related to identified problems facing the public library in adapting to current circumstances' (British Library, 1995).

The Federation of Local Authority Chief Librarians (FOLACL) promoted a major seminar to consider the future of public library research (Goulding, 1994). This recommended the establishment of some kind of mechanism to provide structure and leadership for public library research in the UK. Sumsion (1994) examined some possible research models for UK public libraries, while in the American context, Grenier (1994) considered trends for future research in a book that covered such diverse topics as the links between personality and reading and the possible use of retail location theory as an aid to siting branch libraries. At the international level, it is expected that the 1995 IFLA Conference in Istanbul will include a major session on theory and research in public libraries.

A research base is also being established by staff and students in the departments of library and information studies to be found in universities across the world. Elkin (quoted in Goulding, 1994) told the FOLACL conference that a survey of library schools had produced a very positive response on public library research. Some of this is funded research, but much useful work is also being undertaken by Master's and Doctoral students. As Feather (1994) observed, many departments 'regularly solicit suggestions for possible research projects for . . . Master's students, an exercise which has proved useful to [the schools], to . . . students and to the libraries'.

Despite the difficulties of formal Research Assessment Exercises, which mean that departments compete with departments, there is some cooperation between the British schools. Sheffield and Loughborough Universities, for example, have a joint project examining total quality management in public library services. There are also some examples of international cooperation, for instance, the work of Sturges *et al.* (1992) on African development, and a public library research seminar proposed for June 1995, which will involve research students from the Sheffield and Stuttgart schools.

Conclusion

From America, a respondent (Dougherty, 1994, personal communication) reports that workshops are now being held with the aim of 'Transforming Visions into Realities'. It is intended that these will enable librarians to create their preferred visions as opposed to predicted visions and then to transform these visions into realistic action plans.

However, despite the best efforts of IFLA and UNESCO, it is no longer clear that public librarians have a shared vision. As the above indicates, the world of public libraries is increasingly one of competing ideas, based on different assumptions about the purpose and function of the public library. Thus commercialism competes with community, populism with professionalism, and fee with free. Such ideas need not be mutually exclusive, but it is essential to keep discussion open and to recognize that we may not have a great deal of time in which to come up with the right answers. To quote those writers and artists who wrote to the press (Cleese et al., 1994), 'future generations will not forgive us if we allow further erosion of one of our most precious cultural, educational and economic assets'.

Acknowledgements

My thanks to all those members of the Editorial Advisory Board and other colleagues overseas who supplied me with information and documentation.

References

Abbas, H.A. (1994) Public libraries in Saudi Arabia. In: M. Wise and A. Olden (eds) *Information and libraries in the Arab world.* London: Library Association Publishing.

Abid, A. (1994) *Missions of the public library.* [Paper presented at the IFLA General Conference, Havana (135-PUB-9-E).]

Alderson, K. (1994) Books and banter on wheels for rural folk. *Times,* 18 October, 10.

All (1994) India Public Library Conference on the Eighth Plan: perspective of public library development in New Delhi 24–25 February 1989. *Granthama,* 4(1) and 4(2) [special issues].

Ashcroft, M. A. (1994) (ed.) *The future of the public library. Proceedings of a seminar held in Stamford on 1 December 1993.* Stamford: Capital Planning Information Ltd.

Aslib (1994) *DNH review of the public library service in England and Wales: draft report.* London: The Aslib Consultancy.

Aslib (1995) *DNH review of the public library service in England and Wales: draft final report.* London: The Aslib Consultancy.

Audunson, R. (1994a) Change processes in public libraries. In: R. Verwer et al. (eds) *The future of librarianship. Proceedings of the Second International Budapest Symposium, January 1994.* Amsterdam: Hogeschool van Amsterdam.

Audunson, R. (1994b) *Public library management in a changing political environment: the quest for institutional leadership.* [Paper presented at 14th Anglo-Scandinavian Public Libraries Conference, Viborg, Denmark.]

Baron, D. (1994) *Library and information studies education for the people of New Zealand: baskets, bridges, gardens.* Wellington: Victoria University, Department of Library and Information Studies. (Occasional Paper, 26).

Batt, C. (1994a) Buddy, can you spare £4,750,000? *Public Library Journal,* 9(6), 167–169.

Batt, C. (1994b) *Information technology in public libraries.* 5th ed. London: Library Association Publishing.

Bibliothèques (1994) au service de la communauté. Paris: BPI / UNESCO.

Booker, D. (1993) (ed.) *Twice paid: user pays and public libraries.* Adelaide: Auslib Press.

Bouri, E.N. (1994) Public libraries development reconsidered. The case of Egypt. *International Information and Library Review,* 26(3), 151–168.

Bringedal, T. (1994) The Norwegian public libraries' path towards Internet. *Scandinavian Public Library Quarterly,* **27**(4), 7–11.
British Library (1995). Research and Development. *Public Library Development Incentive Scheme. Development Funding for Public Libraries.* 1994/95 Progress Report. London: British Library.
British Columbia (1994). Ministry of Municipal Affairs. *Library services accessible and accountable under new legislation.* (News release).
Brooks, R. (1995) Public and local businesses urged to 'top up' library cash. *Observer,* 26 February, 7.
Brophy, P. (1994) BS: a curse or blessing? *Library Association Record,* **96**(6), 320–321.
Bundy, A. (1994) (ed.) *Public Libraries: trading in futures. Proceedings of national conference 1 - 3 February 1994.* Adelaide: Auslib Press.
Calvert, P.J. (1994) Library effectiveness: the search for a social context. *Journal of Librarianship and Information Science,* **26**(1), 15–21.
Carlin, J. (1995) Well-read Newt suggests learn and earn. *Independent,* 3 March, 14.
Casale, M. (1994) How Brent won its own contract. *Library Manager,* 2, 10 -11.
Catlin, I. (1994) Redefining the role of the public library in legislation. *Australian Library Journal,* **43**(1), 49–55.
Chu, J. (1994) Self development of public libraries in China. The current situation and some problems. *Library Review,* **43**(8), 40–44.
Clayton, C. (1994) LA support for needs of users. *Library Association Record,* **96**(6), 319.
Cleese, J. *et al.* (1994) Alarm over public library changes. (Letter). *Times,* 16 May, 17.
Committee (1994) on Public Library Statistics. *A standard for the undertaking of surveys of library users in the United Kingdom.* (Draft). London: Institute of Public Finance.
Cottam, K.M. (1994) Directors of large libraries: roles, functions and activities. *Library Trends,* **43**(1), 15–33.
Curry, A. (1994) The chief officer/councillor relationship in British public libraries. *Journal of Librarianship and Information Science,* **26**(4), 211–224.
Czajka, S. (1993?) Public libraries for the benefit of the local community. The importance of sharing information and experience. In: S. Krzywicki and J. Pasztaleniec-Jarzyńska (eds) *Library and the local community.* Polish Library Association, pp. 115–120.
Daines, G. (1994a) Decisions swinging counties' way? *Library Association Record,* **96**(12), 645.
Daines, G. (1994b) Wide impact overall. *Library Association Record,* **96**(1), 37.
Davis, R. (1994) Global link: deliberate destruction in former Yugoslavia. *Library Association Record,* **96**(4), 193.
Denmark (1994). Ministry of Research. *Info-Society 2000. Report from the Committee on the information society by the year 2000.* Copenhagen: Ministry of Research.
Dolan, M. (1994) Relay team for Europe sprints ahead. *Library Association Record,* **96**(8), 441.
Donaldson, E. (1991) Gingrich promotes free enterprise and reading. *Discovery,* 12 July, 2.
Eichert, C. (1994) Von der Behorde zum Dienstleistungsunternehmen. Anforderungen an die bibliothekarischen Führungskrafts. *Buch und Biliothek,* **46**, 434–439.
Emerek, L. (1994) The future of public libraries. In: R. Verwer *et al.* (eds) *The future of librarianship. Proceedings of the Second International Budapest Symposium, January 1994.* Amsterdam: Hogeschool van Amsterdam.

England, L. (1994) *The library user: the reading habits and attitudes of public library users in Great Britain*. London: Book Marketing Ltd. (BNBRF Report 68).

Every (1994) *kind of people: multicultural library services*. Glasgow: LA Community Services Group in Scotland.

Fakudze, Q.N. (1994) *The Swaziland National Library Service. A progress review*. [Paper delivered to the 10th Anniversary of the Swaziland Library Association Conference and General Meeting, New George Hotel, Manzini, 3–4 June 1994.]

Feather, J. (1994) Creative tension or mutual misunderstanding? LIS departments and professional practice. *Library Association Record,* **96**(1), 30–31.

Fialkoff, F. (1994) Denver's dream library. *Library Journal,* **119**(21), 58–59.

Fire (1994) rekindles debate. *Library Association Record,* **96**(9), 469.

Flagg, G. (1994) PLA faces the future with new ideas at its fifth national conference. *American Libraries,* **25**(5), 391–393.

Fourie, J.A. and Kruger, J.A. (1994) Secondary school pupils as public library users. *South African Journal of Library and Information Science,* **62**(3), 97–104.

Fox, B.L. and Nelson, C.O. (1994) Renovations – and additions – on the rise. *Library Journal,* **119**(21), 41–57.

Freedland, J, (1995) The right stuff. *The Guardian 2,* 31 January, 2–3.

Fuegi, D. (1994) Towards a national standard for a public library user survey. *Public Library Journal,* **9**(2), 49–51.

Gallimore, A. and Connor, D. (1994) Europe: a local issue. *Library Association Record,* 96(8), 442,

Gertzog, A. and Beckermann, E. (1994) *Administration of the public library*. Metuchen, NJ: Scarecrow Press.

Goulding, A. (1994) Public library research – its future organization and funding. *Public Library Journal,* **9**(3), 75–77.

Granheim, E. (1994) Library legislation in the Nordic countries. A comparison. [Paper presented at 14th Anglo-Scandinavian Public Libraries Conference, Viborg, Denmark.]

Grenier, J. (1994) (ed.) *Research issues in public librarianship – trends for the future*. Westport, CT: Greenwood.

Gudauskas, R. (1994) Lithuanian library history. *International Information and Library Review,* **26**(4), 271–287.

Guilhaud, D. (1993) A l'est, quoi de nouveau. *Bulletin d'Informations de l'Association des Bibliothécaires Français,* 158, 55–61.

Gunton, D. (1994) Profession has a proud record of international work. (Letter). *Library Association Record,* **96**(11), 610.

Hafner, A.W. (1993) (ed.) (1993) *Democracy and the public library*, Westport, CT: Greenwood Press.

Hafner, A.W. and Sterling Folker, J. S. (1993) Democratic ideals and the American public library. In: A.W. Hafner (ed.) *Democracy and the public library*. Westport, CT: Greenwood Press, pp. 9–43.

Hall, C. and Richards, D.H. (1994). Kent arts and libraries. A view from the chair(s). *Public Library Journal,* **9**(5), 134–136.

Heintitz, C. (1993) The public library review: an elected member's view. *Public Library Journal,* **8**(6), 161–166.

Hicks, J. (1994) *Library legislation in the United Kingdom: the Emperor's new clothes*. [Paper

presented at 14th Anglo-Scandinavian Public Libraries Conference, Viborg, Denmark.]
Hildenbrand, S. (1994) IFLA meets in Havana during a very 'special period'. *Wilson Library Bulletin*, **69**(3), 45–47.
Hopkins, L. (1994) Local government review: the implications for central support services. *Taking Stock*, **32**(2), 20–26.
Hughill, B. (1995) Children to jump library queue. *Observer*, 5 March, 7.
Hyperfutures (1994) and cash realities. *Library Association Record*, **96**(11), 612 - 613.
Into (1994) the third age: reassessing the needs of elderly people. Glasgow: LA Community Services Group in Scotland.
Jordan. T. (1994) Give us a byte. *The Scotsman*, 17 November, 17.
Kinder, R. (1994) (ed.) (1994) *Librarians on the Internet: impact on reference services.* Binghampton, NY: Haworth Press.
Kinnell, M. and MacDougall, J. (1994) *Meeting the marketing challenge: strategies for public libraries and leisure services.* London: Taylor Graham.
Klinec, P. (1994) Public responsibility for public library services concerning law, funding, staffing and networking. *Libri*, **44**(2), 111–122.
Kolodziejska, J, (1994) *Five years of freedom in culture in the Polish experience.* [Paper presented at the IFLA General Conference, Havana (020-READ-4-E).]
Kolodziejska, J. and Luckham, B. (1994) Reading habits of children and youth: issues from a multi-national study. *Newsletter of the Round Table on Research in Reading*, 11 July, 1–38.
Kommission (1994) des Deutschen Bibliotheksinstituts für Organisation und Betrieb, Expertengruppe. *Controlling in öffentlichen Bibliotheken; Deutsches Bibliotheks-institut.* Berlin: Deutsches Bilbiotheksinstitut.
KPMG/CPI (1994) *DNH study: contracting-out in public libraries. Draft report by KPMG and CPI for public consultation.* London and Stamford: KPMG/CPI.
Krzywicki, S. and Pasztaleniec-Jarzyńska, J. (1993) (eds) *Library and the local community.* Warsaw: Polish Library Association.
Kuzmin, E. (1994) *Russian libraries in the context of social, economic and political reforms.* [Paper presented at the IFLA General Conference, Havana (105-CONTR-I-E).]
Largest (1994) public library survey in the world. *The Bookseller*, 28 October, 6.
Leach, A. and Verbeek, J. (1993) The reading habits of adults in anglophone sub-Saharan Africa: a historical overview. *African Journal of Library Archives and Information Science*, **3**(2), 95–106.
Library Association (1994) *Local government reorganisation in England.* [A briefing paper on the effects of Local Government Review on public library services.]
Maj, J. (1993) Public libraries in Poland: hopes, chances and threats. *Polish Libraries Today*, 2, 33 - 40.
Marchant, M.(1994) *Why adults use the public library. A research perspective.* Englewood, CO: Libraries Unlimited.
Marks, L. (1994) Marketing and the public sector library: some unresolved issues. *Australian Library Journal*, **43**(1), 17–27.
McClure, C.R. et al. (1994) *Public libraries and the internet: study results, policy issues and recommendations. Final report 1994.* Washington, DC: National Commission on Libraries and Information Science.
McDonald, T. (1993) *Te ara tika; Maori and libraries: a research report.* Wellington: New Zealand Library and Information Association/Te Rau Herenga o Aotearo.

Midwinter, A. and McVicar, M. (1993) Population size and functional efficiency in public library authorities: the statistical evidence. *Journal of Librarianship and Information Science,* **25**(4), 187–196.

Midwinter, A. and McVicar, M. (1994) *The size and efficiency debate: public library authorities in time of change.* London: Library Association Publishing.

Milner, E. *et al* (1994) Quality management: the public library debate. *Public Library Journal,* **9**(6), 151–157.

Minns, A. (1994) A rising tide of enthusiasm in Havana. *Library Association Record,* **96**(11), 620–621.

Mittermeyer, D. (1994a) Public libraries without autonomous boards: what the evidence shows (a matter of filter and noise). *Canadian Journal of Information and Library Science,* **19**(2), 23–39.

Mittermeyer, D. (1994b) The public library boards of trustees versus the committees of city hall: a power game. *Canadian Journal of Information and Library Science,* **19**(1), 1–17.

Moahi, K.H. and Monau, R.M. (1993) Library and information needs of disabled persons in Botswana. *African Journal of Library Archives and Information Science,* **3**(2), 125–140.

Muffett, D.J.M. (1993) Opportunities and dangers in the opting out of schools. *Public Library Journal,* **8**(6), 173–176.

Munkøe, L (1994) *Library management in relation to the political level.* [Paper presented at 14th Anglo-Scandinavian Public Libraries Conference, Viborg, Denmark.]

Myers, J. (1994) Stable, quiet retreats, or bustling with innovation? *Library Association Record,* **96**(8), 426–427.

Needs (1994) *of Adult Learners.* Mold: Library and Information Service, Clwyd County Council, on behalf of the Plail Project.

Niegaard, H. (1994) *UNESCO's 1994 Public Library Manifesto.* [Paper presented at the IFLA General Conference, Havana (099-PUB-6E).]

Nilsson, E. (1994) Editorial. *Scandinavian Public Library Quarterly,* **27**(1), 3.

Nuhu, A. (1994) Public librarianship in Northern Nigeria: limitations and challenges. *African Journal of Library Archives and Information Science,* **4**(1), 27–34.

Oda, M. (1993) *Public libraries in Japan. Overview.* [Unpublished paper by author, who was Visiting Fellow at the Department of Information and Library Studies, Loughborough University.]

Pallet, F. (1994) Book selection in children's libraries. *Artes Natales,* **13**(2), 3–7.

Papp, I. (1993) Library policy and financing of public libraries in Hungary. In: *The role of libraries today, tomorrow and beyond.* Amsterdam: Hogeschool van Amsterdam.

Parker, J. (1994) *Public Lending Right.* London Library Information Technology Centre. (Library and Information Briefings 51).

Pateman, J. (1994) Don't forget achievements of Communist states. *Library Association Record,* **96**(10), 548.

Pienaar, R.E. (1994) *Survival information: the role of the public library in the social and cultural development of disadvantaged communities.* [Paper presented at the IFLA General Conference, Havana (108 CONTR 3-E).]

Plaister, J. (1994) Public libraries. In: *Librarianship and information work worldwide.* East Grinstead: Bowker Saur, pp. 9–24.

Pop, J.J.H. (1994) Libraries must maintain close links with local government. *Bibliotheek en Samenleving,* **22**(1), 17–20.

Positive (1994) opinion poll. *Library Association Record,* **96**(1), 34–35.
Powledge, T. (1994) Maryland opens first cyber-library. *Independent,* 8 July, 13.
Preston, B. (1994) New chapter with cliffhanger ending opens for libraries: musty municipal backwater transformed by retail revolution. *Times,* 18 October, 10.
Quality (1994): taking a stand on good standard policy. *Library Association Record,* **96**(6), 318–321.
Raseroka, H.K. (1994) Changes in public libraries during the last twenty years: an African perspective. *Libri,* **44**(2), 153–163.
Rowley, J. (1994) Customer experience of libraries. *Library Review,* **43**(6), 7–17.
Savige, D. (1994) Public libraries: trading in futures. Report on the strategic planning forum Friday 4 February 1994. *Australasian Public Libraries and Information Services,* **7**(1), 6–19.
Scheppke, J. (1994) Who's using the public library. *Library Journal,* **119**(17), 35–37.
Schulte-Nolke, P. (1993) Das problem der betrieblichen Leistunga - mesung von Biblotheken. *Bibliothek Foorschung und Praxis,* 17, 7–28.
September, P.E. (1993) Public libraries and community information needs in a changing South Africa. *Journal of Librarianship and Information Science,* **25**(2), 71–78.
Services (1995) *under threat: the crisis in funding for local authorities.* London: Association of County Councils, Association of District Councils and Association of Metropolitan Authorities.
Shongwe, N.F. (1994) Report on an attachment to the National Library Service in Malawi: Extra-mural Services Department from 27 July to 18 October 1993. *Swaziland Library Association Journal,* 10, 1–10.
Simmons, M. (1995) Gummer blows cold on wind of change. *Guardian,* 3 March, 5.
Skuodyte, E. (1994) Lithuanian libraries: conditions and perspectives. [Paper presented at 14th Anglo-Scandinavian Public Libraries Conference, Viborg, Denmark.]
Smita, D. (1994) The Latvian public libraries. [Paper presented at 14th Anglo-Scandinavian Public Libraries Conference, Viborg, Denmark.]
Stephens, D. and Hallam, M. (1994) Commercialising the State library of Queensland *Australian Library Journal,* **43**(1), 3–8.
Strategies (1994) for service quality. *New Library World,* **95**(1113) [Special issue].
Stroud. G. and Usherwood, R. (1994) Towards a model statement of standards for public library services. *Information Research News,* **26**(3), 135–140.
Sturges, P. et al. (1992) The indigenous knowledge base in African development. *Journal of Economic and Social Intelligence,* 2, 5–29.
Sumsion, J. (1994) Strategic research areas and possible research models for UK public libraries. *Library Review,* **43**(4), 7–26.
Tang, S. (1994) A brief introduction to the development of public library service in China. *Focus,* **25**(2), 78–82.
Taylor, R. (1994) Emerging from the closed access trap. *Library Association Record,* **96**(9), 490–491.
Thomas, B. (1994) *Thirty Years without library legislation.* [Paper presented at 14th Anglo-Scandinavian Public Libraries Conference, Viborg, Denmark.]
Turock, B. (1994) The new case for federal library support. *Library Journal,* **119**(3), 126–129.

UNESCO (1995) Public Library Manifesto 1994. *IFLA Public Library News. Newsletter of the Section of Public Libraries*, (12).
Usherwood, R. (1994a) Librarianship: a profession in retreat? In: R. Verwer *et al.* (eds) *The future of librarianship. Proceedings of the Second International Budapest Symposium, January 1994*. Amsterdam: Hogeschool van Amsterdam.
Usherwood, R. (1994b) Local politics and the public library service. *Journal of Librarianship and Information Science,* **26**(3), 135–140.
Usherwood, R. (1994c) Public library management – the political perspective. [Paper presented at 14th Anglo-Scandinavian Public Libraries Conference, Viborg, Denmark.]
Valm, T. (1994) Estonian libraries today. [Paper presented at 14th Anglo-Scandinavian Public Libraries Conference, Viborg, Denmark.]
Van House, N.A. and Childers, T.A (1993a) *The public library effectiveness study*. Chicago, IL: American Library Association.
Van House, N.A. and Childers, T.A (1993b) *What's good? Describing your public library's effectiveness*. Chicago, IL: American Library Association.
Verstraete, J. (1994). Love me tender . . .. *Library Association Record,* **96**(12), 668–669.
Verwer R. *et al.* (1994) (eds) *The future of librarianship. Proceedings of the Second International Budapest Symposium, January 1994*. Amsterdam: Hogeschool van Amsterdam.
Vestheim, G. (1994) Public libraries, cultural institutions on the crossroads between purposive and humanistic rationality. In: R. Verwer *et al.* (eds) *The future of librarianship. Proceedings of the Second International Budapest Symposium, January 1994*. Amsterdam: Hogeschool van Amsterdam.
Walker, G. (1994) *Enabling or disabling? The voluntary contract tendering of Brent Council's library service 1994*. [Available from the author at 121 Wilmot Street, London E2 OBU.]
Waters, R.L. (1994) Library users: how the public library has changed their lives. *Public Library Quarterly,* **14**(1), 21.
Watt, I. (1994) Quality: taking a stand on good standard policy. *Library Association Record,* **96**(6), 318–319.
Westbrook, L. (1994) Qualitative research methods: a review of major stages, data analysis techniques, and quality controls. *Library and Information Science Research,* **16**(3), 241–254.
Wise, M. and Olden, A. (1994) (eds) *Information and libraries in the Arab world*. London: Library Association Publishing.
Woolfrey, L. Omar, L. (1993) *An investigation of public libraries in the Greater Cape Town area*. Cape Town: Library and Information Workers Organisation.
Yamaguchi, G. (1993) The public library: its problems and perspectives [In Japanese]. *Toshokan-Kai* (The Library World), **45**(1), 8–17.

Academic libraries 4

Janet Wilkinson

Introduction

Despite all that has been said this year about financial constraints and shrinking budgets, there has been much excitement in 1994 about the 'library of the future'. The emphasis has been mostly on information technology (IT) developments, especially the shift from holdings to access strategies – assisted by developments in electronic publishing, document delivery, and the availability of information through local, national and global networks. As the general media hype indicates, this has also been the year of the Internet, and our professional literature reflects this trend.

Academic libraries are, none the less, passing through a transition. Despite constraints on all fronts – space, equipment, materials, staff, etc. – impressive progress has been made, although basic information provision, such as books for students, is still a major concern. Surveys show that students cannot get hold of more than about 60% of what they need (Line, 1994a and 1994b; Lyon, 1994). In resource-constrained environments, concern is also growing over how institutions will be able to support IT investment to sustain the new vision. The future of electronic information is still *terra incognita*. There are justifiable concerns and insecurities about our ability to cope, and the librarian's future role. Libraries – still a powerful totem within the academic community – not librarians are accorded the higher value. As the 'virtual library' emerges, will we also become virtual librarians? At one end of the spectrum there are the traditionalists who worry about the loss of values, while others are painting a picture of Utopia – the electronic library. Historically, academic librarianship has emphasised artefacts, rather than people, but the focus is shifting as libraries are becoming increasingly user-led. The challenge we face is less the management of technological change than the management of change within a service culture. 'The good librarian has always been an entrepreneur, receptive to innovation. Those who are not, are going to find survival hard' (Hunt, 1993).

An overview

The dominant factor is the rapid expansion of student numbers, followed closely by yet another year of substantial price increases and a continuation of the so-called 'information explosion'. Waddell's (1994) description of the crisis facing UK academic libraries can easily be applied to libraries worldwide. Reports indicate that, while European library managers share similar problems – as they struggle with mass underfunded systems of higher education, while trying to introduce new technologies in teaching and learning – they are still acting in national contexts (Hunt, 1993).

In the UK, the year was dominated by the Follett Report (Joint, 1993), which appeared at the very end of 1993. Academic libraries are in the limelight for the first time since the Parry Report of 1967, and everyone is writing about Follett (Akeroyd, 1994; Brindley, 1994; Campbell, 1994; Harris, 1994; Law, 1994a; Line, 1994a, 1994b; Roberts, 1994; Stoker, 1994). One particular comparison of UK academic libraries in 1986–87 and 1991–92, although flawed, does provide supporting evidence for some of the main conclusions of the report (Sumsion, 1994). Universities and colleges have seen a 40% increase in students, with at least a corresponding rise in library activity. Increased demands have been accompanied by a reduction in book acquisitions, staff, seats, space, etc. Despite Parry's recommendation for 6% of institutional budgets to be spent on libraries (when four per cent was the actual figure), by 1994 actual spending had dropped to three per cent. In response to the funding crisis (Lyon, 1994), the Follett Report has led to libraries being moved up the higher education agenda, not least by making available £140 million for library space and £20 million for developments in IT. The Report clearly has a relevance for higher education instutions worldwide.

Australia, like the UK, has ended the binary divide and at the same time increased student numbers. Open learning has also increased, and concern exists for the problems facing students (Cavanagh, 1994; Pinson, 1994). Denise and Woods (1994), in their survey of Australian chief librarians, remark upon the passive, reactive attitude that prevails, as institutions wait for funding. There is a need for a proactive, strategically informed approach if academic libraries are not to become increasingly marginalized. However, Denise and Woods are critical of the implications of Follett for academic libraries worldwide and argue that Wolpert's (1991) vision for libraries in 2001 is more visionary and alert to changing social forces. The electronic library concept, after a hesitant start in the late 1980s in Australia, has developed vigorously as institutions have experimented with various approaches at the Australian National University Library. The growing awareness among Australian librarians of the potential (and problems) of electronic library development and the capabilities of AARNet has owed much to the efforts of individuals based in Canberra.

Student expansion in France coincided with a halt in library development. Use increased by over 71% between 1984 and 1990. Van Dooren (1993), Bisbrouck (1994) and Carbone (1994) examine the Miquel Report (Miquel, 1989) and note that, after a long period of funding constraint, significant injections of government funds were made in terms of new buildings, increased budgets, staff, acquisitions and opening hours, and an automated union catalogue. This expansionist phase has now slowed and a huge imbalance in resources exists between libraries. In Paris, in particular, with massive student numbers, matters have deteriorated since Miquel. An original shortage of 6,000 seats has reached 12,000–20,000. Carbone (1994) laments such a decline after ten years of significant development of university libraries in France, and calls for continued modernization and government funding if libraries are to catch up with their North European and American counterparts. The first phase of the state's Schéma Université 2000 (1991–1995), which includes several new library buildings and extensions, will raise the seating capacity by 50%. The initiative also takes into account the need to move contemporary collections from closed to open access, for multimedia collections, the integration of IT, flexible study space and increased staff numbers to provide longer opening hours.

Barral (1994) explains the need to generate income as part of normal library activity through the example of Compiègne Technical University, which has built links with local business by providing a fee-paying service. Problems are not solely economic, however, and attention needs to be paid to structures (Pallier, 1993). A higher profile for librarians and a greater degree of integration within the universities are called for by Chauveinc (1994). An improved understanding of teaching and research activities by librarians would also benefit the collections, and there is a need for library directors to take an active part in planning and policy-making. Indeed, since 1992 planning has been organized at national level for the exploitation of IT in libraries, and this is seen as a means of maximizing resources, facilitating interlending and widening access (Pellé, 1994).

Major changes have taken place in German libraries since the fall of the Berlin Wall. The Bundesvereinigung Deutscher Bibliotheksverbände (1994) published a total plan for libraries in Germany which replaces the 1973 plan, and deals with restructuring and the impact of reunification. Cockrill and Broady (1994) outline the key macroeconomic factors influencing British and German university libraries. Political changes in both countries have resulted in reduced funding but, unlike the British situation, it is only recently in Germany that this has resulted in an increased emphasis on accountability, effectiveness and efficiency. University librarians in Germany have instead had to face problems associated with inadequate technology at a time when student numbers are escalating. In Britain, libraries have had to cope with increasing competitiveness within the education sector, with shrinking funds and almost continual change in terms of the expectations and demands being made upon them. Recommendations include the need for long-range strategic planning. The financial situation in German academic libraries has been dealt with by Griebel (1993; 1994) and Griebel *et al.* (1994), with special reference to collection building and acquisitions policies in university libraries, including the scientific research libraries.

Nordic libraries have achieved a high level of technical development, and are encouraged by Mendes (1994) to take a more dynamic role as a European model. Indeed, Tőrnudd (1994) evaluates the national resource library network in Finland as an information model for developing nations. Evaluation has become a major topic throughout Scandinavia, and much discussion centres around how academic libraries should adapt to the electronic world. In Danish libraries in particular, but also in Sweden, lively debate is taking place over the need to introduce charges for interlibrary loans (Cotta-Schønberg and Winkel-Schwarz, 1994; Harnesk, 1993, 1994).

In the former Eastern bloc, Poland demonstrates typical trends, with significant increases in student numbers and the creation of new universities. Increases in resource allocations to science and education are desperately needed to accelerate change. However, although academic staff numbers have increased, growth has not been matched by the development of libraries (Jazdon and Olszewski, 1994). Budgets are unpredictable and do not allow for staff development, while staff recruitment itself has been based on negative selection. However, in post-Communist society, staff shortages have been compensated for, in part, by greater efficiency. Library automation is the current lively topic in Poland, with three conferences organized in 1994. All the same, automation is still in its initial phases, and with no standardardized coordination, some libraries have embarked on their own projects with whatever financial help they can secure. Krakow, Lublin, Łodz and Poznan have agreed to automate jointly. The Andrew W. Mellon Foundation has funded development of the VTLS intergrated system in several Polish academic libaries (Gdansk, Wrocław, Cracow, Lublin, Warsaw, Torun). All academic libraries are now connected to the Internet through NASK and are in the process of introducing CD-ROM networks (Diehl, K., 1994, personal communication).

Reports from a fairly diverse number of sources offer a snapshot of what has happened worldwide. Ghana, for example, is a developing country plagued with stringent and controversial economic measures and debilitating repayments of huge foreign debts. For Ghana's five university libraries, the most obvious solution is cooperation, particularly with respect to interlibrary loan facilities (Korsah, 1994a and 1994b).

The library without walls

As more and more services can be delivered to the remote desktop, many authors (and hence librarians) now refer to the 'virtual library' and the opportunities it provides for users to bypass conventional libraries. Despite fairly vehement criticisms which have questioned the very concept (Oppenheim, 1994a), the 'electronic library' (which is perhaps a more accurate description) is as exciting as it is inevitable (Larsen, 1994). Geleijnse and Grootaers (1994) summarize what they regard as important aspects of the library of the future, and the strategy for achieving this at the University of Tilburg.

Networks are seen as the solution to many problems, for, as Hawkins (1994) argues, the financial crisis makes it clear that the traditional library will not survive into the next decade. However, networks are not a solution to the escalating costs of publication as long as publishers demand current revenues and control copyright ownership (Bell and Koepp, 1994). Computer networks are not in themselves agents of change, but, as Heseltine (1994b) reminds us, an enabling technology. For him, the major challenge is not so much the development of an information superhighway as the transformation of higher education, but unfortunately he gives no clues as to how this will be achieved. Arnold *et al.* (1994) see the benefits of an electronic library as multiple, remote and intelligent access to information, as well as a reduction in the need for labour- and space-intensive provision of traditional library collections. Bjornshauge (1993) raises questions about how libraries should adapt to the electronic future. The working papers of the IT Sub-committee of the HEFC Libraries Review in the UK (*Libraries*, 1993) discuss how technology might be harnessed to underpin change in the support of teaching and research. The idea of the electronic library as a reality is still an illusion – not for technological reasons, but because of logistical, organizational, financial and legal obstacles (Hawkins, 1994). Today, it is hard to imagine an end to print, despite the increasing availability of electronic equivalents and the fast growing expectations of staff and students. Saunders (1993) collection of papers from the 7th Annual Computers in Libraries Conference provides a hypothetical but optimistic vision of the future academic library. Traditional centralized public services will become increasingly irrelevant to the needs of customers. The walls of the academic library will gradually be removed as students and staff access databases etc. from their offices, laboratories, classrooms and residences. Orum (1993) argues that libraries are losing their status as sole providers of information and calls for the profession to develop a new identity to deal with the competition.

The librarian's role

The increasing emphasis on technology is causing much debate about the future role of both the library and the librarian. Cooper (1994) asks whether the library building's function as a repository of materials should be replaced by a concept of the library as a point of network access where expert help is available. Brophy (1993), Blagden and Ford (1994), Kitt (1994), W.P. Leonard (1994), MacDonald (1994), Owen (1994) and Raitt (1994) ask the more frequent question, whether librarians will disappear in a world dominated by end-user searching. Køfoed (1993) and Glover (1994) are somewhat reassuring, and disagree that the librarian's role as intermediary will diminish. They contend that librarians will continue to act as information guides. Overall, the papers provide an optimistic portrayal of the library of the future, but often raise more questions than answers.

Heseltine (1994a), in his otherwise optimistic article on the role of global networks in the transformation of higher education, is depressingly pessimistic about the librarian's future – in fact, we do not appear to have one. There are others who totally resist the technological changes, such as Quinn (1994) and Wisner (1994), who call on us to stop the madness. The focus on technology is seen as having compromised academic librarianship's scholarly values, and there is a call for a renewal of neglected teaching functions and a reaffirmation of traditional values. Both authors warn of the danger of reducing knowledge to information, and contend that libraries are contributing to the dehumanizing of education. Snow (1994), on the other hand, believes that the greater the dehumanization by technology, the more the need for librarians to provide a human component.

If librarians do not adapt by taking themselves outside the library they are in danger of becoming mere warehouse custodians. It will be up to them to introduce their users to new forms of publication, including electronic journals, if they do not wish them to go elsewhere. It is Rodgers's (1994) view that librarians must seize the opportunity to manage, develop policies and procedures, and keep pace with developments. None the less, libraries are evolving in respect to recent changes. Dusoulier (1994) and MacDonald (1994) are persuasive in arguing that the future belongs neither to the makers of technology nor to the information providers. It will be user-led, and the librarian's challenge is to manage change in service cultures. Tomlinson (1994) talks of a potential end-user revolution. As the incentive for a trip to the library building diminishes, librarians must make themselves available to their remote customers, who will need more detailed assistance in coping with the intricacies of an ever expanding range of information resources (Creth,1994). Dworaczek and Wiebe (1994) and McMillan (1994) remind us that the acquisitions process of electronic journals is similar to that for printed serials and we could face unprecedented problems in selecting, receiving and providing information in this format. The phrase 'mark it and park it' has not lost its relevance in the virtual library and, as Butter (1994), Fisher (1994), Gardner (1994) and Taylor (1994) all tell us, librarians have been doing this for a long time. We must combine these skills with improved service delivery. W.P. Leonard (1994) refers to field service librarians being faced with the difficult task of staying abreast of hardware and network advances, and being conversant with a number of national and international databases.

Edwards *et al.* (1993), writing on the IMPEL Project (Impact on People of Electronic Libraries), pay particular attention to the changing role and function of academic libraries, to management structures and to the increasing reliance on networks. Librarians or information providers must understand the technology, develop the electronic collection, be prepared to tackle user information overload, train staff and users, and develop close links with the organization's total information resource (Creth, 1994).

The Internet

The Internet seems unstoppable. The rate of growth is over 1,000,000 users a month, and although the USA is still the major user, Europe has seen massive growth rates (Ashley, 1994). 1994 has also seen an increase both in new Internet providers and the range of services offered. Navigational tools have multiplied and become available in more powerful versions running under a number of operating systems. Web clients, especially Mosaic and Netscape, although still relatively primitive, became the favourite network tools in an attempt to bring order to the chaos (Obenaus, 1994). Glover (1994) is confident that librarians will continue to have a role in developing search strategies, guiding users towards what is available and helping them to make best use of it. As Fisher (1994) and Taylor (1994) point out, principles for the organization of printed information, which have been laboriously worked out by technical services librarians during the last century and a half, are now being used by others to develop online services.

Coverage in the literature has been international, although by far the highest number of papers has been produced in the USA. Many libraries have been quick to recognize the potential of the Internet as an essential component of the virtual library. Swain (1994) writes on the use of the Internet in Canada; Cherhal *et al.* (1993), writing on France, recognize the wealth of information available and describe how to access the main services. In Germany, coverage is provided by Michold (1994) and Osswald and Koch (1994), and in South America by Ferreira (1994), where the Internet is becoming a growing issue. O'Brien (1994) also briefly traces the development of the AARNet in Australia and the changes it has brought to the information market. Goodacre (1993) and Metcalfe (1994) provide an excellent overview of the opportunities brought by networking in Australia. Through her collection of eighteen papers, including eight case studies, Goodacre includes studies of the distributed national collection in Australia, the University of Western Australia's participation in the Multimedia ISDN Library Link trial, and RMIT's Telelibrary.

In spite of this worldwide coverage, it is still early days if one tries to assess the impact of the Internet on patterns of scholarly communication. In academia,

106 *Academic libraries*

the Internet is becoming a key research tool – for e-mail, bulletin boards, electronic journals, access to (over 700) online public access catalogues (OPACs), databases and document stores – its size and diversity dwarfing the electronic information that libraries have provided in the past. The challenge is to find and evaluate what is out there and to let the users at it (Gartner, 1994).)

Overall, the Internet poses a series of threats, challenges and opportunities for librarians, but it is hard to view recent changes as anything other than an asset. Nevertheless, as Lanier and Wilkins (1994) warn, the virtually limitless and highly volatile information to which we all now have access is likely to strain the staff resources of many reference departments. The need to re-equip libraries and retrain staff has become a priority. Librarians cannot afford to ignore the Internet as an information resource, and must plan for its incorporation into their work. O'Donovan (1994) notes that the development of information resources across the Internet has been so swift that many library and information service professionals have been left behind, and may find themselves in a position where library users know more about the sources than they do. Librarians need to make up this ground by cooperating with computing services and by developing a knowledge of Internet tools through training and self-familiarization. Kitt (1993) believes that librarians can influence the way the Internet changes their roles, by using it to add value to the information derived from it, and by training customers in how to make use of the information supplied.

Convergence

The move towards converged services in the UK is now taking place at a faster rate than in the USA, as universities and their funding bodies demand new information strategies and aim to integrate IT with teaching and research. In many countries, institutions have begun to recognize that it is no longer appropriate to separate the two services within the management structure; elsewhere, services have simply grown closer together on an informal basis. In order to satisfy user expectations for the delivery of integrated services to the desktop, librarians are having to form alliances with other experts (Brophy, 1993). The trend, particularly in the UK, is for planned merger, although the degree to which this has occurred has been dependent on personalities as well as institutional policy (Lovecy, 1994). The debate has also become confused with the need for managerial efficiency. The Scientific, Technical and Medical Information System in the UK review (*Scientific*, 1993) rightly highlights the impact on services of these symbiotic relationships. Creth (1993) argues the need to do away with the mistrust on which the relationships between computer professionals and librarians were formerly based. Both sectors can provide service orientation and leadership in the integration of IT in innovative and thoughtful ways in the 21st century (Creth, 1994; Langenberg, 1994). Gardner (1994) believes that the ability of libraries to change will depend largely on novel forms of cooperation and the dismantling of hierarchical ways of working. In Australia, the work of Brian Cook and Tom Cochrane is applauded by Schauder (1994a) as having provided examples of how a tight integration of library and computing functions can foster electronic library-style access.

There appears to be no single model and no easy answer to the integration of campus-based information services. The difficult question, according to Branin *et al.* (1993), is the level in the chain of information support services where organizational integration should take place. There is general agreement that the work of subject librarians and computer support personnel is drawing closer together – it is hard to see how this can be avoided. End-users clearly benefit from service integration and, overall, the use of IT in libraries and the growing reliance on networks has increased the pressure for convergence, especially as librarians become aware that IT is altering the power structures in their institutions (Branin *et al.*, 1993). According to Pitkin (1992), many feel the need to redefine the library's role within the organization, but are uncertain about direction and approach. Lyon (1994) believes that most universities will go the way of the few that have already merged their services, and even those that do not will see librarians and computer people working together much more closely. Esin (1994) sets out the strategic planning process for integration.

The newest development in the electronic campus is probably the campus-wide information service (CWIS), which provides an excellent example of effective collaboration between libraries and academic computing departments. Extensive coverage of the creation of these powerful information tools is provided by Rothnie (1993), Barry and Stanton (1994), Biddiscombe and Watson (1994), Powell (1994, Seiden *et al.* (1994), Westell (1994) and Tedd (1995).

Access or ownership?

Academic librarians have been talking for years about the 'current serials crisis'. The vicious cycle of cancellation due to high costs, resulting in lower print runs, leading to yet higher subscription prices, is all too familiar, especially for science libraries. Forecasts indicate some slowing, but prices are still outpacing inflation, and librarians continue to accuse publishers of market pricing. Added to this is the increase in worldwide publication output and the decline in library funding. Such an erosion of purchasing power has led to a decline in books acquired by academic libraries since the late 1980s (Perrault, 1994). Woodward and Pilling (1993) demonstrate the problems caused by pressure on academics to publish for career reasons: the costs for commercial publishers and for libraries. Graham (1994) presents the publishers' line, with which librarians are all too familiar. Waddell's (1994) interpretation of the Council of Academic and Professional Publishers' (CAPP) annual report on book and periodical spending in the UK confirms the publishers' reasons for concern and reiterates the need for action by all involved in education. Similarly, Ketcham and Born (1994) report on a survey of the cost history of international periodicals. Contemporary problems are easy to identify – too much information, too little funding – so that librarians are caught between an over-supply of literature and an under-supply of funds.

Academic libraries worldwide are particularly hard hit. Australia, for example, with a relatively small population spread over a large land mass, and a small publishing output of its own, is dependent on the purchase of foreign publications. Libraries have found that cooperation is one approach to the problem. Leonard (1994b) discusses collection management in Australian academic libraries focusing on eight libraries.

Poland offers an interesting example because, until recently, acquisitions policies of academic libraries were not coordinated or targeted to support research in specific subject areas. All libraries aimed to be comprehensive in their collections, which proved to be impossible. There is now a recognition of a need for cooperation to build more focused collections. Jazdon and Olszewski (1994) give a good account of acquisitions policies and the need for a change in the law to deal with copyright deposit.

In a more general context, Harloe and Budd (1994) explore the relationship between collection development and scholarly publication. Attempts are being made to maintain and develop print collections while decisions are simultaneously made about the provision of electronic sources (Syliva and Lesher, 1994). McCarthy (1994) describes how some libraries are trying to meet the challenge of providing access to journals through document delivery or through a coordinated cancellation policy. Many librarians see the opportunities offered by IT developments, although it would be wrong to expect electronic alternatives to be cheaper, and copyright is still a major stumbling block. Interestingly, Pastine and Kacena (1994) give a breakdown of costs for automation, networking and other aspects of new technology in academic libraries.

This is a transition period in which publishing is moving towards an electronic environment. Bennion (1994) certainly does not see electronic journals as the automatic replacement, particularly if they only mimic printed journals with their inherent cost problems. Reduced funding is forcing libraries to turn to new ways of producing services. Libraries are beginning to redirect their budgets away from print and are looking into cooperative arrangements for issues such as acquisitions, storage, database access and the purchase of electronic access and document delivery. For libraries other than the great research libraries, the goal is becoming one of purchase when needed rather than in case it is needed.

Resource sharing and cooperation

IT has undoubtedly assisted library cooperation, from automated union catalogues linking collections to shared responsibility for acquisitions, from document delivery to sharing of databases. Blunden-Ellis (1994) outlines the planning involved in setting up CALIM (Consortium of Academic Libraries in Manchester). Motais de Narbonne (1994) cites the automation of cataloguing in France, which led in 1987 to the beginning of a union catalogue of university and large research libraries – the Pancatalogue – as a turning point for cooperation and interlending. The catalogue now contains 1.5 million records of the holdings of some 80 libraries.

McDonald (1994) examines current resource sharing among academic libraries, particularly the technical and organizational issues, including the digitization of information. The implications for acquisitions and document delivery are considerable. Electronic resource sharing provides opportunities for libraries that will permit a much wider access to information. MacDonald (1994) also has great expectations that a combination of the electronic library and increased resource sharing will help to reduce rapidly escalating operating costs. Such opportunities will, however, enhance both awareness and demand, and, while cost-effective and cost-beneficial, they will not be cheaper (White, 1994). There is a need for investment in technology, and libraries will be expected by their institutions to absorb these costs. Comprehensive planning involving institutional management is called for, rather than the current piecemeal approach.

As the library evolves within a new information environment that focuses on scholarly communication rather than scholarly publishing, the assembling of local collections will, for many libraries, become less important. Harloe and Budd (1994) predict that coordinated collection development and cooperative shared access will become more important. Larsen (1994) goes further, in his belief that cooperation among libraries will become fundamental to their success. This is borne out by Carbone (1994), who describes the creation of the CADIST (Centres d'Acquisition et de Diffusion de l'Information Scientifique et Technique), which links a group of libraries with shared responsibilities for collections and acquisitions to support research. Similar cooperation also exists over preservation and conservation. Law (1994b), on the other hand, regards as implausible the idea of cooperative acquisition as a means of eking out limited resources. He believes that, in the UK, Follett funding will contribute largely to the emergence of a 'superleague' of research libraries, safeguarding the resources of these libraries in the interests of the wider academic community. The UK research assessment exercise cycle is seen as anti-cooperative, in that individual libraries will tend to preserve their own research strengths rather than consider the collective good. A form of natural selection in library collections will result.

The USA, on the other hand, appears to be ahead in the cooperation game. Nicklin (1994) describes a growing trend to save money by sharing administrators and by making joint faculty appointments. This process extends to include library cooperation, by electronically linking library collections. Dedrick (1994) reports on the benefits of cooperation in terms of cost saving and service enhancement. Tuten and Washington (1994) also report on a study of collection development policies in South Carolina.

In Canada, the move to cooperation has not been smooth, particularly in respect of collection rationalisation and project implementation. Other priorities at home institutions, the overriding accountability to the parent institution, a lack of contractual agreement between libraries or of commitment to the idea of resource sharing and its connotations are to blame (Fry, 1994a, 1994b). More recently, however, there has been a renewed sense of the necessity for cooperation. COPPUL (Council of Prairie and Pacific University Libraries) has been revived for consortium purchasing, collection rationalization, staff development, courier service, document delivery and storage. There is worldwide evidence outside North America and Europe of a more genuinely cooperative approach. From Ghana, for example, Kisiedu (1994) reports on the advantages of cooperative acquisitions for cutting costs and maximizing resources. As with all developing countries, if hardware shortages can be overcome, considerable gains are to be made by networking information, and universities in Ghana are about to automate and network their systems as a result of a World Bank-funded programme. Edwards *et al.* (1993) write positively about the benefits of resource sharing in South African libraries as a way of providing a higher level of service than would otherwise be possible given reduced budgets. There is a growing trend for libraries in close proximity to each other or sharing similar interests to cooperate in terms of acquisition, storage, staff training and informal networking. However, Edwards is careful to point out the dangers of unrealistic expectations and stresses the need for planning and monitoring. Across the continent, there are also studies being carried out by the Association of African Universities to establish new electronic networks in universities and research institutions. The major advantage will be connectivity with similar organizations worldwide.

In Chile, high levels of expenditure on periodicals have led to a feasibility study, funded by the Andes Foundation, to create a centre that will enable universities to buy and share periodicals (del Sol *et al.*, 1994). Cooperation is also the order of the day in the Nordic countries, through the NORDUNET academic network (Skogmar, 1994). There is a particular emphasis on library and information networking in Sweden, where cooperation in collection development is essential owing to the expansion and decentralization of higher education and the boom in the price of scientific publications – a trend discussed earlier.

'Just in case' or 'just in time'

Discussion of ownership versus access is persistent in current library literature. The issue is not new, but appears to be a current international preoccupation because of the growing recognition that no single library can be totally self-sufficient. Financial constraints are, according to Elliott (1994), a large contributing factor; but they also note a new awareness of the real costs of maintaining large collections, studies in patterns of use, a growing acceptance of the potential of IT and an explosion of the demand for services. Many continue to ask whether access can perform well enough to substitute for ownership (Brophy, 1993). As was noted earlier, we should not expect to see the end of print; while Harloe and Budd (1994) expect a gradual increase in electronic scholarly publication, some publishers will also continue to produce both conventional and electronic versions. They believe that to talk simply of access versus ownership over-simplifies the issue and they present a more complex argument, with a strategy for collection development in the era of electronic access. In any case, as the discussion of resource sharing and cooperation indicated, academic libraries, instead of continuing to build their own collections which would meet most needs of local users (just in case), will gradually move to a 'collection of collections' mediated by new electronic networking technology (just in time). Kelly (1994) reports on the fact that some academic libraries are using available networking technology and services to overcome the limitations of their own collections.

Electronic publishing

As discussed earlier, many libraries, particularly in the sciences, have begun the process of replacing traditional printed academic journals – especially non-core materials – with electronic surrogates. Naylor (1994) believes that this is due to the now longstanding publishing crisis and that it will be the economic case which forces libraries down this route.

Academic libraries are the most heavily committed to the use of electronically published services, since researchers need access to information services that can now be provided only in this way. In the new strategic plan of the University College of Southern Queensland, preference has been given to electronic rather than print-based sources (McPherson, 1994). It is early days yet, but Schauder (1994b) concludes that the real contribution of electronic publishing lies in greater diversity and choice in the marketplace. There is a call for the forging of new relationships among academics, publishers, libraries and universities. One wonders if this will be achievable after reading Donovan (1994), who, hardly surprisingly as a publisher, cautions us against our excitement about the electronic revolution. His concern is for quality if the traditional journal disappears. Redmond (1994), on the other hand, argues that the term 'cybrarian' reflects not so much a change in what librarians do, but in how they do it.

CD-ROM

Two or three tears ago, CD-ROMs were predicted to become an obsolete form of information technology (McSean and Law, 1990). To date, however, there has been a huge increase in the number of CDs produced and the networking of CD-ROMs has become commonplace, providing multi-user access combined with fast retrieval. Bevan (1994) actually points to a number of areas where CD-ROMs will continue to be useful. Early problems associated with a lack of standardization are beginning to be overcome as more products are designed to run under Windows. Harry and Oppenheim (1993) remind us of the advantages of CD-ROMs, particularly their popularity with end-users, and Lambert (1994), who is also a fan, acknowledges the huge impact that CD technology has had on the way academic libraries function and the services they offer. A paper by Adeniran *et al.* (1994) provides a study of CD-ROM use in Nigerian libraries.

Conkling and Osif (1994), on the other hand, express concern for users relying on CD-ROM databases for literature retrieval at the expense of other tools. CDs alone may not provide sufficient coverage. One crucial question now being addressed is that of duplication costs and the luxury of maintaining more than one subscription, e.g. print and CD formats. Other drawbacks include networking price structures, the fact that disks are often now too small for the larger databases, and the lack of currency. Law (1994c) discusses the current level of spending on CD-ROMs and the limits of this technology.

We are moving beyond CD because better solutions are appearing and, more importantly, central funds are being poured in in an unprecedented way into the development of networked information services. This poses a threat to the custodial and physical role of the library. We have the collective task of redefining our profes--sional future and skills. Hanson (1993) and Casale (1994) recognize that the distribution of online data by suppliers like University Microfilms Inc. (UMI), Silver Platter (SP) and Institute of Scientific Info (ISI), and the development of locally mounted databases are attractive alternatives, but appear to share Bevan's (1994) view that we should regard CD-ROMs in general terms as a replacement for printed material rather than as a competitor to other forms of electronic information.

Pricing

The ability of publishers to meet the demand from academic libraries for electronic journals is less technically difficult than it is financially challenging, particularly with respect to new pricing structures (Hunter, 1993). Singleton (1994) examines the complex issues faced by the publishing industry and various pricing models. It is unlikely that the electronic journal will ever be cheaper than its printed equivalent; publishers will be sure to calculate their pricing structures according to current levels of revenue. Those who have already faced this reality are almost certainly looking towards document delivery. Law (1994b) suggests that we need to consider using academic bulletin boards on the Internet (of which there are currently about 5,000), as an alternative to traditional means of peer-review and validation. We have fallen into the trap of assuming that electronic publishing needs all the superstructure of conventional publishing. Gasson (1994) appears to endorse Law's view and believes that the Internet poses a real threat to academic publishing. Although the academic networks on the Internet were primarily set up to provide a new means of scholarly communication, there is a strong feeling that they should also replace the traditional means of disseminating scholarly research.

In terms of the monograph, for storage reasons alone, librarians may well look forward to electronic alternatives. McRobbie (1994) highlights the need for publishers to provide specialist books at affordable prices, and recognizes that they may choose to become more particular about what is produced, leading to a print-on-demand scenario. However, continuing growth in print output raises questions about the demise of the book. Mowat (1994) and Warlock (1994) remind us that electronically published output is not yet a satisfactory equivalent to the printed monograph.

Olsen (1994) and Schauder (1994b) argue that scholars are not reluctant to accept the concept of the electronic journal in place of print, as long as the electronic form is able to meet their needs. Performance requirements have still to be met: ergonomics (such as the discomfort of reading large amounts of text on a screen), and the psychological need of authors for a permanent record in hard copy, will be significant factors. Building a computerized system of journal literature will require a new frame of mind, an imaginative approach and an unconventional configuration of technology (Olsen, 1994).

Document delivery

Academic libraries have reached a crossroads in terms of collection building, as the online resources available to local university libraries are now international in character. With only one per cent of academic titles currently in electronic format, library collections will continue to be largely paper-based for some time to come. Copyright is still a major barrier to the delivery of the scanned image, and the transition from holdings to access is likely to depend either on greater collaboration between institutions or large research libraries providing a service on a commercial basis. Brandreth and MacKeigan (1994) refer to the need for holding libraries to maximize the investment in their collections by expanding their customer base through document delivery. This is entirely consistent with Heseltine (1994b), who rightly points out that if a document is not available in electronic form, then library access policies are dependent on someone to do the holding. Braid (1994) and Hugenholtz (1994) examine the legal, technical and organizational issues raised and the reasons we are still obliged to deliver the physical object by fax, post or courier.

A number of new players – subscription agents, publishers and online bibliography providers – have wisely invaded the commercial document delivery market in the last two or three years, creating fierce competition. These suppliers have received much attention in recent literature (Fuseler, 1994; Machovec, 1994; Moline *et al.*, 1994; Quint, 1994). More specifically, reviews are available on the following: Blackwell's Uncover (Bauwens, 1994; Rowley, 1994; Whittaker, 1994); BIDS and BODOS (Smethurst, 1994); OCLC's FirstSearch (Bauwens, 1994); Swetscan and Swetdoc (Rowley, 1994); Inside Information (Bauwens, 1994; Rowley, 1994); ADONIS and INIST (Bauwens, 1994).

Elliott (1994), writing on New Zealand university libraries, describes the emergence of large fee-based international document delivery systems accessible via existing electronic networks. Libraries are urged to review the current free domestic interlibrary loan system in order to provide users with a choice based on need between foreign-based document supply and domestic interlibrary loan. The Victoria University of Wellington, New Zealand, is one library among many which is now capping the growth of its own collections. Widdicombe (1993) describes in positive terms the library of Stevens Institute of Technology in the USA, which, he claims, has delighted its users by an emphasis on article access using electronic sources, such that it now has no periodicals on its shelves.

Nilsson (1994) sees interlending as the cornerstone of the cooperative library, with Sweden, as a research-intensive country that publishes little itself, as a European leader. Problems for net lenders are becoming acute, however, and charging is currently under discussion in an attempt to avoid the collapse of library cooperation. The same trend applies to most of the Nordic countries.

An increasing number of home-grown experimental projects for document delivery are also reviewed. Barwick (1994) provides a summary of 65 articles covering several local experiments. Electronic delivery is often being achieved through special collaborative arrangements with publishers in order to overcome copyright problems.

The Canada Institute for Scientific and Technical Information [CISTI] in

Ottawa has been supplying documents to one of its branches using imaging workstations. Much more flexibility is needed, however, to extend this to a more varied Canadian clientele, and the facilities are currently unsuitable for high volume demand. The ability to rationalize library collections is, however, seen as an important consequence, and work continues towards a generic workstation able to transmit to a variety of receivers over long distances (Brandreth and MacKeigan, 1994).

Smith (1994) discusses the technical aspects of Project ION (Interlending Open Systems Network) – an EC-funded international interlending project involving affiliated libraries in the UK, France and the Netherlands through LASER, SDB/SUNIST and Pica.

In the Netherlands, Geleijnse (1994) describes a project for delivery of full-text scanned documents in economics, applied computer sciences and social science, based on the pilot online contents database project between Elsevier Science and Tilburg University. This project, which is similar to TULIP (Zijlstra, 1994) in the USA, aims to develop an interface between the two types of databases – those based on text, and those on graphic images in order to allow switching between bibliographic searches and image browsing. Although this is technically feasible, Roes and Dijkstra (1994) question the wider economic and legal viability (particularly with regard to copyright) given that the project is based solely on bilateral agreements with publishers.

In the UK, ELINOR (Electronic Library Project), a joint venture between the British Library, De Montfort University and IBM UK, is described by Arnold (1994). An electronic library system which contains a collection of the full contents of the most frequently used books, journals, course materials and multimedia learning packages can be accessed directly by students and staff via workstations. As this is a small-scale project (about 35,000 pages), there are obvious limitations, but the results are interesting. A survey found that it was faster to locate electronic books containing answers to given questions, but slower to find the answer from the electronic book than the printed book. However, ELINOR is seen as a useful alternative to printed books, with the obvious advantages of 24-hour and simultaneous access, and the project is now being expanded.

Williams (1994) describes the British Library Document Supply Centre's (BLDSC) experiments with document imaging, although, as Line (1994a, 1994b) points out, the future of document delivery as anticipated by the Follett Report seems to rely more on the use of networks than on the services of the British Library. Vickers (1994) would almost certainly endorse this opinion, given his rather pessimistic view of BLDSC's dealings with publishers. Baker and Wood (1994) report on the experimental project investigating electronic document delivery from the BLDSC to the University of East Anglia, which started in September 1993 and by June 1994 was handling twenty documents a day. Also on a small scale, a SuperJANET project involving five university libraries is outlined by Friend (1994). A small sample of only 312 documents suggests a satisfaction rate as low as 25%. The British Library Research and Development Department has also funded a joint project with five publishers at the Institute of Physics for the distribution of electronic journals. The broadband capabilities of SuperJANET allow true remote browsing to be supported (Rees, 1994).

Concerns exist about the effectiveness of these services. A review of the literature over the last decade reveals that consistency and reliability are the most persistent obstacles in substituting ownership for access. Truesdell (1994) attempts to reassure us by describing the evaluation of services based on cost, speed and success rate. As a result of technological advances, the existence of an organizational infrastructure and the proliferation of options, the potential exists to guarantee rapid and reliable document delivery. Only when we can say with confidence, at the time a request is made, that a document will be available within so many hours will access rather than ownership become a reality. Bjarno (1994) describes a model developed with some Danish university libraries that enables the recording of both the cost of tasks performed and the performance – speed of delivery, fill rate, etc.

Wooliscroft (1994) examines two Australian trials of the cost-effectiveness of document delivery. In particular, the quality of faxed images is still unacceptable for many purposes. Ellis *et al.* (1994) give an account of how the University of Western Australia responded to difficulties caused by the increasing cost of scientific and engineering serials by linking the two concepts, the virtual library and access versus ownership – serial subscriptions were cancelled to fund a rapid document delivery service. Kurosman and Durniak (1994) examine the cost and response times of traditional interlibrary loan services as compared with four commercial document delivery suppliers. Their findings were, surprisingly, that traditional services are more cost-effective and only one day slower. Kinnucan (1993) reports on a consumer survey in Canada using the conjoint analysis approach. Price is regarded as the most important factor; overall, therefore, respondents expressed more willingness to use their library's interlibrary loan scheme than a commercial service.

The electronic scanning of documents, coupled with transmission over high-speed networks, offers one long-term answer. However, unless progress is made in the area of copyright law, the potential of information technology is unlikely to be realized. Rosenberg (1994a and 1994b) predicts that the new information superhighways will make it virtually impossible to protect intellectual property from illegal copying and distribution. Publishers must, therefore, explore both alternative sources of revenue and the means to protect their resources. This should lead to a healthy restructuring of the industry.

Reference services

The volume of literature discussing reference librarianship seems to have increased (W.P. Leonard, 1994; Nofsinger, 1994), not least because it is now widely recognized that the role of the traditional reference service is changing rapidly, particularly as a result of technology (Barbuto and Cevallos, 1994). The near future is likely to bring developments that will change the librarian's job for ever (Dunsire, 1994). Salisbury (1994) highlights the issues involved in integrating technology in reference services and suggests how we can provide timely information to the right users. Choices include locally mounted databases accessible through OPACs, document vendors and, of course, the Internet.

Increased student numbers and rising user expectations have also had an effect. As attempts are made to reduce costs, we should expect a similar review of other library operations. Libraries are beginning to abandon the traditional reference desk and replace it with an information desk, often staffed by para-professionals or, as other countries adopt the American model, by graduate students. Quick-to-answer queries are increasingly being handled in this way, freeing time for reference librarians to deal with referrals and more lengthy enquiries. In the ideal world, the librarian would replace library instruction – currently disguised as reference help – with a personalized literature search (Mood, 1994). In order for academic libraries to survive and prosper, they need to offer special services, streamlined so that user needs are met and met quickly. While the concept of tailored services is no doubt a good one, one wonders, given current staffing levels, how such services can be promised to the large numbers of students who frequent our libraries in the 1990s. Equally, has Mood missed out on the advantages to the customer of end-user searching?

A key assumption is that the creation of client-based services requires reference librarians to move away from the classic professional model that placed users in a dependency relationship. Current IT allows and encourages individuals to use tools without intermediaries, but these tools have to be shaped to meet the needs of users. Reference librarians can fill these new roles only if academic libraries are appropriately structured.

Lewis (1994) is perhaps more realistic when he complains that too little attention has been paid to the organizational changes that are required. We cannot assume that reference librarians will be able to balance a broad range of tasks – including desk services, consultations, training, collection development and the implementation of new IT – and at the same time have a generalized background. Technologies will continue to change and evolve as campus networks develop, and a structured planning process is needed that will encourage reference librarians to adopt new roles.

Lipow (1993) ties together many of the threads of discontent with current models of reference service, and emphasizes the need for a quality user-centred approach that adds value. Both he and Bicknell (1994) call for reference librarians to search for new foundations for services, based on an aggressive needs-assessment process. J.D. Brown (1994) reminds us of the importance of improving the quality of our answers.

No review of reference services can be considered complete without a look at the way in which the Internet is influencing enquiry services. Scott *et al.* (1994) provide references to five articles which describe specific Internet resources. A sixth article deals with the practical applications of Internet information and the new role for reference librarians. Cromer (1994) and Diaz *et al.* (1994) discuss the integration of electronic resources with traditional reference services, the possibilities for remote services provided by the electronic library and the effect of the Internet on communication between reference librarians. Training both for users and staff is covered by Cromer (1994), McLaughlin (1994) and Schiller (1994).

Quality

Library and information services have not been exempt from the implementation of quality management which characterized much US and Japanese manufacturing industry in the 1990s. Many are therefore writing, some with scepticism, about the need for libraries to review their operations and improve effectiveness.

Both France and Germany appear to be particularly preoccupied with accountability and value for money. In France, this topic dominates the literature (Fraisse and Renoult, 1994; Lapelerie, 1994; Van Cuyck, 1994). Renoult (1994) also observes that libraries have become much more self-critical and self-aware. Roda (1994) notes that the need for public accountability has led to the development of performance indicators and argues that it is no longer adequate to rely on a straightforward counting of resources. Automation has helped to provide more information, but he rightly recognizes the need to put the information to good use and to ensure that services are developed in the light of the management information collected. The challenge is to introduce performance measurement as a norm within the library profession.

German academic libraries have also only recently begun to be interested in performance measurement, largely because the trend of funding authorities to examine cost-effectiveness began later than in the UK and USA. German libraries used to rely on a fixed budget every year, but now, as money has become more scarce and the general trend has developed for evaluating public institutions, interest has grown in methods of evaluation for libraries. Poll (1993) notes, with special reference to Münster University Library, that the impulse came from a working group of IFLA, which was trying to draw up guidelines for performance measurement. Intensive discussion about 'the library as a concern'

('Bibliothek als Betrieb') has encouraged work on quality management, financial autonomy and global budgeting (Poll, 1994; Stäglich, 1994; Wätjen, 1994).

Quality is also receiving considerable attention throughout Scandinavia. In Denmark, Cotta-Schønberg and Line (1994) took an impressively empirical approach to performance measurement in the Copenhagen Business School, avoiding the rather theoretical approaches adopted by many other libraries. Garnes (1994) evaluates two reports (Kinnell, 1994; Strandvik, 1994) on quality assessment in Nordic academic libraries. Kinnell's work (1994) is largely an overview of literature on total quality management (TQM) in British academic libraries, with a list of four recommended areas for research and development work. Strandvik's (1994) work is with specific reference to the University of Bergen.

In Australia, where universities have been involved with continual quality assurance since 1992, Judge (1994) describes the trend towards TQM as an important tool for reshaping library planning and operation. Winkworth (1993) summarizes the history and current status of the use of performance indicators in UK academic libraries, with an emphasis on current developments and an analysis of recent external influences.

Not surprisingly, librarians have chosen to adopt techniques used in industry for the evaluation of their services. Measurement of reference services was particularly popular in the literature of 1994, beginning with Larson and Dickson (1994), who examine performance goals and standards based on objective, observable criteria. C.C. Brown (1994) discusses the use of concepts of business quality, especially the effective delivery of accurate answers, and suggests methods of reference service evaluation. Similarly, Crawford (1994) investigates the potential of conjoint analysis, much used by market researchers to develop commercial products. Inevitably, user preferences vary, so the final product must involve trade–offs, but the results are still interesting: of paramount importance to users was the cost of the service (it must be free), with opening hours taking second place (it must be open all the time the library is open).

In 1993, Hunt (1993) predicted an explosion in TQM techniques in British academic libraries, and evidence suggests that he was right. More prominent in the 1994 literature is an interest in collection evaluation (Nisonger, 1994) and book availability (Mitchell *et al.,* 1994; Stopforth, 1994). Kemp (1994) describes three studies undertaken in Egypt, Senegal and Hungary to determine availability, providing a minimum standard of provision with costs. Ifidon (1994) writes on book scarcity in Nigeria, and Ekoja (1994) appraises user satisfaction with services of Sokoto State Library. De Jager (1994) reports the results of a book use study at Cape Town University Library, aimed at establishing the proportion of books in the library which were circulating, and whether the accepted phenomenon of decline in use with age, or obsolescence, would be supported in an environment where a reduction in the purchase of new books was evident. Unlike Anglo-American libraries, there is no particular tradition in French libraries for collection evaluation, but Cressent (1993) argues the need to make this a core area of library activity in order to develop a coherent acquisitions policy. He advocates the use of the Conspectus methodology, despite its imperfections. Rehman *et al.* (1994) describe an analysis of book availability carried out in a university in Malaysia, providing a list of reasons for failure and the implications for the library of this type of study.

Conclusion

If any single theme can be identified in this overview of academic libraries in 1994 it is the impact of technology. The dominance of information technology in many of the issues discussed in this chapter – be it the role of the 'virtual library', the Internet, electronic publishing, the use of CD-ROM or electronic document delivery – is enough in itself to explain the move towards the convergence of libraries and computing services which is being seen in many places throughout the world. Most, if not all, of the other matters discussed, on issues as wide-ranging as academic publishing, resource sharing and quality measurement, again have a clear IT component. For many people, technology may seem to offer a panacea for the problems created by increased demand and underfunding. However, for the librarian, the real challenge is to find a meaningful role in this 'brave new world'.

References

Adeniran, O.R. *et al.* (1994) Availability and use of CD-ROM products in Nigerian libraries and information centres. *Electronic Library*, **12**(3), 155–168.
Akeroyd, J. (1994) The Follett Report: another view. *Relay*, (40), 5–6.
Arnold, K. *et al.* (1994) Electronic library for higher education: an experiment at De Montfort University, Milton Keynes. *Journal of Information Networking*, **1**(2), 117–135.
Ashley, C. (1994) It's in the numbers (Internet statistics). *Information World Review*, (89), 20.
Baker, D. and Wood, A. (1994) Document delivery: the UEA experience. *Vine*, (95), 12–14.
Barbuto, D.M. and Cevallos, E.E. (1994) The delivery of reference services in a CD-ROM LAN environment: a case study. *RQ*, **34**(1), 48–58.
Barral, S. (1994) Choix économiques dans une bibliothèque: l'expérience de Compiègne. *Bulletin des Bibliothèques de France*, **39**(3), 34–37.
Barry, A. and Stanton, D. (1994) CWIS. *Access*, **11**(1), 75–86.

Barwick, M. (1994) Interlending and document supply – a review of recent literature. *Interlending and Document Supply*, **22**(3), 27–34.

Bauwens, M. (1994) Four document delivery services: how well do they really deliver? (BLDSC, INIST, UnCover, Firstsearch). *Information World Review*, (89), 14–16.

Bell, H.K. and Koepp, D. (1994) Networking not the answer to escalating costs of publication. *Library Management*, **15**(1), 36–7.

Bennion, B.C. (1994) Why the science journal crisis? *Bulletin of the American Society for Information Science*, **20**(3), 25–26.

Bevan, N. (1994) Transient technology? The future of CD-ROMs in libraries. *Program*, **28**(1), 1–14.

Bicknell, T. (1994) Focusing on quality reference service. *Journal of Academic Librarianship*, **20**(2), 77–81.

Biddiscombe, R. and Watson, M. (1994) Developing a hypertext guide to an academic library. *Program*, **28**(1), 29–41.

Bisbrouck, M-F. (1994) The new development program for the French academic library buildings 1991–1995. *Liber Quarterly*, (4), 39–50.

Bjarno [sic, for Bjarnø, H. (1994) Cost finding and performance measures in ILL management. *Interlending and Document Supply*, **22**(2), 8–11.

Bjornshauge, L. (1993) Forskningsbibliotekerne i en brydningstid. *DF-Revy*, (6), 152–156.

Blagden, J. and Ford, J. (1994) The electronic library: a view from academia and the computer industry. *Managing Information*, **1**(6), 36–38.

Blunden-Ellis, J. (1994) The Consortium of Academic Libraries in Manchester (CALIM): strategic and development planning of a new consortium. In: *Resource sharing: new technologies as a must for universal availability of information. Proceedings of the 16th International Essen Symposium*, eds A.H.Helal and J.W. Weiss. Essen: Universitätsbibliothek, pp. 99–114.

Braid, A. (1994) Electronic document delivery: vision and reality. *Libri*, **44**(3), 224–236.

Brandreth, M. and MacKeigan, C. (1994) Electronic document delivery – towards the virtual library. *Interlending and Document Supply*, **22**(1), 15–19.

Branin, J.J. et al. (1993) Integrating information services in an academic setting: the organizational and technical challenge (at University of Minnesota). *Library Hi-Tech*, **11**(4), 75–83.

Brindley, L.J. (1994) Joint Funding Council's Libraries Review Group (the Follett) Report: the contribution of the IT Sub-committee. *Program*, **28**(3), 279–286.

British Journal of Academic Librarianship: Special issue on the Joint Funding Councils' Libraries Review Group Report (The Follett Report).

Brophy, P. (1993) Networking in British academic libraries. *British Journal of Academic Librarianship*, **8**(1), 49–60.

Brown, C.C. (1994) Creating automated bibliographies using Internet-accessible on-line library catalogues. *Database*, **17**(1), 67–71.

Brown, J. D. (1994) Using quality concepts to improve reference services. *College

and Research Libraries, **55**(3), 211–219.
Bundesvereinigung Deutscher Bibliotheksverbände (1994) *Bibliotheken 93: Strukturen, Aufgaben, Positionen*. Berlin and Göttingen: BDB.
Butter, K.A. (1994) Red sage: the next step in delivery of electronic journals. *Medical Reference Services Quarterly*, **13**(3), 75–81.
Campbell, R. (1994) How will academic libraries manage? What hope does the Follett report offer? *Learned Publishing*, **7**(2), 75–78.
Carbone, P. (1994) Les bibliothèques universitaires: dix ans après le Rapport Vandevoorde. *Bulletin des Bibliothèques de France*, **37**(4), 46–58.
Casale, M. (1994) End of the road for CD-ROM networks? *Managing Information*, (November), 17–18.
Cavanagh, A.K. (1994) Open learning students and libraries. *Australian Academic and Research Libraries*, **25**(2), 95–105.
Chauveinc, M. (1994) Cathédrale ou chappelle? Recherche d'un modèle pour bibliothèque universitaire. [To be published in: *Les 'Mélanges Thirion'*, end 1995.]
Cherhal, E. *et al*. (1993) Internet ou la recherche interconnectée. *Bulletin des Bibliothèques de France*, **38**(4), 8–12.
Cockrill, A. and Broady, J. (1994) Opportunities and threats: the macroeconomic environment of British and German university libraries. *Journal of Librarianship and Information Science*, **26**(2), 83–92.
Conkling, T.W. and Osif, B.A. (1994) CD-ROM and changing research patterns, *Online*, **18**(3), 71–74.
Cooper, W. (1994) Integrating information technologies for the library environment, *Library Administration and Management*, **8**(3), 131–134.
Cotta-Schønberg, M. and Line, M.B. (1994) Evaluation of academic libraries: with special reference to the Copenhagen Business School Library. *Journal of Librarianship and Information Science*, **26**(2), 55–69.
Cotta-Schønberg, M. and Winkel-Schwartz, A. (1994) Greyber imellem bibliotekerne for interurbån. *DF-Revy*, (2), 27–29.
Crawford, G.A. (1994) A conjoint analysis of reference services in academic libraries. *College and Research Libraries*, **55**(3), 257–267.
Cressent, J-P. (1993) L'évaluation des collections des bibliothèques. *Lettres Actuelles*, 1–2 (Juin - Septembre).
Creth, S.D. (1993) Creating a virtual information organization: collaborative relationships between libraries and computer centers. *Journal of Library Administration*, **19**(3/4), 111–132.
Creth, S.D. (1994) The information arcade: playground for the mind. *Journal of Academic Librarianship*, **20**(1), 22–23.
Cromer, D.E. (1994) Internet's impact on reference services. *Reference Librarian*, (41–2), 55–137.
Cummings, A.M. (1992) *University libraries and scholarly communication: a study prepared for the Andrew W. Mellon Foundation*. Washington, DC: Association of Research Libraries.

Dedrick, A.J. (1994) Shared academic library facilities: the unknown form of library co-operation. *College and Research Libraries*, **55**(5), 437 - 443.

de Jager, K. (1994) Obsolescence and stress: a study of the use of books on open shelves at a university library. *Journal of Librarianship and Information Science*, **26**(2), 71–82.

del Sol, P. *et al.* (1994) Knowledge art: management and technology for the co-operative acquisition and use of periodical publications in Chile. *Interlending and Document Supply,* **22**(2), 12–18.

Denise, O.H. and Woods, G. (1994) The future of Australian academic libraries. *Australian Academic and Research Libraries,* **25**(3), 149–158.

Diaz, K.R. *et al.* (1994) Introducing Internet services. *Reference Librarian,* (41–42), 3–54.

Donovan, B. (1994) Two cheers for the electronic revolution. *Bookseller,* (21 October), 18–21.

Dunsire, G. (1994) The potential of the Internet and networks for library acquisitions. *Taking Stock,* **3**(2), 44–49.

Dusoulier, N. (1994) New technologies, new sources, new users – or only new words? *Electronic Library*, **12**(3), 191–195.

Dworaczek, M. and Wiebe, V.G. (1994) E-journals: acquisitions and access. *Acquisitions Librarian,* (12), 105–121.

Edwards, C. *et al.* (1993) Key areas in the management of change in higher education libraries in the 1990s: relevance of the IMPEL project. *British Journal of Academic Librarianship,* **8**(3), 139–177.

Edwards, H.M. (1994) Library co-operation and resource sharing in South Africa: considerations for the future. *South African Journal of Librarianship and Information Science,* **62**(3), 113–119.

Ekoja, I.I. (1994) An appraisal of user-satisfaction with the services of Sokoto State Library, Sokoto. *Lagos Librarian: Journal of the Nigerian Library Association,* (15), 57–64.

Elliott, V. (1994) Acquisition and access in academic libraries: the case for access, today. *New Zealand Libraries,* **47**(10), 200–203.

Ellis, A. *et al.* (1994) Network document access: planning an electronic document delivery service; a case study. *Australian Library Review,* **11**(1), 67–74.

Esin, J.O. (1994) Strategic planning for computer integration in higher education through the year 2000. *Journal of Educational Media and Library Sciences,* **31**(2), 129–144.

Ferreira, S.M.S.P. (1994) Electronic networking in Brazil, *FID News Bulletin*, **44**(11), 282–285.

Fisher, S.R. (1994) The electronic bookmobile: librarians on the information highway. *Feliciter,* **40**(7/8), 6–12.

Fraisse, E. and Renoult, D. (1994) Les ensignants du supérieur et leurs bibliothèques universitaires. *Bulletin des Bibliothèques de France*, **39**(4), 18–25.

Friend, F. J. (1994) Electronic document delivery through library co-operation. *Interlending and Document Supply,* **22**(4), 17–21.

Fry, H. (1994a) Coppul Part 1. *Newsline (Manitoba Library Association)*, **19**(10), 7–11.
Fry, H. (1994b) Coppul Part 2. *Newsline (Manitoba Library Association)*, **19**(11), 7–11.
Fuseler, E.A. (1994) Providing access to journals – just in time or just in case? *College and Research Libraries News*, **55**(3), 130–132, 148.
Gardner, N. (1994) Itch to flee the flea pit. *Times Higher Education Supplement: Multimedia News*, (14 October), x-xi.
Garnes, K. (1994) Kvalitetsbedømming ved nordiske forningsbibliotek. *Nordinfo-Nytt*, **17**(3), 54–57.
Gartner, R. (1994) Bodleian's BARD on-line access. *Computers in Libraries*, **14**(5), 53–57.
Gasson, C. (1994) Fear and loathing in cyberspace (Internet replacing the learned journal). *Bookseller*, (24 June), 20, 22, 24.
Geleijnse, H. (1994) Journal articles on the desktop. *Managing Information*, **1**(6), 34–35.
Geleijnse, H. and Grootaers, C. (1994) (eds) *Developing the library of the future: the Tilburg experience*. Netherlands: Tilburg University Press.
Glover, H. (1994) The Internet – what is it? what does it offer? and what will its impact on libraries be? *ITs News* [UK Library Association], (29), 28–31.
Goodacre, C. (1993) (ed.) *Networking and libraries in Australia: technology in the library,1*. Port Melbourne: ALIA Press/D.W. Thorne.
Graham, G. (1994) *As I was saying: on the international book business*. London: Hans Zell.
Griebel, R. (1993) Etatsituation der wissenschaftlichen Bibliotheken in den alten und neuen Bundesländern 1993. *Zeitschrift für Bibliothekswesen und Bibliographie*, **40**(6), 485–526.
Griebel, R. (1994) Etatsituation der wissenschaftlichen Bibliotheken in den alten und neuen Bundesländern 1994. *Zeitschrift für Bibliothekswesen und Bibliographie*, **41**(6),585–625.
Griebel, R. et al. (1994) *Bestandsaufbau und Erwebungspolitik in universitäten Bibliothekssystem: Versuch einer Standortbestimmung* (Kommission des DBI für Erwebung und Bestandsaufbau: Expertengruppe Bestandsentwicklung in wissenschaftlichen Bibliotheken). Berlin: Deutsche Bibliotheksinstitut.
Hanson, T. (1993) A future for CD-ROM as a strategic technology? In: T. Hanson and J. Day (eds) *CD-ROM in libraries: management issues*. London: Bowker-Saur, pp. 241–253.
Harloe, B. and Budd, J.M. (1994) Collection development and scholarly communication in the era of electronic access. *Journal of Academic Librarianship*, **20**(2), 83–87.
Harnesk, J. (1993) Avgiftsriktlinjer för fjärrlån. *Bibsamnytt*, (2), 5–6.
Harnesk, J. (1994) Fjärrlåneavgifter – inte bare i Sverige. *Bibsamnytt*, (1), 1–3.
Harry, V. and Oppenheim, C. (1993) Evaluations of electronic databases, part 1: criteria for testing CD-ROM products. *Online and CD-ROM Review*, **17**(4), 211–222.

Hawkins, B.L. (1994) Creating the library of the future: incrementalism won't get us there! (Planning for a national electronic library). *Serials Librarian*, **24**(3/4), 17–47.

Heseltine, R. (1994a) A critical appraisal of the role of global networks in the transformation of higher education. *Alexandria*, **6**(3), 159–171.

Heseltine, R. (1994b) Vices and virtues in the virtual library. *Times Higher Education Supplement: Multimedia News*, 14 October, iv–v.

Hugenholtz, P.B. (1994) Copyright and electronic document delivery services. *Interlending and Document Supply*, **22**(3), 8–14.

Hunt, C.J. (1993) Academic library planning in the United Kingdom, 1993. *British Journal of Academic Librarianship*, **8**(1), 3–16.

Hunter, K. (1993) The changing business of scholarly publishing. *Journal of Library Administration*, **19**(3/4), 23–38.

Ifidon, B.I. (1994) Book scarcity in Nigeria: causes and solutions. *African Journal of Library,Archives and Information Science*, **4**(1), 55–62.

Jazdon, A. and Olszewski (1994) Problems in the management and operation of academic libraries in Poland during the transition period. *Library Review*, **43**(8), 31–39.

Joint (1993) Funding Councils' Libraries Review Group *Report.*[Chairman: Sir Brian Follett]. Bristol: HEFCE.

Judge, P. (1994) Changing the culture of the mindset. *Incite*, **15**(3), 18–20.

Kelly, P. (1994) Academic libraries: towards commonwealth and coalitions.*Library Technology News*, (12), 70–84.

Kemp, I. (1994) *Higher education library services research and policy studies. An evaluation of studies in Egypt, Senegal and Hungary.* London: British Library Research and Development Department. (BLRDD Report 6138).

Ketcham, L. and Born, K. (1994) Projecting serials costs: banking on the past to pay for the future. *Library Journal*, **119**(7), 44–50.

Kinnell, M. (1994) Quality issues for academic and industrial library and information services. *Nordinfo-Nytt*, **17**(3), 3–20.

Kinnucan, M.T. (1993) Demand for document delivery and interlibrary loan in academic settings. *Library and Information Research*, **15**(4), 355–374.

Kisiedu, C.O. (1994) Networking in Ghana: a national profile. *FID News Bulletin*, **44**(11), 272–277.

Kitt, S. (1993) The Internet: a new meaning to networking – part I. *One-Person Library*, **10**(9), 4–6.

Kitt, S. (1994) The Internet: a new meaning to networking – part II. *One-Person Library*, **10**(10), 3–5.

Køfoed, P. (1993) Biblioteket pa det elektroniske informationsmarked – få documentleverandor til informationsvejleder. *DF-Revy*, (5), 123–129.

Korsah, J.E. (1994a) University libraries in Ghana: some observations. *Aslib Proceedings*, **46**(10), 235–241.

Korsah, J.E. (1994b) Towards effective utilization of university library resources: the situation in University of Cape Coast, Ghana. *Aslib Proceedings*, **46**(11/12), 263–266.

Kurosman, K. and Durniak, B.A. (1994) Document delivery: a comparison of commercial document suppliers and inter-library loan services. *College and Research Libraries News*, **55**(2), 129–139.

Lambert, J. (1994) Managing CD-ROM services in academic libraries. *Journal of Librarianship and Information Science*, **26**(1), 23–28.

Langenberg, D.N. (1994) Information technology and the university: integration strategies for the 21st century. *Journal of American Society for Information Science*, **45**(5), 323–325.

Lanier, D. and Wilkins, W. (1994) Ready reference via the Internet. *RQ*, (3), 359–368.

Lapèlerie, F. (1994) L'évaluation d'une bibliothèque par la méthode de Kantor. *Bulletin des Bibliothèques de France*, **39**(4), 55–66.

Larsen, R.L. (1994) The role of networks in achieving academic library goals. In: *Proceedings of the Clinic on Library Applications of Data Processing, Illinois University at Urbana-Champaign, 4–6 April 1993*, ed. A.P. Bishop. Urbana, IL: University of Illinois Press, pp. 215–222.

Larson, C.A. and Dickson, L.K. (1994) Developing behavioral reference desk performance standards. *RQ*, **3**(3), 349–357.

Law, D. (1994a) The Follett Report: panacea or placebo? *Relay*, (40), 3–4.

Law, D. (1994b) The role of academic libraries in the scientific information system. *Learned Publishing*, **7**(3), 159–162.

Law, D. (1994c) Beyond the CD-ROM: wider horizons in the provision of electronic information. *Health Libraries Review*, **11**(1), 52–56.

Leonard, B.G. (1994a) A view from across the Pacific: the role of the academic librarian in the selection of monographs. *Australian Academic and Research Libraries*, **25**(1), 55–9.

Leonard, B.G. (1994b) Collection management in Australian academic libraries: an American perspective. *Library Acquisitions: Practice and Theory*, **18**(2), 147–56.

Leonard, W.P. (1994) On my mind: libraries without walls, field service librarianship. *Journal of Academic Librarianship*, (March), 29–30.

Lewis, D.W. (1994) Making academic reference services work. *College and Research Libraries*, **55**(5), 445–456.

Libraries (1993) and IT: working papers of the Information Technology Sub-Committee of the HEFCs' Libraries Review. Bath: UKOLN.

Line, M.B. (1994a)The implications of declining library resources and improving electronic technology for document access and supply: a review article. *Interlending and Document Supply*, **22**(2), 19–23.

Line, M.B. (1994b) The importance of Follett. *Serials*, **7**(1), 69–72.

Lipow, A.G. (1993) *Rethinking reference in academic libraries*. Berkeley, CA: Library Solutions Press.

Lovecy, I. (1994) Convergence of libraries and computing services. *Library and Information Briefings*, (54), 1–11.

Lyon, J. (1994) What next for academic libraries, *Library Manager*, (2), 17–18.

McCarthy, P. (1994) Serial killers: academic libraries respond to soaring costs. *Library Journal*, **119**(11), 41–44.

MacDonald, A.H. (1994) The survival of libraries in the electronic age. *Feliciter*, **40**(1), 18–22.

McDonald, D.R. (1994) The philosophical and practical dimensions of resource sharing. In: *Resource sharing: new technologies as a must for universal availability of information. Proceedings of the 16th International Essen Symposium,* eds A.H. Helal and J.W. Weiss. Essen: Universitätsbibliothek, pp. 163–172.

Machovec, G.S. (1994) Key elements in an advanced document delivery and ILL system. *Online Libraries and Microcomputers*, **12**(1), 1–5.

McLaughlin, P.W. (1994) Embracing the Internet: the changing role of library staff. *Bulletin of the American Sciety for Information Science*, **20**(3), 16–17.

McMillan, G. (1994) Technical processing of electronic journals in libraries. *Learned Publishing*, **7**(2), 93–98.

McPherson, M. (1994) Necessity and invention in a new regional university. *LASIE*, **24**(4/5), 70–76.

McRobbie, S. (1994) Supply and demand in a bespoke market (academic publishing on demand). *New Scientist*, (1928), 40–41.

McSean, A. and Law, D. (1990) Is CD-ROM a transient technology? *Library Association Record*, **92**(1), 837–841.

Mendes, H.R. (1994) Nordisk bibliotekssamarbete i EU-perspektiv. *Nordinfo-Nytt*, **17**(1), 3–5.

Metcalfe, M. (1994) (ed.) VALA 1993: state of the states and territories. *Australian Library Journal*, **43**(1), 56–78.

Michold, U. (1994) Das Internet für Bibliothekare: eine Einführung. *Bibliotheksdienst*, **28**(7), 1100–1124.

Miquel, A. (1989) *Les bibliothèques universitaires: rapport au ministre d'Etat, ministre de l'Education nationale, de la Jeunesse et des Sports*. Paris; Documentation Française.

Mitchell, E.S. *et al.* (1994) Book availability: academic library assessment. *College and Research Libraries*, **55**(1), 47–55.

Moline, S. *et al.* (1994) Campus-wide access to OCLC's First Search: a study of use at the University of Minnesota. *Reference Services Review*, **22**(1), 21–28.

Mood, T.A. (1994) Of sundials and digital watches: a further step towards the new paradigm of reference. *Reference Services Review*, **22**(3), 27–32.

Motais de Narbonne, A-M. (1994) Pancatalogue: un catalogue collectif de livres pour l'enseignement supérieur. *Bulletin des Bibliothèques de France*, **39**(1), 28–38.

Mowat, I.R.M. (1994) The future of the book in the academic library. *Assistant Librarian*, **87**(4), 60–63.

Naylor, B. (1994) 'Just in case' vs 'just in time': a librarian ruminates about journals, technology and money. *Logos*, **5**(2), 101–104.

Nicklin, J.L. (1994) Cost-cutting consortia. *Chronicle of Higher Education*, **40**(31), 51–52.
Nilsson, K. (1994) Planning for document supply: Sweden and Scandinavia. *Interlending and Document Supply*, **22**(1), 3–6.
Nisonger, T.E. (1994) Collection evaluation in academic libraries: a literature guide and annotated bibliography. *Collection Management*, **18**(3/4), 157.
Nofsinger, Mary M. (1994) Roles of the head of reference: from the 1990s to the 21st century. *Reference Librarian*, (43), 87–99.
Obenaus, G. (1994) The Internet – an electronic treasure trove. *Aslib Proceedings*, **46**(4), 95–100.
O'Brien, L. (1994) AARNet and libraries. *Australian Library Review*, **11**(1),37–52.
O'Donovan, K. (1994) The Internet – library and information service management issues. *Information Management Report*, (August), 1–4.
Olsen, J. (1994) Electronic journals: implications for scholars. *Learned Publishing*, **7**(3), 167–176.
Oppenheim, C. (1994a) The virtual library: some common sense. *Managing Information*, **1**(1), 26–27.
Oppenheim, C. (1994b) The Internet. *On-line and CD Notes*, (April), 3–5.
Orum, A. (1993) Forandringer, faglig identiteter og forskingsbiblioteker. *DF-Revy*, (2), 42–45.
Osswald, A. and Kock, T. (1994) Internet and Bibliotheken – ein einführender Überlick. *Zeitschrift für Bibliothekswesen und Bibliographie*, **41**(1), 1–31.
Owen, T. (1994) Don't get enmeshed in the Net. *Information World Review*, (88), 18–19.
Pallier, D. (1993) Les sections des bibliothèques universitaires. In: *Rapport annuel de l'inspection général des bibliothèques*, pp. 35–67.
Pastine, M. and Kacena, C. (1994) Library automation, networking, and other on-line and new technology costs in academic libraries. *Library Trends*, **42**(3) 524–536.
Pellé, F. (1994) Direction de l'information scientifique et technique et des bibliothèques: le schéma directeur informatique des réseaux de bibliothéques universitaires. *Bulletin des Bibliothèques de France*, **39**(1), 24–27.
Perrault, A.H. (1994) The shrinking national collection. A study of the effects of the diversion of funds from monographs to serials on the monograph collections of research libraries. *Library Acquisitions: Practice and Theory*, **18**(1), 1–22.
Pinson, J. (1994) Providing public services to remote users. *Australian Library Review*, **11**(1), 130.
Pitkin, G.M. (1992) (ed.) *Information management and organizational change in higher education: the impact on libraries*. Westport, CT: Meckler.
Poll, R. (1993) Quality and performance measurement: a German view. *British Journal of Academic Librarianship*, **8**(1), 35–48.
Poll, R. (1994) Qualitätsmanagement in Hochschulbibliotheken. In: H. Lohse (ed.) *Arbeitsfeld Bibliothek. 6. Deutsche Bibliothekskongreß, 84. Deutsche Bibliothekartag in Dortmund*. Frankfurt am Main: Klostermann, pp. 84–99.

Powell, J. (1994) Adventures with the World Wide Web: creating a hypertext library. *Information System*, **17**(1) 59–60, 62–66.

Quinn, D.B. (1994) The information age: another giant step backward. *Journal of Academic Librarianship*, **20**(3), 134–135.

Quint, B. (1994) Found money (the burst in document delivery). *Information Today*, **11**(8), 7–9.

Raitt, D. (1994) The future of libraries in the face of the Internet. *Electronic Library*, **12**(5), 275 -276.

Redmond, M. (1994) Librarians and cybrarians: new roles in an electronic age. *NFAIS Newsletter*, **36**(10), 109–11.

Rees, F. (1994) Electronic journals on SuperJANET (Institute of Physics project). *Information Management Report*, (April), 9–10.

Rehman, S.U. *et al.* (1994) Availability analysis: conduct, comparison and applications. *Australian Academic and Research Libraries*, **25**(1), 19–26.

Renoult, D. (1994) *L'offre des bibliothèques universitaires face à la demande étudiante.* Paris: Éditions du Cercle de la Librarie.

Roberts, J.K. (1994) One librarian's reaction to Follett. *Relay*, (40), 6–9.

Roda, J-C. (1994) L'évaluation des bibliothèques: pourquoi faire? *Bulletin des Bibliothèques de France*, **39**(1), 54–60.

Rodgers, D.L. (1994) Scholarly journals in 2020. *Serials Librarian*, **24**(3/4), 73–76.

Roes, H. and Dijkstra, J. (1994) Ariadne: the next generation of electronic document delivery systems. *Electronic Library*, **12**(1), 13–20.

Rosenberg, V. (1994a) Is copyright an effective stop sign on the information highway? *NFAIS Newsletter*, **36**(3), 25–26, 30.

Rosenberg, V. (1994b) Copyright (on the Internet) RIP? *On-line and CD-ROM Review*, **18**(3), 184–185.

Rothnie, L. (1993) Campus-wide information system development at three UK universities (Birmingham, Bradford, Stirling). *Vine*, (93), 18–30.

Rowley, J. (1994) Revolution in current awareness services. *Journal of Librarianship and Information Science*, **26**(1), 7–14.

Salisbury, L. (1994) Integrating technology in reference services: the issues. *Library Administration and Management*, **8**(3), 167–172.

Saunders, L.M. (1993) (ed.) *The virtual library: visions and realities.* Westport, CT: Meckler.

Schauder, D. (1994a) Development of the E-library concept, with special reference to Australian academic libraries. *Australian Library Review*, **11**(1), 5–30.

Schauder, D. (1994b) Electronic publishing of professional articles: attitudes of academics and implications for the scholarly communication industry. *Journal of the American Society for Information Science*, **45**(2) 73–100.

Schiller, N. (1994) Internet training and support. Academic libraries and computer centres: who's doing what? *Internet Research*, **4**(2), 35–47.

Scientific (1993), *The Technical and Medical Information System in the UK: a study on behalf of the Royal Society, the British Library and the Association of Learned and Professional Society Publishers.* London: British Library. (BLR & DD Report 6123).

Scott, R.L. *et al.* (1994) Selected sources on the Internet. *Reference Librarian*, (41–42), 55–137.

Seiden, P. *et al.* (1994) Progress with the Internet. *Reference Librarian*, (41–42), 275–385.

Singleton, A. (1994) Charging for information – pricing policies and practice. *Learned Publishing*, 7(4), 223–232.

Skogmar, G. (1994) Information networking in the Nordic countries: a Swedish perspective. In: *Resource sharing: new technologies as a must for universal availability of information. Proceedings of the 16th International Essen Symposium*, eds A.H.Helal and J.W. Weiss. Essen: Universitätsbibliothek, pp. 115–140.

Smethurst, B. (1994) BIDS and BODOS – whence and whither: the background to and the development of the BIDS Bibliographic Services and the BIDS Online Document Ordering Service. *Vine*, (95), 29–35.

Smith, P. (1994) Project Ion (Interlending Open Systems Network). *Vine*, (95), 15–24.

Snow, M. (1994) Forward with people. *Journal of Academic Librarianship*, 20(3), 142–143.

Stäglich, D. (1994) Finanzautonomie (Globalhaushalt) an nordrhein-westfälischen Hochschulen: Chancen or Risiko für Bibliothekare. In: H. Lohse (ed.) *Arbeitsfeld Bibliothek.*
6. [Sechste] *Deutsche Bibliothekskongress, 84, Deutsche Bibliothekartag in Dortmund.* Frankfurt am Main: Klostermann, pp. 226–248.

Stoker, D. (1994) From Parry to Follett: the changing world of the university librarian. *Journal of Librarianship and Information Science*, 26(2), 51–53.

Stopforth, C. (1994) Provision of reading list texts in an academic library. *Library Management*, 15(3), 14–20.

Strandvik, T. (1994) Kvalitet i bibliotekstjanester urtt strategisk perspektiv. *Nordinfo-Nytt*, 17(3), 21–43.

Sumsion, J. (1994) *Survey of resources and users in higher education libraries: UK, 1993.* Loughborough: Library and Information Statistics Unit.

Swain, L. (1994) Overview of the Internet: origins, future, and issues. *IFLA Journal*, 20(1), 16–21.

Syliva, M. and Lesher, M. (1994) Hard choices: cancelling print indexes. *Online*, 18(1), 59–64.

Taylor, A. G. (1994) The information universe: will we have chaos or control? *American Libraries*, (July/August), 629–632.

Tedd, L. (1995) Introduction to sharing resources via the Internet in academic libraries and information centres in Europe. *Program*, 29(1), 43–61.

Tomlinson, J. (1994) Will you survive the electronic library? *Serials*, 7(1), 37–41.

Törnudd, E. (1994) Library co-operation for national information provision. *Information Development*, 10(1), 29–34.

Truesdell, C.B. (1994) Is access a viable alternative to ownership? A review of access performance. *Journal of Academic Librarianship*, **20**(4), 200–205.

Tuten, J.H. and Washington, N. (1994) Collection management and resource sharing in academic libraries in South Carolina. *Southeastern Librarian*, **43**(4), 84–6.

Van Cuyck, A. (1994) Construction par l'usage et construction du réel: les étudiants et les bibliothèques à l'université: Jean-Moulin. *Bulletin des Bibliothèques de France*, **39**(1), 48–52.

Van Dooren, B. (1993) En finir avec la crise des bibliothèques universitaires. *Esprit*, (9), 143–158.

Vickers, P. and Martyn, J. (1994) *The impact of electronic publishing on library services and resources in the UK: report of the British Library Working Party on Electronic Publishing*. London: BLRDD. (LIR Report 102).

Vickers, S. (1994) Recent developments at the British Library Document Supply Centre. *Vine*, (95), June, 7–11.

Waddell, C. (1994) 1993 CAPP book and journal spending report. *Serials*, **7**(1), 65–8.

Warlock, D.R. (1994) Is there a future for the electronic book? *Learned Publishing*, **7**(4), 233–237.

Wätjen, H-J. (1994) Hochschulbibliotheken und Globalhaushalt am Beispiel Niedersachsens – Chancen und Risiken. *Zeitschrift für Bibliothekswesen und Bibliographie*, **41**(4), 433–446.

Westell, M. (1994) CWIS: a grassroots development model. *Feliciter*, **40**(3), 53–55.

White, H.S. (1994) Electronic resource sharing: it seems obvious, but it's not as simple as it looks. In: *Resource sharing: new technologies as a must for universal availability of information. Proceedings of the 16th International Essen Symposium* eds A.H.Helal and J.W. Weiss. Essen: Universitätsbibliothek, pp. 1–12.

Whittaker, M. (1994) UnCover: the article access solution. *Bulletin of the Medical Library Association*, **82**(2), 181–182.

Widdicombe, R.P. (1993) Eliminating all journal subscriptions has freed our customers to seek the information they really want and need: the result - more access, not less. *Technology in Libraries*, **14**(1), 3–13.

Williams, B. (1994) Automated document delivery at the British Library Document Supply Centre (demonstrator). *Information Management and Technology*, **27**(1), 36–37, 40.

Winkworth, I.R. (1993) Into the house of mirrors: performance measurement in academic libraries. *British Journal of Academic Librarianship*, **8**(1), 17–34.

Wisner, W.H. (1994) Back toward people: a symposium. *Journal of Academic Librarianship*, **20**(3), 131–133.

Wolpert, A.J. (1991) Libraries in the year 2001. *Information Technology and Libraries*, (December), 331–337.

Woodward, H. and Pilling, S. (1993) (eds.) *The international serials industry*. Aldershot: Gower.

Wooliscroft, M. (1994) Access and ownership: academic libraries' collecting and service responsibilities and the emerging benefits of electronic publishing and document supply. *New Zealand Libraries*, **47**(9), 170–180.

Zijlstra, J. (1994) The University Licensing Program (TULIP): a large scale experiment in bringing electronic journals to the desktop. *Serials*, **7**(2), 169–172.

Parliamentary libraries 5

Ernst Kohl

Introduction

Parliamentary libraries are small in number, and are usually not in the limelight of the library profession. They have never been dealt with by *Librarianship and information work worldwide* before, and this is also true of most major library journals. As many readers may, therefore, be unfamiliar with the specificities of parliamentary librarianship which distinguish it from other types of libraries, I shall discuss them in some detail, on the basis of the literature of the last four years.

Parliamentary libraries have been quite extensively documented in 1993/94, thanks to the sustained joint efforts of the Section of Parliamentary Libraries of IFLA and of the Reference and Research Services of the German Bundestag, resulting in the publication of two international directories recording all parliamentary libraries at the **three territorial levels** where parliaments wield sovereign powers, i.e. member states of federations at the low end, the intermediate level of the nation state, and the supranational level at the top end. The *World directory of parliamentary libraries of federated states and autonomous territories* lists 398 parliaments or chambers of 389 territories at the sub-national level, which roughly corresponds to a 90% coverage of these legislatures (Kohl, 1993c), whereas the fifth edition of the *World directory of national parliamentary libraries,* in addition to 243 parliaments or chambers of 191 sovereign states, includes, for the first time, some parliaments at the supranational level, too (Kohl, 1994).

Consequently, there is hardly any national arena for addressing the particular issues of parliamentary librarianship, with the exception of large federations like the USA, Canada, Germany, India, or Australia. Like other very specific types of libraries which are equally small in numbers, parliamentary libraries are, therefore, very much dependent on having an international forum of expression. IFLA pays particular attention to otherwise disregarded groups of libraries; parliamentary libraries have been fortunate, in that IFLA instituted, in 1976, a Section of Parliamentary Libraries, which has since come to be the prime agent in fostering the advance of parliamentary librarianship throughout the world (Kohl, 1992).

The wave of democratization in Eastern Europe and the former Soviet Union in the 1990s, and in Latin America and parts of Africa, was recognized by the Section as both a challenge and an opportunity for parliamentary librarianship, which could support progress towards parliamentarization in these countries (Kohl, 1991b; Barbier-Wiesser, 1993; Molinelli, 1994). At the Stockholm IFLA Conference, a plan of action was devised (Alexanderson, 1991) to highlight the various essentials of parliamentary librarianship. In consequence, the Section held, in addition to the Open Meetings at IFLA Conferences, both Workshops and Pre-Conference Seminars of its own and also supported regional meetings of parliamentary libraries. Moreover, the Section was successful in compiling and publishing guidelines for the management of parliamentary libraries (Englefield, 1993). As a result, quite a few studies on a wide range of aspects of parliamentary librarianship are now available, on which this chapter draws.

The conceptual foundation of parliamentary librarianship

It is almost a definition of parliamentary librarianship to say that it is a very distinctive kind of information work. None of the various parliamentary support services is more pre-eminently linked to the long-term operational success and, hence, authority of parliament. Some recent comments exemplify this:

> While its electoral linkage helps legitimize the actions of the legislature in a formal sense, the efficacy of its actual lawmaking performance is what induces citizen support and lends binding authority to its actions (Robinson, 1994).

> In any parliamentary system the key to an effective legislature is the knowledge and information that permit it both to play an active role in the policymaking process and to make reasoned choices for society on specific policy issues (Robinson, 1995).

> Vested interests, ethical values, and ideologies may all be moving forces in political life, but as politics are first and foremost concerned with practical matters, political decision making is primarily dependent on information, i.e. on some knowledge on the part of the decision makers about facts and people's opinions, and on their proper apprehension of the latest authoritative results of research, science, and technology. Otherwise political decision makers would

be unable to calculate the consequences of their decisions, thereby risking to eventually lose their position (Kohl, 1991a).

To avoid giving the impression that parliamentary librarians overrate their importance, let us turn to assessments by parliamentarians themselves. The most impressive account of Members' 'incessant and relentless need for information' is by a British MP, the Chairman of the House of Commons Library Sub-Committee (Shepherd, 1991):

> Nothing can prepare the newly elected Member for the full blast of their constituents' expectation of what they believe their Member will know, will want to know and on what matters an opinion will be expected which is both authoritative and accurate.... Be it mass lobby, mass write-in campaign, explosive TV programme, individual letter or other communication, the recipient MP will want to know: How much of the story have I been told? What is the other side of the coin? What is the background of the matter? What is the scale in size and time? Why is it being raised now? Is there a story behind the story? What are the arguments involved? Without full knowledge of the matter over and above that which has been presented by the lobbyist, the further questions of overtone, sectoral interest, knock-on effects or implications, financial and political etc., cannot be assessed. Corralling the various elements of information enables an appropriate plan of action to be evolved.... What is needed, therefore, is a reservoir, from which can be drawn, as required, in a dispassionate and disinterested manner, the background information pertinent to the proposals made.

Similar assessments have been made by parliamentarians of various Latin American countries at the First Ibero-American Meeting of Parliamentary Libraries in Mexico City in 1993 (Paoli Bolio *et al.*, 1994).

These general statements are complemented by a few studies on the kind of information needed for particular activities of parliamentarians, e.g. their daily routine (Russell, 1991), committee work (Silk, 1991), legislation (Paoli Bolio, 1994), or international relations (Lamadrid Sauza, 1994). Clements (1991) examines the importance of statistical materials for parliamentarians. The most detailed investigation into the information needs of parliamentarians, however, has been carried out in Australia, based on empirical data obtained through questionnaires and interviews (Parr and Ransome, 1991).

It can be concluded from these assessments that, as Englefield (1990, p. 8) once put it, 'parliamentarians regard themselves as professionals in the *use* of information . . . But Members don't often regard themselves as professionals in the *gathering* of information. This distinguishes them from the student or academic using his university library'.

From these statements, both the *raison d'être* and the modes of operation of a parliamentary library, as distinct from other types of library, can be derived:

The place of the parliamentary library ... is that of an intermediary, identifying, locating, analyzing, selecting or extracting, interpreting, condensing, and popularizing the information ... finally actively disseminating the results ... In doing so the parliamentary library must be an honest broker of analysis and information' (Kohl, 1991b).

This involves the outreach function to gather information; ... sifting and evaluating the raw data for relevance and quality; compressing and simplifying the information to make it digestible by busy, non-technical legislators; adding value to the raw information by recasting it into relevant formats that highlight problem causes, possible solutions, and their impacts (Robinson, 1994).

To fulfil this mission effectively, high-quality staff of some size is paramount. 'A noticeable impact can be obtained with a staff of 25 - 50 of the right kind of specialists' (Robinson, 1994), consisting of 'professional librarians', 'graduates in economics, law, international relations, and the physical and social sciences' including, in particular, 'statistics' and 'modern history' (Lock, 1991).

Parliamentary oversight committee

It is an indication of parliamentarians' awareness of their dependence on legislative information support services that in almost all fully developed democratic parliaments there is a parliamentary oversight committee for its library, which signals that, unlike in other types of libraries, in the parliamentary library the user really is the boss. The Library Committee of Members is the effective lever for exercising user control. Institutionally, the oversight committee may be a full committee of parliament, or a sub-committee of the Council of Elders or of another central steering committee. In bicameral legislatures with a common parliamentary library, there may be, as in the USA, a Joint Committee on the Library. The frequency of meetings varies considerably. The parliamentary librarian, as a rule, acts as the secretary, and is obliged to report to the chairman of the library committee.

Parliamentary libraries are usually governed by statutory library rules, which are either made, or have at least to be approved, by the parliamentary oversight committee. Though, in the years under report, there have been amendments of the library rules of some parliaments, no academic investigation has apparently been made, nor has there been any study of general library administration.

Whereas parliamentary library committees do not want to be troubled with the details of library administration (with the notable exception of the annual budget), they will see to it that the significant decisions and developments do not run counter to Members' views. This is why parliamentary oversight committees are particularly important in the first legislative term of new parliaments, as is ascertainable from the history of the Library Committee of the German Reichstag installed in 1873 and later the Library Committee of the German Bundestag installed in 1949, subsequently reduced to become (until 1994) a commission of the Council of Elders (Hahn, 1995).

Apart from decision-making and supervisory library committees, there are also advisory bodies consisting of parliamentarians, staff, and outside experts. A thorough investigation of the influence that may be exercised by such a body is Ryle's account (1991) of the Study of Parliament Group in the UK: 'The Group has proved its value in providing a continuous critique of the functioning of Parliament, and in advocating practical and sensible ways in which its functioning can be reformed'.

Library committees and study groups are, vice versa, also instrumental in involving Members and building parliamentary support for the library. To employ support-building methods is paramount for a parliamentary library in view of its dependence on Members' high esteem. This was the theme of the Parliamentary Libraries Section at the Havana IFLA Conference; various means of building support were suggested by the individual papers presented at its Open Meeting (Bannenberg, 1995; Çelik, 1994; Feliú and Délano, 1994; Michalowski, 1994).

Parliamentary libraries as institutions

Parliamentary librarianship being in essence an information support service, which can be organized effectively in very different ways, it is not surprising that parliamentary libraries as institutions do not constitute a uniform type of library. The shapes and sizes of the individual parliamentary libraries that exist in the world depend, in fact, on a number of determinants, the most important of which are:
- the constitutional as well as the real sovereign powers of the parliament concerned;
- the educational level of parliamentarians and whether their competence is increased through personal support staff;
- the size of the parliament, the length of its sessions and the definition of the boundaries of the legislature and, hence, the terms of reference of the library;
- the financial and intellectual resources of the country;
- the information infrastructure of the capital or seat of parliament.

Scales of parliamentary powers

Some determinants need no explanation at all, whereas others have been the subject of recent investigations. In relation to the relative weight of the legislatures in policymaking, Robinson (1994; 1995) offers an enlightening typology correlating the progression of real powers wielded by the individual parliaments to their information needs. Robinson's progression of models starts with the vestigial **'rubber-stamp legislature'** characteristic of the former Soviet Union and its erstwhile satellites at the low end, 'which lacks resources and legal authority to play an effective role in governance', moving up the continuum to the nascent, **'emerging legislature'** with 'at least a minimum level of staff and equipment ... to process legislative demands', through the **'informed legislature'** with personal staff being attached to the individual legislators 'to extend their effectiveness', 'professional committee staff, central research staff, computers and other telecommunications equipment to significantly enhance information processing for the legislature', to the **'transformative legislature'** at the high end, which is 'characterized by a generous allotment of personal staff, strong and well-staffed committees, research and analysis at the party level, and large central research groups that are capable of developing policy options'.

A number of recent case studies can illustrate how parliamentary libraries operate at the different levels of this typology. At the low end, if there is a parliamentary library at all, its function for parliamentarians is recreational rather than informational, mainly serving the staff of the parliament as an administrative library. Hahn (1994) records the history of the Library of the People's Chamber of the German Democratic Republic, whereas the modes of existence of the parliamentary libraries of the Soviet Union (Gavrilenko, 1991), Russia (Shraiberg and Andreeva, 1992), Czechoslovakia, Poland and Hungary (Sosna *et al.*, 1991; Ronai and Bryant, 1992) in the Communist era are alluded to in studies otherwise devoted to the future developments of these libraries, reaching out to the levels of the emerging and perhaps even the informed legislature. At the Havana IFLA Conference, two papers on parliamentary libraries in Cuba were presented (Pagés Hernández, 1994; Torréns Valdés, 1994).

According to Molinelli (1994), most of the nineteen case studies of Latin American parliamentary libraries submitted to the First Ibero-American Meeting of Parliamentary Libraries (Encuentro, 1994, pp. 145–267) are illustrative of parliamentary libraries at the level of the emerging legislature, their services being bibliographic and documentary, but stopping short of policy analysis and research. Another two extensive case studies submitted to the Ninth International Conference of the Section of Parliamentary Libraries in Madrid, on Argentina (Raed, 1993), and on Mexico (Fernández de Zamora and Liahut Baldomar, 1993) describe more advanced services.

At the high end, there are recent case studies of the kind of services expected by, and extended to, transformative legislatures, including the US Congress (Robinson 1994; 1995), the UK Parliament (Englefield, 1991; Tanfield, 1993), the German Bundestag (Schick and Hahn, 1994) and the Sansad of India (Malhotra, 1995).

Federal systems of government

In federations and comparable systems, sovereign powers are divided between the legislatures at the national and at the regional levels. This has an influence not only on the individual parliamentary libraries, but also on the structure of the framework in which they operate. Kohl (1993c) presents a comparative review of the constitutional division of powers in federative and similar systems of government. The Section of Parliamentary Libraries has studied the operations of parliamentary libraries in these systems on two relevant occasions, at the IFLA Conferences in India (Bhardwaj, 1995) and in Spain (Bibliotecas, 1993). Case studies of **parliamentary libraries at the sub-national level** are, therefore, available for Indian state legislatures, some of the largest of which, such as Uttar Pradesh, with its bicameral legislature of 534 parliamentarians representing 140 million citizens, or Bihar, with its bicameral legislature of 420 parliamentarians representing 90 million people, are larger than most national parliaments (Debnath, 1995; Gupta, 1995; Rajamani, 1995), and for the Autonomous Communities of Spain (Gil i Albert, 1993; Vintró i Castells, 1993) and for the Autonomous Regions of Portugal (Pita, 1993). Obra Sierra (1993) gives an overview of the situation in Spain and García de la Oliva (1993) specifically examines the cooperation between the national parliamentary libraries in Spain and those of the Autonomous Communities. In this context, it should also be mentioned that national associations of parliamentary librarians exist in Canada and in the USA.

Finally, case studies exist for **parliamentary libraries at the supranational level** (González Dubón de Pazos, 1994; Michaels Valderrama, 1994; Sarría, 1994), a notable gap being the European Parliament, the most powerful of the supranational parliaments.

Parliamentary libraries as institutions vary considerably from each other. Comparative analysis, however, enables us to devise a classification scheme in which the following categories of parliamentary libraries can be distinguished:

- parliamentary libraries proper;
- hybrid parliamentary libraries;
- contractual parliamentary libraries.

Organizational attributes

There is no parliament without a book. None can exist without at least some basic reference works, such as directories or dictionaries, but books alone do not constitute a library. The entry for the Bahamian House of Assembly in the fifth edition of the *World directory of national parliamentary libraries* serves as an illustration: 'There is no parliamentary library. However, within the Speaker's Chambers there is a selection of parliamentary books and papers. Also in book cases in the lobby of the House there are *Laws* and *Votes and proceedings*, from 1729 onwards, which Members may peruse' (Kohl, 1994, p. 35).

The entry for the Bahamas is exemplary for small parliaments, in session for only a few sitting days per year, both at the national and, in particular, at the sub-national level. A number of additional attributes are necessary for a parliament to realize that its book collection has risen to the status of a parliamentary library (Kohl, 1991d, pp. 4–6). In the entry for the Legislative Council of Hong Kong, a second attribute is added to the collection of books: 'A parliamentary library in the proper sense of the word does not exist, but Members have a reading room where some publications are available for their reference and information' (Kohl, 1993c, p. 415). Adding another two organizational attributes to its book collection of 800 volumes and a reading room with four seats, *viz.* a small annual budget of about US$ 1,000 for collection development purposes and a responsible – part-time – officer (the Sergeant-at-Arms), the Solomon Islands National Parliament quite rightly claims to have an institutionalized parliamentary library (Kohl, 1994, p. 447).

Parliamentary libraries proper

The institutional characteristics of this category of parliamentary libraries are that they are in-house libraries provided for by the parliament, and forming an integral part of the overall support services of the parliament. Taking into account that 'a staff of 25 - 50 is needed to obtain a noticeable impact' in terms of reference and research activities (Robinson, 1994), only parliaments of some size and with corresponding financial resources can afford this type of parliamentary library as effective legislative support services.

Two main organizational variants can be distinguished. It is a common characteristic of parliamentary libraries following the British tradition that they also include research services, whereas, in Continental European parliaments, the parliamentary library, in turn, forms an integral part of a larger Directorate-General of Reference and Research Services. Recent case studies of fully developed parliamentary libraries of the Anglo-Saxon type deal with the British House of Commons (Lock, 1991; Tanfield, 1991 and 1993), Chile (Feliú and Délano, 1992 and 1994), and India (Malhotra, 1995). Recent studies on the German Bundestag (Schick and Hahn, 1994), the Spanish Cortes (Gonzalo, 1993 and 1994; Martín González and López Alsina, 1993; Paesa, 1993), and the Polish Sejm and Senate (Kulisiewicz, 1993; Mezynski, 1993; Nawrocka, 1993; Michalowski, 1994) illustrate the Continental European version.

Hybrid parliamentary libraries

Small states or less developed countries, having to pool their national economic resources, have devised a number of hybrid forms of parliamentary library in order to achieve effective information services for parliament. While this category of parliamentary library is still provided for by the parliament and named accordingly, it is, in fact, a combination of a parliamentary library and a special or general library serving the public as well as parliamentarians. Because of this dual function, it can be equipped with sufficient resources in terms of qualified personnel (professional librarians, subject specialists) and finances in order to maintain the necessary information resources and to make an intelligent use of them for the benefit of the parliament.

In the years under review, two models of hybrid parliamentary libraries have been investigated by the IFLA Section of Parliamentary Libraries. At the Section's Pre-IFLA Conference Seminar in Helsinki with the theme 'Review of parliamentary libraries in Eastern Europe', Tammekann (1991) described the Finnish Library of Parliament, setting out the advantages of a parliamentary library functioning equally as the 'central research and national resource library' for law and political science. The second concept of a hybrid parliamentary library, i.e. the combination of the functions of the parliamentary library and the central law library of the country, is discussed by Pröhle (1993) in her paper presented at the Barcelona IFLA Conference.

Another instance of a hybrid parliamentary library is that which serves as the national library of the country. This concept is particularly appealing to democratic societies insofar as the parliament, in addition to its constitutional function of representing and integrating the nation as a body politic, is also instrumental in giving visible expression to the cultural identity of the nation. The American Library of Congress is the best known instance of this grand democratic notion, and has set an example to the establishment of parliamentary libraries of this type in Australia, New Zealand, and, after the Second World War, in Japan.

There is, however, a danger inherent in this construction: in the long run, service to the nation at large may outweigh the information support service to parliament. In Australia and New Zealand, for example, the functions of parliamentary library and national library were eventually separated in the 1960s. The solution which the USA devised, in the Legislative Reorganization Acts of 1946 and 1970, was the establishment within the Library of Congress of a Congressional Research Service; this is an exclusively Congressional support service, with its own library of 100,000 volumes, 5,000 current periodicals, and more than 800 staff. With the establishment of its Research and Legislative Reference Bureau in 1984, the National Diet Library in Japan followed suit. The operations of the Congressional Research Service, the largest of all legislative information support services, have recently been described in detail by Robinson (1991, pp. 118–124; 1993a, pp. 65–77; 1993b, pp. 47–51).

Contractual parliamentary libraries

If, for whatever reason, a parliament does not have its own library, parliamentarians and staff may either individually consult other libraries in the area or, preferably, the parliament may select the largest neighbouring library – usually the national library – officially assigning to it the status of parliamentary library. The duties of the contractual library in relation to its services to parliament are stipulated in its charter.

In the wake of the disintegration of the former Soviet Union, many national, and, in particular, second-tier, parliaments had no parliamentary library of their own, and were obliged to look for effective information support services. The IFLA Section of Parliamentary Libraries, realizing that this was a question of vital concern for many parliaments in Eastern Europe and the former Soviet Union, invited papers on this subject for the 59th IFLA Conference. According to Eenmaa (1993), there are common characteristics in the way contractual libraries commit themselves to their additional function as parliamentary libraries. The first move is to create a parliamentary information department, sometimes located in parliament, which is responsible for all information services to Members and staff. To provide these, it can draw upon the entire intellectual and material resources of the national library. As a rule, the information services offered are bibliographic and documentary in character, but sometimes analytical services are offered as well. Alternatively, analytical and research services may be supplied by another national research institute. The second major activity of the contractual library consists of maintaining a reading room in the parliament building, with a reference collection, periodicals and newspapers.

According to Shraiberg (1993), a number of parliaments in the former Soviet Union have gone this way. Sometimes, the contractual library supplements a small parliamentary reference library, as in Latvia and Lithuania (Eenmaa, 1993).

In this set-up, basic reference and newspaper clipping services are supplied from the parliament's own resources, but more sophisticated library and information services are provided by the national library.

Terms of reference

If the parliamentary libraries listed in the two international directories are to be attributed to one of the three categories in this typology, the predominant model is the parliamentary library proper, although many parliaments with a small and rather inadequate library of this type would be well advised to consider the alternative models. While it is clear that the other types, in addition to serving parliamentarians, in varying degrees also serve other user groups, the terms of reference of parliamentary libraries proper are at present very much subject to discussion.

Kohl (1991b) argues that 'parliamentary librarianship, in order to be effective, has to be based on a thorough analysis of the political processes in the societies concerned, for *political power is larger than parliament*'. As far as contemporary pluralistic societies are concerned, he goes on to state that 'in the decision-making processes of today, political parties, mass institutions and autonomous collectivities within society, *e.g.* trade unions or the churches, special-interest or lobbying groups, the civil servants of the higher bureaucracy, citizens' action groups, and, of course, the mass media are all involved, and quite a few parliaments now make use of hearings as an adequate instrument for responsive rule'. 'Following the principle of participatory democracy, the government and parliament in Western societies allow a large number of persons and groups . . . to take a direct and active part in the formulation of public policy, and even invite them to do so [by way of hearings] at an early stage in the decision-making process' (Kohl, 1991a).

The still controversial definition of the boundaries of legislatures must affect the terms of reference of parliamentary libraries. To alert parliamentary librarians to this fact, a discussion of the target groups who are legitimately to be served under contemporary political conditions was made the theme of the Open Meeting of the Parliamentary Libraries Section at the Barcelona IFLA Conference (Kohl, 1993b). While there are still some cases, e.g. the Irish Oireachtas or the Australian Commonwealth Parliament, where the parliamentary library is 'really a private library for Members' (Englefield, 1990, p. 16), and a large number of others only admit the government bureaucracy (and scholars by special permission) as users, Kohl (1993a) advocates that the entire political class should be regarded as legitimate users of a parliamentary library. Some other parliaments, e.g. the Swedish Riksdag or the Italian Camera dei deputati, go even further, by opening their parliamentary libraries to the public at large.

Collections

The attentive reader having followed this review this far will not be surprised to be told that, in terms of collections and collection development policies, parliamentary libraries differ greatly. Without taking the hybrid and contractual forms of parliamentary library into account, the sizes of the collections vary between more than a million volumes (Argentina, Greece, Germany) and less than a thousand (Benin, Burkina Faso, Dominica, Mali, Niger, Solomon Islands, Tuvalu, Vanuatu and others). The middle-size collections range from 4,500 volumes in Africa to over 100,000 in Western Europe.

The collection development policies of fully consolidated parliamentary libraries have been examined in detail by Kohl (1991c), Heavner (1993) and Lindley (1993b). With a view to the various information requirements of political decision makers, *viz.* information about:

- facts, events, personalities, and ideas;
- the latest authoritative results of research, especially in science and technology;
- public opinion;
- the declared preferences of groups in society who are affected by a specific issue or legislative proposal;
- directives and targets of international and supra-national organizations that may have to be observed;
- solutions which other bodies politic have found for particular problems (Kohl, 1991d, pp. 83–84),

they identify six primary categories of materials:

- reference books, including statistical compilations and cartographic materials;
- press and other media information;
- current affairs materials, including a comprehensive collection of periodicals;
- publications of organized interest groups, mass organizations and political parties;
- government and other official and semi-official publications, including the publications of public corporations and the courts, and of international organizations;
- parliamentary documents, including national, regional and foreign legislation.

Such a collection development policy is based on the assumption that a library with a large general collection, as well as some special libraries, exist at the location of parliament as back up libraries. This is the typical library infrastructure of most capitals. Where this is not the case, as in Germany, where there is no large federal library in Bonn, the parliamentary library has to build up its own general collection on law, administration, international relations, political science, economics, commerce, agriculture, social welfare and education (Kohl, 1991c). The consequences of the availability of a back up library can best be seen from a comparison of three equally advanced parliamentary libraries. The German Bundestag Library has, in the 45 years of its existence, built up a collection of well over a million volumes, whereas the much older British House of Commons Library contents itself with just 600,000 volumes, and the Canadian Library of Parliament, after a considerable collection weeding in the 1980s, transferred more than 200,000 publications to the National Library of Canada and is now satisfied with only 350,000 volumes.

An authoritative bibliography on reading room reference collections has been compiled by the Congressional Research Service (1991). A detailed study of the specific reference collection requirements of European parliaments has been undertaken by Grau and Gonzalo (1992).

Cataloguing, indexing, and catalogue maintenance

Research libraries usually index their materials by specific subject headings; parliamentary libraries typically use a more general thesaurus with descriptors. A thesaurus is particularly suited to their specific kind of information work designed for use by the non-specialist, 'because a didactic, knowledge acquisition component is inherent in every thesaurus' (Kohl, 1991a). The parliamentarian is a generalist who is required to make informed decisions on very specific and complex issues. He or she has to be led by the indexing system of the parliamentary library, by means of a hierarchical chain, from the most general terms down to more specific ones. The advantages which a thesaurus offers for parliamentary information work have been examined by Kohl (1991a).

Common or compatible thesauri also facilitate the exchange of information between parliamentary libraries. One of the most interesting developments in this area is the European Union's thesaurus, EUROVOC (European Parliament, 1992), which is one of the most elaborate parliamentary thesauri, becoming a sort of standard parliamentary thesaurus in Europe. Being available in all the official languages of the European Union, with the European Parliament actively promoting translations into East European languages, EUROVOC is serving as a model for East European parliaments in designing their indexing system. The investigation of Fernández Mera (1993) into the adaptation of EUROVOC by the Spanish parliament is, therefore, a very timely study. It is a major flaw of the *Guidelines for legislative libraries* that, apart from two passing remarks (Lindley, 1993b, p. 21; Walker, 1993, pp. 119–120), it contains no chapter on cataloguing, indexing, and the management and maintenance of thesauri.

Services and products

Its services and products being the field where the value of parliamentary librarianship is put to the test, publications abound in the years under review. Personalized reference services responding to specific requests include:
- looking up specific facts and sources;
- preparing synopses, abstracts and extracts of publications;
- the provision of reader assistance points: first, a reading room, with a reference collection (in technically advanced parliaments also a multimedia room with facilities for the consultation of microfilms, microfiches and CD-ROMs and for online searches); secondly, a circulation and lending desk.

Reference and information services in the form of bibliographic materials are a mandatory model of operation. The most comprehensive survey of the various kinds of bibliographic products to recommend is still the *Bibliography of bibliographic services of European parliamentary libraries* (Kohl, 1990), but a number of more specific studies having been published subsequently. Common current services of parliamentary libraries include:

- a daily newspaper indexing and clipping service, sometimes complemented by an indexing of relevant radio and television programmes (Floistad, 1993);
- frequent bibliographies of periodical articles;
- a – preferably annotated – accessions list of monographs;
- an abstracting and indexing service of ongoing indigenous legislative activities (Walker, 1993; Schick and Hahn, 1994, pp. 13–14);
- a select bibliography of ongoing and completed foreign legislation (Lamaro, 1992);
- subject bibliographies for current political activities anticipating subjects under parliamentary discussion (Holt, 1992).

As distinct from these bibliographic products for the general benefit of all users, technically advanced parliamentary libraries also offer SDI services, i.e. individuated bibliographic services according to a specific user profile (Çelik, 1994).

A second, more advanced, model of operation is the production of documentary evidence and of factual and analytic reports. It is exemplified by the written products of the Congressional Research Service and the Reference and Research Services of the German Bundestag (Robinson, 1993a, pp. 69–72; Schick and Hahn, 1994, pp. 20–21). These include:

- background papers or bulletins with information on current issues, programmes or problems;
- information packs, i.e. collections of materials most consistently in demand in order to respond to questions raised by constituents, including clippings and other products produced for fast-breaking issues;
- legal reports containing the progress of Bills, summary descriptions and analysis of legislation, and legislative histories of major enactments;
- issue briefs on topics of current legislative interest, providing an analysis of the issue and tracing legislative activity and other sources of information;
- option papers describing a legislative issue, but also providing an array of alternative actions and analysing the options;
- topical court rulings which briefly describe and explain their political relevance;
- memoranda, i.e. personalized responses originating as a specific question asked by a Member, but of interest to others as well.

The Reference and Research Services of the German Bundestag publish a quarterly bibliography, *Auswahlverzeichnis*, containing a selection of the most important memoranda, background papers and issue briefs. They also publish a series, *Der aktuelle Begriff*, in which the origin and meaning of new terms used in political debate are explained. It is also annually published in book form.

Whereas the first model of operation is indisputably a library activity, the second one is more or less an activity of the research services, and can be undertaken by the parliamentary library only in environments in which the concept of the parliamentary library goes beyond the usual notion of a library and encompasses analytical services.

Automation

Since the publication of Cabral's comprehensive compendium (1991; 1992) on the *Automation of parliamentary libraries, documentation and information services*, only a few specific studies of the automation of parliamentary library services have appeared. Among them, Ku's paper (1992) for the New Delhi IFLA Conference can be particularly recommended as being the most comprehensive overview. The *Guidelines for legislative libraries* also contains instructions, as it were, for automating parliamentary libraries (Lindley, 1993a). The role of automation in a parliamentary library's strategy of winning Members' support is the subject of

148 *Parliamentary libraries*

an investigation by Çelik (1994). Major case studies describe the British House of Commons (Wainwright, 1991), Russia (Shraiberg and Andreeva, 1992) and Spain (Macía, 1993).

Cooperation

Given the interdependence of nations, as well as the fact that many political issues are not restricted to one country alone, but are regional or even global issues, parliamentary libraries inevitably have to rely greatly on cooperation and mutual assistance. In the last two decades, parliamentary libraries have, therefore, established both worldwide and regional associations. The IFLA Section of Parliamentary Libraries has been mentioned before (Kohl, 1992). Regional associations that have come into existence cover Australia and Oceania (founded in 1972), Europe (founded in 1977, disbanded in 1994) and Asia (founded in 1990). Regional conferences intended as a first step to the establishment of a regional organization have been held in Latin America in 1993 and in Eastern and Southern Africa in 1994.

Cooperation is also practised outside these associations. In John's (1991) assessment of library twinning projects in IFLA, the parliamentary libraries stand out. One of the most successful projects has been the establishment of parliamentary libraries in the South West Pacific region, recorded by MacLean (1991). The history of the most ambitious current project of parliament-to-parliament assistance, however, has still to be written, i.e. the assistance being given by the US Congress to the parliaments of Eastern Europe and the former Soviet Union.

Inter-parliamentary associations have also had a share in aid projects. Kordon's (1993) account of the library assistance programme of the Inter-Parliamentary Union, an association of more than 130 national parliaments with headquarters in Geneva, is impressive evidence of this. In the community of French-speaking countries, the Assemblée Internationale des Parlementaires de Langue Française (1993) has launched an extensive cooperation and assistance programme, PARDOC; this is a most timely programme in view of the parliamentarization of a number of Francophone countries in Africa. Barbier-Wiesser (1993) describes the components and activities of this programme.

Conclusion

The areas of parliamentary librarianship which have been the subject of publications in the last few years have been determined largely by the dominant political event of the period: parliamentarization in Eastern Europe and the former Soviet Union, and in Africa and Latin America. The need to convince parliamentarians that it is worth their while to have an independent information support service has provoked a noticeable number of articles and papers on the conceptual foundations of parliamentary librarianship. The second focus of attention has been on the information services and products which parliamentary libraries must offer in order to be recognized as effective. By comparison, other areas, such as cataloguing, classification and indexing, internal organization and administration, including library rules, statistics, or buildings and equipment, have been covered to a much lesser degree or not at all. Parliamentary libraries are characterized by a wide range of activities, on the one hand, and by their small numbers on the other; it is understandable that their output of publications is somewhat selective, reflecting the major fields of interest of the day. In the first quinquennium of the last decade of the 20th century, the primary challenge to parliamentary libraries was the wave of parliamentarization throughout the world, and I hope to have demonstrated here that there is reason to believe that they have stood the test with some honour.

References

Alexanderson, B. (1991) Assistance to parliamentary libraries in Central and Eastern Europe. In: E. Kohl (ed.) *Soviet and East European parliamentary libraries at the dawn of the post-communist era*. Bonn: Deutscher Bundestag, pp. 25–34.

Assemblée Internationale des Parlementaires de Langue Française (1993) *L'information au service des parlementaires francophones: programme d'appui à l'organisation des services documentaires des Parlements du Sud*. Paris: AIPLF.

Bannenberg, N. (1994) *Building Member understanding and support for the parliamentary library*. IFLA Journal, **21**(2), 102–05.

Barbier-Wiesser, F-G. (1993) *Le programme AIPLF PARDOC*. [Paper presented at the Meeting of the Section of Parliamentary Libraries during the 59th IFLA General Conference, Barcelona, 25 August 1993.]

Bhardwaj, R.C. (1995) (ed.) *Library and information services to the Sansad*. New Delhi: Lok Sabha Secretariat.

Bibliotecas (1993) *y servicios de documentación de las regiones autónomas de la Península ibérica*. Barcelona: Parlament de Catalunya.

Cabral, A. (1991) *Automation of parliamentary libraries, documentation and information services*. Lisboa: Assembleia da República.

Cabral, A. (1992) *Automation of parliamentary libraries, documentation and information services*. Lisboa: Assembleia da República.

Çelik, H. (1994) *Using automation and electronic services to build support for the parliamentary library*. [Paper presented at the 60th IFLA General Conference, Havana (024-PAR-4-E).]

Clements, R. (1991) Parliamentarians and figures. In: D. Englefield (ed.) *Workings of Westminster: essays in honour of David Menhennet* . . . . Aldershot: Dartmouth, pp. 121–132.

Congressional Research Service (1991) *Parliamentary reference library bibliography of core materials.* Washington: US Government Printing Office.

Debnath, S. (1992) Tripura Legislative Assembly Library: a study. In: R.C. Bhardwaj (ed.) *Library and information services to the Sansad.* New Delhi: Lok Sabha Secretariat, pp. 116–120.

Eenmaa, I. (1993) *Serving the parliamentarians by serving the nation: the establishment of parliamentary library and information services by national libraries in the Baltic states.* [Paper presented at the 59th IFLA General Conference, Barcelona (061-PAR-E).]

Encuentro (1994) Iberoamericano de Bibliotecas Parlamentarias. *Memoria del Primer encuentro iberoamericano de bibliotecas parlamentarias, Ciudad de México, 20–23 de octubre de 1993.* México: Cámara de Diputados.

Englefield, D. (1990) (ed.) *Parliamentary libraries and information services: a directory of the member legislatures of the European Communities and the Council of Europe.* Roma: Camera dei deputati.

Englefield, D. (1991) (ed.) *Workings of Westminster: essays in honour of David Menhennet, Librarian of the House of Commons, 1976–1991.* Aldershot: Dartmouth.

Englefield, D. (1993) (ed.) *Guidelines for legislative libraries.* München: Saur (IFLA publications, no. 64).

European Parliament (1992) *Thesaurus EUROVOC: user manual.* Luxembourg: Office for Official Publications of the European Communities.

Feliú, X. and Délano, M. (1992) *Rethinking a library: knowledge for legislators and the Library of Congress of Chile.* [Paper presented at the 58th IFLA General Conference, New Delhi (039-PAR-3-E+F).]

Feliú, X. and Délano, M. (1994) *User-oriented services: a feedback strategy for understanding and support for the parliamentary library.* [Paper presented at the 60th IFLA General Conference, Havana (022-PAR-2-E).]

Fernández de Zamora, R.M. and Liahut Baldomar, D.M. (1993) *Los servicios bibliotecarios y de documentación del parlamento de los Estados unidos méxicanos.* [Paper presented at the Ninth International Conference of the Section of Parliamentary Libraries, Madrid, 18–19 August 1993 (with English summary).]

Fernández Mera, M.V. (1993) *El tesauro EUROVOC en el Congreso de los Diputados.* [Paper presented at the Ninth International Conference of the Section of Parliamentary Libraries, Madrid, 18–19 August 1993 (with English summary).]

Floistad, B. (1993) Mediating news and public opinion to Members of Parliament. In: D. Englefield (ed.) *Guidelines for legislative libraries.* München: Saur, pp. 79–90. [Earlier version in: E. Kohl (ed.) *Soviet and East European parliamentary libraries at the dawn of the post-communist era.* Bonn: Deutscher Bundestag, pp. 91–98.]

García de la Oliva, A. (1993) *La cooperación documental entre las Cortes y las Assambleas de las Comunidades autónomas.* [Paper presented at the Ninth International Conference of the Section of Parliamentary Libraries, Madrid, 18–19 August 1993 (with English summary).]

Gavrilenko, N. (1991) The Library of the USSR Supreme Soviet Secretariat: history, current status, and prospects. In: E. Kohl (ed.) *Soviet and East European parliamentary libraries at the dawn of the post-communist era.* Bonn: Deutscher Bundestag, pp. 145–151.

Gil i Albert, T. (1993) *La biblioteca del Parlamento de Cataluña*. [Paper presented at the 59th IFLA General Conference, Barcelona (123-PAR(WS)-S + E).]

González Dubón de Pazos, I. (1994) Parlamento Centroamericano. In: Encuentro Iberoamericano de Bibliotecas Parlamentarias. *Memoria del Primer encuentro iberoamericano de bibliotecas parlamentarias, Ciudad de México, 20–23 de octubre de 1993.* México: Cámara de Diputados, pp. 111–114.

Gonzalo, M. (1993) *Las funciones de las Direcciones de Estudios y Documentación del parlamento español*. [Paper presented at the Ninth International Conference of the Section of Parliamentary Libraries, Madrid, 18–19 August 1993 (with English summary).]

Gonzalo, M. (1994) Los letrados y los servicios de información de las Cortes de España. In: Encuentro Iberoamericano de Bibliotecas Parlamentarias. *Memoria del Primer encuentro iberoamericano de bibliotecas parlamentarias, Ciudad de México, 20–23 de octubre de 1993.* México: Cámara de Diputados, pp. 60–66.

Grau, R.M. and Gonzalo, M.A. (1992) The European Communities: reference works and documentary sources of the Spanish parliament. *Advances in Librarianship*, **16**, 183–215.

Gupta, C.P. (1995) Library, reference and research services in the Rajasthan Legislative Assembly. Library, Jaipur. In: R.C. Bhardwaj (ed.) *Library and information services to the Sansad*. New Delhi: Lok Sabha Secretariat, pp. 107–115.

Hahn, G. (1994) Die Volkskammerbibliothek der DDR: Abriss ihrer Geschichte. *Bibliotheksdienst*, **28**(3), 337–345.

Hahn, G. (1995) *Die Reichstagsbibliothek zu Berlin: das Parlament im Spiegel seiner Bibliotheksgeschichte*. Düsseldorf: Droste.

Heavner, P.F. (1993) Research: collections. In: D. Englefield (ed.) *Guidelines for legislative libraries*. München: Saur, pp. 34–44.

Holt, L. (1992) *Special bibliographic services – special subject bibliographies: the experience of the Folketinget*. [Paper presented at the Tenth Meeting of the Working Group Parliamentary Libraries of the European Centre for Parliamentary Research and Documentation, Vienna, 14–15 April 1992.]

John, N. (1991) IFLA projects on twinning of libraries. *IFLA Journal*, **17**(3), 315–325.

Kohl, E. (1990) (ed.) *Bibliography of bibliographic services of European parliamentary libraries*. Bonn: Deutscher Bundestag, Wissenschaftliche Dienste.

Kohl, E. (1991a) Bibliographic information work for political decision making. *INSPEL*, **25**(2), 115–126.

Kohl, E. (1991b) The challenge of change in Eastern Europe to the parliamentary libraries of the West. *IFLA Journal*, **17**(2), 128–134.

Kohl, E. (1991c) Collection development policies of parliamentary libraries. In: E. Kohl (ed.) *Soviet and East European parliamentary libraries at the dawn of the post-communist era*. Bonn: Deutscher Bundestag, pp. 83–90. [Abridged version in *IFLA Journal*, **17**(4), 389–394.]

Kohl, E. (1991d) (ed.) *Soviet and East European parliamentary libraries at the dawn of the post-communist era*. Bonn: Deutscher Bundestag, Wissenschaftliche Dienste.

Kohl, E. (1992) IFLA: Parliamentary Libraries Section. *Constitutional and parliamentary information*, 3rd series, (164), 150–153.

Kohl, E. (1993a) *Die politischen Entscheidungsträger als die legitimen Nutzer der Parlamentsbibliothek*. [Paper presented at the 59th IFLA General Conference, Barcelona

(060-PAR-G + S + E).]
Kohl, E. (1993b) *Whom should the parliamentary library serve?* [Paper presented at the 59th IFLA General Conference, Barcelona (058-PAR-E).]
Kohl, E. (1993c) (ed.) *World directory of parliamentary libraries of federated states and autonomous territories.* Bonn: Deutscher Bundestag, Wissenschaftliche Dienste.
Kohl, E. (1994) (ed.) *World directory of national parliamentary libraries: including multinational parliamentary libraries.* 5th ed. Bonn: Deutscher Bundestag, Wissenschaftliche Dienste.
Kordon, D. (1993) *Programme d'étude et de promotion des institutions représentatives.* [Paper presented at the Eleventh Meeting of the Working Group Parliamentary Libraries and Information Services of the European Centre for Parliamentary Research and Documentation, Warsaw, 14–15 October 1993.]
Ku, K.M. (1992) *Developmental strategies of computerized legislative information services.* [Paper presented at the 58th IFLA General Conference, New Delhi (037-PAR-2-E).]
Kulisiewicz, W. (1993) *La Bibliothèque de la Diète: les services prêtés aux Députés et aux Sénateurs.* [Paper presented at the Eleventh Meeting of the Working Group Parliamentary Libraries and Information Services of the European Centre of Parliamentary Research and Documentation, Warsaw, 14–15 October 1993.]
Kurian, G.T. (1995) (ed.) *World encyclopedia of parliaments and legislatures.* Washington: Congressional Quarterly Inc.
Lamadrid Sauza, J.L. (1994) Información para el tratamiento de las relaciones internacionales. In: Encuentro Iberoamericano de Bibliotecas Parlamentarias. *Memoria del Primer encuentro iberoamericano de bibliotecas parlamentarias, Ciudad de México, 20–23 de octubre de 1993.* México: Cámara de Diputados, pp. 58–60.
Lamaro, E. (1992) *Special bibliographic services: experience of the Camera dei deputati.* [Paper presented at the Tenth Meeting of the Working Group Parliamentary Libraries of the European Centre for Parliamentary Research and Documentation, Vienna, 14–15 April 1992.]
Libraries (1993) *and information services of the autonomous regions of the Iberian Pensinsula.* Barcelona: Parlament de Catalunya.
Lindley, J.A. (1993a) Information technology. In: D. Englefield (ed.) *Guidelines for legislative libraries.* München: Saur, pp. 91–108.
Lindley, J.A. (1993b) Reference services. In: D. Englefield (ed.) *Guidelines for legislative libraries.* München: Saur, pp. 17–33.
Lock, G. (1991) Subject specialists in the House of Commons Library. In: D. Englefield (ed.) *Workings of Westminster: essays in honour of David Menhennet . . ..* Aldershot: Dartmouth, pp. 87–98.
Macía, M. (1993) *Las bases de datos parlamentarias.* [Paper presented at the Ninth International Conference of the Section of Parliamentary Libraries, Madrid, 18–19 August 1993 (with English summary).]
MacLean, H. (1991) Australia and the Southwest Pacific: an exercise in parliament-to-parliament assistance. *Inter-Parliamentary Bulletin*, **71**(1), 53–59.
Malhotra, G.C. (1995) Library, reference, research, documentation and information services to Members of Parliament. In: R.C. Bhardwaj (ed.) *Library and information services to the Sansad.* New Delhi: Lok Sabha Secretariat, pp. 82–100.
Martín González, A. and López Alsina, M. (1993) *La Biblioteca del Congreso de los Diputados.*

[Paper presented at the Ninth International Conference of the Section of Parliamentary Libraries, Madrid, 18–19 August 1993 (with English summary).]

Mezynski, A. (1993) *Les services de recherches et d'information à la Chancellerie de la Diète*. [Paper presented at the Eleventh Meeting of the Working Group Parliamentary Libraries and Information Services of the European Centre for Parliamentary Research and Documentation, Warsaw, 14–15 October 1993.]

Michaels Valderrama, D. (1994) El Parlamento andino: hacia una nueva dimensión en los procesos de integración. In: Encuentro Iberoamericano de Bibliotecas Parlamentarias. *Memoria del Primer encuentro iberoamericano de bibliotecas parlamentarias, Ciudad de México, 20–23 de octubre de 1993*. México: Cámara de Diputados, pp. 107–111.

Michalowski, J. (1994) *The importance of advertising: the use of brochures and highly visible services to attract Members' attention and encourage use of the library*. [Paper presented at the 60th IFLA General Conference, Havana (023-PAR-3-E).]

Molinelli, N.G. (1994) *Information and policy analysis in a democratic legislature: a Latin American perspective*. [Paper presented at the Tenth International Conference of the Section of Parliamentary Libraries, San José, 18–19 August 1994.]

Nawrocka, E. (1993) *Information services of the Senate of Poland Chancellery Research and Analysis Office*. [Paper presented at the Eleventh Meeting of the Working Group Parliamentary Libraries and Information Services of the European Centre for Parliamentary Research and Documentation, Warsaw, 14–15 October 1993.]

Obra Sierra, S. (1993) The documentation, library, and archive services of the autonomous parliaments: some considerations. In: *Libraries and information services of the autonomous regions of the Iberian Pensinsula*. Barcelona: Parlament de Catalunya, pp. [39–44].

Paesa, M. (1993) *Los servicios de documentación del Congreso de los Diputados y del Senado*. [Paper presented at the Ninth International Conference of the Section of Parliamentary Libraries, Madrid, 18–19 August 1993 (with English summary).]

Pagés Hernández, R. (1994) *Biblioteca y servicio de información a los parlamentarios cubanos*. [Paper presented at the 60th IFLA General Conference, Havana (068-PAR(WS)-5-S + E).]

Paoli Bolio, F.J. (1994) La importancia de la información para el trabajo legislativo. In: Encuentro Iberoamericano de Bibliotecas Parlamentarias. *Memoria del Primer encuentro iberoamericano de bibliotecas parlamentarias, Ciudad de México, 20–23 de octubre de 1993*. México: Cámara de Diputados, pp. 51–56.

Paoli Bolio, F.J. et al. (1994) Los legisladores como usuarios de la información legislativa. In: Encuentro Iberoamericano de Bibliotecas Parlamentarias. *Memoria del Primer encuentro iberoamericano de bibliotecas parlamentarias, Ciudad de México, 20–23 de octubre de 1993*. México: Cámara de Diputados, pp. 125–138.

Parliamentary (1995) *libraries of Latin America and Iberia*. München: Saur. [In preparation.]

Parr, E. and Ransome, A. (1991) *The information marriage: the parliamentary library and the personal staff of Senators and Members*. Canberra: Australian Government Publishing Service.

Pita, M. (1993) *La Bibliothèque et les services d'information dans l'Assemblée Législative Régionale de Madère*. [Paper presented at the 59th IFLA General Conference, Barcelona (124-PAR(WS)-F + E).]

Pröhle, E. (1993) *The library of parliament as the national law library: the model of Hungary*. [Paper presented at the 59th IFLA General Conference, Barcelona (059-PAR-E).]

Raed, E. (1993) *Los servicios bibliotecarios y de documentación del parlamento de Argentina*. [Paper presented at the Ninth International Conference of the Section of Parliamentary Libraries, Madrid, 18–19 August 1993.]

Rajamani, S. (1995) Library and information services in Andhra Pradesh Legislative Assembly Library. In: R.C. Bhardwaj (ed.) *Library and information services to the Sansad*. New Delhi: Lok Sabha Secretariat, pp. 101–106.

Robinson, W.H. (1991) Building a parliamentary research capability. In: E. Kohl (ed.) *Soviet and East European parliamentary libraries at the dawn of the post-communist era*. Bonn: Deutscher Bundestag, pp. 99–124. [Abridged version in *IFLA Journal*, **17**(4), 379–388.]

Robinson, W.H. (1993a) Research: services of research and analysis in a legislative environment. In: D. Englefield (ed.) *Guidelines for legislative libraries*. München: Saur, pp. 59–77.

Robinson, W.H. (1993b) Research: staffing and organization. In: D. Englefield (ed.) *Guidelines for legislative libraries*. München: Saur, pp. 45–58.

Robinson, W.H. (1994) El papel de la información en una legislatura democrática: el caso del Servicio de Investigación del Congreso. In: Encuentro Iberoamericano de Bibliotecas Parlamentarias. *Memoria del Primer encuentro iberoamericano de bibliotecas parlamentarias, Ciudad de México, 20–23 de octubre de 1993*. México: Cámara de Diputados, pp. 82–96. [Original English version to be published in *Parliamentary libraries of Latin America and Iberia*. München: Saur.]

Robinson, W.H. (1995) Parliamentary libraries: the role of information in the legislative process. In: G.T. Kurian (ed.) *World encyclopedia of parliaments and legislatures*. Washington: Congressional Quarterly Inc. [Forthcoming.]

Ronai, I. and Bryant, M.N. (1992) The role of Hungary's parliamentary library in fostering democratic decision making. *Libri*, **42**(2), 136–143.

Russell, R. (1991) Distributing Parliament's documents: the work of the Vote Office. In: D. Englefield (ed.) *Workings of Westminster: essays in honour of David Menhennet . . ..* Aldershot: Dartmouth, pp. 133–140.

Ryle, M. (1991) The Study of Parliament Group. In: D. Englefield (ed.) *Workings of Westminster: essays in honour of David Menhennet . . ..* Aldershot: Dartmouth, pp. 193–205.

Sarría, A.M. (1994) Parlamento latinoamericano. In: Encuentro Iberoamericano de Bibliotecas Parlamentarias. *Memoria del Primer encuentro iberoamericano de bibliotecas parlamentarias, Ciudad de México, 20–23 de octubre de 1993*. México: Cámara de Diputados, pp. 114–123.

Schick, R. and Hahn, G. (1994) *The Reference and Research Services of the German Bundestag*. Bonn: Deutscher Bundestag. [Revised fourth edition of the German version *Wissenschaftliche Dienste* forthcoming in 1995.]

Shepherd, C. (1991) The Members' need for information. In: D. Englefield (ed.) *Workings of Westminster: essays in honour of David Menhennet . . ..* Aldershot: Dartmouth, pp. 25–30.

Shraiberg, Y. (1993) *National Library with function of a parliamentary one or a separate parliamentary library: the choice of Russia and other new countries of the former USSR*. [Paper presented at the Informal Meeting of the Section of Parliamentary Libraries at the 59th IFLA General Conference, Barcelona, 23 August 1993.]

Shraiberg, Y. and Andreeva, I. (1992) *The Russia Parliamentary Library: its history, functions, and proposed automation.* [Paper presented at the 58th IFLA General Conference, New Delhi (038-PAR-2-E).]

Silk, P. (1991) Select committees and information. In: D. Englefield (ed.) *Workings of Westminster: essays in honour of David Menhennet . . ..* Aldershot: Dartmouth, pp. 41–54.

Sosna, K. *et al.* (1991) Parliamentarism in Czechoslovakia, Hungary, and Poland: past and present. In: E. Kohl (ed.) *Soviet and East European parliamentary libraries at the dawn of the post-communist era.* Bonn: Deutscher Bundestag, pp. 35–44.

Tammekann, E.-M. (1991) Internal and external tasks of the Library of Parliament, Helsinki. In: E. Kohl (ed.) *Soviet and East European parliamentary libraries at the dawn of the post-communist era.* Bonn: Deutscher Bundestag, pp. 17–23.

Tanfield, J. (1991) The House of Commons Library in the 1990s. In: D. Englefield (ed.) *Workings of Westminster: essays in honour of David Menhennet . . ..* Aldershot: Dartmouth, pp. 207–218.

Tanfield, J. (1993) *Services for Members - services for the public: the dual mandate of the Library Department of the House of Commons.* [Paper presented at the 59th IFLA General Conference, Barcelona (079-PAR-E).]

Torréns Valdés, R. (1994) *Servicios bibliotecarios y de información brindados a los integrantes de los órganos de base del Poder Popular.* [Paper presented at the 60th IFLA General Conference, Havana (069-PAR(WS)-6-S + E).]

Vintró i Castells, J. (1993) *El Parlamento de Cataluña: organización y funciones.* [Paper presented at the 59th IFLA General Conference, Barcelona (125-PAR(WS)-S + E).]

Wainwright, J. (1991) Parliament's papers and proceedings: the use of computers. In: D. Englefield (ed.) *Workings of Westminster: essays in honour of David Menhennet . . ..* Aldershot: Dartmouth, pp. 109–120.

Walker, A. (1993) The indexing of a parliament's papers and proceedings. In: D. Englefield (ed.) *Guidelines for legislative libraries.* München: Saur, pp. 109–122.

Bibliographic control and access

6

Giles Martin

Introduction

Over the last year, the most striking feature of library cataloguing has been its increasing internationalization. This has been a result of the influence of computer systems and networks, especially the Internet, on cataloguing. There have been more:

- Regional, national and international cooperation in cataloguing, with sharing of records and authority control.
- Internationalization of data: multilingual catalogues and non-Roman character sets in catalogues, moving away from catalogues in just the English language and the Latin alphabet.
- Access to materials throughout the world outside the conventional library system – the 'virtual library', including Gopher and the World Wide Web.

One particularly significant impact of the Internet on cataloguers has been greater communication between cataloguers in different countries, through discussion groups on the Internet and through electronic publication replacing print publication of articles about cataloguing (as can be seen in the bibliography of this chapter). A considerable body of library cataloguing resources is already available on the Internet, and is listed in a useful guide by Sha (1994).

The other major feature has been the increasing acceptance of the online public access catalogue (OPAC) as the norm, replacing card and microfiche catalogues in an increasing number of libraries. The OPAC has meant a re-examination of the principles and practice of cataloguing. We can now carry out catalogue use studies via logs of terminal sessions, finding out what users really do at our catalogues; and we can look at cataloguing rules and catalogue displays in the context of the more flexible and powerful OPAC.

Cooperation, sharing of records and authority control

Computer networks such as the Internet are making cooperation in cataloguing easier, while economic pressures on libraries are making it more necessary. Two examples of state-wide cooperation in the United States are ILLINET Online and OhioLINK. ILLINET is an OPAC shared by 800 libraries in Illinois. Within ILLINET, authority control is coordinated over the whole network. Preece and Henigman (1994) describe how this state-wide authority control is managed. OhioLINK is an OPAC shared by eighteen academic libraries in Ohio. This system was encouraged by a financial carrot offered by the state, and has provided both benefits and savings to the participants (Kohl, 1993; Best, 1994).

Within Australia and New Zealand respectively, the Australian Bibliographic Network (ABN) and the New Zealand Bibliographic Network (NZBN) have been examples over the last ten years of cooperative cataloguing within their two countries. However, as Naun (1994) points out, the ease of communication of the Internet now opens them up to competition from overseas bibliographic utilities. If cataloguers cannot find bibliographic records within their own country, they may *turn* to utilities like OCLC and RLIN rather than do staff-intensive original cataloguing.

ABN and NZBN are presently being redeveloped as the National Document and Information Service (NDIS) (Cathro, 1994). The NDIS is an internationally cooperative venture that will provide access to and delivery of documents for Australians and New Zealanders – end-users as well as libraries.

The other facet of national cooperation in Australia is the 'Distributed National Collection' (DNC) (ACLIS, 1994). The Distributed NationarCollection is a recognition of the fact that no library in Australia can be self-sufficient in its resources, and an attempt to use mechanisms such as ABN and Conspectus to coordinate collection building and sharing of resources so that the country as a whole can approach self-sufficiency. Without a national bibliographic database – without ABN or the NDIS – the DNC could not work.

During 1994, there were some landmarks in international cooperation in the English-speaking cataloguing world:

- British Library (BL) records were input to the Library of Congress (LC) name authority file (British, 1994).
- LC discussed cooperation in authority control with the Chair of the Australian Bibliographic Network Standards Committee (Australian, 1994).
- The National Library of Canada (NLC) started contributing headings to *Library of Congress Subject Headings* (LCSH) (National, 1994)
- The BL, LC and the NLC discussed the future alignment of the CANMARC, UKMARC and USMARC formats (MARC, 1994).

- LC and NLC discussed cooperating in an Anglo-American authority file with BL (NLC, 1995).

All these developments should make it easier in the future for English-speaking libraries and library systems to share catalogue records.

At another extreme, libraries in Germany are more individualistic. They do not share a common MARC format or a common subject thesaurus corresponding with LCSH in the Anglophone world. Nevertheless, there has been cooperation in the development of 'Allegro' as a bibliographic database. Allegro was developed by the Braunschweig Technical University Library, and is widely used in Germany (Eversberg, 1994).

Moving from card catalogue-oriented to computer screen-oriented display

What have we gained, and what have we lost in moving from cards to OPACs? Baker (1994), as a lay person, warned us that we may be losing significant information as we convert to OPACs and discard our card catalogues. Although he provoked a hostile response from some cataloguers on discussion lists such as OPAC, Baker does make some useful points, such as warning about quick and cheap retrospective conversions. He also welcomes the positive features of OPACs, including his ability to search remote catalogues on the Internet.

Although OPACs are increasingly popular, both with librarians and with their clients, they still present problems. Norgard *et al.* (1993) look at some of the difficulties that users have with catalogues, in formulating searches and handling the results of their searches. Many solutions have been proposed and developed to deal with these difficulties, and ever-increasing computer power at decreasing cost should make better solutions possible in the future. Allen (1993) looks at how the OPAC opens up possibilities for a more client-centred catalogue. She proposes separating the creation of bibliographic data from its presentation to the client. However, while I agree with her point that the OPAC should adapt itself to the client's needs, I do not understand how you can create bibliographic data without understanding how it might be used by a client: the whole process of preparation and presentation of bibliographic data should be client-centred.

There are many OPAC systems available now, of an increasingly high standard. Boss (1993) offers a detailed evaluation of commercially available OPACs: 30 for multiple-user systems, and thirteen for PC and Macintosh based systems. The report was compiled by asking the vendors to respond to a model Request For Proposal (RFP) for an OPAC. The report found that average vendor compliance with the RFP had risen by 20% between 1989 and 1993; from 65% to 85% for multiple-user systems, and from 47% to 69% for PC/Mac systems. This is an impressive rise in performance in this industry. Cherry *et al.* (1994) surveyed OPACs in twelve Canadian academic libraries, and evaluated them against a checklist of desirable features gathered from the literature. Their basic conclusion was that subject searching is the area where the OPACs are weakest.

Descriptive cataloguing rules and rule interpretations

Consistency is important, both within catalogues and across shared cataloguing systems, so that the data can be easily understood by the user and shared between different catalogues. This is why we have cataloguing standards such as *Anglo-American Cataloguing Rules* (AACR) and the MARC format.

AACR

The rules for descriptive cataloguing commonly used in the English-speaking world, AACR, continue to be debated by librarians. Although (as Gorman and Oddy (1993) and Gorman (1994) suggest) there may not be an AACR3 in our future, it is certain that there will be revision of the present AACR2, to take into account both new forms of publication and new forms of catalogue. In addition, AACR is being converted to electronic form, using SGML (Duke, 1994).

Even concepts as basic as 'main entry' continue to be debated. Bierbaum (1994) asks if main entry is still relevant in the MARC record, and concludes that it is not. She distinguishes the main entry heading (in the catalogue record) from the main entry record (in the catalogue), and argues that the main entry heading should be transformed into the 'principal access point'. Where I believe her argument fails is that it treats the main entry heading as providing a unique identifier for a person. Its real function (along with uniform title) is to provide a unique identifier for a *work*, regardless of what it is called or to whom it is attributed in particular manifestations.

Crawford (1994a) criticizes several descriptive cataloguing practices, including the non-recording of changes in serial publishers and the non-cataloguing of chapters in books. On the other hand, there are those who want to further 'simplify' cataloguing: Marker and Reagor (1994) want the catalogue records in bibliographic utilities to ignore any variation in place of publication, in order to avoid having very similar records. Warrick (1994) looks at whether users understand the abbreviations used in the 'physical description area' of AACR, and finds that in general they do not.

LCRIs

The Library of Congress has been looking at whether its Rule Interpretations (LCRIs) can be simplified, by setting up a Task Group on LC-Issued Descriptive Cataloging Documentation. LCRIs do not just affect LC, but affect all libraries that use catalogue records from LC. So while it is probably inevitable that there will be some LCRIs, it is to be hoped that their number can be reduced (CPSO/CCC, 1994b). However, not all simplification of LCRIs is welcomed by librarians: Schimizzi (1993) finds that LC, in simplifying its presentation of the 'Bibliography' note, has lost consistency and made LC catalogue records less useful.

'Works', 'versions' and 'manifestations'

One of the major issues for descriptive cataloguing is how to handle 'works', 'versions' and 'manifestations'. There are two facets of the problem:

- How different must two different manifestations be in order to justify the creation of a new bibliographic record?
- How do you link different manifestations or versions of the same l work?

In the first of a proposed series of articles to be published in *Cataloging and Classification Quarterly* on what 'work' means in descriptive cataloguing, Yee (1993) looks at the concept for moving image materials. In another article, Yee (1994) looks at the general concepts of 'manifestations' and 'near-equivalents', and then goes on to apply them to moving image materials. She proposes that the same bibliographic record be used more often for near equivalents, so that cataloguer users will not be confused by large numbers of records for the same work.

One technique that has been proposed for near-equivalent manifestations is 'multiple versions'. This is intended to be applied to mechanical reproductions of a work, rather than to versions with significant differences in content (Hoffmann, 1994). The Multiple Versions Forum held in 1989 looked at three different models for multiple versions, and chose a two-tier technique (Huthwaite, 1994) using the USMARC holdings format (Nicholas, 1994). However, that technique presents some difficulties, and may not be the one adopted in practice (Wells, 1994). In particular, in Australia, there have been problems in implementing US decisions for multiple versions: problems that need to be addressed in the design of the National Document and Information Service currently being developed for Australia and New Zealand (Pearce and Trainor, 1994).

Special materials

Special materials often need special descriptive cataloguing treatment; for example, audiovisual material often has inconsistent data from title screens, labels, container and accompanying documents. Title screens usually give fuller data (Weimer, 1994). Bandyopadhyay and Mookerjee (1994) discuss how computer files are treated by AACR2. Maben (1993) analyses how AACR is applied to primary state legal material from the USA.

Subject headings

The other side of access to library materials is subject access, usually provided by controlled subject headings such as LCSH, and less often by uncontrolled key words or by classification schemes such as Dewey Decimal Classification (DDC) and Universal Decimal Classification (UDC).

It is not easy to define what the 'subject' of a book is, or to explain how you decide what the subject is (Todd, 1993). Moreover, after cataloguers have decided what the subject of a book is, they have to express that concept with a term or terms from a controlled vocabulary or thesaurus. Subject headings such as LCSH, being based on natural language, will have the limitations of natural language, including cultural biases of language. The IFLA satellite meeting on 'Subject Indexing: Principles and Practices in the 90s', held in Lisbon in August 1993, looked both at subject heading practice in various countries and at the principles of subject access. In spite of its limitations and biases, LCSH has been adapted and translated for use in many different countries, including Britain, Canada, France, Iran and Portugal (Holley, 1993; Beall, 1994).

Little (1993) describes the problems that need to be solved in constructing a specialized subject thesaurus: what do terms mean? What are their relationships? It is not as easy as it seems. Thesauri for non-book material present different problems, such as the question of what subject aspects you are trying to cover, as Walker (1993) shows in describing the creation of a subject thesaurus for the collection of historical photographs of the New South Wales Government Printing Office. Early printed books may need different treatment, because how authors view subjects has changed over the centuries, and because existing projecs to catalogue them have emphasized the descriptive side over subject access (Bourke and Salmond, 1993). Then there is fiction, which has not in the past been given subject access by LC. However, since 1991, OCLC has been adding subject and genre access for fiction, using *Guidelines for subject access to individual works of fiction, drama, etc.* (Denehy, 1993).

LCSH

LC subject headings are representations in natural language of concepts. The usual problem is to go from the concept to the appropriate heading. Franz *et al.* (1994) go the other way, and look at how well end-users understand the concepts expressed by subdivided LC subject headings. They find that end-users can successfully describe about 40% of subdivided headings, and that the longer the heading is, the less likely it is that the end-user can describe it.

As a general subject heading system, LCSH does not handle a specialized area like veterinary medicine very well, but nor does a specialized thesaurus like MeSH when trying to cover materials outside its specialty (Pelzer, 1993). Some subject thesauri, such as MeSH's 'Tree structures', have an explicit classification scheme. LCSH's classification of knowledge is implicit in its 'See' and 'See also' references. Weinberg (1993) explores the implicit classification hierarchy for Judaica in LCSH, and finds that it contains more levels than the corresponding parts of the LC Classification.

Classification: the arrangement of books and knowledge

The other side of subject access is classification, which can be used both to arrange the physical items in a library's collection and to organize access to the collection.

Although physical arrangement in libraries is dominated by the pragmatic schemes originating in the 19th century (DDC and LC Classification), classification theory in this century has been dominated by Ranganathan's theories and his faceted Colon Classification (Neelameghan, 1993; Xiao, 1994). DDC is increasingly becoming a faceted classification within the notation first developed by Dewey: the two areas which are being revised for the 21st edition (350–354 Public administration and 560–590 Life sciences) both use faceted notation (Trotter and Woodhouse, 1993).

The use of classification for information retrieval is explored by Micco and Popp (1994), who have developed a prototype called 'Improving Library Subject Access' (ILSA). ILSA clusters MARC records based on the DDC classification and the main subject heading. It then links other keywords from titles and tables of contents to those clusters, to create a scheme which takes the user from a natural language query to the most relevant MARC records. This builds on the hierarchical structure of DDC to provide control to the user over how specific or general the results will be.

Multilingual catalogues and non-Roman scripts

Many libraries, including libraries in countries where a single language predominates, need to provide access to materials in a variety of languages and scripts for their users. Academic and school libraries need to support the teaching of foreign languages, and national public libraries need to deliver services to linguistic minorities. In addition, the international exchange of bibliographic information must be supported by systems that can maintain records in many different languages.

Cousins and Hartley (1994) summarize the problems faced by creators of multilingual OPACs, including character sets, different name headings in different languages, and multilingual subject thesauri. They also describe some existing systems giving multilingual access, particularly in Europe and Canada. An IFLA meeting on 'Automated systems for access to multilingual and multiscript library materials' was held in Madrid, on 18–19 August, 1993 (McCallum and Ertel, 1994; Murtomaa, 1994). As well as looking at some current library systems that support multiple languages or multiple scripts, this seminar looked to the future, when Unicode (as described in ISO/IEC 10646) will be implemented (Aliprand; Cain, 1994). Using sixteen-bit characters, Unicode can support all living languages, including the ideographic characters of Chinese, Japanese and Korean. However, Unicode is not yet used in library applications.

Wells (1993) reminds us that multilingual catalogues are also required in Australia: a country where English is the predominant language, but where there are significant non-English-speaking communities.

Non-Roman scripts

Non-Roman scripts, particularly those of Asian languages, present particular difficulties for control and access. You need staff with proficiency in the different languages, and you need systems which can handle the various scripts. The alternative of romanization is less satisfactory, and still requires language knowledge for such things as word division (Stokes, 1994).

Aliprand (1993) describes how non-Roman scripts are handled in the USMARC record and, in particular, the USMARC authority record. 'Alternate graphic representations', i.e. headings in non-Roman scripts, are held in 880 fields and linked with the romanized form in other fields. The most serious problem is that the AACR rules for headings and USMARC authority format are based on the Latin alphabet and do not cope well with non-Roman scripts. An example is given of authors who have different names in Chinese characters, but whose names have the same romanized form. She makes recommendations on how non-Roman scripts might be better handled in MARC authority records.

East Asian scripts, including the ideographic Han script used in Chinese, Japanese and Korean (CJK), present the greatest challenge for cataloguers. Kaneko (1993) describes the use of the RLIN CJK system by the East Asian library community since the system became operational in 1983. More than a million records had been added to the system in the first ten years. Wu (1993) describes options for retrospective conversion of East Asian cataloguing records, including use of OCLC and RLIN's CJK system. Problems include changes in cataloguing practice over the years, including changing romanization of the same characters.

Even if you avoid using vernacular scripts, you have the problem of choosing which romanization scheme to use. This problem exists for any languages, but is worst with Chinese, with the choice between Wade-Giles (the predominant system in North America, including the 1,000,000 plus records in RLIN) and Pinyin (the system preferred in China and used by most speakers and learners of Chinese). Studwell *et al.* (1993) look at the Wade-Giles/Pinyin problem and urge the Library of Congress to switch to Pinyin, since that is the scheme preferred world-wide.

Specific non-English cataloguing systems

There are considerable problems in adapting Anglocentric cataloguing tools such as AACR and LCSH in non-English-speaking communities. Murtomaa and Greig (1994) describe some of the problems in linking authority files in different languages. They suggest possible international standards for linking different headings for the same entity.

While Greek culture goes back further than most European cultures, and has had a great influence on Western civilization, Greece now depends on bibliographic records from the Library of Congress. Raptis and Salaba (1994) describe how the Central Library of the Aristotle University of Thessaloniki adapts LC's practice in Greece by the use of bilingual authority files. Thus they use the Greek 'Πλατων' instead of the English 'Plato'.

Latvia has the problem of just starting library automation and creation of bibliographic records. Kreslins *et al.* (1994) look at how English-language subject thesauri can be adapted or translated for use in Latvia. In particular, they examine the difficulties of translating a thesaurus like LCSH into a language with different syntax, and how the different syntax might affect keyword retrieval.

New Zealand is a bilingual community, with a minority indigenous Maori community. Barrie and Powell (1994) describe 'He Puna Kupu Maori' ('The Maori Wordnet'), which is a subject thesaurus developed for that community. This is not a translation of LCSH, even though English-speaking New Zealand libraries use LCSH extensively.

In Spain, there are regional languages which are now recognized by the state, and which need to be supported by cataloguing systems. Only Catalan has a well-developed catalogue at present (Altuna, 1994). In addition, the Spanish Biblioteca Nacional needs to provide access to collections in Arabic, Greek and

Hebrew (Jaudenes Casaubon and Torres Santo Domingo, 1994).

Within the Uralic language family (which includes Hungarian, Finnish, Estonian, and about sixteen minority languages in Scandinavia and Russia), there is a project to create a bibliographic database called *Bibliographia Studiorum Uralicorum*. This database has to cope with two scripts – the Latin and Cyrillic alphabets – as well as linguistic and cultural differences (Aho, 1994).

Each country and each language community has to make its own decisions: how much will they use the English language cataloguing tools, and how much effort will they put into developing their own cataloguing tools?

Cataloguing practice: processing more with less, and doing it better

There are conflicting expectations of cataloguers these days. On the one hand, they are being asked to catalogue in more detail, particularly by giving tables of contents in catalogue records. Rast and Studwell (1994) provocatively suggest that cataloguing in more detail will require fewer intermediaries between the user and the catalogue: more work done by cataloguers means less work for reference librarians. On the other hand, cataloguers are expected to be increasingly efficient and do the same or more work with fewer staff.

Intner (1993) treats some of the issues facing cataloguing managers as ethical issues. Although 'ethics' may not be the right word, certainly there are some difficult issues to resolve in delivering a high quality catalogue to the patron at a reasonable cost. LeBlanc (1993) outlines a number of ways to manage the cataloguing crisis of the 1990s, without sacrificing quality for quantity: greater acceptance of catalogue copy from other libraries, higher standards of original cataloguing in bibliographic utilities like OCLC, and making cataloguing backlogs accessible to library users by putting them under partial control.

One option that is suggested is minimum level cataloguing (MLC). Camden and Cooper (1994) describe how MLC has been used at the University of Virginia to reduce a cataloguing backlog and to provide at least some access for users. However, as Intner (1994b), points out, MLC is not suggested for the best-sellers, which users will find anyway: rather it is suggested for 'the most sophisticated, the most unusual or the most difficult to catalogue', that is, for the material that should receive fuller cataloguing.

Callahan and MacLeod (1994) surveyed entry level cataloguers to find out how cataloguers can be recruited and retained, at a time when there is a shortage of good cataloguers. Their solutions include improving the image of cataloguing and better cataloguing education. In Australia, library technicians are doing an increasing share of both copy cataloguing and original cataloguing (Clayden,

1993). What should be the relationship between technicians and professional librarians?

Team cataloguing has been adopted in many libraries to try to increase productivity and morale. Schuneman and Mohr (1994) surveyed academic libraries in the USA and found ambivalent results on the question of whether productivity and morale had improved. On the other hand, S.J. Smith (1994) reports that cooperative team cataloguing at the University of Illinois at Urbana-Champaign has increased productivity by 17%.

Bibliographic databases

In the English-speaking cataloguing world, at least, most libraries get most of their catalogue records from bibliographic utilities like OCLC and RLIN.

For 'mainstream' publications, the bibliographic utilities are extremely successful. Ross (1993) found a 98.4% to 99.8% 'hit rate' for recently published monographs in OCLC and WLN. Of those records, 29.3% in OCLC and 16.9% in WLN were Cataloguing in Publication (CIP) records, reflecting different policies on upgrading of records in the two different systems. WLN allows any participant to upgrade records, and other participants benefit from those upgradings.

However, when you move outside the mainstream, hit rates go down. Sercan (1994) found only a 28% hit rate for current Latin American imprints in RLIN, although the hit rate did improve to 45% after four weeks and 57% after eight weeks. Seymour (1994) found catalogue records for only 20% of East European titles searched in OCLC. Tsao (1994) found hit rates of 50% and 53% respectively for Chinese and Japanese monographs in RLIN. Clearly, there is room for improvement here, which might be brought about by cooperative cataloguing programmes linking the countries of Latin America, Europe and Asia with theAnglo-American cataloguing world. Another form of material with low hit rates on the bibliographic utilities is music. MacLeod and Lloyd (1994) report on large music cataloguing backlogs in many libraries in the USA, partly due to lack of records on OCLC, and partly due to a lack of knowledgeable staff to process them. The two factors are related, as the catalogue records on OCLC must be created by cataloguing staff somewhere.

Quality as well as quantity is involved in finding catalogue records in bibliographic utilities, and material that gives lower hit rates will often also give more errors. Tsao (1994) found that, of 321 Chinese and Japanese records in OCLC, 192 records required revision. Quality control can be helped by automated mechanisms. Zeng (1993a; 1993b) looked at the quality of 1,306 Chinese-language records in OCLC (including 453 loaded from RLIN to OCLC). The first paper divided the different errors into categories; the second looked at the possibility of using a rule-based validation system to identify the different kinds of errors. At least 65% of the errors found could be identified automatically.

However, quality control also needs human intervention. S.J. Smith (1994) looked at how OCLC cataloguing copy is handled at the University of Illinois at Urbana-Champaign. In increasing productivity in a cataloguing unit, both quality and quantity are important.

National bibliographies

Another widely used source of catalogue records is the national bibliography, often on CD-ROM as an alternative to online access (Elliot, 1994). Potentially, if every country had a national bibliography, this could provide universal bibliographic control (UBC). However, we are some distance from UBC, because of differing levels of technological development (Bourne, 1994) and the lack of a common approach in data standards (R. Smith, 1994).

Collection-level cataloguing

Instead of cataloguing some material as individual items, you can describe them at the collection level (Saunders, 1994). This has been proposed for archival video and audio recordings (Haynes *et al.*, 1993) and for vertical file material (Kronenfeld and Howley, 1994). In that last case, non-cataloguing staff were used to carry out part of the cataloguing process. Reference staff used Pro-Cite to control a vertical file at the item level. Entries were created in the OPAC at the collection level, that is, for each folder in the vertical file (Kronenfeld and Howley, 1994).

Outsourcing

One solution to the cataloguing crisis is 'outsourcing': using an outside agency to do your original cataloguing. Alley (1993) supports the decision of Wright State University Libraries to outsource cataloguing to OCLC. Intner (1994a) looks at the push to outsource cataloguing, and wonders what would happen if libraries outsourced any of their other functions.

Government document cataloguing

One genus of material that often causes difficulties is government documents. Sherayko (1994) has edited a survey of how different government documents are processed in various libraries.

Use of automation in the cataloguing process: cataloguers' workstations and expert systems

The OPAC may already appear fully automated: records are created and stored in machine-readable form, and delivered to users by computers and computer networks. However, there is still room for further automation in two areas, in helping the cataloguer to apply cataloguing rules to create the MARC record, and in helping to mediate between the user's needs and the bibliographic database (Dunsire, 1993).

The Cooperative Cataloguing Council (CCC) has looked at what is needed in a 'technical services workstation' to provide acquisitions and cataloguing staff with access to all the tools and databases they need in their work (Kiegel, 1994).

Several authors have proposed the use of expert systems to help automate the cataloguing process. Hawks (1994) presents a useful survey of projects that have used expert systems in technical services, including cataloguing, and, despite the limited sucesses so far, she is optimistic about the future for expert systems. However, the problem is that expert systems have been most successful in limited domains, and cataloguing is not a limited domain. Even descriptive cataloguing must cope with materials in all written languages and in all forms: legal, liturgical and musical, among others. Subject cataloguing must cope with materials on all subjects; it has an unlimited domain. So, successful expert systems must deal with limited domains within the field of cataloguing. Armarego (1993) reports on a research project to use an expert system in applying DDC to Western Australiana at the Library and Information Service of Western Australia. Jeng and Weiss (1994) examine the feasibility of modelling descriptive cataloguing expertise at the National Agricultural Library. Khoo and Poo (1994) propose developing an expert system front end to help in subject searches.

This last approach, using an expert system as a front end to an OPAC, seems to me to be the most promising approach. You would be building on thesauri such as LCSH, which is designed for end-users, and use techniques of experienced searchers to broaden or narrow searches: key words, classification numbers, spelling checkers, or alternative databases such as periodical indexes. Expert systems, such as ILSA developed by Micco and Popp (1994), might also be used to help the cataloguer to match books with subject headings. Would this downgrade the cataloguer's skills, or leave the cataloguer free to spend more time on more creative work? Kartus (1993) believes that, on balance, expert systems would help the cataloguer.

Computers might also be used to make *more* explicit what is explicit in the MARC record. For example, could a program link successive titles of serials, using information found in existing records, and create a cluster record to include the separate records for the different titles? Alan (1993) finds that using the

OCLC control number, ISSN and LCCN in existing successive title records, you could do so 71% of the time. This means that, for 29% of the records, human intervention will be needed to help in the automatic linking of records.

Authority control: linking headings and ideas

Authority control is the iceberg of cataloguing: there is a lot of it there, but the catalogue user only sees the tip. Ignore it, however, and the part that is unseen can cause you trouble when you hit it unawares.

The Library of Congress does more authority control than anyone else – authority control which is taken advantage of by other libraries that use LC bibliographic records and name authority records. In a period of severe budget cuts, LC has been looking at how to make authority control easier. Some of the strateies have been:

- simplifying the process of authority control;
- using authority work done by other libraries through cooperative authority control programmes;
- removing differences in cataloguing practice between LC, the British Library and the National Library of Canada.

This cooperation is moving us from the centralized LCNA and LCSH authority files maintained by LC towards a cooperative 'Anglo-American Authority File', jointly maintained by BL, LC and NLC (NLC, 1995).

Simplifying authority control

Authority control is the process of establishing headings for a catalogue, and building up a structure linking variant and related headings. It continues to be an expensive as well as an important part of the cataloguing process. However, at a time when administrators are questioning the time spent on such work, it is refreshing to learn how valuable the authority file can be in reference work (Olszewski, 1994).

The Library of Congress, as the largest source of authority control in the world, is currently reviewing the process to see how it can be simplified. One task group has looked at 'Issues surrounding maintenance of separate name and subject authority files' (CPSO/CCC, 1994c). It stopped short of recommending the merging of the LCNA and LCSH authority files, but recommended making them more consistent and easier to use. Another task group looked at simplifying the creation of LCSH authority records and revising the LC *subject cataloging manual* (CPSO/CCC, 1994a).

The Series Authority Record Task Group (CCC, 1994b) looked both at whether authority control was required for all series and at how authority control could be simplified. In the Anglo-American Authority File, which tried to cover the requirements of all libraries, control was needed for all series, and fuller rather than brief records were called for, including records for 'series-like phrases' that are not traced.

The CCC Subject Authorities File Task Group (CCC,1994c) found that the LCSH authority file was not a true authority file (as it did not include all headings used) and not a true thesaurus (as it did not include completely explicit rules on how combinations of headings and subheadings may be combined). The recommendations include creation of a 'validation file', and establishment of authority records for subdivisions and valid heading-subdivision combinations, so that all subject headings in records could be automatically validated.

The report of the CCC Task Group on the 670 field in name and series authority records (CCC, 1994a) looked at simplifying the creation of name authority records. It studied the 670 field (the field identifying the sources of information used to create the heading), and asked why the 670 field is created and how its creation could be simplified. It concluded that the 670 field remains important in cooperative authority files, but that less information might be adequate. The report also looks at some promising ways to automate the creation of 670 fields from bibliographic records.

McCurley (1993; 1994) describes how an online series authority file has replaced a card authority file at Auburn University, and lists the benefits of online authority control, particularly for technical services staff.

Catalogue display: what does the user see?

OPAC displays are far more varied than card catalogues ever were. This can be confusing to users, when they can look at hundreds of different catalogues from anywhere on the Internet. Ensor (1993) asks 'Do we need standards for OPAC interfaces?' and concludes that some standardization would be both desirable and feasible.

Part of the problem is that OPAC displays are based on the MARC record, and so are not tied directly to cataloguing rules such as AACR and ISBD (International Standard Bibliographic Description). Wool et al. (1993) compare the OPAC display of bibliographic records in an INNOPAC catalogue with the format prescribed by ISBD. They find 38 kinds of change which can be ascribed to the software, including rearrangement of data and mislabelling of data. So what needs to change: the cataloguing rules, or the OPAC display? Also, should cataloguers take into consideration how their work will be displayed to the catalogue user?

Another part of the problem is that some searches (both in card catalogues and in OPACs) produce a large number of hits. In the card catalogue, under each heading, cards were arranged alphabetically by main entry (one can remember the different shades of grey at the tops of cards which indicated that most users of card catalogues only looked at the first centimetre or so). Buckland *et al.* (1993) argue against this alphabetic arrangement being carried over from card catalogues to OPACs. They suggest other methods, which will display first the hits most likely to be relevant to the user.

Catalogue users have particular difficulty with subject searches, especially if they are faced with a choice of techniques, such as LCSH, keywords in LCSH, keywords in titles, and keywords in table of contents. If they make the wrong choice, they may get either no hits at all or too many hits. Drabenstott and Weller (1994) describe an experimental system using search trees to deliver better results from subject searches.

Catalogue use: how do users get what they want?

Catalogues exist for the benefit of their users, not for the benefit of their creators. Focusing on delivering a high quality product to the client is an important part of modern management and should be part of the cataloguing process (James, 1993). Duckett (1994) asks, 'Do users matter?', and offers a range of suggestions to help catalogue users. Watters and Shepherd (1994) believe that information access is moving from a data-centred to a user-centred paradigm. However, Allen (1993) does not believe that OPACs have moved far enough towards a 'client-centred' model.

Fortunately, cataloguing does seem to be moving in the right direction. Liverpool John Moores University and Liverpool City Libraries have an old microfiche catalogue and an old sheaf catalogue as well as an OPAC. Although the OPAC has shortcomings, users prefer it to the older forms of catalogue (Balaam, 1993; Burton and Hawkins, 1993).

Users are moving in the right direction, too. Sinnott (1993) found that users of OPACs are making fewer errors in author searches now than they were ten years ago. Either users are becoming more familiar with computers, or they are becoming more familiar with OPACs. Caplan (1994a) suggests that users prefer keyboard input for an OPAC, rather than a mouse and a graphical user interface (GUI) – probably because the keyboard must be used to input search strings in any case. This contradicts the conventional wisdom that a mouse and GUI is better because it is more user-friendly.

According to McClellan (1993), subject searching on OPACs is deficient in comparison with commercial journal databases. However, Lancaster *et al.* (1994) discovered that end-users searching on one of those journal databases (ERIC) found only about a third of the important items that skilled intermediaries did. Skilled bibliographic database searchers have to learn many tools and tricks of their trade; the difficulty is to lead unskilled end-users to use the same skills, while making the process still appear relatively simple.

Another approach to the catalogue user is that of Huthwaite (1993). She looks at users' mental models of the catalogue, and how those models might be enhanced to improve subject searching.

Use of transaction logs

One of the advantages of OPACs over card catalogues is that many OPACs can log the inquiries made of them.

Ballard (1994) compares how library users and library staff use an INNOPAC catalogue. Library users tend to stick to the traditional author, title and subject indexes, while library staff use other indexes more – perhaps because they are using call number and OCLC number indexes to find specific titles. Against the author's expectation, patrons use the keyword index more than library staff. Wallace (1993) analyses transaction logs gathered on the CARL system at the University of Colorado: 53% of searches were keyword searches and, since CARL does not provide a controlled subject index, many of these would have been subject searches. The other popular indexes were the name index (22%) and the title index (24%). Of the keyword and name searches, 82% produced between one and 25 hits, with a surprisingly high proportion avoiding the twin perils of no hits and too many hits.

Millsap and Ferl (1993) analyse the transaction logs of remote users of MELVYL at the University of California. Their principal finding was that 40% of users were looking for known items, and were well served by the system. The other 60% conducted longer sessions, often getting either no hits or high numbers of hits. Their problem was a difficulty in describing something that they were still looking for.

The Internet: making the world a single library, without a union catalogue?

While the Internet is very new to most of us, it is already having a profound effect on control of and access to information (McCoy, 1994). Because it is so new, it is often described by using analogies to past experience. Lester (1993), in the first of a series of columns in *Technicalities, uses the image* of *a* 'global metropolis', rather than 'global village', to describe the Internet. Janes and Rosenfeld (1994) use the metaphor of 'navigation' to examine how people find resources on the Internet. McCombs (1994) uses the surfing concept 'point break' to look at how library technical services should use the Internet. Studwell (1994) compares the Internet with the US interstate highway system.

The Internet is already large and is expanding rapidly, although it is spread unevenly, and is often unavailable in Third World countries (Brown, 1994). It is often chaotic (Taylor, 1994), and unreliable (Crawford, 1994b), and can often deliver valuable resources to library users faster than any other medium (Lanier and Wilkins, 1994).

Taylor (1994) believes that the skills developed by librarians over the last 150 years are needed to bring control to the chaos on the Internet. Burrows (1993), on the other hand, believes that librarians must move beyond the traditional concept of a catalogue, to create bibliographic access appropriate to the Internet. Both Taylor and Burrows are right. Taylor is right when she says that 'the online world is desperately in need of the skills we librarians have developed in the area of information organization'. However, those skills need to be applied in new ways, to do things that our card catalogues and our present OPACs cannot do, such as taking the user directly from a catalogue entry to an Internet resource, as Burrows suggests.

Machine-readable texts and e-journals

Within the Internet, there are two extremes of electronic texts: electronic preprints and journals of the very latest scientific research, and electronic texts of material which is so old that it is out of copyright. In the middle is copyright material of commercial value, where publishers are still working out how to charge for electronic texts and get a return on their investment.

Caplan (1994b) argues that the paper preprint is on its way to extinction, and is being replaced by electronic preprints or 'e-prints'. Most libraries do not collect paper preprints: they collect the later versions of those articles in scientific journals. How will libraries collect and provide access to e-prints?

In the same way as e-prints are replacing paper preprints, electronic journals (or 'ejournals') are starting to replace printed journals. Sasse and Winkler (1993) and Lary (1994) describe ejournals as a challenge – and they certainly challenge most of our present ideas about journals, including how libraries should control and provide access to them. Sasse and Winkler (1993) review how electronic journals should be handled in libraries: how patrons should be given access; how they should be indexed and abstracted; how they should be archived, how easy they are to read, and to what extent they will replace printed journals as a means of scholarly communication. Libraries have started to integrate ejournals into their collections, but we are a long way from full acceptance. Lary (1994) looks specifically at how electronic journals should be used for publication within the field of librarianship and information science.

The Columbia Working Group on Electronic Texts met on 22–23 September 1994, bringing together representatives of libraries, publishers and learned societies to look at how the process of scholarly publication should take place in an electronic environment. Sloan and Okerson (1994), in their report on the meeting, describe the problems (including delay and high cost) of present print-based scholarly publication, and the opportunities provided by electronic publication. Two models of electronic publication are proposed: the 'academic server' model, providing fast and cheap access, and the 'prestigious' e-publishing model, providing higher editorial standards.

As well as having access to the latest research, scholars in the humanities have access to the primary source material. Hoogcarspel (1994) describes the *Rutgers inventory of machine-readable texts in the humanities,* which is maintained by the Center for Electronic Texts in the Humanities (CETH) on RLIN. E-texts provide particular difficulties in cataloguing and access, including often inconsistent and incomplete information about the texts.

Virtual libraries

You put together a virtual collection of electronic texts, linked through the Internet, and what do you have? A virtual library! Or perhaps *The* Virtual Library, as the same resources can be available to everyone with access to the Internet. Universal bibliographic control at last, perhaps.

The virtual library is not quite with us yet, although there are working systems, such as the Mann Library Gateway system (Schlabach and Barnes, 1994), which come close. There is a gap between the promise of the virtual library and the current reality, because most information is not yet available in electronic form, and adequate tools do not yet exist to control and provide access to electronic information (Johnson, 1993).

Even if the virtual library does not have the physical limits of a real library, it still has some of the same problems. There are problems of standards for the bibliographic description of documents (Gorman and Oddy, 1993). There are problems with the economics of publishing, and there are legal issues with patents covering technologies for the storage and display of information (Kahin, 1994). Libraries will still provide reference services, even if they will be delivered in new ways (Myers, 1994). If today's libraries are to survive, they need to adapt to and become part of the virtual library of the future. How they adapt will be a combination of evolution (Rooks, 1993) and revolution (Shaw, 1994).

Cataloguing tools for the virtual library

Z39.50

One specific challenge of the virtual library is the variety of user interfaces in the catalogues and databases available on the Internet. One solution to this problem is the ANSI standard Z39.50, which is a standard to allow inquiries of a variety of bibliographic databases using the same commands. This is important to librarians and to library users because it will make searching remote databases easier: they will only need to learn one set of commands, either the Z39.50 commands or the commands of the OPAC in their local library (Ward, 1994).

Corey (1994) describes how this standard was developed by the Z39.50 Implementors' Group (ZIG), and how the Florida Centre for Library Automation developed software for it on the Centre's NOTIS system. Though the original concept was for Z39.50 to operate over Open Systems Interconnection (OSI) protocols, while it was being developed, TCP/IP protocols became more important as a means of communication, so the Z39.50 software was adapted to be able to use both OSI and TCP/IP.

Gopher

Gopher is one way of organizing the virtual library known as the Internet. Using a simple menu interface, which can be run on most computers, you can provide links to documents, databases and other services available on the Internet. Organization of an individual Gopher site depends on the person in charge: often a person who has little idea of how to organize knowledge. However, there are some good examples:

- BUBL (Bulletin Board for British Libraries);
- LC MARVEL (Library of Congress Machine Assisted Realization of the Virtual Electronic Library) (Muns, 1994);
- The University of Minnesota's Internet Gopher (Wiggins, 1993).

World Wide Web (WWW)

Another way of organizing the Internet is the World Wide Web (WWW). This uses 'hypertext' rather than the ASCII text and menus of Gopher. The tools it uses are the hypertext mark-up language (HTML) (Barry, 1994) and Mosaic (Lester, 1994; Morgan, 1994).

The Indiana University-Purdue University Indianapolis (IUPUI) University Library has used Mosaic for its Library Information System (LIS) (Koopman and Hay, 1994). The home page of the LIS (URL: http://www-lib.iupui.edu) provides the library's users with links to useful resources at IUPUI and elsewhere on the WWW. Price-Wilkin (1994b) describes several projects at the University of Virginia to use the WWW to deliver electronic documents. He also lists some limitations of HTML, and describes a gateway that he has developed to overcome these limitations. A later article by the same author (Price-Wilkin, 1994a) gives a technical description of this gateway. Ridley (1994) looks at how the WWW has been integrated into the work of the University of Waterloo Libraries. He emphasizes the need for a flexible, client-centred approach.

A problem with the World Wide Web is that, although every document is linked to other documents, finding a specific piece of information can be difficult. Pinkerton (1994) describes a program that he has developed called 'WebCrawler'. WebCrawler automatically navigates and indexes the WWW, using full text rather than just titles, as titles are often missing or inadequate in the WWW.

Conclusion

Cataloguing is at a crossroads. Can it move out of the traditional physical library and cope with an increasingly interconnected, internationalized and exponentially growing explosion of information? Or does the future lie with automated information assistants that will explore the global network? I believe that in the future there is a place for:

- the analytic skills of cataloguers, to help users to find information in its various forms;
- the control of cataloguing rules and subject thesauri, to cope with the variety of forms of natural language;
- the cooperation that has been shown by librarians in the past, and that is generally seen on the Internet;
- the ever increasing data-processing capacity of computers needed for an ever-increasing body of information.

References

ACLIS (1994) *The Distributed National Collection: a report on progress 1988–1994.* Canberra, ACT: Australian Council of Libraries and Information Services.

Aho, M. (1994) Automation and the Uralic: dreams and reality of the experience of the Uralica database. In: *Automated systems for access to multilingual and multiscript library materials: proceedings of the Second IFLA Satellite Meeting, Madrid, August 18–19, 1993*, eds S. McCallum and M. Ertel. München: K.G. Saur, pp. 55–62.

Alan, R. (1993) Linking successive entries based upon the OCLC control number, ISSN, or LCCN. *Library Resources and Technical Services* **37**(4), 403–413.

Aliprand, J.M. (1993) Linking of alternate graphic representation in USMARC authority records. *Cataloging and Classification Quarterly*, **18**(1), 27–61.

Aliprand, J.M. (1994) Unicode and ISO/IEC 10646: an overview. In: *Automated systems for access to multilingual and multiscript library materials: proceedings of the Second IFLA Satellite Meeting, Madrid, August 18–19, 1993*, eds S. McCallum and M. Ertel. München: K.G. Saur, pp. 87–102.

Allen, L. (1993) Towards a learning catalogue: developing the next generation of library catalogues. *Cataloguing Australia*, **19**(3–4), 125–147.

Alley, B. (1993) Reengineering, outsourcing, downsizing, and perfect timing. *Technicalities*, **13**(11), 1, 8.

Altuna, B. (1994) Considerations and requirements in designing Spanish multilingual library catalogues. In: *Automated systems for access to multilingual and multiscript library materials: proceedings of the Second IFLA Satellite Meeting, Madrid, August 18–19, 1993*, eds S. McCallum and M. Ertel. München: K.G. Saur, pp. 29–44.

Armarego, J. (1993) Subject cataloguing: expert knowledge for an expert system. *Cataloguing Australia*, **19**(3–4), 148–159.

Australian (1994) Bibliographic Network Standards Committee. *LC Cataloging Newsline*, **2**(4). [To retrieve this report, send the following e-mail message to listproc@loc.gov: GET LCCN LCCN-2.04]

Baker, N. (1994) Discards. *New Yorker*, (4) April, 64–86.

Balaam, A. (1993) Approaches to library catalogues. *Library Management*, **14**(5), 9–12.

Ballard, T. (1994) Comparative searching styles of patrons and staff. *Library Resources and Technical Services* **38**(3), 293–305.

Bandyopadhyay, R., and Mookerjee, B.P. (1994) The treatment of computer files in AACR2. *International Cataloguing and Bibliographic Control*, **23**(3), 47–48.

Barrie, A. and Powell, T. (1994) *Seminar on He Puna Kupu Maori / the Maori Wordnet: notes from National Library* [of New Zealand] *seminars on He Puna Kupu Maori*. [Paper presented at New Zealand CATSIG meeting in assocation with Joint ALIA/NZLIA Conference, Wellington, New Zealand, 30 September 1994]

Barry, J. (1994) The hypertext markup language (HTML) and the World Wide Web: raising ASCII text to a new level of usability. *Public-Access Computer Systems Review*, **5**(5), 5–62. [To retrieve this file, send the following e-mail message to listserv@uhupvm1.uh.edu: GET BARRY PRV5N5 F=MAIL.]

Beall, J. (1994) IFLA satellite meeting on subject indexing: Principles and practices in the 90s, Lisbon, 17 and 18 August 1993. *International Cataloguing and Bibliographic Control*, **23**(1), 11–12.

Best, J.J. (1994) The technology information revolution and the university: 'The electronic superhighway is coming . . .' *LIBRES*, **4**(2–3). [To retrieve this file, send the following e-mail message to listserv@kentvm.kent.edu: GET LIBRE4N2 BEST.]

Bierbaum, E.G. (1994) A modest proposal, no more main entry. *American Libraries*, (January), 81–84.

Boss, R.W. (1993) Online catalog functionality in the 90s: vendor responses to a model RFP. *Library technology reports*, **29**(4), 587–745.

Bourke, L. and Salmond, R. (1993) From bibliographer to cataloguer: subject access to early printed books. *Cataloguing Australia*, **19**(3–4), 160–166.

Bourne, R. (1994) Bridging the gap: technological differences in the production of current national bibliographies. *International Cataloguing and Bibliographic Control*, **23**(1), 13–14.

British (1994) Library shares records with LC/NACOfile. *LC Cataloging Newsline*, **2**(3). [To retrieve this report, send the following e-mail message to listproc@loc.gov: GET LCCN LCCN-2.03.]

Brown, J.M. (1994) The global computer nework: indications of its use worldwide. *International Information and Library Review*, **26**(1), 51–65.

Buckland, M.K. *et al.* (1993) Filing, filtering, and the first few found. *Information Technology and Libraries*, **12**(3), 311–319.

Burrows, T. (1993) Bibliographic integration and the Internet: moving beyond 'cataloguing' in academic and research libraries. *Cataloguing Australia*, **19**(3–4), 167–174.

Burton, P.A. and Hawkins, A.M. (1993) Attitudes to an online public access catalogue in an academic library. *Library Management*, **14**(5), 13–15.

Cain, J. (1994) Practical applications of Unicode. In: *Automated Systems for Access to multilingual and multiscript library materials: proceedings of the Second IFLA Satellite Meeting, Madrid, August 18–19, 1993*, eds S. McCallum and M. Ertel. München: K.G. Saur, pp. 103–114.

Callahan, D. and MacLeod, J. (1994) Recruiting and retention revisited: a study of entry level catalogers. *Technical Services Quarterly*, **11**(4), 27–43.

Camden, B.P. and Cooper, J.L. (1994) Controlling a cataloging backlog, or taming the bibliographical zoo. *Library Resources and Technical Services* **38**(1), 64–71.

Caplan, P. (1994a) A user's eye view of the OPAC. *Public-Access Computer Systems Review*, **5**(7), 28–33. [To retrieve this file, send the following e-mail message to listserv@uhupvm1.uh.edu: GET CAPLAN PRV5N1 F=MAIL.]

Caplan, P. (1994b) You can't get there from here: e-prints and the library. *Public-Access Computer Systems Review*, **5**(1), 20–24. [To retrieve this file, send the following e-mail message to listserv@uhupvml.uh.edu: GET CAPLAN PRV5N1 F=MAIL.]

Cathro, W. (1994) *The NDIS Project: an overview of the National Document and Information Service.* [Speech given at National Library of Australia presentations in 1994 and 1995, and posted to NDIS-L@NLA.GOV.AU by B. DeLaMotte on 12 January 1995.]

CCC (1994a) Report of the CCC Task Group on the 670 field in name and series authority records. *LC MARVEL gopher* [URL: gopher://marvel.loc.gov/11/services/cataloging/coop/coop_cncl/cptg670]

CCC (1994b) Series Authority Record Task Group final report. *LC MARVEL gopher.* [URL gopher://marvel.loc.gov 11/services/cataloging/coop/coop_cncl/tgseries.1.]

CCC (1994c) Subject Authorities File Task Group final report. *LC MARVEL gopher.* [URL: gopher://marvel.loc.gov/11/services/cataloging/coop/coop_cncl/tgsubj.1.]

Cherry, J.M. *et al.* (1994) OPACs in twelve Canadian academic libraries: an evaluation of functional capabilities and interface features. *Information Technology and Libraries*, **13**(3), 174–195.

Clayden, J. (1993) Library technicians: merely copy cataloguers? *Cataloguing Australia*, **19**(3–4), 175–182.

Corey, J.F. (1994) A grant for Z39.50. *Library HiTech*, (45), 37–47.

Cousins, S.A., and Hartley, R.J. (1994) Towards multilingual online public access catalogues. *Libri*, **44**(1), 47–62.

CPSO/CCC (1994a) CPSO/CCC Task Group to Revise and Simplify Subject Cataloging Documentation and Procedures, interim report, June 1994. *LC MARVEL Gopher* [URL:

gopher://marvel.loc.gov/11/services/cataloging/coop/coop_cncl/cptgsubj.]

CPSO/CCC (1994b) Interim report of the work of the Task Group on LC-Issued Descriptive Cataloging Documentation. *LC MARVEL Gopher* [URL: gopher://marvel.loc.gov/11/services / cataloging / coop / coop_cncl / cptgdesc.]

CPSO/CCC (1994c) Report of the CPSO/CCC Task Group on Issues Surrounding Maintenance of Separate Name and Subject Authority Files. *LC MARVEL Gopher* [URL: gopher://marvel.loc.gov/11/services/cataloging/coop/coop_cncl/cptgdiv.]

Crawford, W. (1994a) And only half of what you see. Part II: skeletons in the catalog. *Public-Access Computer Systems Review,* **5**(5), 63–66. [To retrieve this file, send the following e-mail message to listserv@uhupvm1.uh.edu: GET CRAWFORD PRV5N5 F=MAIL.]

Crawford, W. (1994b) And only half of what you see. Part III: I heard it through the Internet. *Public-Access Computer Systems Review,* **5**(6), 27–30. [To retrieve this file, send the following e-mail message to listserv@uhupvm1.uh.edu: GET CRAWFORD PRV5N6 F=MAIL.]

Denehy, C.C. (1993) Subject cataloguing of fiction. *Cataloguing Australia,* **19**(3–4), 183–193.

Drabenstott, K.M. and Weller, M.S. (1994) Testing a new design for subject searching in online catalogs. *Library HiTech,* (45), 67–76.

Duckett, B. (1994) Do users matter? *Catalogue and Index,* (111), 1, 3–8.

Duke, J.K. (1994) Slow revolution: the electronic AACR. *Library Resources and Technical Services,* **38**(2), 190–194.

Dunsire, G. (1993) Sex, lies and catalogue cards. *Catalogue and Index,* (109), 1, 3–5.

Elliot, J. (1994) The use of CD-ROMs as a source of catalogue records in the European Community: report of a survey. *Catalogue and Index,* (112), 1–5.

Ensor, P. (1993) Do we need standards for OPAC interfaces? Or, at least card catalogs all looked alike. *Technicalities,* **13**(11), 9–11.

Eversberg, B. (1994) *Allegro: what is it, what does it do, who uses it?* [Report publicized on the AUTOCAT list. To retrieve it, send the following e-mail message to listserv@ubvm.cc.buffalo.edu: GET ALLEGRO REPORT.]

Franz, L. *et al.* (1994) End-user understanding of subdivided subject headings. *Library Resources and Technical Services* **38**(3), 213–226.

Gorman, M. (1994) Michael Gorman and AACR3. *LC Cataloging Newsline,* **2**(5). [Report of talk by Gorman to Library of Congress staff on May 24, 1994. To retrieve it, send the following e-mail message to listproc@loc.gov: GET LCCN LCCN-2.05.]

Gorman, M. and Oddy, P. (1993) Bibliographic standards and the library of the future. *Catalogue and Index,* (110), 1, 4–5.

Hawks, C.P. (1994) Expert systems in technical services and collection management. *Information Technology and Libraries,* **13**(3), 203–212.

Haynes, K.J.M. *et al.* (1993) Cataloging collection-level records for archival video and audio recordings. *Cataloging and Classification Quarterly,* **18**(2), 19–32.

Hoffmann, H. (1994) Multiple versions: history, definition and scope. *Cataloguing Australia,* **20**(1), 3–6.

Holley, R.P. (1993) Report on the IFLA satellite meeting 'Subject Indexing: Principles and Practices in the 90s', August 17–18, 1993, Lisbon, Portugal. *Cataloging and Classification Quarterly,* **18**(2), 87–100.

Hoogcarspel, A. (1994) The Rutgers inventory of machine-readable texts in the humanities: cataloging and access. *Information Technology and Libraries,* **13**(1), 27–34.

Huthwaite, A. (1993) Understanding the user: cognitive aspects of subject searching. *Cataloguing Australia*, **19**(3–4), 200–208.
Huthwaite, A. (1994) Multiple Versions Forum and models. *Cataloguing Australia*, **20**(1), 7–13.
Intner, S.S. (1993) Ethics in cataloging. *Technicalities*, **13**(11), 5–8.
Intner, S.S. (1994a) Outsourcing: what does it mean for technical services? *Technicalities*, **14**(3), 3–5.
Intner, S.S. (1994b) Taking another look at minimum level cataloging. *Technicalities*, **14**(1), 3–5, 11.
James, S. (1993) A question of quality: BS5750 and catalogues. *Catalogue and Index*, (109), 6–10.
Janes, J.W. and Rosenfeld, L.B. (1994) And Magellan thought he had problems: 'navigation' in a network environment. *LIBRES*, **4**(4). [To retrieve this file, send the following e-mail message to listserv@kentvm.kent.edu: GET LIBRE4N1 JANES.]
Jaudenes Casaubon, M. and Torres Santo Domingo, N. (1994) A Mediterranean perspective: Spain's Biblioteca Nacional. In: *Automated systems for access to multilingual and multiscript library materials: proceedings of the Second IFLA Satellite Meeting, Madrid, August 18–19, 1993* eds S. McCallum and M. Ertel. München: K.G. Saur, pp. 45–53.
Jeng, L.H. and Weiss, K.B. (1994) Modeling cataloging expertise: a feasiblity study. *Information Processing and Management*, **30**(1), 119–129.
Johnson, P. (1993) Mind the gap. *Technicalities*, **13**(10), 6–8.
Kahin, B. (1994) Institutional and policy issues in the development of the digital library. *Journal of Electronic Publishing*. [URL: http://sansfoy.hh.lib.umich.edu/jep/works/kahin.dl.html.]
Kaneko, H. (1993) RLIN CJK and the East Asian library community. *Information Technology and Libraries*, **12**(4), 423–426.
Kartus, E. (1993) A fully automated cataloguing workbench with enhanced subject access: the cataloguer's dream or nightmare? *Cataloguing Australia*, **19**(3–4), 209–221.
Khoo, C.S.C. and Poo, D.C.C. (1994) An expert system approach to online catalog subject searching. *Information Processing and Management*, **30**(2), 223–238.
Kiegel, J. (1994) Summary of the Technical Services Workstation Survey. *LC MARVEL gopher*. IURL: gopher://marvel.loc.gov/11/services/cataloging/coop/coop_cncl/tswsurv.]
Kohl, D.F. (1993) OhioLINK, plugging into progress. *Library Journal*, (1 October), 42–46.
Koopman, A. and Hay, S. (1994) Swim at your own risk – no librarian on duty: large scale applications of Mosaic in an academic library. In: *Electronic proceedings of the Second World Wide Web Conference '94: Mosaic and the Web*. [URL: http://www.ncsa.uiuc.edu /SDG / IT94 / LibApps /hay / WWWPap.html.]
Kreslins, K. *et al.* (1994) Online public access catalogues in Latvia: strategies for subject access. *International Information and Library Review*, **26**(1), 31–50.
Kronenfeld, M. and Howley, L. (1994) Theory and implementation of an automated vertical file. *RQ*, **33**(3), 387–394.
Lancaster, F.W. *et al.* (1994) Searching databases on CD-ROM: comparison of the results of end-user searching with results from two modes of searching by skilled intermediaries. *RQ*, **33**(3), 370–386.

Lanier, D. and Wilkins, W. (1994) Ready reference via the Internet. *RQ*, **33**(3), 359–368.

Lary, M. (1994) Electronic journals: challenges for the information profession. *LIBRES*, **4**(4). [To retrieve this file, send the following e-mail message to listserv@kentvm.kent.edu: GET LIBRE4N4 LARY.]

LeBlanc, J.D. (1993) Cataloging in the 1990s: managing the crisis (mentality). *Library Resources and Technical Services*, **37**(4), 423–433.

Lester, D. (1993) An eye on the Internet. What neighborhood do you live in? *Technicalities*, **13**(11), 3–4, 11.

Lester, D. (1994) An eye on the Internet. Getting the best toys: WWW and Mosaic. *Technicalities*, **14**(4), 6–8.

Little, K. (1993) Constructing a thesaurus of environmental protection terms. *Cataloguing Australia*, **19**(3–4), 222–232.

Maben, M. (1993) The cataloging of primary state legal material. *Cataloging and Classification Quarterly*, **18**(1), 103–115.

McCallum, S. and Ertel, M. (1994) (eds) *Automated systems for access to multilingual and multiscript library materials: proceedings of the Second IFLA Satellite Meeting, Madrid, August 18–19, 1993*. München: K.G. Saur.

McClellan, D. (1993) Subject access what degree of sophistication? *Cataloguing Australia*, **19**(3 4), 233–241.

MacLeod, J. and Lloyd, K. (1994) Study of music cataloging backlogs. *Library Resources and Technical Services*, **38**(1), 7–15.

McCombs, G.M. (1994) The Internet and technical services: a point break approach. *Library Resources and Technical Services*, **38**(2), 169–177.

McCoy, P.S. (1994) *Technical Services and the Internet*. [Paper for the American Association of Law Libraries conference, posted to AUTOCAT@ubvm.bitnet on 15 July.]

McCurley, H.H. (1993) Implementation of an online series authority file at Auburn University. *Cataloging and Classification Quarterly*, **18**(2), 41–58.

McCurley, H.H. (1994) The benefits of online series authority control. *Technical Services Quarterly*, **11**(3), 33–50.

Marker, R.J., and Reagor, M.A. (1994) Variation in place of publication: model for cataloging simplification. *Library Resources and Technical Services*, **38**(1), 17–26.

MARC (1994) format alignment. *LC Cataloging Newsline*, **2**(10). [To retrieve this report, send the following e-mail message to listproc@oc.gov: GET LCCN LCCN-2.10.]

Micco, M., and Popp, R. (1994) Improving Library Subject Access (ILSA): a theory of clustering based in classification. *Library HiTech*, (45), 55–66.

Millsap, L. and Ferl, T. (1993) Search patterns of remote users: an analysis of OPAC transaction logs. *Information Technology and Libraries*, **12**(3), 321–343.

Morgan, E.L. (1994) The World Wide Web and Mosaic: an overview for librarians. *Public Access Computer Systems Review* **5**(6), 5–26. [To retrieve this file, send the following e-mail message to listserv@uhupvm1.uh.edu: GET MORGAN PRV5N6 F=MAIL.]

Muns, R.C. (1994) Generic network resource reviews: LC MARVEL: Library of Congress Machine Assisted Realization of the Virtual Electronic Library. *LIBRES*, **4**(4). [To retrieve this file, send the following e-mail message to listserv@kentvm.kent.edu: GET LIBRE4N4 MUNS]

Murtomaa, E. (1994). Second IFLA satellite meeting on automated systems for access to multilingual and multiscript library materials, Madrid, 18 and 19 August 1993. *International Cataloguing and Bibliographic control* **23**(1), 9–11.

Murtomaa, E., and Greig, E. (1994) Problems and prospects of linking various single-language and/or multilanguage name authority files. *International Cataloguing and Bibliographic Control,* **23**(3), 55–58.

Myers, J.E. (1994) Reference services in the virtual library. *American Libraries,* (July–August), 634–638.

National (1994) Library of Canada contributes to LCSH. LC *Cataloging Newsline,* **2**(8). [To retrieve this report, send the following e-mail message to listproc@loc.gov: GET LCCN LCCN-2.08.]

Naun, C.C. (1994) AARNet access and cataloguing procedures in Australian academic libraries. *Australian Library Journal,* **43**(1), 9–15.

Neelameghan, A. (1993) Application of S.R. Ranganathan's postulates and principles of the general theory of knowledge classification to database design and information retrieval. *International Cataloguing and Bibliographic Control,* **22**(3), 46–50.

Nicholas, M. (1994) USMARC holdings format. *Cataloguing Australia,* **20**(1), 14–24.

NLC (1995) and LC name authority practices. LC *Cataloging Newsline,* **3**(1). [To retrieve this report, send the following e-mail message to listproc@loc.gov: GET LCCN LCCN 3.01.]

Norgard, B.A. *et al.* (1993) The online catalog: from technical services to access service. *Advances in Librarianship,* (17), 111–148.

Olszewski, L.J. (1994) Madonna, Brahms, and President Clinton: reference use of the OCLC authority file. *RQ,* **33**(3), 395–403.

Pearce, J. and Trainor, J. (1994) Multiple versions in the Australian Bibliographic Network: present and future. *Cataloguing Australia,* **20**(1), 28–37.

Pelzer, N.L. (1993) Veterinary subject headings and classification: a critical analysis. *Cataloging and Classification Quarterly,* **18**(2), 3–18.

Pinkerton, B. (1994) Finding what people want: experiences with the WebCrawler. In: *Electronic proceedings of the Second World Wide Web Conference '94: Mosaic and the Web.* [URL: http://www.ncsa.uiuc.edu/SDG/IT94/Proceedings/Searching/pinkerton/WebCrawler.html.]

Preece, B.G. and Henigman, B. (1994) Shared authority control: governance and training. *Technical Services Quarterly,* **11**(3), 19–31.

Price-Wilkin, J. (1994a) A gateway between the World Wide Web and PAT: exploring SGML through the Web. *Public-Access Computer Systems Review,* **5**(7), 5–27. [To retrieve this file, send the following e-mail message to listserv@uhupvm1.uh.edu: GET PRICEWIL PRV5N7 F=MAIL.]

Price-Wilkin, J. (1994b) Using the World Wide Web to deliver complex electronic documents: implications for libraries. *Public-Access Computer Systems Review,* **5**(3), 5–21. [To retrieve this file, send the following e-mail message to listserv@uhupvm1.uh.edu: GET PRICEWIL PRV5N3 F=MAIL.]

Raptis, P., and Salaba, A. (1994) Bilingual authority files at the Central Library of the Aristotle University of Thessaloniki, Greece. *International Information and Library Review,* **26**(2), 67–76.

Rast, E. and Studwell, W.E. (1994) When you do more someplace, you usually do less someplace else. *Technicalities,* **14**(8), 2–3.

Ridley, M. (1994) Innovation and implementation: adopting and managing World Wide Web services in academic libraries. In: *Electronic proceedings of the Second World Wide Web Conference '94: Mosaic and the Web.* [URL: http://www.ncsa.uiuc.edu/SDG/IT94/LibApps/ridley/ridley.html.]

Rooks, D. (1993) The virtual library: pitfalls, promises, and potential. *Public-Access Computer Systems Review,* **4**(5), 22–29. [To retrieve this file, send the following e-mail message to listserv@uhupvm1.uh.edu: GET ROOKS PRV4N5 F=MAIL.]

Ross, R.E. (1993) A comparison of OCLC and WLN hit rates for monographs and an analysis of the types of records retrieved. *Information Technology and Libraries,* **12**(3), 353–360.

Sassé, M. and Winkler, B.J. (1993) Electronic journals: a formidable challenge for libraries. *Advances in Librarianship,* (17), 149–173.

Saunders, R. (1994) Collection- or archival-level description for monograph collections. *Library Resources and Technical Services,* **38**(2), 139–147.

Schimizzi, A.J. (1993) The Library of Congress and the 'Bibliography' note. *Cataloging and Classification Quarterly,* **18**(2), 59–70.

Schlabach, M.L. and Barnes, S.J. (1994) The Mann Library Gateway system. *Public Access Computer Systems Review,* **5**(1), 5–19. [To retrieve this file, send the following email message to listserv@uhupvm1.uh.edu: GET SCHLABACH PRV5N1 F=MAIL.]

Schuneman, A., and Mohr, D.A. (1994) Team cataloging in academic libraries: an exploratory survey. *Library Resources and Technical Services,* **38**(3), 257–266.

Sercan, C.S. (1994) Where has all the copy gone? Latin American imprints in the RLIN database. *Library Resources and Technical Services,* **38**(1), 56–59.

Seymour, V.S. (1994) A survey of East European monographic records in the OCLC database. *Library Resources and Technical Services,* **38**(3), 275–279.

Sha, V.T. (1994) *Library Cataloging: Internet Resources.* Version 2.0. [URL: gopher://una.hh.lib.umich.edu/00/inetdirsstacks/libcat:sha.]

Sherayko, C.C. (1994) (ed.) Cataloging government publications online. *Cataloging and Classification Quarterly,* **18**(3–4), 1–208.

Shaw, D. (1994) Libraries of the future: glimpses of a networked, distributed, collaborative, hyper, virtual world. *Libri,* **44**(3), 206–223.

Sinnott, E. (1993) Fewer errors resulting from the users' misconception of the OPAC in 1992 than a decade ago: a comparative study of no direct hits and zero hits in author searches. *Cataloging and Classification Quarterly,* **18**(1), 75–101.

Sloan, E. and Okerson, A. (1994) (convenors) Columbia Working Group on Electronic Texts. *Journal of Electronic Publishing.* [URL: http://sansfoy.hh.lib.umich.edu/jep/works/okerson.columbia.html.]

Smith, R. (1994) National bibliographies on CD-ROM: development of a common approach. *International Cataloguing and Bibliographic Control,* **23**(1), 15–18.

Smith, S.J. (1994) Cataloging with copy: methods for increasing productivity. *Technical Services Quarterly,* **11**(4), 1–11.

Stokes, R. (1994) New information technology: acquiring, processing and accessing resources in Asian languages. *Australian Library Review,* **11**(3), 337–343.

Studwell, W.E. (1994) Are catalogers ready for the 'Information Superhighway'? *Technicalities,* **14**(7), 2–3.

Studwell, W.E. *et al.* (1993) A tale of two decades: the controversy over the choice of an

Chinese language romanization system in American cataloging practice. *Cataloging and Classification Quarterly,* **18**(1), 117–124.

Taylor, A.G. (1994) The information universe: Will we have chaos or control? *American Libraries,* (July–August), 629–632.

Todd, R.J. (1993) Subject access: what's it all about? Some research findings. *Cataloguing Australia,* **19**(3–4), 259–267.

Trotter, R. and Woodhouse, S. (1993) On the road with DDC: a report of the visit of Joan Mitchell, Editor of the Dewey Decimal Classification, to the UK, November 1993. *Catalogue and Index,* (110), 6–8.

Tsao, J.H. (1994) The quality and timeliness of Chinese and Japanese monographic records in the RLIN database. *Library Resources and Technical Services,* **38**(1), 60–63.

Walker, A. (1993) Building an Australian thesaurus: indexing Australian historical photographs. *Cataloguing Australia,* **19**(3–4), 268–279.

Wallace, P.M. (1993) How do patrons search the online catalog when no one's looking? Transaction log analysis and implications for bibliographic instruction and system design. *RQ,* **33**(2), 239–252.

Ward, M. (1994) Expanding access to information with Z39.50. *American Libraries,* (July–August), 639 641.

Warrick, Y.S. (1994) The use of abbreviations in Area V of AACR2. *Technicalities,* **14**(3), 11–13.

Watters, C. and Shepherd, M.A. (1994) Shifting the information paradigm from data-centred to user-centred. *Information Processing and Management,* **30**(4), 455–471.

Weimer, K.H. (1994) A citation comparison of sourcebooks for audiovisuals to AVLINE records: access and the chief source of information. *Library Resources and Technical Services* **38**(2), 119–138.

Weinberg, B.H. (1993) The hidden classification in Library of Congress subject headings for Judaica. *Library Resources and Technical Services,* **37**(4), 369–379.

Wells, A. (1993) Subject access and languages other than English. *Cataloguing Australia,* **19**(3–4), 280–285.

Wells, A. (1994) Multiple versions: American developments. *Cataloguing Australia,* **20**(1), 25–27.

Wiggins, R. (1993) The University of Minnesota's Internet Gopher system: a tool for accessing network-based electronic information. *Public-Access Computer Systems Review,* **4**(2), 4–60. [To retrieve this file, send the following e-mail message to listserv@uhupvm1.uh.edu: GET WIGGINS PRV4N2 F=MAIL.]

Wool, G.J. et al. (1993) Cataloging standards and machine translation: a study of reformatted ISBD records in an online catalog. *Information Technology and Libraries,* **12**(4), 383–403.

Wu, A.H. (1993) With characters: retrospective conversion of EastAsian cataloging records. *Information Technology and Libraries,* **12**(4), 427–431.

Xiao, Y. (1994) Faceted classigeation: a consideration of its features as a paradigm of knowledge organization. *Knowledge Organization,* **21**(2), 64–68.

Yee (1993) The concept of *work* for movmg image materials. *Cataloging and Classification Quarterly,* **18**(2), 33–40.

Yee (1994) Manifestations and near-equivalents: theory, with special attention to moving-image materials. *Library Resources and Technical Services,* **38**(3), 227–255.

Zeng, L. (1993a) Quality control of Chinese-language records using a rule-based validation system. Part 1: an evaluation of the quality of Chinese-language records in the OCLC OLUC database. *Cataloging and Classification Quarterly,* **16**(4), 25–66.

Zeng, L. (1993b) Quality control of Chinese-language records using a rule-based validation system. Part 2: a study of a rule-based data validation system for online Chinese cataloging. *Cataloging and Classification Quarterly,* **18**(1), 3–25.

Libraries in Western Europe: a bird's-eye view

7

Giuseppe Vitiello

National library policies

Remember the good old handbooks of librarianship, where libraries were considered to be the result of a dynamic confluence of a *biblios* and a *theca*. No author today would consider libraries in such a stand-alone way. The shift from collection-based to information access services has broken down walls, and is replacing paper by cables. Libraries are no longer introverted institutions purely serving their visitors; they are seen as essential links in the book and information chains. Moreover, no researcher in librarianship would describe them without having such a holistic approach in mind.

The concept of libraries as the crossroads between the information chain and the book market has received special recognition at international level. Tribute must be paid to UNESCO, which has pioneered such a move since 1977. The General Information Programme (PGI) established a framework for national information policies including all professionals, from librarians to information specialists, and from brokers to archivists. No librarian would deprecate, even now, the importance of programmes like UBC and UAP (respectively, Universal Bibliographic Control and Universal Availability of Publications), which still influence current library activities throughout the world (Chandler, 1982). UNESCO is not, however, the only international organization which has stressed the economic and cultural importance of libraries in the world of books and information.

In 1985, a Resolution of the Ministers of Cultural Affairs of the European Community stated that 'libraries [are] active agents within the information chain', and gave birth to the Library Programme of DG XIII of the European Commission; this is now included in the Fourth Framework Programme for Research and Technological Development (Commission of the European Communities, 1985; Commission of the European Communities, 1994). In 1992, a Recommendation issued at a meeting of the Council of Europe Ministers of Culture stated that 'a sufficiently dense network of bookshops and libraries' should be maintained throughout Europe 'to afford all readers ready access to books, whether for consultation or purchase' (Council of Europe, 1992). The Council of Europe programme 'Books, reading and translations', which was the main outcome of the conference, therefore attaches great importance to library activities provided in cooperation with all other actors along the book chain.

In spite of such authoritative pronouncements, however, libraries have very seldom been put at the core of the information or book policies of European national administrations. Their role as information providers has never been given any special consideration. In one important case, Germany, library policy is not even a national duty, and responsibility rests with the regional Länder. It is worth noting, however, that France has created a Directorate for Books and Reading, in which is concentrated all goverment authority related to the book world, from the publishing industry to the book trade, and from distribution to libraries (Pingaud and Barreau, 1982; Bertrand, 1994). This concept has found imitators in Spain (Dirección General del Libro y Bibliotecas) and in Portugal (Instituto Nacional do Livro e da Biblioteca Nacional).

It would be an exaggeration to say that an overall book policy, led by a central administration, produces a truly integrated approach to the book world by tightening up relations among its different actors. Nevertheless, the advantages are not to be underestimated. In France, an 'Observatory of Book Economics' has been established, which provides accurate statistics on the book trade and reading, and helps to define appropriate policies. Not less important is the fact that a *super partes* forum for all concerned is provided at ministerial level; libraries are given appropriate weight and can counterbalance the influence and the lobbying of other participants. In common sessions, a mutual understanding is more easily reached on controversial issues such as, for instance, copyright, lending right or free library services.

If libraries have become more visible in the book world, there is a long way to go before national administrations fully understand the role of libraries in the information chain. A few years ago, Denmark explored the possibility of general guidelines for a national information policy (Wille, 1991). A report reviewed information providers within the country; as yet, however, no decision has been taken to develop a coherent national information policy.

A practical test to see to what extent libraries play an important role in the book and information chains would be to assess their economic relevance in relation to other sectors. This is easier said than done. Fees and charges levied by libraries as a proportion of total library incomes are hard to assess. As libraries are non-profit organizations, their revenues are only occasionally recorded. A recent report on European library macro-statistics estimated, however, an income of 209 million ecus per year from fees and charges made by libraries for their own services, while the global library expenditure was 6.6 billion ecus per annum; both figures refer to the period 1986–1990, at constant 1990 prices (European Commission, 1995). More than ten per cent of the income (21 million ecus in 1991–92) is represented by the receipts of the British Library Document Supply Centre (BLDSC), by far the largest library document supplier in Europe (British Library, 1992).

By comparison, the European Union publishing industry totalled a turnover equal to 22.6 billion ecus in 1989 (Ancillani, 1992) and the income of the EU electronic information services industry has been estimated at 3.6 billion ecus in 1992 (Information Market Observatory, 1993). Raw figures, however, create crude comparisons. Libraries cannot be considered simply as electronic information providers; in the BLDSC figure quoted above, only half the demands come through non-postal methods of request.

Library networks in Europe

The increasing role of libraries in the information market depends on how library networks are going to develop in the future. Apart from being a formidable tool for cooperation between, and automation of, libraries, networks have undoubtedly boosted library activities. As they are today part of a virtually worldwide interconnected library, via the Internet, the demand for library services is expected to increase at remarkable speed.

Some years ago, in describing library networking in the USA, Hildreth (1987) gave a picture of a market which was flourishing in prosperity and maturity. At that time, four major networks (or 'utilities', as Americans call them) cabled libraries all over North America: OCLC, considered as a 'mass' utility (by far the largest network in the world); 'elitist' RLG, consisting almost exclusively of research libraries; and two regional networks, UTLAS and WLN. Of these, only UTLAS was private, whereas the other three were non-profit organizations. The picture painted by Hildreth has not changed greatly, except for OCLC, which has dramatically expanded overseas and whose specialized services find eager customers in Europe.

The situation in Europe is rather 'Balkanized', as Jacquesson (1992) put it. Library networks require, above all, continuing economic effort and user-friendly interfaces. As they are promoted by national administrations, it is no surprise that every European country, except for Luxembourg, has its own network, and very often more than just one. Networks have been implemented in various ways in Europe; in some cases, a top-down approach has led to abstract patterns of application not always meeting library needs. In categorizing these approaches, four options may be identified: the regional, the administrative, the sectoral and the library system-related option.

The regional approach is particularly notable in the UK and in Germany. In the UK, for instance, three regional networks, BLCMP, SWALCAP and VISCOUNT, were originally developed to connect libraries situated, respectively, in the Birmingham, South-East and South-West regions. In Germany, there are almost as many *Verbundsysteme* as there are *Länder*. Geographical scope is a strong argument for such developments, although new developments, like JANET (Joint Academic NETwork) in the UK, are starting to make it quite obsolete. Achievements are indeed varied and leave gaps in library development. Regional discrepancies may be fatal: SCOLCAP, a Scottish network, which had been long in existence, did not survive its restructuring. Even more sensational has been the disappearance of the Swiss network REBUS (Réseau des Bibliothèques utilisant Sibil), which was recently disbanded by its funding bodies.

The administrative option is typical in countries where a top-down approach for library policy and development is usual. France offers a good example. Theoretically, the Directorate of Books and Reading controls the national library, while the responsibility for public libraries rests with local authorities. In fact, because large funds are controlled at national level, the state maintains an extensive coordinating role in library modernization. For a long time, library automation has been implemented in isolation, with the Bibliothèque Nationale going on a different track form the research libraries. The new project of the Bibliothèque Nationale de France brings together some 20 libraries, mainly academic, for the purpose of cooperative cataloguing and acquisitions; it will lead eventually to the long desired automated French union catalogue (Renoult, 1994a). On the other hand, automation schemes devised by the (Sub)Directorate for Libraries within the Ministry of Education have resulted in remarkable achievements for university libraries, like the *Catalogue collectif national des publications en série*. The result of this top-down option is that the availability of networked information preceded the automation of library functions (Renoult, 1994b).

The sectoral approach is to be found especially in the Scandinavian countries, where the division between public and academic libraries is traditional. Not surprisingly, when automation was implemented, two distinct networks emerged. In Denmark, for example, all public libraries used a bibliographic utility, mostly based on records provided by the Danish National Bibliography. Only a political decision provoked the merging of the two networks some years ago (Højsgaard, 1993).

In recent years, there has been a tendency to interconnect libraries using the same automated library systems. Clubs of users spread out all over Europe. In Spain, for instance, libraries using similar systems (like ALEPH or Tinlib) share resources thanks to the compatibility of their automated functions (Mayol and Massisimo, 1993). Although this option may not be appropriate for all European countries, its easy implementation will certainly make such an approach more and more popular.

'The golden age of networks is now over', in the opinion of Jacquesson (1992, p. 176). Library networks were blossoming during the 1980s, when they represented a real advance in library automation and working methodologies. Nowadays, the growing costs of their maintenance and management, the concurrent development of laser technologies (as optical discs) and the emergence of integrated library systems working with standardized protocols on UNIX platforms have diminished their importance as bibliographic databases. They are no longer considered to be permanent, as the disappearance of REBUS, SCOLCAP and LIBRA (a French network) clearly illustrates. Their existence is in danger, unless they are able to provide new added-value services, as the following example will show.

The Dutch national network, PICA (Project for Integrated Catalogue Automation), was founded in 1969 in the Royal Library at The Hague, with the aim of improving cooperation between the national library and university libraries. By 1983, PICA had developed both as an online shared cataloguing system and as a local library system. The PICA Foundation, established in 1986, moved to its own building in Leiden in 1989 and signed agreements with the Deutsche Bibliothek and the Land of Lower Saxony. In 1992, the third generation of central and local library systems (PICA3 and LBS3) became operational; one year later, a new project for electronic document delivery was started (RAPDOC). Important features of PICA are hospitality and openness: with OLN (Open Library Network), it will be possible for end-users to find, and issue a request for, information required in their own libraries, as well as in other libraries participating in the OLN; they can also search, print and download information from the databases of PICA's Online Retrieval System. In due course, end-users will be able to search the Dutch Union Catalogue, to issue requests via PICA's Interlibrary Lending System and to connect to RAPDOC for document delivery by electronic mail.

What is the lesson to be learnt from this success story? Multiple services, standardization, diversification between central and local library systems and internationalization – these aspects seem to be PICA's recipes for success. Should other networks follow the same pattern of development if they want to survive?

The changing role of national libraries

The role of national libraries today is controversial. Without doubt, their visibility is increasing. In 1996, three of the largest libraries in the world – the British Library, Bibliothèque Nationale de France and Deutsche Bibliothek – will move to huge and functional new buildings. These are not the only examples. Admirable renovation work has been carried out on the 19th century building of the Spanish Biblioteca Nacional, and new and comfortable stores were built in Alcaló de Henares. The National Library in Norway has opened a branch in Mo i Rana, a town located far in the north, hundreds of kilometres from Oslo. Not only professionals are now aware of the importance of national libraries as guardians of the written memory of a nation.

The story of the Bibliothèque Nationale de France has become well known all over the world, albeit for extra-library reasons: the new premises will be located in four towers 79 metres high, with 395 kilometres of shelving. Reading rooms will accomodate no less than 3,500 people, while the annual intake should reach the impressive, and perhaps alarming, figure of two million physical units per year (Renoult, 1994a).

In order to keep up with such great expectations, budgets allocated to national libraries have been proportionally increased. In 1981–1985, the annual average expenditure of European national libraries was equivalent to 401.2 million ecus (expressed at 1990 constant prices), which represented 5.7% of the total budget allocated to libraries; during the years 1986–1990 expenditure grew by 0.9% per year and reached 423.6 million ecus (European Commission, 1995). It is worth noting that, like many other libraries, national libraries are developing forms of self-financing. The production of bibliographic services, once considered as a duty, has become a key aspect of the library industry, with a strong commercial component. National bibliographies are being diversified, both in scope and in media, and their issues often now include books, periodicals, academic dissertations, official publications, sound and/or music recordings, videos and films. As for kinds of media, it is not rare to see them published not only on paper, but also online, on diskette, in microform and as a CD-ROM. As a consequence, their economic value increased: in the UK, receipts for national bibliographic services reached £2,412,300 in 1991–92 (British Library, 1992). This considerable figure does not take into account income related to online records captured by other libraries.

Despite their willingness to soar, national libraries still remain at ground level. Their evident expansion, may be regarded as a result of three major factors. The first is the unrelenting increase in new publications. It has been estimated that the annual intake of monographs via legal deposit in European national libraries is about half a million titles; obligatory copy acquisitions have been cruising along at an annual growth rate of almost five per cent over the past ten years (Vitiello, 1994). The second factor is the deterioration of 19th and 20th-century imprints, which has continued at a devastating pace. Almost one quarter of old book collections is in danger of total destruction and needs urgent (and costly) preservation and conservation work. The third is the increasing number of customers, usually higher education students and teachers, which has boomed in the last 25 years. The example of France is an illustrative one: there were 97,000 students and 7,300 high school teachers in 1945; today, there are, respectively, two million and 58,000 (Renoult, 1994a). What is deemed to be an upheaval in national libraries may therefore prove to be only a twist. In trying to adjust themselves to the consequences of the information boom, national libraries are in fact only adapting their premises to the increased amount of material and number of users. This does not mean that their role is dominant in the new electronic environment. There is indeed evidence of an opposite trend.

Proof of this can be detected firstly in their organizational arrangements. In some cases, in spite of technological upheavals, this has not changed for many years. The French Bibliothèque Nationale had the same structure for years, not to say centuries, since Abbé Bignon, Librarian from 1719 to 1741, subdivided it into departments. Significantly, the new Bibliothèque Nationale de France has been divided into innovative administrative units, such as the Directorates of Public Services, Cultural Developments and Commercial Action and the Directorate of Scientific Developments and Networking. It is too early to say, however, whether this change corresponds to a shift from 'ownership strategy' to 'information access strategy'.

Further proof of the diminishing role of national libraries within the information community is that they are no longer considered, with museums and archives, as the sole guardians of the memory of a nation. The French Bibliothèque Nationale no longer holds 'Toute la mémoire du monde', as film-maker Alain Resnais put it in his 1956 documentary. Other institutions, like the British Film Institute in the UK, the Institut National de l'Audiovisuel and the Centre National de la Cinématographie in France, or the Filmarchiv in the Bundesarchiv, play a key role at national level. In countries where legal deposit of non-book material has been assigned to national libraries, like Spain and Portugal, librarians themselves are pleading for more realistic arrangements (Vitiello, 1994).

National libraries play a still less dominant role within national library systems. Only 20 years ago, the Director of the Bibliothèque Nationale was also in charge of all French libraries and maintained a coordinating function at a national level. Such a powerful position would be unthinkable today. Libraries are, in fact, developing in an autonomous way even in former socialist countries, where national libraries were playing a pivotal role. The widespread diffusion of the Internet is democratizing access to information and abolishing more or less formalized hierarchical levels among libraries. In conclusion, national libraries can still play an important role in the new electronic environment, but only if they are able to coordinate a national plan to access information (Line, 1989; Cornish, 1991).

Public libraries

What is the state of public libraries in Europe? A disturbing piece of literature has pictured libraries in great difficulties, trying to cope with lower budgets and reduced interest of public powers. Stagnation and, in some cases, even a negative trend characterize public library activities after the booming 1960s and 1970s. The question is: to what extent this picture is valid throughout Europe?

An overall overview of public library developments has been given in a very informative book edited by Poulain (1992). She convincingly asserts that public library policies are directly connected with reading habits: intensive reading makes libraries prosperous and, in return, a thriving library system encourages active reading practices. For countries having a level of literacy – and consequently, of library use – below European standards, this observation is significant.

An historical cartographer, Todd (1990), shows how processes of literacy and cultural practices have, for centuries, divided Western Europe in two, with northern regions taking the lead in the 18th century. Reading habits today seem to reflect this historical divide. The percentage of the population registered in public libraries is as high as 65% in Denmark and 58% in the UK, whereas smaller percentages are accounted in the Netherlands (30%), in Ireland (19.5%), in France (17%) and in Germany (between 10% and 15%) (Poulain, 1992). No information is given for Southern European countries; however, the low figure exhibited by the rich and literate region of Lombardy, in Italy (12% of the population) shows the gap that needs to be filled (Regione Lombardia, 1994). Number of patrons is not the only element which makes public libraries differ throughout Europe. For years, a common paradigm (in the sense of shared thoughts) among librarians has taken the Scandinavian/Anglo-Saxon model as a point of reference. Permeated as they are by a philosophy based on free access, non-ideological values in collection development and distribution, and a strong integration with the local environment, the Scandinavian/Anglo-Saxon libraries have been (and still remain) the ideal 'grand tour' for would-be librarians. Over the years, changes to the model have affected the scope of public library activities: large sections are now devoted to minority groups and children, or to the promotion of new library services, like business information. Universal admiration for Scandinavian and Anglo-Saxon libraries has not declined. Evidence for that may be found in the establishment, as early as 1975, of the Bibliothèque Publique d'Information in the Pompidou Centre in Paris, which overtly referred to the Anglo-Saxon model.

Although it could be applicable, this model is not current everywhere in Europe. In some countries, particular features in library developments, whether considered as historical heritage or as national peculiarities, are worth mentioning. A distinctive model, for instance, can be found in Germany, where a *dreigeteilte Bibliothek* ('threefold library') is found in many municipal libraries which have large rare book collections held in historical buildings. Such constraints do not make it possible to arrange library material in a way which closely relates to users' needs; therefore, a distinction is made between a 'far' (*Fernbereich*), a 'middle' (*Mittelbereich*) and a 'near' area (*Nahbereich*). In the *Fernbereich*, brittle books or lesser used items are stored in repositories not open to the public. The *Mittelbereich* is theoretically an open access section; nevertheless, as it holds very large collections, catalogues are needed in order to find a book. The *Nahbereich* is usually situated at the library's entrance; it holds commonly requested books and often displays new acquisitions; for this reason, it may be seen as the library window, which shows the cultural diversity and the social range of the library.

Many public libraries in Italy, Spain and Greece, which also hold rare book collections, have not equipped themselves for popular audiences and still seem to follow the old-fashioned model of the library as an intellectual entertainment for local scholars and intelligentsia. In these countries, a good library infrastructure is far from being considered a 'basic need' of the nation, as for instance it is in Finland. In fact, throngs of secondary school and higher education students, whose demand for books is not met by university and school libraries, use municipal libraries. Professionals speak sometimes of their libraries' 'improper use', but it is worth spelling out at this point that any theoretical model applied to libraries should adapt itself to reading practices and information needs existing at a local level, and not the opposite.

Portugal provides a good example of library policy which pragmatically has taken local needs into consideration. The central planning done by the former Instituto Português do Livro e da Leitura (now, Instituto do Livro e da Biblioteca Nacional) envisaged three kinds of libraries with a minimum standard for books and audiovisual materials in stock. Standards for library development are set according to the number of inhabitants and the availability of resources. The plan, which has been successfully implemented in several phases, is still in progress. Proudly, Portugal can now boast almost 100 brand new libraries, built up in cooperation with local authorities in less than ten years. In a country where illiteracy was still a scourge less than a quarter of a century ago, it is no surprise that such libraries are incredibly popular.

According to most recent statistics, expenditure on public libraries in Europe increased from some 2,812 million ecus in 1981 to 3,338 million ecus in 1990, where both figures are expressed at 1990 constant prices. The annual average increase represents, therefore, 1.9% over the decade. Some 58% of public library expenditure was spent on staff and 17.9% for acquisitions (European Commission, 1995).

Stagnation is the keynote for library budgets, but certainly not for library activities. Especially in Northern European countries, special services are being provided, such as reference services, business information, user-tailored information and community information. It is worth noting that some of the diversification has developed regardless of the free-of-charge principle, which was for years to be one of the basic tenets of public library provision. After animated discussions, the revised Unesco Manifesto for Public Libraries echoed these debates by making a distinction between basic services, which should be free of charge, and added-value services, for which libraries should be able to cover their working costs (Gattégno, 1994). Even before this change was accepted, librarians seem to have taken a pragmatic attitude, keeping principles on one side and using them only for theoretical debates. According to the statistics provided by the European Commission, fees and charges as a proportion of total library income have increased slightly from an average of 2.99% for the quinquennium 1981–1985 to 3.16% for the quinquennium 1986–1990. In the public library sector, however, they grew from some 90 million ecus in 1981 to

110 million ecus in 1990, where both figures are expressed at 1990 constant prices. This represents an annual average increase of 3.6%. The study suggests that this trend reflects 'an emergent "market philosophy", perhaps encouraged by a restraint on government fundings' (European Commission, 1995, p. 31).

Champions of a market philosophy would find even more arguments if their observations were limited to only a few countries. In the Netherlands, income from fees and charges represents 9.6% of the total expenditure on libraries; they have increased, however, by 31% from 1981–1985 to 1986–1990. In spite of a 'weak' increase of 19% from 1981–1985 to 1986–1990, fees and charges in Belgium now total 10% of the global library income. In the UK, data is more controversial: here, too, fees and charges increased by 19% from the first to the second quinquennium; self-financing incomes reach 2% of the overall library expenditure. Charging the users for value-added services, nevertheless, seems to be a trend only in a particular group of countries in Europe. Should historical cartography once again come to the aid of library economics?

Academic libraries

The concept of 'variable geometries' is certainly to be found in the field of academic libraries. Here, all combinations are to be seen: libraries for which responsibility lies with the state (Denmark, Portugal) or with regional governments (Germany); libraries having central coordinating bodies (France) or completely autonomous (UK, Italy, Spain); libraries participating in an exclusively academic network (Sweden, Norway) or sharing networks with public libraries (the Netherlands, Italy). It would be incorrect, however, to think that the more centralized the system, the better the cooperation between its parts. Evidence suggests the opposite. Take the UK, for example: universities are fully autonomous; the Librarian, therefore, generally receives a lump sum to be spent as he likes (in the context of the overall university policy). Yet, the tradition of cooperation has permeated library practices to such an extent that libraries themselves create their cooperative structures. The latest is CURL (Consortium of University Research Libraries), which brings together the most important research libraries in the country. The same can be said for the Netherlands, where the PICA network, apart from gathering a significant number of academic libraries, has a *de facto* national mission.

In general terms, academic libraries are today in an awkward position. On the one hand, benefiting from the tremendous impulse given worldwide to academic research by the development of electronic networking, they seem rather prosperous. On the other hand, their situation is becoming intolerable. Why is there such a paradox?

Universities have always been, and still are, higher education providers and research centres. This principle, however, is starting to be undermined. The unrelenting increase of the number of students, as well as the need to keep pace with changes in the labour market, are altering some universities' fundamental mission, with teaching activities becoming dominant over research. The process of diversification has profoundly changed educational courses and schemes. This is true in many countries. In 1950, for instance, there were no more than 3,500 French university teachers; in 1991–92 there were 55,400. One-third of these are schoolteachers or well qualified students temporarily employed by universities who have not completed a doctoral thesis or an academic dissertation (Renoult, 1994b, p. 129). In the UK, there is evidence that universities will be split in three groups: mainly teaching-oriented universities, mainly research-oriented universities, and mixed institutions, with teaching activities in many disciplines and research carried out in some (Law, 1994).

The number of universities and, as a consequence, of academic libraries has therefore grown tremendously in recent years. What used to be lower -level institutions (Instituts Universitaires de Technologie in France, Polytechnics in the UK, Gesamthochschulen in Germany) are now fully integrated into the university system. A rather astonishing case is Spain, where the number of library administrative units has increased by 29% from 1981–85 to 1986–1990 and service points are expanding at a rate of 7.5% every year. In the single region of Catalonia, five universities (out of eight) were founded in the last five years (Generalitat de Catalunya, 1993).

At a lesser rate, numbers of service points have increased all over the European Union. They were 4,421 in 1981–1985 and 4,874 five years later. What is stagnating is the budget allocated to academic libraries. Staff numbers increased by 9% in five years (from 34,544 to 37,798), yet costs grew at a higher rate (12%). Particularly striking is the gap between, on the one hand, the volume of library acquisitions (+13% in 1986–1990, or 20.3% of all libraries' expenditure) and, on the other, the expenditure for library acquisitions (+14,5%, corresponding to 31.6% of all libraries acquisition expenditure) (European Commission, 1995).

The following statement can then summarize the situation: greater expansion, fewer resources. Academic libraries have tried to optimize the use of information technologies, often successfully. In the UK, services provided by the academic network JANET are of essential concern to libraries. The distribution of bibliographic data provided via JANET by the Institute for Scientific Information through the University of Bath, for example, has 3,000 users every day. Networking is operating so successfully that its internationalization is already a fact: in the field of electronic document delivery, the project ION (Interlending Open Systems Interconnection Network) allows the interconnection of three networks (LASER in the UK, PICA in the Netherlands and PEB in France) for interlending services and electronic mail. ION is now to be followed by the project EDIL, which allows electronic document delivery between the same networks (Commission of the European Communities, 1994).

The high rate of development in technology can create new problems. On the eve of information superhighways, the rapid growth of electronic document services may raise questions about the copyright of documents and restrict rights of reproduction. This question is very far from being resolved, although at least three projects included in the DG XIII Library Programme (COPINET, DECOMATE, JUKE-BOX) tackle this very issue (Commission of the European Communities, 1994) and a study commissioned by the European Commission proposes some solutions and recommendations (Hugenholtz and Wisser, 1994). In Renoult's words, we can say that 'la définition des accords avec les auteurs et les éditeurs est peut-être davantage que les problèmes techniques, le problème majeur des années 1990' (Renoult, 1994b, p. 273).

Towards a European library policy?

Sincere Euro-advocates deem it possible that a convergence of national library policies can be realized through the European Commission Library Programme, included in the Framework Programme for Research and Technological Development. Their hope is well founded, for many reasons. First, the response to the programme has been enthusiatic. In all, 1,590 proposals were generated by the three calls launched by the Commission. This is by far the largest participation in any international programme devoted to libraries. Secondly, the Library Programme has not only involved national administrations, but also companies and private agencies, developing a convincing synergy between the public and the private sectors. It is a confirmation, albeit an unnecessary one, that libraries are today identified as important carriers of information and agents of development of communication technologies. Thirdly, the budget which has been allocated from 1991 to 1994, approximately 22 million ecus, is not negligable (Commission of the European Communities, 1994).

Successful though the Library Programme has been, the question of whether it can be the unique and most appropriate tool for the harmonization of European library policies still remains open to doubt. Such harmonization as a means to reduce regional disparities is explicitly mentioned as an objective of the programme, the others being the creation of modern library services, the introduction of information technologies, and standardization. Yet, after 49 proposals have been approved, and a further call for proposals has been issued in the Fourth Framework Programme, we still have no real evidence that library policies are on the way towards achieving the desired convergence.

The unequal participation of the Member States in the Library Programme certainly diminishes its European ambition. Some states, like the UK and Italy, are fairly well represented in the approved projects, with research libraries and private firms taking the lion's share. Also in a good position are the Netherlands, Denmark and Greece. More disappointing has been the participation of French and German libraries, despite both countries having a relatively good and effective library infrastructure. Such uneven involvement casts some doubts on the development of a Europe-wide library system - just as in the EU as a whole, harmonization of library policies is unthinkable without France and Germany.

The participation of the private sector, although encouraging, is not necessarily a real incentive to European library integration. As 'active agents within the information chain', libraries operate in the free information market; their objective, nevertheless, is not (and should not be) to make money. The library 'industry' still remains a government responsibility and the private sector can be integrated only for particular tasks and selected activities. Conversely, library policies, if any, are set at a national level and involve national and regional bodies. It is an illusion to think, therefore, that the convergence of national library policies will be a result of the natural evolution of the market and not a process resulting from intergovernmental cooperation.

A mutual, well-accepted misunderstanding, based on the exchange of means and ends, has been very productive for the success of the Programme: for DG XIII, libraries are just a means to facilitate the diffusion of the European telecommunication, industry and telematic services; for libraries, technologies are only a means to perform their informational, educational and cultural mission. Either because national administrations are unfamiliar with such logic, or are reluctant to think 'European', or else because of incompatibility between national and EU bureaucracies, it is a fact that some major actors on the library scene do not seem ready to play the European game. On the other hand, 49 proposals and more than 200 partners now involved in relatively small-size projects may also give the impression that investments are distributed in a haphazard way.

The future will tell whether large utilities, major libraries and public library networks, at the moment still national, are ready to expand and/or cooperate internationally. For the moment, the European union of libraries is certainly a possible target, but not for tomorrow.

References

Ancillani, G. (1992) *Il mercato del libro. Le prospettive dell'editoria nel mercato unico europeo.* Perugia: Protagon.
Bertrand, A-M. (1992) *Les bibliothèques municipales: acteurs et enjeux.* Paris: Éditions du Cercle de la Librairie.
British Library (1992) *Nineteenth annual report 1991–92.* London: British Library Board.

Bundesvereinigung Deutscher Bibliotheksverbande (1994) *Bibliotheken '93. Strukturen-Aufgaben-Positionen.* Berlin/Göttingen: Bundesvereinigung Deutscher Bibliotheksverbande.

Chandler, G. (1982) *International and national library and information services 1970–1980.* Oxford: Pergamon Press.

Commission of the European Communities (1985) *Official Journal,* no. 271, 23 October.

Commission of the European Communities (1994) *Libraries Programme. Telematic systems in areas of common interest 1990–1994: libraries. Synopsis of projects (Release: CfP '91, CfP '92 and CfP '93).* [Luxembourg]: Commission of the European Communities, Directorate-General XIII – Telecommunications

Cornish, G. (1991) *The role of national libraries in the new information environment.* Paris: UNESCO. (PGI-91/WS/4).

Costers, L. (1994) Des bibliothèques universitaires en réseau: l'expérience des Pays-Bas. In: D. Renoult (ed.) *Les bibliothèques dans l'université.* Paris: Éditions du Cercle de la Librairie, pp. 308–320.

Council of Europe (1991) *Reading habits in Europe. Moscow Round Table – April 1991 – about the participation in cultural life in Europe.* Strasbourg: Council of Europe.

Council of Europe (1992) *Seventh Conference of European Ministers responsible for Cultural Affairs (Paris, 15–16 October 1992). Reading, books and publishing in Europe report.* Strasbourg: Council of Europe.

European Commission. *Library economics in Europe. An update - 1981–9.* By Phillip Ramsdale. Luxembourg: Directorate - General Telecommunications, Information Market and Exploitation of Research, 1995.

Gattégno, J. (1994) Unesco Public Library Manifesto. *Libri,* **44**(2), 164–170.

Generalitat de Catalunya (1993) *Les biblioteques de les universitats públiques de Catalunya en els anys 90.* Barcelona: Servei de Publicacions de la Universitat Autònoma de Barcelona.

Hildreth, C. (1987) *Library automation in North America: a reassessment of the impact of new technologies on networking.* München: Saur.

Hojsgaard, U. (1993) Danish academic and special libraries: the manifold and the one. *Nordinfo-Nytt,* **15**(1), 3–26.

Hugenholtz, B. and Wisser, D. (1994) *Copyright problems of electronic document delivery: a comparative analysis. Report to the Commission of the European Communities DG XIII.* (Unpublished report).

Information Market Observatory (1993) *Strengths and weaknesses of electronic information services in the European Union.* Luxembourg: Commission of the European Communities. (IMO Working Paper 93/6 Final).

Jacquesson, A. (1992) *L'information des bibliothèques.* Paris: Editions du Cerele de la Librairie.

Law, D. (1994) Les bibliothèques universitaires du Royaume Uni. In: D. Renoult (ed.) *Les bibliothèques dans l'université.* Paris: Editions du Cerele de la Librairie, pp. 299–307.

Line, M.B. (1989) *National library and information needs: alternative means of fulfilment, with special reference to the role of national libraries.* Paris: UNESCO. (PGI-89/WS/9).

Mayol, C. and Massisimo, A. (1993) Libraries and librarianship in Spain. *IFLA Journal,* **19**(2), 131–146.

Pingaud, B. and Barreau, J-C. (1982) *Pour une politique nouvelle du livre et de la lecture.* Paris: Dalloz.

Poulain, M. (1992) (ed.) *Les bibliothèques publiques en Europe*. Paris: Éditions du Cercle de la Librairie.

Regione Lombardia (1994) *Guida alle biblioteche comunali della Lombardia. Censimento al 1992*. Milano: Editrice Bibliografica.

Renoult, D. (1994a) La Bibliothèque Nationale de France. *Documentation et Bibliothèques*, Juillet-Septembre, 139–144.

Renoult, D. (1994b) (ed.) *Les bibliothèques dans l'université*. Paris: Éditions du Cercle de la Librairie.

Todd, O. (1990) *L'invention de l'Europe*. Paris: Seuil.

Vitiello, G. (1994) *Il deposito legale nell'Europa comunitaria. Legal deposit throughout the European Communities*. Milano: Editrice Bibliografica.

Wille, N. E. (1991) A framework for a national information policy, with special regard to libraries and information services. *Nordinfo-Nytt*, **14**(2), 19–24.

Librarianship and information work in Central and Eastern Europe

8

Péter Szántó
and Tibor Futala

During 1989, many countries left the Soviet zone of influence, and, within the Soviet Union itself, trends towards independence and separation began to develop. Not even the political elite could realistically estimate the enormous difficulties involved in the historical transformation that lay ahead. Many were convinced that, after demolishing ideological barriers and party bureaucracy, and when a series of peaceful reforms had been implemented, a period of growth would result that would bring about a substantial improvement in the general living conditions and standards of society.

Political naivety reached many different professional circles, causing unfounded expectations. Librarians and information specialists were no exception to this credulous euphoria. Many were happy to witness an end to ideological constraint, to see the liberation of collection building, an end to directives from above and to the prohibition or limitation of online searches, the cancellation of the technical-technological embargo, and, in general, they welcomed the opportunity to concentrate on meeting user needs.

Although no office, centre or organization has subsequently tried to prevent the realization of these promises, the financial resources necessary to implement them soon vanished. This resulted in every country of the region being faced by a serious crisis, which manifested itself partly in a substantial decline in the number of institutions and partly in a devaluation of professional values.

As recorded in specialist literature, the years 1991 and 1992 were the most crisis-hit, while 1993 and 1994 raised certain hopes of survival and rebirth. For example, it is evident that librarianship and information work in the region has to some degree approached that of the developed countries, with regard to the methods, skills and technologies applied.

The chapters of *Librarianship and Information Work Worldwide 1995* will certainly report on these developments. Nevertheless, it will be useful to describe some characteristic features of librarianship and information work in this region. We hope it will help to better other people's understanding of what is happening in Central and Eastern Europe, and to enrich the forms and opportunities of cooperation between the East and the West.

The demise of the institution

Within socialist librarianship and information activity, the most important measure was the number of institutions. This helped to ensure an increase in the number of readers and users in the year-on-year statistics, and an increase in turnover. In official terms, this meant an increasingly effective contribution to the development of socialist man. Until the collapse of the socialist system, these institutions were able to operate and function effectively as gatekeepers of information. The resulting elimination and/or restriction of their activities was not therefore painless. The following pages describe how this process took place in each of the countries in the region.

The closure of institutions has been most pronounced in the former Soviet Union. The convening board of the heads of large libraries in the Russian Federation found it necessary to express its protest against such actions as early as April 1992. They demanded that the state should cease the further closure of the tens of thousands of libraries, and the wasting of holdings, and accept a plan of action to maintain at least the present standard (Rezolyutsiya, 1992).

According to Kuz'min (1993a; 1993b), head of the Library Department at the Ministry of Culture, of the 336,000 libraries in existence during the Soviet period, 62,000 public libraries, 41,000 school libraries, 20,000 trade union libraries, 3,000 academic libraries and 8,400 special libraries (or, about 40%) have survived. The first group to be threatened by closure were the trade union libraries, but, considering the excessive number of libraries in the Soviet period, Kuz'min questions whether all the endangered libraries should be saved. He favours the saving of collections rather than institutions.

No data is yet available on how many institutions in the scientific-technical information system have ceased to exist. It is known, however, that in the Russian Federation there are just 158 information centres performing efficiently, most of them being large libraries or branch-level centres. The deterioration of the established system was described by Kedrovskiĭ (1992):

> ... this system has practically ceased to exist, with the related normative documents becoming ineffective. Information contacts are being severed, and the channels of financial maintenance frozen. Individual institutions are being liquidated. The acquisition of international scientific and technical information sources is coming to an end, while the quantity of data provided on R & D and other scientific and technical research activities in Russia is decreasing drastically.

If these uncontrolled processes continue, specialists will shortly lack all the sources necessary to judge the value of current science and technology, and to objectively evaluate the quality of new scientific, technical and industrial products.

We can add that the Soviet-directed International Information System on Science and Technology is also a thing of the past.

The professional literature reports infrequently on the current situation in the Commonwealth of Independent States (CIS) and in those countries that are no longer part of the Russian Federation. In summary, it can be said that the libraries and information institutions of these states have suffered even greater hardship than their Russian counterparts in becoming self-dependent, while also experiencing the collapse of the Russian-language 'information store'. Appraisals for the extent of the losses of this institutional sphere only started in 1993 (Shatberashvili, 1993).

In other Central and East European countries, the number of institutions has also been reduced. Data is available for some countries.

In Bulgaria, the number of libraries at the end of 1992 was 8,587: 760 less than in 1989. Among those libraries closed, 494 were special libraries and information centres within industrial firms, while only 31 were public libraries (*chitalište*). The number of librarians has also decreased by approximately 2,000 since 1989; at the end of 1992, their number had fallen to 9,930. Acquisitions budgets were similarly reduced (Yanakieva, 1994).

In the Czech Republic, just 3% of public libraries had officially closed by the end of 1992 (there were 8,364 in 1990), but the number of librarians declined by almost 9%. District libraries were handed over to the self-governing authorities of towns. They became town libraries, and district library networks therefore ceased to function. The nine state research libraries have been maintained since 1991 by the Ministry of Culture; it is expected that, after the much postponed administrative reform, they will be transformed into provincial libraries. Collection development is a concern not only for public libraries, but, to an even greater degree, for research and special libraries. While in principle they can now acquire materials freely, they are restricted in practice by the lack of resources. What is more, they are forced to limit their interlending activities because of the high costs of postage. Frequently, they cannot even accept gifts because of customs duties. Among the research and special libraries, more than 200 institutions were closed during 1993, and presumably the same fate awaits most of those in the medical library establishment. Academic libraries (128 units with holdings of over ten million and a total staff of 636) may feel slightly more secure. Company and factory libraries belonging to the Sci-Tech and Economic Information System fell victim to privatization. Only branch-level information centres have continued to operate. The most highly qualified staff members have found jobs in the emerging information industry (Zpráva, 1993; Burgetová, 1994; Rupešová, 1994).

The Polish library community accepted decline without remorse, entering the new era of public libraries with the following words: 'There will be no funeral . . . '. If these libraries could endure three successive shocks in the recent past (in 1952, their integration into 'people's education', being torn from the system of school and educational libraries; later, the National Library giving up central methodological guidance and development; then in 1975, the ending of district networks), they will surely survive this latest episode (Burakowski, 1992). It appears that indeed they have. In 1990, the number of public and branch libraries was 10,270; in 1991, it was 9,770, and in 1993 it was 9,605. However, the so-called 'library service points' (*punkty biblioteczne*), serving small communities, have suffered greatly. Of the former total of 17,000, 68% had ceased operation by 1993. The number of company and trade union libraries stood at 580 at the end of 1993, but, on the national level, only 380 have any chance of survival (Przybyszewski, 1993; Kuźmińska 1994). The Polish information system for science, technology and organization, SINTO, ceased to exist in May 1990, together with its two leading institutions, the CIINTE and the Centrum INTE (Sordylowa, 1991). Research libraries (approximately 1,200), including the National Library, academic libraries and the libraries of the Academy of Sciences and of research institutions, saw change characterized by reorganization rather than by closure (Sordylowa, 1993). Reorganization has inevitably caused some confusion, but this has been eliminated by the diligent work of recent years (Sójka, 1993).

The number of Hungarian public libraries (maintained by self-governing authorities) in 1988 was 4,410, while the number of company (trade-union) libraries stood at 4,381. In 1993, the number of public libraries had fallen to 3,794, while company libraries had declined more drastically to 1,470. However, while the decline in the number of public libraries had slowed (to just 1.7%, compared with the previous year), the decline of company libraries continued more rapidly (at 25.7%, compared with the previous year). All other operational parameters for these two sectors indicate that public libraries have survived the crisis, while most of those at company workplaces have not, or were compelled to change their functions (Statisztikák, 1993-1994). This change may either mean that the library of the workplace must become a 'public library', or must integrate into a more comprehensive, cultural institution of the trade union, as was the general practice prior to 1945 in Hungary (Skaliczki, 1994).

Special libraries in Hungary with national responsibilities have not, by and large, been threatened with closure, with a few exceptions. Their concern about acquisition has, however, increased (Karbach, 1993). The major research and academic libraries of the country have not only survived, but are regarded as core libraries and mediators of a projected National Specialist Information System. Consequently, their development is actively encouraged (Elózetes, 1994).

In Slovakia, the reform of public libraries, and the creation of self-governing authorities, took place in 1991. District libraries, however, were not restructured in the same way, having been 'spared' by the Ministry of Culture, which preferred to keep them under closer control. Until 1993, the decline in numbers or closure of public libraries and their branches barely exceeded 4%. Nevertheless, compared with 1990, libraries have been closed in 57 settlements, with the number of full-time librarians dropping back by 163; for 418 volunteers, no salaries were payable. Five hundred and forty-eight libraries (20% of the total) did not receive any financial support for acquisitions for a period of two years, while 45 libraries received no general maintenance funds whatsoever. As a result, their buildings deteriorated. The number of registered readers (685,000) is a mere 64% of the figure two years earlier, while the number of loans (eighteen million units) is just 54.5% of the former figure (Kalinová, 1992, 1993).

The 89 town libraries in Slovakia are in a slightly better position, as they rely heavily on sponsorship. They constitute just 3.32% of public libraries, although they have 14.1% of the total holdings, and provide services for 16.75% of registered readers. More than 20% of these libraries participate in regional cooperation schemes (Kalinová, 1994).

As in all other countries of the region, the number of scientific and technical libraries and information workplaces has decreased in Slovakia. In 1989, there were 223, whereas in 1993 there were 109. This seems to be a long-term trend, with only selected libraries in research institutes having any chance of survival (Segešová, 1994).

Professional reaction to the transformation of Central and Eastern Europe's libraries

The trends towards closure and decline have been accompanied by a lively professional debate. The themes of articles have varied considerably. Among them one finds protests and rejections, retrospective explanations of intent, criticisms, radical proposals, pragmatism and ethical warnings. Some characteristic examples are described in this section.

Many protests and rejections have been directed toward those who like to reminisce on past glories and achievements as they face the present-day difficulties. In the former Czechoslovakia, for example, several librarians still recall that a unified library system had existed and that it is now being distorted because of the social-economic upheavals. Who saw a unified system here?, asks Matoušová (1992). Even bibliographic description could not be unified, not to mention classification systems. Not even mutual use and exchange of catalogue cards could be realized. Unified librarianship existed only on paper, not in reality.

Another example is the decline of the scientific, technological and economic information system (UTEI), which several professionals claim is causing enormous damage to the nation's wealth. This kind of rhetoric is often uttered by those who acquired 'socially advantageous' jobs in the former system. Many of them obtained degrees by conducting literature searches using state funds, even though that was illegal. In the scientific, technical and economic information centres, activities were often many-sided, although user needs were nearly always forgotten. The Slovak author, Vontorčik (1993), remembers the knights of 'good old times' and the present 'hostile propagandists' with similar anger and irony.

The Polish author Sordylowá (1991), however, regards the scientific, technical and economic information systems as having had two characteristic deficiencies from their very onset in the late 1940s. They did not consider the information needs of the various user groups, and they duplicated the tasks of libraries, while neglecting many fundamental tasks, such as the dissemination of scientific and technical knowledge.

The founding 'father' of centralized library systems, and his colleagues (Serov, 1993; Serov et al., 1993), later tried to explain themselves in response to the accusations of leading experts and former supporters of the centralized system. The founders argued that centralized library systems should be maintained because there is no alternative for the supply to small communities and those living in housing estates. Several new problems should, however, be addressed, in the field of financing and in the modernization of technological support. What is needed is a clear definition of concepts: centralization in librarianship is not identical to the centralization of networks.

Adamiec (1993) responded, perhaps rather cynically, but succinctly, to the objections of the Polish Society of Bibliology and the Polish Reading Society (Stanowisko, 1993) to the closure of libraries and the disposal of collections. Adamiec believes it is not worth grieving over the closure of libraries, since it has eliminated undesirable marginalization. Similarly, there is no point in sympathizing with those citizens who are no longer within reach of a library service, when they have not needed one for decades. The materials many citizens would like to have seen were not held by their local libraries, and those that were, were high-quality works in which many users had little interest. It is perhaps embarrassing that for decades 'experts' assumed that library users were interested in such works, which were held in their millions.

The head of the Cultural Department in the Wrocław town office was right in many respects (Zlikwidować, 1992) when he proposed the privatization of branch libraries and the allocation of state funds for library use. Naturally, he provoked a storm of protest from the local librarianship elite; however, he pointed out that the sum total of these measures would cost less than the previous budgetary support.

The guidance given to those involved in acquisitions differed little between Hungary and Poland, since the recreational function of the library was recognized fairly early on. An essay by Ladosné Varjú (1994) argued that the role of Hungarian public libraries has always been that of educator, and that works that seemed to be apt for this purpose had to be acquired. As a result, few resources remained to meet local needs, particularly in village libraries, and thus the traditional role of the librarian to monitor and meet the needs of the user could not be met. An identical situation applied in Slovakia and Hungary (Seršiková, 1993).

Kuz'min's (1993b) observations of the past, present and future prospects for Soviet libraries (and in practice therefore for all the former socialist countries) are finally worth noting. In Russia, there are many towns where the population does not exceed 100,000. In each of them there are at least 100 libraries, based on the principle that every Soviet citizen should find a library within a ten-minute walking distance from home. Local governments are disinclined to replace these many small libraries, which neatly correspond with the aims of Soviet cultural policy, with a lesser number of real libraries more able to perform a full range of functions. Soviet cultural policy's aim had been to have the most important works propagated in as many places as possible, and materials which broadened the vision in as few places as possible. While today's media is stimulating a freer and more accessible post-Soviet environment, many libraries, particularly those in the rural areas, still perpetuate the former narrow-minded, totalitarian mentality.

Almost 60% of library users, however, are not satisfied with library services. Some say that the Soviet system did not cater for their needs, while others feel the same is true of today's system. Both statements, however, exaggerate and, at the same time, simplify.

The representatives of the old regime were aware of the need for libraries: their task was to serve Communist propaganda. Libraries were considered to be gateways between information and people. They were expected to control and direct the interest of the reader in the appropriate direction. Naturally, they were supported accordingly.

Even today's elite in librarianship and information work still do not see the social contribution that libraries can make. They fail to recognize in them the guarantee of democracy, self-government and stability. Librarianship and information work in Russia is currently undergoing a critical phase of development; however, this is not the comatose state before death, but rather the weakness of a healing patient. Recuperation will follow.

The preparation of legal regulations

In all sectors of the economies of the former socialist countries, cutbacks in funding and services have been made. While many are perhaps willing to accept change, a large number of professionals wish that at least library and information services could be preserved, and still operate in the good old-fashioned way.

Even in the information profession, time does not stand still, however. For this reason and others, a new library and/or library-information law is being formulated in most of the Central and Eastern European states. A large number of preliminary draft laws are known to have been prepared by 1992; initial reading, however, indicates that most new laws are in fact very similar to the socialist laws that they were intended to replace. In particular, each law is generally intended to cover all types of institutions so that the state guarantees the operation of the largest possible number of institutions, allowing the network organization and network hierarchy to be maintained as well as possible.

Preliminary drafts were followed by others, because it became clear that some requirements could not be met and some areas could not be covered by a single law. This is why the comment by Szántó (1993) is correct, in that 'one law is insufficient' in the information field. Presumably the standpoint that criticizes the legal regulations in preparation which oppose 'unity of librarianship and information work' is also correct. Karvalics (1995, in press) concludes that library and information activity is always an integral part of a specific subject field, or a profession, and not something created by outside forces. As a consequence, library and information-related matters within individual subject fields and professions should be codified within their respective frameworks of law. Unfortunately, the recently passed laws on the Academy of Sciences, on higher education, and on education and culture in many countries do not meet this requirement (Howorka, 1993; Szántó, 1993). Instead, they regard the issue of libraries and information centres as matters of secondary importance.

In spite of the efforts to revise legal regulations, not a single country in the region has been able to introduce a comprehensive new law on librarianship or information work. This is not least because of the uncertainties about direction of services, the designation of duties, and the social and administrative affiliations that exist and result from librarianship and information work. This is why (as recorded in the professional literature of 1994) most countries have preferred to shelve the texts of draft laws: other issues have assumed greater importance. Some of these issues may be the starting point for future laws (e.g. in Georgia), and some are simply ignored (e.g. in Hungary). In the latter case, the faith tends to be in professional understanding rather than in legal regulations.

In spite of these delays, there have been some developments in regulating certain aspects of legal frameworks, particularly regarding legal deposit copies and the status of certain libraries. Illustrative examples from individual countries are offered to demonstrate this.

By far the largest number of draft laws and concepts in the region have been prepared in the Russian Federation; for the most part, during 1992. Generally, those in the field of scientific and technical information have dealt with library and information activities separately. The first draft law (Kedrovskiĭ, 1992) was entitled 'The law of the Russian Federation regarding the Russian State Sci-Tech

Information System' (Zakon, 1992a), which declared that 'the scientific and technical information resources of the state are constituted by the activities of all information institutes, centres, and libraries which generally comprise the State Sci-Tech Information System'. It was stated that these centres and libraries should achieve a predetermined level of domestic and international resources, sufficient for up-to-date information supply to scientists and other specialists. These resources should be acquired using the state budget, and will permanently remain under society's ownership. They cannot be privatized.

With a Presidential Decree, dated 22 January 1992, the Russian State Library (Rossiiskaya gosudarstvennaya biblioteka - RGB), based on the Lenin Library, was established. While such a measure had been generally expected, the related measures were not; these included the dismissal of former management, the appointment of a new one, the creation of a 'dissolving committee' with an undefined task, and the publication of the Schneierson collection. All this caused anger and consternation both within the library and outside (in the Supreme Council), which could be calmed only gradually (RGB, 1992).

In April 1992, an all-Russian conference was organized on the use of information technology and for the development of the domestic information industry. A proposal was outlined and the concept was to be realized during the period 1993 to 1995 (Tereshchenko, 1992a, 1992b).

By the summer of 1992, a draft law had been prepared for all libraries within the Russian Federation, including those maintained by the state and free of charge to users, and also the 'many other types of libraries' known to exist. The draft law includes the obligations of libraries to meet and fulfil a basic element of human rights (Proekt, 1992a). This draft recently successfully went through its first committee hearing. The first task had been completed, as Panova (1994) remarked.

In the early autumn of 1992, the Russian Ministry of Scientific, Higher Educational and Technology Policy (hereafter Minnauki), published a comprehensive report on the state policy regarding information resources (Razrabotka, 1992). The report considers the various sources of information available and indicates their respective location. It also differentiates between cultural centres supported by the state budget (central large libraries, social science information institutes) and non-profit institutions (VINITI, VNTICentr, NPO Poisk, VIMI and so on). The State decided to absolve itself from all responsibility for other institutions, declaring that these would all now operate according to market forces.

The Russian Federation's draft law on all-Russian national libraries (Proekt, 1992b) was written at the same time as this draft report. It differentiates between national libraries with full rights, and the so-called 'para-national' libraries, which embody those institutes known formerly as 'special libraries with national responsibilities'. According to the draft law, these libraries, as yet still unnamed, would be granted a distinctive place in the library system.

In November 1992, a draft document was published in the Russian Federation on information and information protection (Zakon, 1992b). Its scope excluded information on the mass media, information on arts, on historical monuments, on copyright issues and on patents. By the end of 1992, a detailed version of the Minnauki concept had been prepared by its committee (Chernyi et al., 1993).

The efforts of 1992, which had failed in almost every respect *ante portas*, were largely discontinued in 1993 and 1994. The library law was submitted to the relevant parliamentary committee; only a single decree was published as a result, by the Council of Ministers on the statute of the Russian State Library (Polozhenie, 1993). Its main recommendation, with acquisitions in mind, was that, in addition to the domestic imprint and Russia-related foreign literature, the Library should collect literature on the former Soviet Union and on other Soviet issues.

Among the CIS States, Georgia is still pondering a development concept for librarianship and information work which would assign a major role to the country's libraries (Chkhenkeli, 1994). In the Ukraine, the re-regulation of legal deposit copies was put on the agenda (Solyanik, 1994). Libraries insist on maintaining the regional and local legal deposit system. (The alternative within the CIS was that a total of 300 copies should have been deposited for each printed work.)

In Bulgaria, a special committee of the Association of Bulgarian Librarians and Information Specialists is presently working on a new library law (Yanakieva, 1994). A recent law decreed the scope and activity of eight state cultural institutions that are to be of national importance, including the Cyrill and Methodius Library. These institutions are to be funded separately from the budget of the Ministry of Culture (Postanovlenie, 1994).

In the Czech Republic, the National Library began to prepare a new library law almost on the day after the 'Velvet Revolution'. Efforts were proceeding well until the Ministry of Culture decided to assume responsibility. This meant that the former advocates of the 'unified library system' could once again enforce their will. For this reason, the Ministry of Economic Policy and Development produced a proposal under which public information services would 'form a part of the state information system of the Czech Republic, and as such create defined areas of information available to the public and to other economic centres' (Koncepce, 1992). The law received full support from progressive professionals. The laws to be passed in this manner clearly differentiated between basic institutions (for the most part public libraries), and special institutions and agencies; the latter included the National Library, the national information centre, supply agencies, the depository libraries and others.

Following this, a draft law on public libraries was prepared, consigning their care and maintenance to the public purse, and making them compulsory in places where the population exceeds 2,000. The public library law intends to operate within the legal framework defined by the present draft laws on the country's state information system, on the operation of information systems and of public information systems and on the protection of the information within these systems. In addition, the text assumes a separate law will follow on the National Library, and that other laws, e.g. the laws on higher education and archives etc., now in preparation, will cover further library and information activities. It also assumes that national legal regulations will be issued on interlibrary services, on the central registration of foreign publications, and on realizing various aspects of the public library law (Pilař, 1992; Pilař and Hemola, 1992). According to Burgetová (1994), this draft is awaiting hearings, following the reform of state administration.

Other legal regulations are still less certain, such as the law on legal deposit. A ministerial decree of 1964 ordered the deposit of 80 copies, a figure which could not be met under the pressures of a market economy. Legislators therefore accepted a more modest law (ordering the deposit of just sixteen copies) in 1991; however, within six weeks, this had been replaced by an even more modest ruling. The latter no longer includes serials, and calls for an end to the legal deposit copies in the so-called branch libraries. It does, however, extend its coverage to audio, visual and audio-visual materials (Suchánková, 1992). The most recently submitted law annuls regional legal deposit copies, and makes no proposal concerning compensation for the thirteen libraries which formerly received legal deposit. Now, only three copies are deposited; the financial resources involved constitute at least 300-400,000 crowns a year per library. Parliament may have accepted this law which for many libraries appears unjust; however, there has been no reference to it yet in the professional literature (Povinny, 1994).

It is the Poles who are most insistent on the enactment of a new library law. Its supporters acknowledge that an all-inclusive law may not be necessary: one on public libraries would suffice. An adequate legal framework already exists (or will do shortly) for all those libraries which are not public, such as the libraries of the Academy of Sciences, academic libraries, libraries of educational institutions, and so on. These arguments are mistaken, however, for two reasons. First, such widespread regulations as have been referred to also cover public libraries, as in the law referring to cultural activities. Secondly, the sketchy and sometimes contradictory regulations that have been introduced do not constitute the kind of comprehensive library and information system that is necessary for developed countries (Howorka, 1993).

The draft law is increasingly focusing on public libraries, indicating that (a) self-governing authorities are now obliged to maintain public and school libraries; (b) the voivodship [county] library inspects libraries maintained by self-governing authorities within the county, and (c) the system itself is made up of other types of libraries and information institutions which will interact and cooperate (Biliński and Kuźmińska, 1994; Howorka, 1994; Kuźmińska 1994).

A fifth sub-version of this draft recently had to be published, because, instead of undertaking the review of librarianship themselves, the Scientific Research Council assigned the duty to another body: the Council of the National Library-Information System. Unnecessary delay therefore means that preparations are progressing far more slowly than many would like to see (Ustawa, 1994).

In Hungary, a new library draft law was prepared in several versions, in order to encourage reaction from the profession. Consequently, the draft became more concise, until in 1993, consensus was reached on its content. The law would refer only to public libraries maintained by self-governing authorities, the national library/libraries, the national central services and the public research libraries (special libraries with national responsibilities) (Papp, 1993; Szántó, 1993). In 1994, however, all activity regarding the new law came to an end, and many professionals still await its proposals.

The proposals for the revised law on legal deposit were also accompanied by much discussion. In 1986, the proposal that libraries should have just ten copies, instead of the former sixteen, caused great indignation (Sonnevend, 1994). The present draft, however, which proposes the deposit of between one and five or seven copies has caused even greater unfavourable reaction among the library community. The question again arises as to whether libraries are going to be compensated for their losses (Gajtkó, 1994).

Instead of introducing the new library law, however, the 'reformers' have been distracted by other issues. For example, the aim is now to set up a National Special Library and Information System. Having been commissioned by the Secretariat of the Commission of Science Policy at the Office of the Prime Minister, its key characteristics are to be as follows (Előzetes, 1994):

- development of the system based on the current library network;
- access to public databases built on a continuous basis using standard methods;
- for the system to be connected into similar national and international systems; and
- for widespread participation in the work of international library, information and documentation organizations, in order to ensure and encourage compatibility.

It is of the utmost importance that institutions in this system should be connected by an up-to-date data transmission network, facilitating internal and external communication with access to international services. Such a system would be feasible with the use of the IIFP (Information Infrastructure Development Programme), which, as described by Bakonyi (1993), is the only project already established which has continued to exist and become more efficient. Its main purpose is to establish a nationwide computer network and a related infrastructure for the research community. As the system accepts any library as a mediator or a recipient of services, it serves not only to perform library and information tasks, but also public education functions.

The Slovaks have for some years regarded their Integrated Library-Information System (IKIS), which operates together with various cooperative associations of libraries (KZK), as something of an extension to the 'unified library system'.

Indeed, it may be a credible starting point for an up-to-date library-information system (Kalinová *et al.*, 1993; Integrovaný, 1994). However, as a result of the changes in the political system, personal problems have begun to appear around the IKIS system (Katuščák, 1992).

Meeting the needs of ethnic and national minorities

A particular feature of the region's countries is the complicated issue of national minorities. Supplying these groups with literature in their mother tongue has always to a large degree depended on politics. The general trend (in Central Europe until the early 1970s, and until more recently in the former Soviet Union) was that the minorities should get accustomed to the use of literature in the primary language of the state. This happened so unobtrusively that even librarians did not realize that they were being manipulated in this respect. An investigation in 1990 showed that in several republics, however, a very high ratio of the inhabitants still read their mother tongue (Dan'shina, 1992).

Certain government policies and actions, however, have caused whole nations to cease to exist. For example, the Ruthenians of Sub-Carpathia were declared to be Ukrainians, and, as a result, Ruthenian literacy and book and journal publishing ceased. The same happened not only in the Soviet Union but also in the Comecon countries. However, this particular small Slavic language did survive and has developed in certain parts of Yugoslavia, and within groups of Ruthenians who emigrated overseas (Czene, 1994).

Within the region, frequently denied minority groups existed in many places. For example, Belorus librarians became conscious after the changes in the political system that almost 420,000 Polish people lived in their country, and that it would now seem appropriate to supply them with literature in their mother tongue (Demeshko and Krotyuk, 1992). The total number of Polish people living in the CIS countries can actually be put at around 1,126,000.

It goes without saying perhaps that the supply of literature to national minorities in their mother tongue has always been considered an internal affair, since the opportunity to arrange the supply from outside rarely existed. Since the political changes, many of the countries where minorities are known to exist have tried to introduce a wider choice of books and journals (Hodossy, 1993; Okálová, 1993). For libraries, supplies of minority language material have multiplied several fold. This growth has partly resulted through local resources, and partly from donations from libraries in the mother country (Rexa, 1993; Lukáts, 1994).

Hungarians are the largest national minority in the region, and it is evident that they have adapted themselves very quickly to many different forms of support following the political changes. A basis for this is in acquiring the holdings of closed (mainly public) libraries. Another is through a foundation specializing in this (Arató, 1993). In the latter case, the libraries of Hungarian minorities can often receive direct support, while other Hungarian libraries may prefer to establish some form of partnership with a foreign library supplying a Hungarian minority. Foundations have become very popular in Hungary; according to Andrássy (1993), the number of cultural foundations reached 7,000 in 1992, as opposed to the 3,000 foundations known to exist in 1991.

There are various other solutions to the problems of services to minorities. The above are just two examples that try to undertake the task within the constraints of general supply. Examples of the former solution are also known to exist in the national minority libraries of Kishinev (Moldavia) (Kulikovski and Rosca, 1992), and of the latter solution, the supply of minorities in Slovakia, Sub-Carpathia (the Ukraine), Transylvania (Romania), Voivodship (Yugoslavia) and Hungary. The work of such an organization is illustrated by the Library of Mures County (Fülöp, 1993).

The issue was recently raised among Hungarians living in Transylvania who wished to establish separate minority libraries. However, while it was made possible in Kishinev from the state budget, in Transylvania it was only possible thanks to the support of the mother country. The Transylvanian Hungarian Cultural Association has now established five libraries (Kiss, 1994).

As if in support of these efforts, several recent investigations have shown that the reading skill of Hungarian minorities living in neighbouring countries is not inferior to that of those living in the mother land. To take the example of one ethnic group; the Csángós, living on the other side of the Carpathian Mountains, do not understand works written in contemporary Hungarian. A consignment of books was sent to the Csángós living in Moldavia; however, they were of little use since they spoke only the form of Hungarian language used prior to the first language reform. Instead, it was said, the 100,000 Csángós would need a Hungarian priest and a school, although they would also gladly welcome tractors to assist their economic development (Ungár, 1994).

There are also other nationalities in the region, for whom books in their mother tongue are 'like the blind receiving colour images as a gift. We need Slovak kindergartens and Slovak primary schools in all places where Slovaks are living, as we have been in need of them for almost a century. When all this becomes a reality, books can also come . . .', writes a Slovak living in Hungary to the Matica Slovenska, the Slovak National Library (List, 1993).

Finally, a reflection from Poland on the support of Poles living in the CIS countries (Skaradziński, 1994): it is not of real assistance if the mother country supplies Polish language books and newspapers, notes and films, patriotic postcards and memorabilia. How many of them are able to read original Polish literature? It should rather be considered how best to prepare these people for the emerging capitalist environments which are also establishing themselves in the CIS countries.

In almost all the region's states, Gypsies abound. Not all of them have Romany as a mother tongue; some of those living in Slovakia are Hungarians, and some in Hungary are Romanians. Their concentration in any one place is never high, even though an increasing number of examples do exist. Romany language publications are seldom found anywhere, and therefore the question of library provision remains unsolved. It can only realistically be addressed when Romany organizations decide to establish a cultural centre. Special literature dealing with Gypsies is, of course, available to researchers in appropriate libraries.

The signs of evolution

Clearly, librarianship and information work in Central and Eastern Europe have been pushed to new and higher limits, because of advances in automation and telecommunications. By contrast, Russia is still forced to struggle while it proceeds slowly with social and economic reforms under ever-burgeoning financial constraints. Reforms are delayed, or even made impossible, by the country's backwardness. This is all the more emphasised by, and indicates the need for, an adequate automated information structure. The situation is especially bad at the regional level. The reason for this is that, in the last 20 to 30 years, development objectives have changed very frequently, and all of them were just adequate to satisfy research ambitions. These objectives covered many things, but not average user needs. Users did not wish for anything except to enjoy the benefits of these objectives.

It has become increasingly clear at various exhibitions that Russian information technology is not able, and cannot be made able, within the next two to three years, to resolve the difficulties faced by the library community, especially at a regional level. There seems to be no alternative but the mass application of western technology.

Mediated and assisted by new commercial structures progressive information technologies will become increasingly available, including electronic mail, electronic publishing, and the linking of information networks by telecommunications (Tereshchenko, 1992a, 1992b). It is advisable that these developments should be integrated, according to the new draft law on information policy already mentioned (Zakon, 1992b).

In some countries where information practice has been more purpose-oriented, the situation has been somewhat more favourable. Alas, not everywhere. In Romania, for example, in 1992, there was still not a single computerized network available (Parusi, 1992).

The long preparation process has, however, brought its benefits. Specialists, such as new graduates, have been able to get acquainted with the latest trends, at least within the constraints of Comecon equipment, and to familiarize themselves with technology. Confronted by today's machines, they are able rapidly to achieve very clear results. It is therefore in the West's interest to assist in the reorganization of the library and information environment and its practices in the East, using new technologies. A lecture by Cornish (1994) in Prague, for example, looked forward to increased interlibrary lending and document supply.

In the Czech Republic, many articles have been written on issues relating to the State Information System (SIS). Subjects include its global architecture (Goldšmid, 1993), the information technologies currently available and those to be used in the future (Dudik, 1993), and its current achievements and future projects (Matoušová and Feistner, 1993). The library and information system in the Czech Republic has good professional reasons to adjust itself to the model solutions of the SIS, a computerized system which today is reaching into even the remotest parts of the country.

In Slovakia, a decree was passed in 1992 by the Council of Ministers announcing a programme which would oversee the gradual introduction and increased use of information technology in the country (Národný, 1992).

In Hungary, such a programme is the blueprint for the realization of the National Library and Information System (Előzetes, 1994), although it is elaborated in more detail.

New information technology

It appears that the construction and provision of databases have taken priority in the countries of Central and Eastern Europe. Courage and Butrimenko (1994) listed a total of 1,918 public databases, 60.8% of which have been established in Russia, with the remaining 39.2% located as follows: Bulgaria (8.4%), the Ukraine (6.4%), Hungary (5%), Poland (3.6%), Romania (3.1%), Czech Republic and Slovakia (2.8%), Latvia (2.2%), Belorus (2.0%), other countries (5.5%). Sixty-five per cent of these databases cover the fields of science, technology and patents, while 20% feature economics, social sciences and the arts. Of the 1,918 databases, only 214 are accessible online. Of these 214, 136 are to be found in Russia, while 70 are in Hungary. Of the 72 English language databases available, 33 are based in Hungary.

In addition to the publicly accessible databases in Russia, there are approximately 20,000 non-public databases in operation, although, on the world scale, the country has a modest share of the world market of databases. Approximately one quarter of these databases are of a standard that would be acceptable on the world market, should they possess the necessary certification. However, even a system for certification still needs to be established (Antopol'skii and Vigurskii, 1993).

Furthermore, an adequate computer network and telecommunications infrastructure is needed, as well as a flourishing internal and external market. In 1992, 97% of infrastructure development was import-based, carrying a value of 778,000 US $. In 1993, the total domestic revenue generated form the use of these databases was estimated at around 2-2.5 million roubles. Little revenue was generated, however, from abroad. Summarizing, Molchanova *et al.* (1993) view the present situation as being still very unfavourable to any form of progress, development or growth.

In the smaller countries of the region, only databases that are of some national interest tend to be developed (Vásárhelyi, 1994), while in other cases priority is given to online access to foreign and international databases, most commonly in business information (Huszár, 1994; Roboz, 1993, 1994b). In Hungary, a separate organization operates to protect the interests of database suppliers (Roboz, 1994a).

CD-ROM technology has been available for some time in the various countries of Central and Eastern Europe, even before the political changes. Domestic CD-ROMs started to appear soon after. In the Czech Republic, for example, the Czech National Bibliography has been published on CD-ROM. This includes data on items published during the period 1991 to 1993, and includes a total of 164,000 records, 80,000 of them covering books published in the period 1983 to 1993; some 5,000 records covering journal and newspaper titles, and approximately 3,000 doctoral theses. According to a recent review, further revisions are necessary (Brožek, 1994).

In Hungary, a publishing company cooperates closely with several large libraries and information centres to publish databases of national interest on CD-ROM, using the ARCTIS publishing platform (Biszak, 1994). The more important of these databases (Hazai, 1994) include: the national bibliography of books, with over 100,000 individual records and approximately 200,000 analytical records; the national periodicals database, with bibliographical data and details of library holdings (for foreign periodicals available in Hungary (Tószegi, 1993); HUNPATÉKA, the database of Hungarian patents for the period 1920 to 1994 (Vadász and Biszak, 1994); PRESSDOK, containing the bibliographic data of Hungarian press articles dating back to 1989; Hungarian standards, and even The Bible, a full-text, hypertext database based on the first full Hungarian language translation.

There are some other experiments with hypertext in Hungary (Koltay, 1993; Lengyel, 1993). Slovak experiments have also been referred to in the literature. Russian hypertext research has until now tended to concentrate on algorithmic navigation; these systems include HYPERLOG, HYPERNET, BAHYS, and SEMPRO (Gilyarevskiĭ and Subbotin, 1993).

Intensive work is presently under way to develop shared cataloguing in Hungary (Tószegi, 1994a; E. Vajda, 1994b).

In some countries (Hungary: Kokas, 1992; Poland: Dobrowolski, 1994), the establishment of integrated library systems began with general discussion in the professional press, later developing towards increasing numbers of installations. One of the most popular pieces of software thus far appears to be ALEPH (for the Czech Republic, see Svoboda, 1994; for Hungary, Árosy, 1994; Frank, 1994, and for Slovakia, Sližová and Prokop, 1994). Other systems are also in use, however, particularly in Hungary: DOBIS/LIBIS (Horvát, 1993); Dynix Marquis (Mohor and Szelle, 1994); ORACLE Libraries (Tószegi, 1994d; M. Vajda, 1994); TINLIB (Cserey and Tapolcai, 1994; Varga, 1994) and Voyager (Kertész, 1993; Gombá, 1994).

Machine translation was a traditional field of research at VINITI (the All-Union Institute of Sci-Tech Information) in Russia. Their latest innovation is an interactive system that can be used for the translation of English-Russian and Russian-English multi-subject scientific and technical texts. The system is based on a dictionary of some 250,000 expressions, collected between 1983 and 1991.

Automation is characteristic not only of research and special libraries, but also of public libraries. In this respect, county and town libraries take a leading role (Tolnai, 1992; Horváth, 1993; Przybyszewski, 1993; Szymanowski, 1994a). More conservative rural librarians, however, still naturally exhibit certain anxieties about new technology.

Miscellaneous

In education and training, areas formerly accused of conservatism, great efforts are being made to adapt the system to the demands of a changed and constantly evolving environment. In Russia, for example, there is no single library school without a module focusing on library marketing or management (Klyuev, 1993; Fonotov, 1994; Klyuev and Suslova, 1994). In some cases, these subjects are even over-emphasized. The same situation exists concerning extension training (Dzherelievskaya, 1994), part of which has already been taken over by privately-owned organizations (Yastrebova, 1993). Library education is being revised at a rapid pace in Hungary too (K. Vajda, 1994). In Slovakia, library science has become a separate subject in the training of researchers (Nováková, 1994). On the creation of an infrastructure for training, and the overall modernization of its contents, it is worth mentioning that the first areas to be supported from the West were in higher education.

To begin with, librarianship and information work were analysed in some of the Central European countries, including Hungary and the Czech Republic, by Western (mainly British) experts. The reports were useful when requesting support (Trancygier, 1992), or at least to act as a guideline to some programmes already in existence, such as, the European Union's PHARE project, TEMPUS, which focused on some of the needs that had been formerly identified (Iván,

1995, in press). The TEMPUS programme now covers eleven countries in the region. Thanks to its three-year support (45.5 million Forint), Hungarian library and information science education has fundamentally changed, particularly as regards its computer infrastructure and its content. It is now comparable with that in other European countries (Fülöp, 1993a, 1993b; Blumendorf, 1994). Support has also taken the form of gifts. The Sabre and Soros Foundations have donated around 450,000 volumes of American books to Hungary during the period from 1986 to 1992 (Kovács, 1993). Some financial transactions, including a World Bank loan to Hungarian academic libraries, are still being prepared (Huszár, 1993; Martos *et al.*, 1993).

Besides PHARE, support is provided from other programmes. The Czech and Slovak Library Information Network for example has benefited from the American-supported CASLIN project which undertook (from 1994) to modernize information on holding libraries (Hemola, 1994; Svoboda, 1994), while professional training at a secondary level has been offered in the Czech Republic by the Dutch AMBI project (Siman, 1993). Many Slovak librarians have been using mobile libraries, also with assistance and support from the Netherlands (Kalinová and Hrabinská, 1994). In addition, the European Union has established information centres both in Budapest (Arnóth, 1993) and in Bratislava (Chudá, 1994).

To achieve the technical advances highlighted in this chapter, librarianship and information work in Central and Eastern Europe has had to make certain sacrifices. In particular, librarians and information professionals have been required to carefully examine their beliefs and working philosophies. These revisions of attitude and the resulting reforms and trends have extended to, and influenced, the development of networks (Horváth, 1994), methodology (Szymanowski, 1994b), collection building and resource sharing (Zarzębski, 1993; Tószegi 1994c; Vasilenko, 1994), library education and the revision of information activity (Čejpek, 1992; Tereshin, 1993; Tyulina, 1993; Skvortsov, 1994); have encouraged new forms of cooperation (Dudzińska and Wojciechowska, 1993; Skandera, 1994); have affected school libraries (Szocki, 1994), and have caused almost complete reform of services in large libraries and information centres (E. Vajda, 1994a). The use of modern technology has also been detailed in articles with regard to disadvantaged readers (Dianskaya, 1993 ; Czajkowski, 1994).

Politics today does not tend to interfere in professional issues to the extent that it used to. As a result, the mass media started to rigorously cover what were previously unthinkable issues. In Poland, for example, the question was raised as to why there is not more religious literature on the shelves of libraries (Mylik, 1993). In the interest of saving money, however, the state does not relinquish all rights to offer 'sound' advice. Some examples include the merging of cultural centres and libraries (Piaczyńska, 1994), or the combining of school and public libraries (Blońska, 1994). Objecting to or debating these suggestions still remains something of an exercise in diplomacy.

Finally, let us focus on some individual achievements.

The Russian author Artamonov (1993) sees an unusual analogy in the first chapter of the Gospel according to St John:

> In the beginning was the Word and the Word was with God, and the Word was God.
> He was in the beginning with God.
> All things came into being through Him, and apart from Him nothing came into being which has come into being.

If we interpret the word 'Word' as 'information', and the word 'God' as 'society', we obtain a definition of the social role of information. Taking this a step further, the role of information can better be defined by the Holy Trinity. If we interpret 'God the Father' as 'society', 'God the Son' as 'man', and 'God the Holy Spirit' as 'information', it might indicate the basic law of information science: the three-part concept of society, man and information.

The Czech author Cejpek (1993) takes a post-modernist viewpoint of information science. The post-industrial society, for example, as defined by Daniel Bell in the mid-1970s (in which the leading concept is the system) is frequently referred to as an information society:

> Its main power manifests itself in controlling the knowledge stored, the cognition fixed in information systems, similarly to controlling the soil in Feudalism or the productive forces in Capitalism. For man, and for society, it is not the mere concept of system (information system) that is dangerous, as long as it is considered as a method, and as a tool. It becomes dangerous only when it is interpreted as the point and essence of things, persons, phenomena and events. After that, the internal inertia of the concept will start to act, and may intervene in the affairs of any man-made phenomenon, organization, institution, policy, science, technology and art, even into that of war. The system interpreted as an aim and essence becomes impersonal and alienated. How can we protect ourselves? V. Havel briefly replies: the intentions of the system should be surpassed by the intentions of life.

This is no simple task, however, given that in the field of information science, artificial language is calculable and can be planned, while natural language cannot. Still, we should resolve not to fall victim to the artificial world of information imposed upon us.

In Russia, two new disciplines or approaches have been founded. Grachev (1993) praises library 'socionomics' that offer efficient methods to explore and evaluate the characteristics of individuals belonging to a group.

Muranivskiř (1993) announces the birth of 'infornomics', its basic law being the information cycle. This begins with the creation of information, includes the flow of information, and concludes with information use and eventually with the creation of new information. While information science (as interpreted by

Mihailov-Chernyĭ-Gilyarevskiĭ) has been seeking an answer on 'how' information can be found, stored, rapidly transmitted and received, infornomics deals with 'what', i.e. what information is worth storing, transmitting and receiving. Russia was the birthplace of this new discipline, because problems about information activity have been raised there more sharply than in the West. Intellectual rebirth and raising cultural standards are specifically Russian problems.

The Hungarian author Tószegi (1994a) recently wrote a monograph on pictorial information. It is the great accomplishment of her work that it analyses the subject from both theoretical and historical aspects, and thus lays the foundations for related practical work.

The Library of the Presidential Administration of the Russian Federation, writes Zajtsev [Zajcev] (1993), is not an example of individual accomplishment, but of the presidential power which in a very short time established a modern and well-equipped library from three formerly closed party libraries. The equipment had been delivered by the American firm MERISEL; the TEXTO/Logotel software was purchased from the French firm CHEMDATA.

Summary

Librarianship and information work in the region will without doubt survive the quantitative losses described in this review. Many of the losses indeed are not worth grieving for, given the new working philosophy. Indications exist that this, and modern-day technology, have already led to substantial achievements.

It should be noted that the authors of today's state-of-the-art reports are the representatives of the profession, and not government officials. Osipova (1993), for example, observes that it is the profession itself that is now taking an active role in its own transformation and organization. A degree of unity among the national libraries within the CIS has been maintained, and services have now started to be tailored to individual needs.

The activities of the profession, and the increasing efficiency of its associations, have become characteristic in all countries. In Hungary, for example, a three-tier system for safeguarding interests was established. The trade unions fought for the financial support of librarians, the library association for the recognition of professional interests, and the Chamber of Libraries and Information Institutions for institutional interests (Zalainé Kovács, 1994).

In recent years, West European ideas, products and practices have been increasingly criticized, although those religiously adopting them are happy to hear such comments as: 'Do not make the same mistakes we did' (Richards, 1994).

The professional press in Central and Eastern Europe has, for the most part, survived the most difficult years. Only a small number of journals have ceased publication (e.g. *APID* in Poland), although there have been many title changes (e.g. the Soviet *Bibliotekar'* became *Biblioteka*, the Hungarian *Könyvtáros* became *Könyv*, *Könyvtár*, *Könyvtáros*, and from many Russian titles the adjective 'sovetskoe' and the adverb of place 'v SSSR' was omitted) and mergers (the Slovak *Citatel* and *Kniznice a Vedecké Informácie* have been merged and given the title *Kniznice a Informácie*, while the Czech *Technická Knihovna* and *Ceskoslovenská Informatika* now continues as *i*). Several new journals have also appeared on the market (e.g. the Hungarian *Könyvtári Levelező/lap*).

This new breed of professional press has tried to report on the national processes and international trends in such a way that the latter has had a favourable effect on the former (Hanáková, 1994).

Acknowledgements

The authors express their thanks to Ms Ilona Hegyközi, National Széchényi Library and Mr Jerome Simpson, National Technical Information Centre and Library of Hungary for their contribution to the English version of this text.

References

Adamiec, W. (1993) O paru paradoksach księgozbiorowych. *Przęglad Biblioteczny*, (3–4), 263–268.
Andrássy, L. (1994) Az alapítványi intézmény története. *Könyvtári Figyelő*, 39(2), 198–205.
Antopol'skiĭ, A.B. and Vigurskiĭ, K.V. (1993) Sertifikatsiya baz dannykh i rynok informatsionnoĭ produkcii. *Nauchno-Tekhnicheskaya Informatsiya Ser.1*, (12), 1–4.
Arató, A. (1993) A Kölcsey Ferenc Alapítvány a határon túli olvasókért. *Könyvtári Levelező/lap*, (8), 11–12.
Arnóth, K. (1993) Látogatás az Európa Tanács magyar információs központjában. *Könyvtári Levelező/lap*, (9), 7–8.
Árosy, A.L. (1994) Számítógéppel támogatott állománygyarapítás az OMK-ban. *Tudományos és Műszaki Tájékoztatás*, 41(10), 392–402.
Artamonov, G.T. (1993) Problemy teoreticheskoĭ informatiki. *Nauchno-Tekhnicheskaya Informatsiya Ser.1*, (6), 25–27.
Bakonyi, P. (1993) Az Információs Infrastruktúra Program nyolc éve. *IIF Hírek*, (6), 1–2.
Belogonov, G.G. *et al.* (1993) Interaktivnaya sistema russko-angliĭskogo i anglo-russkogo mashinnogo perevoda politematicheskikh nauchno-tekhnicheskikh tekstov. *Nauchno-Tekhnicheskaya Informatsiya Ser.2*, (3), 20–27.
Biliński, L. and Kuzmińska, K. (1994) Status organizacyjny wojewódskich bibliotek publicznych, ich finansowanie oraz niektóre zadania. *Poradnik Bibliotekarza*, (3), 1–6.
Biszak, S. (1994) Az ARCTIS szövegvisszakereső rendszer. *Tudományos és Műszaki*

Tájékoztatás, **41**(9), 350–355.
Błońska, L. (1994) Biblioteki szkolno-publiczne w świetle informacji wojewódskich ośrodków metodycznych. *Poradnik Bibliotekarza*, (2), 9–11.
Blumendorf, P. (1994) Az ELTE három éves TEMPUS projektjének mérlege. *Tudományos és Műszaki Tájékoztatás*, 41(3–4), 120–125.
Brożek, A. (1994) Česká národní bibliografie na CD-ROM. *i*, 36(10), 263–264.
Burakowski, J. (1992) Pogrzebu nie będzie . . . Uwagi o kondycji bibliotek publicznych. *Bibliotekarz*, (11–12), 13–16.
Burgetová, J. (1994) Bibliotekarstwo czeskie w okresie przejściowym. *Bibliotekarz*, (7–8), 23–25.
Čejpek, J. (1992) K informační funkci veřejných knihoven. *Čtenář*, **44**(3), 74–76.
Čejpek, J. (1993) Informační věda z pohledu postmoderního myšlení. *i*, **35**(12), 300–303.
Chernyĭ, A.I. *et al.* (1993) Gosudarstvennaya sistema nauchnoĭ i tekhnicheskoĭ informatsii Rossiĭskoĭ Federatsii: proekt programmy sozdaniya i razvitiya. *Nauchno-Tekhnicheskaya Informatsiya Ser.1*, (3), 1–30.
Chkhenkeli, T.I. (1994) Kontseptsiya gosudarstvennoĭ bibliotechno-informatsionnoĭ sistemy Respubliki Gruziya. *Nauchnye i Tekhnicheskie Biblioteki*, (7), 34–37.
Chudá, S. (1994) Predstavujeme informačné a dokumentačné stredisko o Rade Európy v Bratislave. *i*, 36(10), 255–256.
Cornish, G.P. (1994) Mezinárodní spolupráce knihoven – sjednocuje nebo rozdeluje Evropu. *i*, 36(5), 116–121.
Courage, M.A. and Butrimenko, A. (1994) Elektronikus információszolgáltatások – adatbázis-előállítás és használat. *Tudományos és Műszaki Tájékoztatás*, **41**(11–12), 457–462.
Cserey, L. and Tapolcai, Á. (1994) Változó feladatok az Állatorvostudományi Egyetem Könyvtárában. *Tudományos és Műszaki Tájékoztatás*, **41**(7–8), 294–295.
Czajkowski, Fr. (1994) Prawo do czytania. 10 lat działalności Ośrodka Chorych i Niepolnosprawnych w Toruniu. *Poradnik Bibliotekarza*, (6), 9–12.
Czene, G. (1994) Tiltott nemzetiség: a ruszin. *Népszabadság*, 8 November, 13.
Dan'shina, I.V. (1992) Mnogonatsional'naya literatura i massovaya biblioteka. *Sovetskoe Bibliotekovedenie*, (1), 51–62.
Demeshko, L. and Krotyuk, N. (1992) Pol'skaya kniga v Belorussii. *Biblioteka*, (11–12), 9–11.
Dianskaya, G.P. (1993) Bibliotechnoe obsluzhivanie nezryachikh studentov. *Nauchnye i Tekhnicheskie Biblioteki*, (13), 11–18.
Dobrowolski, Z. (1994) Wybór systemu zintegrowanego. *Bibliotekarz*, (6), 9–13.
Dudik, J. (1993) Informačné technológie v knižnično-informačnom systéme. *Knižnice a Informácie*, 25(10), 431–433.
Dudzińska, E. and Wojciechowska, A. (1993) Współpraca bibliotek sieci I. Centralnej Biblioteki Technicznej w nowych warunkach społeczno-ekonomicznych. *Przegląd Biblioteczny*, (3–4), 273–280.
Dzherelievskaya, I.K. (1994) CBS v usloviyakh perekhoda k rynochnym otnosheniyam. (Po rezul'tatam delovoĭigry.) *Bibliotekovedenie*, (1), 46–48.
Előzetes (1994) rendszerterv az Országos Szakirodalmi Információs Rendszer megvalósítására. *Könyv, Könyvtár, Könyvtáros*, (Special issue), 4–106.
Fonotov, G. (1994) Marketing: obreteniya i poteri. *Biblioteka*, (4), 26–29.

Frank, R. (1994) Az ALEPH integrált könyvtári rendszer a BME Könyvtárában. 2. *Tudományos és Műszaki Tájékoztatás*, **41**(7–8), 283–288.

Fülöp, G. (1993a) A budapesti ELTE Könyvtártudományi-Informatikai Tanszékének TEMPUS-kapcsolata. *Könyv, Könyvtár, Könyvtáros*, (November), 34–39.

Fülöp, G. (1993b) Információs szakemberek Magyarország számára – a TEMPUS segítségével Európába. *Könyvtári Figyelő*, **39**(4), 561–565.

Fülöp, M. (1993) Vizsgálódások, felismerések a Maros Megyei Könyvtárban. *Könyv, Könyvtár, Könyvtáros*, (December), 49–53.

Gajtkó, É. (1994) A kötelespéldány törvény tervezete. *Könyv, Könyvtár, Könyvtáros*, (May), 3–8.

Gilyarevskii, R.S. and Subbotin, M.M. (1993) Russian experience in hypertext automatic compiling of coherent text. *Journal of the American Society for Information Science*, **44**(4), 185–193.

Goldsmid, I. (1993) Globální architektúra státního informačního systému České republiky. *i*, **35**(4), 86–88.

Gomba, Sz. (1994) A debreceni Universitas számítógépes könyvtári rendszere. *Tudományos és Műszaki Tájékoztatás*, **41**(7–8), 276–282.

Grachev, V.I. (1993) Bibliotechnaya socionika – novoe napravlenie izucheniya bibliotechnoĭ zhizni. *Nauchnyie i Tekhnicheskie Biblioteki*, (7), 18–39.

Hanáková, J. (1994) O redagování a redaktorech, *i*, **36**(2), 29–30.

Hazai (1994) termés. *Tudományos és Műszaki Tájékoztatás*, **41**(9), 349.

Hemola, H. (1994) Služby čtenářum. *Národní Knihovna pro Čtenáře*, (3), 1–2.

Hodossy, D. (1993) Problematika doplňovania, spracúvania a sprístupňovania literatúry mad'arskej národnostnej menšiny na Slovensku. *Knižnice a Informácie*, **25**(5), 221–223.

Horvát, Á. (1993) Az OSZK online olvasói katalógusa. *Könyv, Könyvtár, Könyvtáros*, (January), 20–22.

Horváth, T. (1993) Könyvtárgépesítés a magyar közművelődési könyvtárakban. *Könyv, Könyvtár, Könyvtáros*, (April), 8–12.

Horváth, T. (1994) Szilánkok a hálózati gondolathoz és a hálózat szó használatához. *Könyvtári Levelező/lap*, (8), 4–6.

Howorka, B. (1993) Czy ustawa o bibliotekach jest potrzebna? *Poradnik Bibliotekarza*, (7–8), 1–6.

Howorka, B. (1994) Biblioteki szkolne I pedagogiczne a projekt nowej ustawy bibliotecznej. *Bibliotekarz*, (5), 7–12.

Huszár, E. (1993) VB projekt. *Könyv, Könyvtár, Könyvtáros*, (March), 3–5.

Huszár, E. (1994) Üzlet-e az üzleti információ? *Tudományos és Műszaki Tájékoztatás*, **41**(1), 3–6.

Integrovaný (1994) knižnično-informačný systém. Výklad pojmu. *Knižnice a informácie*, **26**(10), 444–448.

Kalinová, V. (1992) Realita l'udových knižníc. *Knižnice a Informácie*, **24**(6), 254–257.

Kalinová, V. (1993) Stanú sa l'udové knižnice ohrozenými kultúrnymi inštitúciami? *Knižnice a Informácie*, **25**(6), 259–262.

Kalinová, V. (1994) Mestské knižnice v Slovenskej republike. *Knižnice a Informácie*, **26**(10), 401–407.

Kalinová, V. and Hrabinská, T. (1994) Bibliobuszok – egy holland-szlovák projekt. *Könyv, Könyvtár, Könyvtáros*, (June), 56–61.

Kalinová, V. et al. (1993) Kooperačné združenie knižníc. Knižnice a Informácie, 25(3), 128–133.

Karbach, E. (1993) Az országos feladatkörű szakkönyvtárak helyzetéről és finanszírozásáról. Könyvtári Figyelő, 39(3), 361–370.

Karvalics, L. (1995). The science of history information in libraries. Tudományos és Műszaki Tájéboztatás, 42(1), 7–16.

Katuščák, D. (1992) Integrováný knižnično-informačný systém. Riešenie, problémy, perspektívy. Knižnice a Informácie, 24(3), 104–110.

Kedrovskiĭ, G.V. (1992) O sisteme nauchno-tekhnicheskoĭ informatsii v Rossii. Nauchno-Tekhnicheskaya Informatsiya Ser.1, (1), 1–3.

Kertész, A. (1993) A Voyager integrált könyvtári rendszer. Könyvtári Figyelő, 39(1), 22–30.

Kiss, J. (1994) Magyar könyvek és könyvtárak Romániában. Könyvtári Figyelő, 40(3), 391–393.

Klyuev, V.K. (1993) Marketingovaya podgotovka menedzherov bibliotechnogo dela. Nauchnyie i Tekhnicheskie Biblioteki, (3), 26–35.

Klyuev, V.K. and Suslova, I.M. (1994) Sovremennaya kontseptsiya novogo bibliotechnogo kursa 'Bibliotechnyĭ menedzhment'. Nauchnyie i Tekhnicheskie Biblioteki, (6), 22–42.

Kokas, K. (1992) Új integrált könyvtári rendszerek a hazai piacon. Tudományos és Műszaki Tájékoztatás, 39(7–8), 311–331.

Koltay, T. (1993) Hipertextet írok: néhány tapasztalat, szembesítve a szakirodalommal. Tudományos és Műszaki Tájékoztatás, 40(8), 340–343.

Koncepce (1992) rozvoje veřejných informačních služeb. i, 34(9), 198–202.

Kovács, D. K. (1993) Amerikai ajándékkönyvek 1992–ben és elosztásuk. Könyvtári Levelező/lap, (1), 5–6.

Kulikovski, L. and Rosca, E. (1992) Sericiul de biblioteca pentru minoritatile nationale municipiul Chisinau. Biblioteca, 3(5), 4–5.

Kuz'min, E. (1993a) At a crossroads: Russian libraries face the future. Wilson Library Bulletin, 67(5), 52–58, 118.

Kuz'min, E. (1993b) From totalitarism to democracy. Russian libraries in transition. American Libraries, 24(6), 568–570.

Kuźmińska, Kr. (1994) Sytuacja w bibliotekarstwie po raz trzeci od r. 1990 na forum Sejmowej Komisji Kultury i Środkow Przekazu. Poradnik Bibliotekarza, (7–8), 1–4.

Ladosné Varjú, I. (1994) Célok a tanácsi könyvtárügyben. Szervezetszociológiai elemzés. Könyvtári Figyelő, 40(1), 49–60.

Lengyel, M. (1993) Számítógépes könyvtári kalauzok. Tudományos és Műszaki Tájékoztatás, 40(11–12), 458–461.

List (1993) z Budapešti. Slovenské Pohl'ady, (2), 126–127.

Lukáts, J. (1994) Tanácskozás a hazai németek könyvtári helyzetéről. Könyv, Könyvtár, Könyvtáros, (July), 38–39.

Martos, B. et al. (1993) Magyarországi könyvtárak számítógép-hálózati infrastrukturális ellátása. Tudományos és Műszaki Tájékoztatás, 40(9–10), 391–398.

Matoušová, M. (1992) Informační služby v České republice – minulost, budoucnost a mýty. i, 34(12), 291–292.

Matoušová, M. and Feistner, J. (1993) Komise vlády ČR pro státní informačný systém. Ohlédnutí ze činnosti. i, 35(10), 243–244.

Mohor, J. and Szelle, B. (1994) ELMESO: összefogás három egyetem könyvtári rendszerének megújításáért. *Tudományos és Műszaki Tájékoztatás,* **41**(7–8), 289–293.

Molchanova, O.P. et al. (1993) Analiz rynka informatsionnykh sredstv Rossii. *Nauchno-Tekhnicheskaya Informatsiya Ser.1.,* (9), 8–19.

Muranivskii, T.V. (1993) Infornomika – novaya nauchnaya distsiplina. *Nauchno-Tekhnicheskaya Informatsiya Ser.1,* (6), 9–14.

Mylik, M. (1993) Czasopisma i książki religijne w bibliotekach. *Bibliotekarz,* (2), 9–11.

Národný (1992) program informatizácie Slovenskej republiky. *Knižnice a Informácie,* **24**(10), 429–434.

Nováková, M. (1994) Knižničná a informačná veda ako samostatny obor. *Knižnice a Informácie,* **26**(7), 317–318.

Okàlová, M. (1993) Literárna produkcia nàrodnostných menšin na Slovensku a jej odraz v automatizovanom systéme Slovenskej nàrodnoj bibliografie. *Knižnice a Informácie,* **25**(5), 218–221.

Osipova, I.P. (1993) Kontury pereobrazovanii. *Bibliotekovedenie,* (3), 3–13.

Papp, I. (1993) Javaslat az új könyvtári törvényben rendezendő kérdéskörökre. *Könyv, Könyvtár, Könyvtáros,* (November), 3–7.

Parusi, G. (1992) Libraries and cataloguing at present. *Probl. Inf. Doc.,* **26**(4), 234–238.

Piaczyńska, M. (1994) Biblioteki publiczne – problemy łączenia z ośrodkami kultury i bibliotekami szkolnymi. *Bibliotekarz,* (2), 25–27.

Pilař, J. (1992) Pokus o nácrt obsahu knihovnického zákona. *Knižnice a Informácie,* **24**(8–9), 392–401.

Pilař, J. and Hemola, H. (1992) Návrh zásad 'knihovnickeho zákona' z komentárem. *i,* **34**(6), 145–147.

Polozhenie (1993) o Rossiiskoi gosudarstvennoi biblioteke. *Bibliotekovedenie,* (5–6), 3–10.

Postanovlenie (1994) No. 128 ot 11 yuli 1994 godina za opredelanie statusa i finansiraneto na darzhavni kulturni instituti s nacionalno znachenie. *Biblioteka,* **2**(9), 3–4.

Povinny (1994) výtisk podruhé. *i,* **36**(4), 85–86.

Proekt (1992a) zakona Rossiiskoi Federatsii 'O bibliotechnom dele'. *Nauchnye i Tekhnicheskie Biblioteki,* (8), 5–25.

Proekt (1992b) zakona Rossiiskoi Federatsii ob obshcherossiiskikh natsional'nykh bibliotekakh. *Nauchnye i Tekhnicheskie Biblioteki,* (9), 7–14.

Przybyszewski, W. (1993) Biblioteki publiczne w 1992 r. *Bibliotekarz,* (7–8), 24–28.

Razrabotka (1992) gosudarstvennoi politiki v oblasti sozdaniya i ispol'zovaniya informatsionnogo resursa i programma modernizatsii sistemy NTI. *Nauchno-Tekhnicheskaya Informatsiya Ser.1,* (9), 9–21.

Rexa, D. (1993) Starostlivost' státu o knižnice v národnostne zmiešanych oblastiach Slovenska. *Knižnice a Informácie,* **25**(5), 217–218.

Rezolyutsiya (1992) Vserossiiskogo soveshchaniya rukovoditelei krupnykh bibliotek po proektu Zakona Rossiiskoi Federatsii o bibliotekakh. *Nauchnye i Tekhnicheskie Biblioteki,* (8), 32–33.

RGB (1992): stroya budushchee, cherpat' vse tsennoe iz proshlogo. *Sovetskoe Bibliotekovedenie,* (5–6), 3–16.

Richards, P.S. (1994) 'Ne povtorite nashikh oshibok' – preduprezhdayut kollegi iz SShA. *Biblioteka,* (5), 11–15.

Roboz, P. (1993) Közép- és kelet-európai üzleti online adatbázisok. *Tudományos és Műszaki Tájékoztatás,* **40**(7), 283–385.

Roboz, P. (1994a) Bemutatjuk a Magyar Adatbázisforgalmazók Kamaráját. *Tudományos és Műszaki Tájékoztatás*, **41**(3-4), 126-130.
Roboz, P. (1994b) Piaci tanulmányok online keresése. *Tudományos és Műszaki Tájékoztatás*, **41**(10), 404-412.
Rupešová, M. (1994) Vychodiská koncepce veřejných informačných služeb na vysokých skolach. *i*, **36**(10), 245-251.
Segešová, L'. (1994) Vývoj, súčasný stav a perspektívy činnosti technických knižníc a informačných stredísk v Slovenskej republike. *Kniznice a Informácie*, **26**(6), 237-240.
Serov, V. (1993) Neozhidannii povorot. *Biblioteka*, (5), 55-56.
Serov, V. *et al*. (1993) Lomat' – ne stroit'. 1-2.ch. *Biblioteka*, (2), 10-13; (3), 14-17.
Seršiková, A. (1993) Knihovnicka profesia a etika. *Knižnice a Informácie*, **25**(5), 234-237.
Shatberashvili, O.B. (1993) Informatsionnaya politika Gruzii v perekhodnyj period. *Nauchno-Tekhnicheskaya Informatsiya Ser.1*, (5), 1-6.
Siman, P. (1993) Podaří se zvýšit úroveň středoškolsky vzdelaných pracovníků v informatice? *i*. **35**(10), 259-260.
Skaliczki, J. (1994) Szubjektív számvetés a munkahelyi közművelődési könyvtárak rendszerváltás utáni helyzetével. *Könyvtári Figyelő*, **40**(2), 182-186.
Skandera, B. (1994) VTEI v Polsku: příklad pro nás? *i*, **36**(7-8), 203.
Skaradziński, B. (1994) Sprawa ciężka z propozycją happy endu. *Więz*, **37**(2), 163-167.
Skvortsov, V.V. (1994) O metodologii sovremennogo bibliotekovedeniya. *Bibliotekovedenie*, (1), 39-42.
Sližová, D. and Prokop, I. (1994) Koncepčné otázky a hlavné problémy informatizácie v Matici slovenskej. Systém ALEPH: jeho uplatnenie v Slovenskej národnej knižnici a d'alších ústavoch MS. *Knižnice a Informácie*. **26**(10), 412-416.
Sójka, J. (1993) Wybrane problemy bibliotek szkół wyższych w 1992 r. *Preglad Biblioteczny*, (1-2), 37-45.
Solyanik, A. (1994) V novykh usloviyakh – starymi metodami. O podkhodakh k organizatsii sistemy obyazatel'nogo ekzemplyara na Ukraine. *Biblioteka*, (4), 61-62.
Sonnevend, P. (1994) A tudományos célú köteles példányok szolgáltatását szabályozó törvény koncepciója. *Könyvtári Figyelő*, **40**(2), 175-181.
Sordylowa, B. (1991) Biblioteki i informacja naukowa w dobe przemian. *Przęglad Biblioteczny*, **59**(2), 135-145.
Sordylowa, B. (1993) Rola i zadanie bibliotek naukowych w nowych warunkach ekonomiczno-spolecznych. *Przęgląd Biblioteczny*, (1-2), 15-25.
Stanowisko (1993) Polskiego Towarzystwa Bibliotecznego i Polskiego Towarzystwa Czytelniczego wobec trybu likwidacji bibliotek oraz losów ich zbiorów. *Przęglad Biblioteczny*, (3-4), 269-271.
Statisztikák (1993-1994) a magyar közművelődési és szakkönyvtárak 1992. évi, illetve a magyar közművelődési könyvtárak 1993. évi működéséről. Könyv, Könyvtár, Könyvtáros, (July), 52-55; *Könyvtári Levelezőlap*, (4), 16-17.
Suchánková, A. (1992) Současný stav v oblasti povinných výtisků. *Čtenař*, **44**(3), 85-88.
Svoboda, M. (1994) CASLIN v roce nula. *i*, **36**(6), 152-154.
Szántó, P. (1993) Javaslatok a könyvtári törvényhez. Az OMK javaslatai. *Könyv, Könyvtár, Könyvtáros*, (December), 6-9.
Szocki, J. (1994) O bibliotekę na miarę reformującej się szkoły. *Bibliotekarz*, (7-8), 36-38.
Szymanowski, W. (1994a) O niektórych problemach bibliotek publicznych w 1994 r.

Bibliotekarz, (3), 4-6.

Szymanowski, W. (1994b) Prawno-społeczne uwarunkowanie działalności instrukcyjnometodycznej i nieco wnioskow. *Bibliotekarz,* (1), 3-7.

Tereshchenko, S.S. (1992a) Informatizatsii Rossii – novyř temp i novoe kachestvo. *Nauchno-Tekhnicheskaya Informatsiya Ser.1,* (3-4), 1-80.

Tereshchenko, S.S. (1992b) K razrabotke kontseptsii informatizatsii Rossii na period 1993-1995 gg. *Nauchno-Tekhnicheskaya Informatsiya Ser.1,*(6), 1-5.

Tereshin, V.I. (1993) Rukovodstvo chteniem? Net, bibliotechnaya pedagogika sotrudnichestva. *Nauchnye i Tekhnicheskie Biblioteki,* (7), 43-54.

Tolnai, G. (1992) A hazai könyvtárgépesítés a megváltozott világban. *Tudományos és Műszaki Tájékoztatás,* **39**(7-8), 303-309.

Tószegi, Zs. (1993) A Nemzeti Periodika Adatbázis CD-ROM-on. *Könyv, Könyvtár, Könyvtáros,* (November), 20-25.

Tószegi, Zs. (1994a) A képi információ. Budapest: Országos Széchényi Könyvtár. /Az Országos Széchényi Könyvtár füzetei 6./ Reviewed by T. Futala. *Tudományos és Műszaki Tájékoztatás,* **41**(10), 413-415.

Tószegi, Zs. (1994b) A Nemzeti Periodika Adatbázis (NPA) rendszer bővítése a rendelési és a könyvtárközi kölcsönzési alrendszerrel, felkészülés az osztott katalogizálás bevezetésére. *Tudományos és Műszaki Tájékoztatás,* **41**(3-4), 109-115.

Tószegi, Zs. (1994c) Magfolyóiratok Magyarországon. *Tudományos és Műszaki Tájékoztatás,* **41**(11-12), 431-439.

Tószegi, Zs. (1994d) Az ORACLE Libraries integrált könyvtári rendszer. *Tudományos és Műszaki Tájékoztatás,* **41**(11-12), 448-455.

Trancygier, T. (1992) Britskí experti o knihovníctve v ČSFR. *Knižnice a Informácie,* **24**(6), 241-248.

Tyulina, N.I. (1993) Informatsionnaya funktsiya biblioteki. *Bibliotekovedenie,* (1), 3-11.

Ungár, T. (1994) A csángók, a kulturális autonómia és a Vatikán. Kallós Zoltán a kisebbségi létről. *Népszabadság,* 7 November, 17.

Ustawa (1994) o bibliotekach. Projekt, wersja V.5. z 29. VI. 1994 r. ØStatut Rady Krajowego Systemu Biblioteczno-Informacyjnego. Projekt. Versja 1.2. *Bibliotekarz,* (7-8), 2-12.

Vadász, Á. and Biszak, S. (1994) HUNPATÉKA: a magyar nemzeti szabadalmi archívum optikai lemezen. *Tudományos és Műszaki Tájékoztatás,* **41**(9), 343-348.

Vajda, E. (1994a) A magyar nyelvű referáló és bibliográfiai tájékozatás távlatairól. *Tudományos és Műszaki Tájékoztatás,* **41**(6), 232-235.

Vajda, E. (1994b) A műszaki szakterületen tervezett osztott katalogizálás jelenlegi helyzete, a fejlődés irányai és a megvalósítás feltételrendszere. *Tudományos és Műszaki Tájékoztatás,* **41**(3-4), 99-108.

Vajda, K. (1994) Vita a könyvtárosképzésről. *Könyv, Könyvtár, Könyvtáros,* (June), 3-6.

Vajda, M. (1994) Bemutatjuk az ORACLE Libraries integrált könyvtári rendszert. *Könyvtári Figyelő,* **40**(3), 368-373.

Varga, S. (1994) A Bádogember lépeget. *Tudományos és Műszaki Tájékoztatás,* **41**(6), 223-231.

Vásárhelyi, P. (1994) A Magyar Kultúra Adatbankja. *Tudományos és Műszaki Tájékoztatás,* **41**(6), 245-248.

Vasilenko, G.I. (1994) Komplektovanie fondov natsional'nykh bibliotek v usloviyakh rynochnykh otnoshenii. (Na primere RGB.) *Bibliotekovedenie,* (1), 63-70.

Vontorčik, E. (1993) Slovenská asociácia knižníc a prestavba slovenského knihovníctva. *Knižnice a Informácie*, **25**(6), 283–286.

Wozniak, E. (1994) Komercjalizacja bibliotek w świetle opinii czytelników. *Bibliotekarz*, (7–8), 13–20.

Yanakieva, T. (1994) SBIP – sastoyanie i perspektivi. *Biblioteka*, **2**(7–8), 3–7.

[Yastrebova] Jastrebova, E. (1993) Bibliomarket in Russland. *Bibliotheksdienst*, **27**(6), 899–902.

Yavraeva. U.V. (1993) Podgotovka menedzherov dlya bibliotek. *Nauchnye i Tekhnicheskie Biblioteki*, (1), 22–32.

[Zajtsev] Zajcev, V.G. (1993) Biblioteka Administratsii Prezidenta Rossiĭskoĭ Federatsii segodnya. *Nauchnye i Tekhnicheskie Biblioteki*, (10), 3–13.

Zakon (1992a) Rossiĭskoĭ Federatsii 'O Gosudarstvennoĭ sisteme nauchno-tekhnicheskoĭ informatsii Rossii'. (Proekt.) *Nauchno-Tekhnicheskaya Informatsiya Ser.1*, (1), 3–5.

Zakon (1992b) Rossiiskoĭ Federatsii ob informatsii, informatizatsii i zashchite informatsii. (Proekt. Versiya ot 10. 11. 92.) *Nauchno-Tekhnicheskaya Informatsiya Ser.1*, (12), 3–9.

Zalainé Kovács, É. (1994) Beszámoló a Könyvtári és Informatikai Kamara munkájáról. *Könyv, Könyvtár, Könyvtáros*, (August), 14–19.

Zarzębski, T. (1993) Specjalizacja zbiorów i bibliotek. *Bibliotekarz*, (9), 25–30.

Zlikwidować (1992) biblioteki publiczne we Wrocławiu? *Bibliotekarz*, (10), 16–18.

Zpráva (1993) o stavu veřejných informačních služeb v České republice. *i*, **35**(9), 215–218.

Librarianship and information work in Southeast Asia

9

Mark Hepworth
and Michael Cheng

[Editor's note: Some of the personal names in the text and references of this chapter may appear to Western eyes to be in unusual forms. However, I am told by the authors that these are according to the conventions used in Singapore libraries; I have therefore chosen to leave them as they were supplied to me.]

Introduction

In writing about Southeast Asia, we are referring to the geographical region made up of two major physical blocs: namely, the mainland countries of Cambodia, Laos, Myanmar (the former Burma), Thailand, and Vietnam, and the island states of Brunei Darussalam, Indonesia, Malaysia, the Philippines and Singapore. The total land area covered by them is approximately 4.49 million square kilometres and the population figure at the end of 1994 has more than doubled since ten years ago to 480 million. While it may be said that there exists some degree of physical unity in terms of climate, geological evolution and culture, yet the differences between them in economic status, literacy levels, political development and library development are quite large. A number of these nations (Brunei Darussalam, Indonesia, Malaysia, Singapore, the Philippines and Thailand) have joined together to form the Association of Southeast Asian Nations (ASEAN) for the purpose of working together to promote economic growth and cooperation in various other areas like culture, education, technical assistance and sports. Vietnam is scheduled to join the group in July 1995, and will be followed by Cambodia at a later stage.

In recent years, the world has seen a dramatic shift in global economic activity away from the west to Asia. The Southeast Asian region is now one of the fastest growing economic regions in the world: the annual growth in GDP within some of the Southeast Asian countries has been most impressive – Singapore (10.2%), Malaysia (8.9%), Thailand (7.4%) and Indonesia (6.7%). Even post-war Vietnam has shot into the limelight, with an annual growth of 8.5% (*Asiaweek*, 1994).

In viewing the progress of librarianship in this region, we can see that those countries which have made the most economic progress, e.g. the ASEAN group, are the ones which have enjoyed a long period of political stability and are actively developing their countries' information infrastructure. Malaysia, Thailand and Singapore provide good examples. Singapore, for instance, with its IT2000 (Neo, 1993) and Library 2000 (*Library*, 1994) blueprints, is a country that has been steadily forging ahead in establishing itself as an 'intelligent island', with a stated aspiration of becoming the hub for the Asian information highway. While efforts have been expended to look at the planning of national, academic and public libraries, as well as rural library services for the countries with wide expanses of agricultural land, services to children, regional library co-operation and the promotion of reading, literacy and book development, it is clear to the policy makers and planners that the development of information technology on a country-wide scale is a vital preliminary to the linking of resources, manpower and services together effectively. In many places, developments are now being speeded up because of the growing sense of the need for regional cooperation and sustained economic growth. It must be admitted, however, that not all the Southeast Asian nations are able to develop at the same pace. Progress in key areas like education, health, literacy and the promotion of reading may often vary drastically, sometimes hampered by the extensive land areas, or by the lack of well-trained personnel, or by a large percentage of the population not having even a basic education, or (worse) by a lack of government support. The literacy rate in Thailand, for example, is estimated at 93.8%, in stark contrast to the 37.8% in Cambodia, slowly recovering as it is from the ravages of a war which has destroyed much of the country's cultural heritage. The literacy rates for the other Southeast Asian countries range from 80.0% in Malaysia to 93.5 % in the Philippines (*Asiaweek*, 1994), which augurs well for the region even when it seems that more could be done in developing public and school libraries to supplement the great hunger for knowledge among the young.

A survey of library activities indicates that, as a whole, the libraries in the ASEAN region have made greater progress in terms of collection development, library education, computerization, cooperative projects, manpower training and service improvements than have the other newly-emerging countries like Cambodia, Laos, Myanmar and Vietnam, which are slowly making attempts to restore much of what was destroyed through years of war and neglect (Nguyen, 1993). Foreign-aid agencies, international organizations and overseas libraries have ongoing programmes, e.g. the Vietnamese Union Catalogue Project (Cross and Jarvis, 1993) and the Vietnam Microforms Project (Microfilming, 1993; Henchy, 1994), to assist in restoring and developing libraries in these countries (Dommen, 1993). The need to train a large pool of people to provide effective library services, not only to the city areas, but, in many instances, to remote rural districts, is a matter which requires urgent assistance from the more developed nations.

In line with the ASEAN concept, the library associations of Indonesia, Malaysia, the Philippines, Singapore and Thailand, and their national libraries got together to form the Congress of Southeast Asian Librarians (CONSAL); inaugurated in 1970, it has met nine times since then. CONSAL IX was held in Bangkok in 1993, when Brunei Darussalam was formally received as a member. CONSAL X will be held in Kuala Lumpur in 1996. Other regional cooperative programmes are carried out by such organizations as the International Serials Data System-Southeast Asia (ISDS-SEA) Regional Centre, the National Libraries Group (NLG), and the Southeast Asian Regional Branch of the International Council on Archives (SARBICA). Another group of regional centres includes libraries attached to various international bodies whose main or regional offices are in Southeast Asia. These include the specialized agencies like the Asian Development Bank (ADB) in the Philippines, the International Development Research Centre (IDRC) in Singapore, the Southeast Asian Ministers of Education Organization (SEAMEO) in Thailand, the Asian Mass Communication Information Centre (AMIC) in Singapore, and the Regional Centre for the Teaching of Science and Mathematics (RECSAM) in Malaysia.

Because of their historical link and physical proximity, Malaysia and Singapore show many similarities in the various areas of their library development. Hence, the library associations of the two countries have been able to meet biennially for a joint conference to discuss such relevant issues as acquisition of Malaysian and Singapore materials, developments in academic, public and school libraries, joint cooperative projects and, following the latest trends in information technology, networking and computerization of library services. The last such conference was held in Penang, Malaysia, 19–24 September 1994, on the theme 'Towards Achieving High Performance Libraries'; it was attended by librarians not only from these two countries, but from the neighbouring Southeast Asian and Pacific regions as well. Both associations are long-established members of the Commonwealth Library Association (COMLA) and IFLA.

Libraries in Asia have, in the past, patterned their developments very much along the lines of what had been taking place in leading libraries in the USA, Canada, the UK, and a few other European countries. This has, of course, enabled the development process to be accelerated. A slow-down in development in such instances would generally be caused by lack of funds or qualified personnel. Now the libraries are seriously exploiting the available technology to gain quick access to, and retrieval of, an enormous pool of information located throughout the globe. The libraries can now 'focus on the extensiveness of the information worldwide, instead of the size of their physical collections' (*Library 2000*, 1994).

One feature that marks the Southeast Asian countries is the wide diversity of languages and dialects used, many of them with no common roots; this makes communication between races difficult. However, it is becoming clear that if ever there would be a language to link these nations it would have to be English. Singapore, Malaysia and Myanmar had a head start as English was very much the common language of communication during colonial days. However, this cannot be said of the remaining Southeast Asian nations, some of which came under the rule of other European peoples during a part of their history, such as the Dutch in Indonesia and the French in Vietnam. There is now a noticeable effort on the part of these nations to introduce English as a practical second language, so that they may read the major portion of the world's scientific and business publications, and thus participate in the global community of information technology, scientific development and business transactions.

In trying to identify the relevant literature on library and information science published during the past year, we had great difficulty in locating articles published in the English language. Hence, a high proportion of the literature reviewed would seem to have been published in Singapore and, to a lesser extent, Malaysia. We also had to rely on some publications issued outside this region. It must also be pointed out that publications in the vernacular languages which touch on the topics we have covered do not exist in large numbers, mainly because writing about such topics is something that does not come easily to the practising librarians. It is hoped that, as economic progress enables the Southeast Asian nations to turn their attention towards the modernization of their library resources and services, greater efforts to record the achievements can be traced to a larger output of published materials as recorded in bibliographies, indexes, documentation and library journals, and even through the electronic media such as the Internet.

Publishing and libraries

The interconnection between the publishing environment, the writers, readers and distributors – for example, libraries – is charted by Anuar (1994). She notes that any one weak link in this chain will cause problems. Chong (1993) raises the issue of the huge, rapidly-growing potential market for books among Chinese readers. On a less positive note, at a seminar for publishers, booksellers and librarians in Singapore, P. Lim, a Research Fellow at the Institute of Southeast Asian Studies, notes the lack of contact between librarians and publishers and also the lack of coordinated information about the availability of books (quoted by Teo, 1994; *Towards*, 1994). She suggests the online availability of *Singapore Books in Print* (SBIP) and the sharing of bibliographic resources, including those of the Singapore Integrated Library Automation Service (SILAS), between libraries as well as the book trade through networking facilities. L.U.W. Lim (1994) also highlights the issues concerning the role of booksellers and their interaction with libraries. Comparisons are made between foreign 'jobbers' and local publishers. Examples are given of opportunities for local publishers. Ramachandran (1994b) also points out the increased demand for books, and the concomitant opportunity for local and regional publishers to develop their services and become more proactive.

A brief survey of recent developments in publishing and reading (Recent, 1994) is perhaps indicative of a number of developments, including increased interest in electronic publishing. Publishers in Malaysia are said to be investing in computerized systems. In Indonesia, it is noted that 50% of production is concerned with educational publishing; in Thailand, the number of books for children is increasing significantly, whereas in the Philippines romance books and self-help books seem to be what most people are reading. In Laos, publishing is relatively underdeveloped with approximately 100 titles are published each year (Nguyen, 1993): of these, about 7% are novels and the rest are mostly government publications.

Library services (national libraries and national plans)

Two countries in the region seem to be particularly involved in preparing a co-ordinated national plan. These are Malaysia and Singapore. In many Asian countries, one can see, to a greater or lesser extent, some connection between the country's national aspirations, for example, the need to create a knowledge-based society or the need to diversify away from traditional forms of industry or agriculture, and the development of libraries, their collections and the services provided. Currently, these aspirations are increasingly translated into the acquisition and application of technology and materials, rather than, for instance, increasing the number of people required to manage and develop the services. Funds seem less readily available for the development of expertise through increased manpower training than for the application of information technology (IT). This is perhaps not surprising, since IT can be implemented relatively quickly, whereas training an information professional takes a longer period of time. Furthermore, the benefits of IT are more widely understood than those of the skills associated with information management.

Nevertheless, several countries, most noticeably Singapore and Malaysia, have published and announced long-term plans that involve and effect the provision of library and information services at a national level. In Singapore, the eagerly-awaited report of the Library 2000 Review Committee (*Library 2000*, 1994) was released in March 1994. This was the result of work conducted by a committee initially appointed in June 1992 by the Minister for Information and the Arts, BG

(Res) George Yeo. The report follows on from the IT2000 plan (Neo, 1993) and an IT usage survey conducted in 1992 (*Singapore*, 1993) which set the scene for the National Information Infrastructure (NII).

Ramachandran (1994a) summarizes the main points of the Library 2000 plan in his conference paper. Essentially, the plan seeks to 'establish a constellation of libraries of varying sizes, services and capabilities to serve the variegated needs of the population and to achieve better reach' (*Library*, 1994). The Reference Service Division of the National Library will become the National Reference Library, supported by a network of specialist libraries such as the Law and Medical Libraries of the National University of Singapore. It also recommends that two new special libraries be established: one for the Arts and another for Business. Public libraries will be linked through a more extensive network made up of regional libraries, community libraries and neighbourhood libraries (PM, 1994). The latter will be located in the 'void decks', the generally empty ground floors of blocks of flats located in housing estates (Void-deck, 1994), as well as community centres. The report also recommends that Singapore works towards establishing a network of 'borderless libraries' utilizing the NII. Other recommendations include:

- building up collections in the various spoken languages (especially Chinese, Malay and Tamil);
- setting up a library warehouse for less-used materials;
- ensuring that the education of librarians and technicians is monitored and kept up to date;
- that a 'new wave' of librarians should be attracted to the profession through better training programmes, more competitive remuneration and greater career opportunities.

In general, a phased implementation is expected over the next ten to fifteen years. Prototyping is a stated strategy for the new services. The Tampines Regional Library is the key site for prototyping some of the new ideas (see below). One of the most significant new developments will be the setting up of a new statutory board to implement the Library 2000 recommendations (Republic of Singapore, 1995). This should enable a more focused and centralized approach to be taken to library provision in Singapore, although it is unclear whether the proposed Board will take responsibility for school libraries and academic/special libraries or not. The main thrust of the development plan is to link up all the libraries within the island state, and also to enable users to access other resources from overseas (New-age, 1994).

In Malaysia, there has also been an initiative to develop an integrated strategy for the development of library services. This has come from the National Library, but it has also had the support of the government. The role of the National Library of Malaysia is defined in the National Library Amendment Act 1987, which includes responsibility for coordinating the information infrastructure of the nation. Awareness of the importance of information can also be clearly detected in the working paper 'Malaysia: the way forward' (now better known as the Vision 2020 paper) presented by the Prime Minister of Malaysia, Y.A.B. Dato' Seri Dr. Mahathir Mohamad, in which he emphasized the importance of information as a national resource (Ahmad, 1993).

In 1993, the Deputy Director-General of the National Library, Shahar Banun Jaafar, stated its future goals to be:

- strengthening the infrastructure;
- balancing resources of the states;
- achieving a minimum standard in all libraries;
- helping to develop more special libraries;
- ensuring the availability of computer facilities to create local databases;
- establishing a national bibliographic database;
- enabling good access via document delivery throughout the country;
- implementing reading campaigns and user education;
- establishing a National Reference and Referral Centre for Malaysian information;
- repackaging and creating value-added goods;
- establishing standards and a drive for quality library services.

Much emphasis has been placed on the networking and linking up of libraries as well as access to global networks. The Jaringan Ilmu (knowledge networks) project (Shahar, 1994) is the key to this and will be discussed later.

In her paper defining objectives for high performance in academic and special libraries in Malaysia, Zaiton (1994) attempts to relate these objectives to the Vision 2020 document.

Other countries in the region are, of course, active, but are hampered to some extent by the lack of resources, or do not have the same government backing. Indonesia is perhaps representative, in that the lack of a centralized responsibility for libraries throughout the country has impeded development. Concern over issues such as conservation and preservation (Hardjoprakoso, 1993), readership, the emerging cooperative efforts between national and government libraries (Hariyadi and Gani, 1993) and also the lack of urgently-needed professional staff are fundamental themes that are echoed throughout the region. At the same time, in contrast, there are examples of hi-tech information solutions, either proposed or implemented, which affect the information infrastructure. Such solutions are usually government-backed and are often managed by quasi-governmental technology agencies.

In Laos, the National Library has an ongoing project to publish both a current and a retrospective bibliography (Nguyen, 1993). More bibliographic activities can now be seen to be taking place with assistance from libraries and organizations outside the country.

In Myanmar, due to a turbulent history and an extended period of isolation, the National Library has experienced significant challenges. Currently, the library has about 22,332 square feet of floor area, which is insufficient for proper library functions; however, it is hoped that new premises will be found. There are 39 staff, of whom eight are trained professionals. In general, librarians are aware of the need to update their library resources, to acquire computers and skills in providing online information services, and to develop a plan for library automation. The Universities' Central Library (UCL) is one of the few libraries that has automated some of its functions; it is connected through a local area network to most departments of Rangoon University. It is likely that this library may become a model for future developments, particularly in the area of access to electronic sources of information (E.O.F. Reid, 1994, personal communication).

Library services (reading and user education)

Information about reading and user education seems to be rather lacking in the library literature of this region. Documented examples are difficult to come by, although it would seem, from a review of past activities, that the promotion of reading has been more of a major component of public library services and that user education programmes are more actively pursued by academic libraries. Two reports on surveys of reading habits and interests carried out in Singapore (Kiang-Koh, 1994; Ngian, 1994a) give fairly comprehensive accounts of this topic. These showed that, out of a sample of 1,000 respondents aged twelve and above, the reading of newspapers, books or magazines ranked second among leisure activities. The most popular subjects were fiction (62%), followed by hobbies, cooking and decoration (29%), philosophy and religion (28%), family and health care (26%), sports (22%) and travel (21%). In general, 31% of the population are members of the library. A survey of school children showed that 84% of them watch television for two hours each evening, and 35% of them read only course books. A curriculum highly oriented towards examination success, and competitive early streaming, probably also discourage 'leisure' reading.

Ng et al. (1993) describe methods used to familiarize students with the resources and services of the library. In the academic setting, these include bibliographic instruction or library tutorials, and the introduction of computer-assisted instruction. Nanyang Technological University, for example, introduced a computer-assisted library instruction package in 1994. The other libraries of tertiary institutions are known to conduct user education programmes for new students and teaching staff on a regular basis, especially at the beginning of an academic year.

One study of users of CD-ROM services at the Ngee Ann Polytechnic (D.F.C. Chan, 1993) was undertaken to determine their problems in searching, and how the interfaces could be improved to eliminate the need for help of an intermediary.

With regard to the public library environment and the use of the library resources by children, Butterworth (1994) discusses how new user interfaces aimed at children such as Book Wizard or Kid's Carl may be used to encourage reading among the young. A collection aimed at another community was also brought to the reader's attention (Azizah, 1993). This discussed the role of the Singapore National Library in providing a clearing-house on 'Women in development', the objective being to build up a good collection of literature on women in general and, in particular, on women in Singapore and Southeast Asia.

A similar set-up in Kuala Lumpur, Malaysia, called the Malaysia Information Clearinghouse on Women in Development, is described by Khoo (1994) as an example of how access to information can be improved through cooperation. In Sabah, Malaysia, readership is being encouraged by the setting up of village libraries in each of the 48 constituencies (Sabah, 1994). It was also reported that the Malaysian Chinese Association (MCA) is discussing the setting up 500 libraries in the new villages throughout Malaysia, so that the educational standards of Chinese children in rural areas can be raised (MCA, 1993).

Thailand has an interesting project, which is being carried out in a very different setting. Called 'Rural Development Through Reading Activities and Continuing Education', it was launched by the Academic Resource Center in cooperation with the Department of Library Science at Srinakharinwirot University. An update of this project is given by Boonyakanchana (1993).

Public libraries

Throughout the region, the resources of public libraries vary greatly. In Indonesia, where there is a combination of national library, regional libraries acting as its agents, public libraries in the cities or regencies, branches in the sub-districts and villages, and also a mobile service, the impression is one of an understaffed and under-resourced public service (Hardjoprakoso, 1993). The total public holdings were 4,556,238 volumes for a total population of over 180 million spread out over two million square kilometres of territory. It is possible that the lack of a centralized coordinating body in Indonesia may have been a constraint, in comparison with Malaysia, for example, which has such a body.

In the Philippines, lack of adequate public library facilities in rural areas, where the majority of people live, has been a concern (Bolos, 1993); this has led to plans for the purchase of fifteen new bookmobiles for the rural areas to revitalize the services. These will be equipped with a television set, video player/recorder, karaoke and projectors. The aim is to provide equal opportunities for readers and non-readers alike to acquire information.

In Thailand, there is a general initiative to enlarge and upgrade old libraries and to establish new ones, in order to provide a more extensive library service to the people. Cooperation among libraries is seen as an important step towards the achievement of an effective library network system; it may also bring more financial support from the government (Kanakamani, 1993).

Two exciting developments have taken place in Singapore and Malaysia. In Singapore, it is the opening of the new Tampines Regional Library (TRL), which will be developed as a prototype for new concepts and services (Library, 1993). Among the new services offered are an electronic library of CD-ROMs, 'Interactive tv', laser disc players, Teleview (a public viewdata service) and CDIs. Users can use a personal computer to access electronically the audiovisual collection, the National Library online public access catalogue system (NLine), INtv services and a selection of popular CD-ROM titles. Remote dial-up access to the library is also available, and home delivery of books has been instigated. The library incorporates an information technology showcase and a theatre, and even a bookshop in the foyer; colourful displays make the children's area an attractive environment (Koh, 1994).

The opening of the new National Library in Kuala Lumpar was, as with Tampines, prestigious and presented as a significant national event. Visually dramatic, the tiled roof is built in the style of the tengkok (the traditional male headgear), symbolizing pride and respect. Inside the 238,000 square foot room for 1,000 readers there is a collection of over one million books; of these, 20,000, mostly in Malay and English, are available for loan. In addition, access is provided to internal databases (*Bunar* for publications, *Mentari* for academic and research articles, *Pancaram* for Malaysian conference proceedings) and also to external databases provided by *Bernama* (mostly financial data, news and company information) and *NSTP Online* (the full text of New Straits Times Publications). Wheelchair access is provided, as are facilities for the visually handicapped such as talking books and text-enlarging facilities.

At the less glamorous end of public librarianship, Tan and Sulaiman (1994) in Singapore describe and discuss some local initiatives to attract readers. These include programmes for children (e.g. story telling and classroom visits), for teenagers (drama workshops and talks by well-known personalities on topics related to teenage issues), for adults (e.g. programmes on health, the environment, self-improvement, etc.), and for the disadvantaged, including story-telling and the starting of a collection of large print books.

Academic libraries

Nera (1993) provides reports on different countries, giving a good overview of concerns and issues within the region. Collection development, information technology, involvement in the academic curriculum, cooperation, and responding to national aspirations are common themes.

The Philippines paper (Angeles, 1993) stresses the need to formulate appropriate rather than idealistic, and often elitist, standards. Other concerns of the Philippines academic libraries include the role of the library in the educational process, particularly in the area of bibliographic instruction, and the importance of involving the library in general university administration.

A similar concern with standards was expressed in the paper on Brunei Darussalam (Sharifah, 1993). In addition, the need for cooperation is emphasized. In most cases, academic libraries there do not have separate budgets, and are therefore dependent on the institutional head. This affects collection building and services to users. Qualified staffing is raised as a significant issue; for example, only 24 out of the 70 academic librarians are qualified, and 75% of those are in the Universiti Brunei Darussalam Library.

The Indonesian paper (Mudjito, 1993) emphasizes the need for cooperation on an ASEAN-wide basis to support resource-sharing and networking. All the 45 government universities and institutions of higher education are equipped with relatively good libraries; and in the private institutions (numbering about 400–500) a library is one of the requirements for accreditation. A Library Development Coordination Unit and a Library Advisory Group have been set up by the Government to look into ways of optimizing the development of library services for higher education.

In Singapore, space and staffing constraints are presented as significant issues (Yap, 1993). However, to some extent, this has probably encouraged the adoption of new technologies such as self-service circulation systems (Ong, 1994). Libraries in Singapore need more space to accommodate rapidly increasing collections and new library services such as CD-ROMs. In a number of academic institutions, including Nanyang Technological University and the National University of Singapore, CD-ROM services have been networked so that they are readily available to academic staff and students. With the advent of the use of automated systems, new forms of user education are taking place in the academic institutions (New, 1993).

Shaikha (1993) describes the background to academic libraries in Malaysia, where there are seven university libraries with collections ranging from 100,000 to one million volumes (Shahar, 1994). Issues raised include the increase in the use of audiovisual material, despite some budget cut-backs, the extension of library services to the commercial sector, and increased coordination and networking both at an organizational level and in a technological sense. Zaiton (1994) discusses the national Vision 2020 concept and defines the implicit role of the academic and research library in supporting the transformation of the economy, the advancement of science and technology, and human resource development. She emphasizes the need for academic libraries to be involved in the educational process both by providing relevant services and by understanding the user environment – for example, the process of research. Other themes highlighted are the need to use merit rather than seniority as a criterion for promotion in libraries, the need for effective management, the need for new collections and new media, the need for adequate remuneration and sound training to encourage good staff (particularly in the area of science), and also the application of technology with a view to the concept of the borderless library.

Although less well-documented, the academic libraries of Thailand seem comparatively developed in terms of the services offered to the user. Recent new services have included current awareness service, selective dissemination of information and networking. Future developments are expected to include fee-based services (Chintawong, 1993) and expansion in the area of information technology (see below).

Myanmar has three universities and several institutes specializing in subjects such as economics, technology, education, agriculture, medicine and animal husbandry. As mentioned above, developments have been limited, hampered by lack of funds. However, recent initiatives have been put in place to start to address some of the areas needing improvement. At the Universities' Central Library (UCL), bibliographies have been developed using the Pro-Cite software, which enables the incorporation of Burmese characters, and also CDS/ISIS software (E.O.F. Reid, 1994, personal communication).

School libraries

In Brunei Darussalam, the school library is a recent social phenomenon. However, all newly built schools now have libraries or resource centres. In 1988, it was found that, out of 114 schools visited, 90% had libraries. The Sixth Form Centre had the largest stock, with 22,100 volumes (Ali, 1992). In 1993, there were 108 library posts; only two post-holders were professionals (Nellie, 1993).

In Indonesia, as in Singapore, the school library is usually managed by a teacher and, in most cases, is only an additional duty along with all the other teaching responsibilities (Gobel and Wardaya, 1992). The conditions of most school libraries are generally poor (Mudjito, 1993). Despite this situation, the National Library in Indonesia has, in the last decade, organized 120 hours of short introductory library training for teachers. A decree by the Minister of State for State's Apparatus Efficiency number 18/1992 was announced, on awarding credits for librarians. It means that a librarian can be promoted by accruing credits: this will encourage people to choose librarianship as a possible career. The Centre for Library Development has established 26 model school libraries, one in each of the provinces, intended to be models for other schools in the area (Mudjito, 1993). Gobel and Wardaya (1992) make a number of recommendations, which include establishing regional model school libraries, centralized acquisition systems for each province, cooperation and rotation of material in some areas, formalizing further the teacher librarian's role, and setting standards for the school collection.

Jamaiah and Omar (1994), who work for the Educational Technology Division of the Ministry of Education, describe the developing role of the Malaysian school resource centres; the need is expressed for integration of the resource centre role in the educational process and its involvement in developing generic information handling skills. Sajjad (1993) gives a more detailed account of the training of personnel in such resource centres, and also discusses the status and prospects related to the job.

Special libraries

Mariah (1993) describes Brunei Darussalam's current position of having twelve government special libraries and one semi-governmental institution, the Brunei Darussalam Shell Petroleum Company Sendiran Berhad. The law library, with a collection of over 50,000 books, is probably the most significant (Nellie, 1993). One is given the impression that special libraries there are at the early stages of development.

Contrasting numbers are evident in Indonesia, where it is estimated that there are 620 special libraries, 81% of them in government organizations (Rompas, 1993). One issue highlighted here is the problem of collection development within an economically tight environment.

Although Malaysia has fewer special libraries than Indonesia, they fall into a larger number of different types. Out of the total number of 337, 175 are in government departments, 50 are in statutory organizations, 44 in private organizations such as legal, accounting and oil companies, 38 in banks and financial institutions (an area that has grown in recent years), 19 in professional and voluntary organizations and 11 in embassies and international organizations (Zainab, 1993). These figures are, to some extent, similar to those found in Thailand (Tontyaporn, 1993). Zainab discusses current issues like staffing, budgets and space, and points out the shortage of statistics concerning the activities of special libraries. From a professional point of view, she highlights the problem of getting access to information on particular disciplines, the difficulty of identifying sources and the lack of formal networking among special libraries.

In both Malaysia and Singapore, special libraries have been involved in automation; for example, in Singapore, the Attorney Gencral's Office has been involved with the setting up of Lawnet, the local legal database (Tan, 1993). Another recent example has been the Singapore Broadcasting Corporation Library (now renamed the Television Corporation of Singapore Library) which is in the process of developing a multimedia 'one stop' resource centre held digitally on a centralized system (Mah, 1993). In July 1994, a contract was signed with IME Ltd (Information Management Engineering) to develop the multimedia library automation segment of the two million Singapore dollar system. Several other special libraries, like the DBS Bank Library, the Monetary Authority of Singapore (MAS) Library and the Ministry of Information and the Arts (MITA) Library, have existing optical storage databases for press cuttings. The latter is available for use by government departments, including the National Library.

Computerization

Computerization has been a key issue throughout the region, to the extent that a publication covering the ASEAN libraries was devoted to this topic (Chan, 1993). Computerization has taken a number of forms, including library automation, the installation of CD-ROMs (in some cases in a networked environment) (Chollampe and Anaprayot, 1993), access to overseas online databases (although this is limited and often restricted to accessing DIALOG), the development of local databases, and also the use of the Internet. Computerization tends to be more developed in the government organizations, especially the more technical, and also in libraries at tertiary institutions. Other developments have included the introduction of self-checkout systems – partly perhaps in response to the shortage of staff now faced by many libraries.

Library automation itself has taken place to a lesser or greater extent throughout the region, varying from systems based on micros or minis (running, for example, CDS/ISIS provided by UNESCO) to mini or mainframe solutions (running, for example, ATLAS, URICA, VTLS), and recently a couple of TINLIB sites. In Brunei Darussalam, most computer systems are for retrieval of data or information by staff (Azhari, 1993); whereas, in Thailand, Singapore and Malaysia, publicly accessible databases have been developed. In writing about library automation, Azhari highlights a common theme, that is, the inadequacy or absence of local support by library automation vendors.

As previously mentioned, the SBC (Singapore Broadcasting Corporation) Library has signed an agreement to install a library automation system, BLISS, that will be accessed by end-users from their desks (IME, 1994). It is different from the usual text-based library systems in that it will include multimedia components such as the selection and previewing of key frames of audiovisual materials. BLISS is a client-server system serving more than 1,700 users on the network; it enables the user to navigate from one entity to another during the search, allowing instant switching from an author search to a subject search and from a book to an article (SBC, 1994).

Again in Singapore, an interesting technical development at the public library level has been the setting up of the Tampines Regional Library system. Here, the system enables the user (among other things) to browse, select and view any of 3,000 audiovisual titles, including feature films, documentaries, music albums, etc. The CDDI network, which runs at 100 million bits per second [Mbps], is one of the first of its kind in the region: 26 personal computers in the library are currently connected via the network file server (K.C. Lim, 1994).

In Indonesia, computerization has not developed as fast as expected, even though the issues of library automation have been discussed since the early 1970s (Setiarso and Sudarsono, 1993). This slow development has been attributed to lack of resources, in particular of manpower and equipment; automation has therefore not been a priority in library development programmes. At present, most computerization in libraries is still based on microcomputers: the most popular software is Micro CDS/ISIS, provided by UNESCO. The main activity has been the creation of bibliographic databases in the National Library and special libraries. One of the more advanced systems is at the Centre for Scientific Documentation and Information – Indonesian Institute of Sciences (PDII-LIPI), which successfully completed a union catalogue of serials as one of its earliest projects. In 1992, an upgrade in its computer system has enabled it to embark on several new projects, like implementing an area local network for integrated library operations and increasing its public services. Also in the pipeline is the creation of specialized databases to produce the *Index of Indonesian Research Reports*, the *Index of Indonesian Learned Periodicals Articles*, the *Index of Indonesian Conference Proceedings* and the other regular bibliographic publications of PDII-LIPI which have been published manually since 1960. In line with the awareness that 'an ever increasing variety, quantity and quality of information are needed by the users' is the realization that training and education programmes must be provided for the librarians, so that they will be able to administer, operate and manage the computerized networks which are needed to link the many libraries and information centres throughout the country.

At the national level, two bibliographic databases have received wide publicity. These are the formation of the Malaysian Bibliographic Network, of which MALMARC forms the core (Begum, 1993), and the Singapore SILAS system, which promotes shared cataloguing as well as maintaining the national union catalogue. A detailed write-up of the work of SILAS is given by its Head of Bibliographical Control (A.E. Lim, 1993) and by its Assistant Director (Lai, 1993). The *Singapore National Bibliography* (SNB) is now available in CD-ROM format.

Special and academic libraries have been responsible for the evolution of local databases. Examples of these include *PALMSEARCH*, developed by the Palm Oil Research Institute of Malaysia Library (Begum, 1993); the *PATS* database, developed by the Ministry of Trade and Industry's Department of Statistics in Singapore; *AGRIASIA*, a database on agricultural literature developed by the Agricultural Information Bank for Asia (AIBA), Philippines; and *BIZNET*, an electronic information network containing data supplied by the Registry of Companies and

Business in Singapore.

Less well-publicized, but probably as significant, have been the developments in Thailand. The Computer Network Project has been initiated to link all the science and technology databases created by eleven universities. THAIPOPIN is a national population information network linking eighteen institutes. There is also the Provincial University Library Network (PULINET), as well as the Documentation Centre of the Asian Institute of Technology, which has created the Thailand Inter-University Network (ATUNET) and seventeen other databases (Siriwongworawat, 1993). These developments are also reflected in the more recent implementation of Internet applications.

In Malaysia, the paper by Shahar Banun Jaafar (1994) describes current plans and developments involving the setting up of a coordinated network of national, regional and special libraries with common access to local databases and international information systems and services such as the Internet. This followed the signing of a Memorandum of Understanding to set up a nationwide library network under the Jaringan Ilmu project; work will be undertaken by the Malaysian Institute of Microelectronic Systems (MIMOS) in conjunction with the National Library. This project will involve the development of a research network, a knowledge network, an education network, a public network and an agricultural network. Emphasis is placed on developing local electronic products and services for the community as a whole. Further applications of library networking are to be found in the papers of a seminar on global information networking (*Seminar*, 1994).

In the Philippines, the extensive use of computers by libraries to handle information is in an early stage of development. The National Committee on Libraries and Information Services, headed by the Director of the National Library, is currently undertaking a nationwide survey of library resources in the country. One part of this will cover the computerizarion of libraries. Problems such as budgetary constraints and inadequate supply of trained personnel to develop and maintain the systems are deemed to be the cause of the slow development. However, several of the larger libraries attached to institutions and organizations have been able to computerize their information activities through the help of external agencies like the World Health Organization and UNESCO; this has enabled them to participate in regional and national networks. Examples are the libraries at the Southeast Asian Fisheries Development Center (SEAFDEC), the International Rice Research Institute (IRRI) and the Agricultural Information Bank for Asia (AIBA). Other libraries are also using the mini-micro CDS/ISIS software package developed by UNESCO (Mascapac, 1993).

In the academic environment, a good example of networked applications is offered by the Ngee Ann Polytechnic in Singapore (Introducing, 1994). At this location, application software, courseware, electronic books, specialized databases, CD-ROM databases, the online public access catalogue (OPAC) and bulletin board are made available to the entire campus.

One development that is affecting, though not strictly taking place within, the region demonstrates a trend: the launch of the *INTANMAS* database by the Northern Territory University in Australia. *INTANMAS* contains references to the literature on northern Australia and eastern Indonesia and on Australia's relations with Indonesia (Mulliner, 1993). This database reflects the increased Australian library involvement in the Southeast Asia and China region.

Computerization in Myanmar is in its early stages. The Universities' Central Library (UCL) in Yangon (formerly Rangoon) has automated its circulation and bibliographic search functions and has recently connected to most university departments through a local area network. CDS/ISIS and Pro-Cite software are being used to create bibliographies of local resources. One other library, the Institute of Medicine, has installed CD-ROM as a result of a collaboration with the World Health Organization.

The use of the Internet has received much attention around the world: Southeast Asia is no exception. Reid (1995) provides a good overview in her conference paper. All of the countries in Southeast Asia, except Brunei Darussalam, have some type of connection to the Internet; however, it is only relatively recently that Indonesia and the Philippines have provided full access to it. The libraries which are proactively using the Internet are either academic or special libraries: examples of the latter group would be the National Computer Board and the Ministry of Education in Singapore or the National Electronics and Computer Technology Center in Thailand. Currently, in each country, the following have either World Wide Web (WWW) (own home page) and/or Gopher sites: Indonesia, with nine active academic sites and two government or quasi-government sites; Malaysia, with five; the Philippines, with six; and Singapore, with five. The sites in Malaysia, Singapore and Thailand are providing access to local OPACs and/or internal databases.

Training and education

The training and education of librarians is a constant topic of discussion within the profession around the world. Stueart (1993) reiterates the diversity of schools, from library science to information science or information management, and the range of programmes from part-time to full-time, certificate to postgraduate. The education of librarians and information professionals in Southeast Asia reflects, to some extent, these differences. However, there seems to be a consensus in the region that more trained librarians and information professionals are required.

In Indonesia, several universities offer diplomas in library science. Only the University of Indonesia offers a Master's degree, which has been available since

1990; three other universities offer the sarjana programme, which is equivalent to a bachelor's degree. In addition, special sarjana programmes have been offered to help to develop unqualified practitioners (Sulistyo-Basuki, 1993). In the Philippines, there are currently three programmes: the Bachelor of Library Science, the Master of Library Science and the Diploma in Librarianship, which was introduced in 1990 (Vallejo, 1993a, 1993b). Malaysia is in a similar situation with, until 1992, only one training centre for information professionals, at the Institut Teknologi MARA. The International Islamic University of Malaysia has been running a Master's degree in library science since 1992 (Abdullah, 1993).

In Singapore, the only source of professional training for many years was a part-time, two-year, postgraduate diploma course in library and information science, run by the National Library and the Library Association. After considerable research into the need for information professionals, a Master's degree course was set up at the Nanyang Technological University in July 1993, with a full-time faculty (Butterworth, 1993a; Sabaratnam, 1993). The programme at present takes two years to complete on a part-time basis; a Master's degree through research and a PhD programme are also offered.

In contrast to other countries in the region, Thailand offers six Master's programmes and seven bachelor's degree programmes (Premsmit, 1993). Graduate programmes in library and information science are available at most public universities except Chiang Mai and Khon Kaen, which are expected to offer Master's programmes in the near future.

Professional training in Myanmar is currently being offered by the Universities' Central Library (UCL) and is taught at diploma level. The urgent need for a bigger pool of professionally trained librarians cannot be over-emphasized, as the country is attempting to catch up with its more developed neighbours: a great deal of developmental work has to be carried out to restore and upgrade the library collections which have seen neglect for a good number of years.

Although there is a growing demand for higher education programmes, there is also a need for ongoing professional development, short courses or continuing education programmes and even in-service training programmes (Amanah and Shahrozat; Mohd and Norma, 1994). In their paper, Amanah and Shahrozat discuss the importance of such training and provide some information on the training programmes that are being conducted by the National Library of Malaysia.

In Singapore, the Temasek Polytechnic and the Library Association of Singapore jointly conduct a six-month course leading to a certificate in library and information studies. Temasek Polytechnic is also planning to offer an information science and management course which aims to train people who will need to manage information when their institutions, such as libraries or private companies, are linked to global networks (Temasek, 1994).

Management

Significant interest has been shown in the many aspects of the management of information services. One theme, expressed during a seminar organized by the Library Association of Singapore, was the incorporation of market-oriented strategy and the need to 're-engineer' the library (Butterworth, 1993b). Another theme is the urgent need for well-trained professional staff. In the Philippines Arlante and Tarlit highlight the importance and significance of legislation recognizing the professional role of the librarian (Arlante and Tarlit, 1993). At the 1994 Joint PPM/LAS Congress in Penang, the themes were performance and its measurement (Ngian, 1994b), the issue of quality in libraries and training (Mohd and Norma, 1994) and the future role of librarians (Hepworth, 1994).

In Thailand, an ALP (Advancement of Librarianship in the Third World Programme) Workshop organized by Thammasat University Library, IFLA-ALP and IFLA Regional Standing Committee for Asia and Oceania (RSCAO), brought together participants from Brunei Darussalam, Cambodia, Indonesia, Laos, Malaysia, Pakistan, the Philippines, Vietnam and Thailand. The objective of the meeting was to identify major regional needs and to help formulate proposals for projects that could be submitted to funding agencies (ALP, 1994). Papers presented at the workshop can be found in the published proceedings (Guaysuwan, 1994).

Preservation

Throughout the region, the issue of preservation is apparent (Mariam and Siti, 1994), although perhaps not as conspicuously as other topics such as technology or education. In Vietnam, a major project is under way, with North American funding, to establish microfilming facilities and the skills for preservation filming and stabilization of the original sources (Henchy, 1994). In connection with the IFLA/National Library of Australia workshops held in Bangkok and Hanoi, Lyall (1994) highlights some of the key issues concerning preservation in the Southeast Asia and Pacific Region. She is of the opinion that, in order for effective national preservation programmes to be developed, three major issues will have to be addressed, namely:
- support for funding;
- an environment of cooperation; and
- significant increases in government funding.

Many libraries in Southeast Asia have historical collections, some of which date back more than a century. If not properly maintained, these priceless collections will soon be useless; steps must be taken to restore and preserve them, using modern technology. Weather, wars, thefts, ignorance and neglect have all contributed to the destruction of this rich heritage and record of mankind's achievement. It is not too soon for some action to be taken by all parties concerned to ensure that the process of decay is halted.

Conclusion

Countries in Southeast Asia show great disparity in their economic development; disparities also occur between urban and rural settings. However, significant changes are taking place. These disparities and changes can be seen to be reflected in the library activities and services in the region. As in many countries, the library sector is not at the forefront of the politician's mind. Nevertheless, in the more developed countries, such as Malaysia and Singapore, policy documents and strategies show some appreciation of the value of libraries and the development of an information sector. In the newly-emerging countries, such as Vietnam and Myanmar, programmes are focused on the restoration, preservation and development of library collections. One common underlying theme, however, that is echoed throughout the region is the need for more trained information professionals.

The future will hold more dramatic changes in all these countries. It is hoped that makers of policy and sources of finance will perceive the value and necessity of the 'content', that is, the information and its effective organisation and management, and are not charmed into thinking that the 'conduit', that is, the technology, is an acceptable alternative.

References

Abdullah Yaacob (1993) The training of library and information professionals in Malaysia. *Asian Libraries*, 3(4), 78–80.

Ahmad Sarji Abdul Hamid (1993) (ed.) *Malaysia's Vision 2020: understanding the concept, implications and challenges*. Petaling Jaya, Selangor: Pelandok Publications, p. xv.

Ali bin Haji Kayum (1992) School libraries and challenges ahead, with special reference to Brunei Darussalam. In: Soekarman and S.S. Wardaya (eds) *Introduction to ASEAN librarianship: school libraries*. Jakarta: ASEAN Committee on Culture and Information, pp. 1–18.

ALP (1994) Workshop, 10–12 May 1993, Bangkok, Thailand. *IFLA Journal*, 20(1), 79–80.

Amanah Ahmad and Shahrozat Ibrahim (1994) In-service training for a productive library workforce. In: *Towards achieving high performance libraries: vision for the future. 1994 Joint*

PPM/LAS Congress: proceedings, vol.1. Penang: Universiti Sains Malaysia Library and Persatuan Perpustakaan Malaysia, pp. 137–146.

Angeles, B.B. (1993) Academic libraries in the Philippines. In: C.M. Nera (ed.) *Introduction to ASEAN librarianship: academic libraries.* Jakarta: ASEAN Committee on Culture and Information, pp. 61–85.

Anuar, H. (1994) Twenty-five years of book development. *Singapore Book World,* (23), 1–8.

Arlante, S.M. and Tarlit, R.Y. (1993) The professionalization of librarians: a unique Philippine experience. *Asian Libraries,* 3(2), 13–22.

Asiaweek (1994), Vital signs. (14 December), 65.

Azhari bin Haji Suhaimi *Asiaweek,* (1993) Library automation: its development in Brunei Darussalam with special reference to Institut Teknologi Brunei Darussalam. In: T.S. Chan (ed.) *Introduction to ASEAN librarianship: library computerization.* Singapore: ASEAN Committee on Culture and Information, pp. 1–38.

Azizah Sidek (1993) The status and development of the Clearinghouse on Women in Development (Singapore). *Singapore Libraries,* (22), 60–66.

Begum, R. (1993) Computerization of library operations in Malaysia: an overview. In: T.S. Chan (ed.) *Introduction to ASEAN librarianship: library computerization.* Singapore: ASEAN Committee on Culture and Information, pp. 51–68.

Bolos, A.M. (1993) Library development and future trends in the Philippines. In: *CONSAL IX papers: future dimensions and library development, Bangkok, 2-7 May 1993.* Bangkok: CONSAL, pp. A26–A42.

Boonyakanchana, C. (1993) Rural development through reading and continuing education. In: *CONSAL IX papers: future dimensions and library development, Bangkok, 2-7 May 1993.* Bangkok: CONSAL, pp. 154–165

Butterworth, M. (1993a) New course offered at NTU: MSc in information studies becomes reality. *Singapore Libraries Bulletin,* 4(1), 15.

Butterworth, M. (1993b) Strategic planning for the 21st century –a seminar. *Singapore Libraries Bulletin,* 4(2), 3.

Butterworth, M. (1994) The book behind the terminal: electronic tools help children find what they want in bookshops and libraries. *Singapore Book World,* (24), 5–10.

Chan, D.F.C. (1993) Direct searching of a CD-ROM database by library users: a study. *Singapore Libaries,* (22), 15–25.

Chan, T.S. (1993) (ed.) *Introduction to ASEAN librarianship: library computerization.* Singapore: ASEAN Committee on Culture and Information.

Chintawong, W. (1993) Academic libraries in Thailand. In: C.M. Nera (ed.) *Introduction to ASEAN librarianship: academic libraries.* Jakarta: ASEAN Committee on Culture and Information, pp. 107–120.

Chollampe, K. and Anaprayot, P. (1993) CD-ROM networking in Thailand. *Asian Libraries,* 3(2), 44–52.

Chong, K.Y. (1993) The relationship between Singapore Chinese readers and the Chinese market. *Singapore Book World,* 23(1), 13–21.

Cross, N. and Jarvis, H. (1993) The challenge of building an international union catalog: the Vietnamese experience. *Asian Libraries,* 3(2), 36–43.

Dommen, A.J. (1993) Survey of Laos research. *CORMOSEA Bulletin,* 22(2), 2–5.

Gobel, R. and Wardaya, S.S. (1992) School library services in Indonesia. In: Soekarman and S.S. Wardaya (eds) *Introduction to ASEAN librarianship: school libraries.* Jakarta:

ASEAN Committee on Culture and Information, pp. 19–36.
Guaysuwan, P. (1994) (ed.) *The advancement of librarianship: a workshop to identify and assess needs in South-East Asia and to formulate proposals. Proceedings of the Workshop held in Bangkok, Thailand, 10-12 May 1993.* Bangkok: Thammasat University Press.
Hardjoprakoso, M. (1993) Library development and future trends in Indonesia. In: *CONSAL IX papers: future dimensions and library development, Bangkok, 2-7 May 1993.* Bangkok: CONSAL, pp. A7–A25.
Hariyadi, U.and Gani, F. (1993) The National Library of Indonesia. *Asian Libraries*, 3(2), 11–12.
Henchy, J. (1994) Vietnam Microforms Project. *CORMOSEA Bulletin*, 23(1), 12–16.
Hepworth, M. (1994) The virtual library: perceptions, realities and roles. *Singapore Libraries*, (23), 13–26.
IME (1994) International selects Singapore for regional office. *Singapore Libraries Bulletin*, 4(4), 6–7.
Introducing (1994) the electronic library at the Ngee Ann Polytechnic campus. *Singapore Libraries Bulletin*, 4(3), 9–10.
Jamaiah Osman and Omar Samsuri (1994) Malaysian school resource centres: impetus to quality education. In: *Towards achieving high performance libraries: vision for the future. 1994 Joint PPM/LAS Congress: proceedings, vol.1.* Penang: Universiti Sains Malaysia Library and Persatuan Perpustakaan Malaysia, pp. 85–93.
Kanakamani, T. (1993) Library development and future trends in Thailand. In: *CONSAL IX papers: future dimensions and library development, Bangkok, 2-7 May 1993.* Bangkok: CONSAL, pp. A56–A77.
Khoo, S.M. (1994) Pusat Sumber Maklumat Wanita Dalam Pembangunan Malaysia (Malaysia Information Clearinghouse on Women in Development): an example of improving access through cooperation. In: *Towards achieving high performance libraries: vision for the future. 1994 Joint PPM/LAS Congress: proceedings, vol.1.* Penang: Universiti Sains Malaysia Library and Persatuan Perpustakaan Malaysia, pp. 63–76.
Kiang-Koh, L.L.(1994) The reading environment in Singapore. *Singapore Libraries*, (23), 34–40.
Koh, B.S. (1994) Plugged into global information: cable TV, computers, plays all-in-one library. *Straits Times*, (30 November), *Supplement*, 5.
Lai, Y.P. (1993) Computerization of library operations in Singapore: an overview. In: T.S. Chan (ed.) *Introduction to ASEAN librarianship: library computerization.* Singapore: ASEAN Committee on Culture and Information, pp. 85–104.
Library (1993) of the future makes appearance. *Singapore Libraries Bulletin*, 4(2), 10–11.
Library (1994) *2000: investing in a learning nation. Report of the Library 2000 Review Committee.* Singapore: SNP Publications.
Lim, A.E. (1993) National bibliographic network: the Singapore experience. *Singapore Libraries*, (22), 3–14.
Lim, K.C. (1994) Tampines Regional Library: a vision for the future. *Singapore Libraries*, (23), 3–12.
Lim, L.U.W. (1994) Serving the library's needs – a book publisher's perception. *Singapore Libraries*, (23), 67–75.
Lyall, J. (1994) Developing managing preservation programmes in the South-East Asian and Pacific regions. *IFLA Journal*, 20(3), 262–275.

Mah, C.K. (1993) The SBC Library: library services. *Singapore Libraries Bulletin*, **4**(2), 13.
Mariah Haji Kamis (1993) Special libraries in Brunei Darussalam. In: Shahar Banun Jaafar et al. (eds) *Introduction to ASEAN librarianship: special libraries.* Kuala Lumpur: ASEAN Committee on Culture and Information, pp. 1–16.
Mariam Abdul Kadir and Siti Rodziah Othman (1994) Developing a preservation policy of library material for future users. In: *Towards achieving high performance libraries: vision for the future. 1994 Joint PPM/LAS Congress: proceedings, vol.2.* Penang: Universiti Sains Malaysia Library and Persatuan Perpustakaan Malaysia, pp. 67–83.
Mascapac, G.A. (1993) Computerization of library operations in the Philippines: an overview. In: T.S. Chan (ed.) *Introduction to ASEAN librarianship: library computerization.* Singapore: ASEAN Committee on Culture and Information, pp. 69–84.
MCA (1993) officials to discuss plan for 500 rural libraries. *Straits Times*, (11 February), 14.
Microfilming (1993) and preservation project in Vietnam. *CORMOSEA Bulletin*, **22**(2), 6.
Mohd Sharif Mohd Saad and Norma Abu Seman (1994) Education and training of library professionals: trends and perspectives. In: *Towards achieving high performance libraries: vision for the future. 1994 Joint PPM/LAS Congress: proceedings, vol.2.* Penang: Universiti Sains Malaysia Library and Persatuan Perpustakaan Malaysia, pp. 125–142.
Mudjito (1993) Higher education libraries in Indonesia: condition and its development program. In: C.M. Nera (ed.) *Introduction to ASEAN librarianship: academic libraries.* Jakarta: ASEAN Committee on Culture and Information, pp. 26–38.
Mulliner, K. (1993) New databases and online resources. *CORMOSEA Bulletin*, **22**(1), 14.
Nellie Dato Paduka Haji Sunny (1993) *Library development and future trends: Brunei Darussalam.* [Paper presented at CONSAL IX, 2–7 May 1993, Bangkok.]
Neo, B.S. (1993) *IT2000: Singapore's vision of an intelligent island.* Singapore: Information Management Research Centre, Nanyang Technological University.
Nera, C.M. (1993) Academic libraries in the ASEAN countries: an overview. In: C.M. Nera (ed.) *Introduction to ASEAN librarianship: academic libraries.* Jakarta: ASEAN Committee on Culture and Information, pp. 1–6.
New-age (1994) public libraries with global reach planned. *Straits Times*, (7 March), 1.
New (1993) students learn how to use the library's computer catalogue. *Singapore Libraries Bulletin*, **4**(1), 12.
Ng, K.K. et al. (1993) Supporting teaching, supporting learning: the NUS Library's programmes. *Singapore Libraries*, (22), 26–30.
Ngian, L.C. (1994a) Singaporeans: their reading habits and interests. In: *National Reading Seminar 1994, organized by the National Library under the sponsorship of the ASEAN Committee on Culture and Information.* Singapore: National Library, pp. 13–30.
Ngian, L.C. (1994b) Surveys and feedback channels: a perspective from the public libraries of Singapore. In: *Towards achieving high performance libraries: vision for the future. 1994 Joint PPM/LAS Congress: proceedings, vol.1.* Penang: Universiti Sains Malaysia Library and Persatuan Perpustakaan Malaysia, pp. 113–121.
Nguyen, P.T. (1993) Acquisitions trip to Laos. *CORMOSEA Bulletin*, **22**(1), 3–4.
Ong, K. (1994) Check out your own books at the library. *Straits Times*, (28 June), 9.
PM (1994) wants 100 libraries for kids 10–15 years; 4 new ones next year based on neighbourhood concept. *Straits Times*, (26 June), 3.
Premsmit, P. (1993) Library and information science education in Thailand: a summary. *Asian Libraries*, **3**(4), 87–88.

Ramachandran, R. (1994a) Library 2000 – vision for Singapore. In: *Towards achieving high performance libraries: vision for the future. 1994 Joint PPM/LAS Congress: proceedings, vol.2.* Penang: Universiti Sains Malaysia Library and Persatuan Perpustakaan Malaysia, pp. 29–40.

Ramachandran, R. (1994b) The book trade and industry: a librarian's perception. *Singapore Libraries,* (23), 78–91.

Recent (1994) developments in publishing and reading – from the results of the questionnaire to the APPREB meeting participants. *Asian Pacific Book Development,* **25**(1), 6–7.

Reid, E.O.F. (1995) *Internet and digital libraries: implications for libraries in ASEAN region.* [Paper to be presented at the Digital Libraries Conference held in Singapore, 29–30 March 1995.]

Republic of Singapore (1995) National Library Board Bill, no.5 of 1995. *Government Gazette,* (23 January).

Rompas, J.P. (1993) Special libraries in Indonesia: conditions and developmental problems. In: Shahar Banun Jaafar *et al.* (eds) *Introduction to ASEAN librarianship: special libraries.* Kuala Lumpur: ASEAN Committee on Culture and Information, pp. 17–32.

Sabah (1994) to set up more village libraries. *New Straits Times,* (21 June), 6.

Sabaratnam, S. (1993) Library education and training in Singapore: an update. *Asian Libraries,* **4**(3), 83–86.

Sajjad ur Rehman (1993) The training of school center personnel in Malaysia: status and prospects. *Asian Libraries,* 3(3), 43–55.

SBC (1994) Library takes step towards Library 2000. *Singapore Libraries Bulletin,* **4**(4), 1–2.

Seminar on Global Information Networking for Library Applications - Recommendations Resolutions, 17 December 1994, INTAN, Bukit Kiara. (1994) Organized by International Islamic University of Malaysia in cooperation with MIMOS and the National Library of Malaysia.

Setiarso, B. and Sudarsono, B. (1993) The development of library computerization and computerized network in Indonesia. In: T.S. Chan (ed.) *Introduction to ASEAN librarianship: library computerization.* Singapore: ASEAN Committee on Culture and Information, pp. 39–50.

Shahar Banun Jaafar (1994) Jaringan Ilmu: libraries' gateway to global information resources. [Paper presented at: *Seminar on Global Information Networking for Library Applications - Recommendations Resolutions, 17 December 1994, INTAN, Bukit Kiara.* Organized by the International Islamic University of Malaysia in cooperation with MIMOS and the National Library of Malaysia.]

Shaikha Zakaria (1993) Academic libraries in Malaysia. In: C.M. Nera (ed.) *Introduction to ASEAN librarianship: academic libraries.* Jakarta: ASEAN Committee on Culture and Information, pp. 39–50.

Sharifah Naema Syed Mansor Al-Idrus (1993) Academic library developments in Brunei Darussalam. In: C.M. Nera (ed.) *Introduction to ASEAN librarianship: academic libraries.* Jakarta: ASEAN Committee on Culture and Information, pp. 7–25.

Singapore (1993) *IT usage survey 1992.* Singapore: National Computer Board.

Siriwongworawat, S. (1993) Computerization of library operations in Thailand: an overview. In: T.S. Chan (ed.) *Introduction to ASEAN librarianship: library computerization.* Singapore: ASEAN Committee on Culture and Information, pp. 105–140.

Stueart, R.D. (1993) Information studies education: the key to an information society. In: *CONSAL IX papers: future dimensions and library development, Bangkok, 2-7 May 1993.* Bangkok: CONSAL, pp. B37–B44.

Sulistyo-Basuki (1993) Library education and training in Indonesia. *Asian Libraries,* **4**(3), 41–48.

Tan, D. and Sulaiman, F. (1994) Public libraries and reading: the Singapore experience. In: *Promoting reading in an urban environment, 26-27 May 1994, organized by National Library of Singapore,* pp. 49–55.

Tan, M. (1993) Special libraries in Singapore. In: Shahar Banun Jaafar *et al.,* (eds) *Introduction to ASEAN librarianship: special libraries.* Kuala Lumpur: ASEAN Committee on Culture and Information, pp. 115–122.

Temasek (1994) to offer information science and management course. *Straits Times,* (20 July), 25.

Teo, P. (1994) Towards service excellence in the book community. *Singapore Libraries Bulletin,* **4**(4), 9–10.

Tontyaporn, B. (1993) Special libraries in Thailand. In: Shahhar Banun Jaafar *et al.* (eds) *Introduction to ASEAN librarianship: special libraries.* Kuala Lumpur: ASEAN Committee on Culture and Information, pp. 123–134.

Towards (1994) *service excellence in the book community: a seminar for publishers, booksellers and librarians, 19 March 1994.* Singapore: [Jointly organized by] Library Association of Singapore, Singapore Booksellers Association and Singapore Book Publishers Association [to be published].

Vallejo, R.M. (1993a) Library and information science education in the Philippines: a summary. *Asian Libraries,* **4**(3), 81–82.

Vallejo, R.M. (1993b) Library education at the Institute of Library Science, University of the Philippines. *Asian Libraries,* **4**(3), 49–57.

Void-deck (1994) libraries for children a big success. *Straits Times,* (12 June).

Yap, S.S.B. (1993) Academic libraries in Singapore: a country report. In: C.M. Nera (ed.) *Introduction to ASEAN librarianship: academic libraries.* Jakarta: ASEAN Committee on Culture and Information, pp. 86–106.

Zainab Ibrahim (1993) Special libraries in Malaysia. In: Shahar Banun Jaafar *et al.,* (eds) *Introduction to ASEAN librarianship: special libraries.* Kuala Lumpur: ASEAN Committee on Culture and Information, pp. 33–78.

Zaiton Osman (1994) Vision 2020: defining objectives for high performance in academic and special libraries in Malaysia. In: *Towards achieving high performance libraries: vision for the future. 1994 Joint PPM/LAS Congress: proceedings, vol.2.* Penang: Universiti Sains Malaysia Library and Persatuan Perpustakaan Malaysia, pp. 41–57.

Document supply 10

Peter Johan Lor

Introduction

About ten years ago, I was collecting literature with a view to research which led to a doctoral thesis on monitoring South African interlending traffic. It then seemed a perfectly sensible and useful topic to study. There was no lack of literature about interlending. It was dominated by Maurice Line, the British Library Lending Division (BLLD), and Universal Availability of Publications (UAP). UAP placed interlending in a chain, linking publisher and user (contemporary and future), encompassing publishing, distribution, acquisition, interlending and retention. Thus, interlending was quite a well-connected topic in the literature of librarianship, being related to topics such as the centralization and decentralization of national information resources, resource sharing, networking, bibliographic control, and national information policy generally.

Commercial document delivery, although growing, was still something of a fringe activity. Librarians wrote articles comparing the performance of commercial suppliers and interlending partners. The use of computer networks in interlending, electronic document ordering, electronic transmission of documents and electronic journals were among the fringe topics covered in my mid-1980s literature search. One of the most promising technologies was fax. Experiments in its use for transmission of documents were being written up, and it seemed that, after decades of unfulfilled promise, its time had come. As this chapter will reflect, much has happened since the mid-1980s.

Scope and methodology

This is the first chapter in *Librarianship and information work worldwide* (*LIWW*) that is devoted to document supply. It has been difficult to decide on its parameters. For example, where does document supply stop and electronic publishing begin? Does document supply include the supply of documents to an institution's own users by means of electronic delivery of instructional materials, an electronic reserve collection or a commercial full-text CD-ROM subscription? Is it still necessary to give full coverage to conventional interlending as part of document supply? It seemed unwise to make these decisions *a priori*. Instead, this year's coverage is inclusive, leaving the scope to be narrowed down in subsequent years.

The bulk of the literature on document supply is published in North America and Western Europe. As far as these countries are concerned, the literature reviewed has largely been restricted to that published in 1994. However, an attempt has been made to include as much literature as possible on document supply in other countries. In these cases, material published in 1993 has been selectively included.

Literature for this review was identified by scanning current issues of library and information science journals received by the State Library, Pretoria. This covers almost all of the major English-language journals and newsletters and some in Dutch, French and German. Issues of *Information science abstracts*, *Library and information science abstracts (LISA)* and Aslib's *Current awareness abstracts* were scanned as they arrived, as were the literature reviews (Barwick, 1994b; Barwick, 1994c) and bibliographies (Bibliography, 1994a; Bibliography, 1994b) published in *Interlending and document supply*. Early in 1995 online searches were done in the *LISA* and UnCover databases. Members of the editorial board of *Librarianship and information work worldwide* also supplied me with references to materials published in their countries. Unfortunately use of some of this material was inhibited by the language barrier. The task of writing this chapter was a sobering object lesson in the limitations of document supply in my working environment and of my own absorptive capacity. Undoubtedly much material published in the second half of 1994 remains to be dealt with next year.

Terminology

The term 'interlending' or 'interlibrary loan' is no longer adequate as a generic term for the various types of transactions that have in the past been lumped under it. This is illustrated by the decision of the IFLA Section on Interlending and Document Delivery to change its name to Section on Document Delivery and Interlending (Mark and Fuchs, 1994; Section, 1994). During the 1970s and 1980s the provision of photocopies replaced lending as the dominant activity. In the 1990s the emphasis shifted from moving documents or copies thereof to transmitting images of documents using various technologies. In addition, the supply of documents is no longer the prerogative of libraries. Various other agencies have entered the market, and many document suppliers are directly serving the end user (Section, 1994).

There is no consensus on whether interlending should be considered to be subsumed under document delivery (Jackson, 1994a; Rice, 1994a; Section, 1994). Some consider interlending to be a form of document delivery (cf. Cornish, 1994c; Goodacre, 1994); others argue that the two should be distinguished on the basis that interlending is concerned with returnable materials (i.e. materials provided on loan) while document delivery is concerned with the provision of materials (such as photocopies) that do not have to be returned (Behrens, 1993; Gassaway, 1994). Other criteria for distinguishing between document delivery and interlending have been suggested: whether delivery is on a commercial or non-commercial basis, and whether delivery is to 'internal' or 'external' clients (Boykin, 1994; Gassaway, 1994; Hugenholtz, 1994). Excluding the provision of original books or journals, and the provision to the library's own ('primary') users of copies made from the library's own collection or obtained through interlibrary loan, Gassaway (1994) restricts document delivery proper to fee-based document delivery:

> True document delivery is defined as the providing of photocopies or electronic copies to external constituencies either on a cost-recovery or a profit-making basis. The latter . . . is the equivalent of commercial document delivery (p. 25).

In this chapter 'document delivery' is defined as above. The term 'interlending' is used as defined in the *Model national interlibrary lending code*, drawn up by the IFLA Office for International Lending, as

> . . . the process whereby one library obtains from another specified library materials requested by its users and not available from its own stock. The requested material may be sent as a temporary loan or a copy may be supplied or transmitted instead (Model, 1984, p.15).

As an umbrella term, Goodacre (1994) suggests a new term, 'SOD' (search, order and deliver), while Line (1994c) proposes 'document access and supply' as appropriate for the loan of books as well as for journal articles delivered by mail or electronically. Here the term 'document supply' is used as the umbrella term for interlending and document delivery, whether undertaken commercially or otherwise. 'Document supply' has the advantage over 'document delivery' of being able to accommodate the full range of delivery modes, old (i.e. including interlending), new (i.e. including electronic delivery of images of documents), and those as yet undiscovered, and to encompass the infrastructure which supports delivery as well as the processes preceding and following it. It is in this sense that the term will be used in this chapter.

In the following sections, factors in the technological and business environments that are influencing the evolution of document delivery are first outlined. Then conventional interlending and pre-electronic document delivery are described, with particular attention being paid to interlending and document delivery in Eastern Europe and the developing world. After this, electronic document delivery is dealt with in a roughly evolutionary order of increasing integration and sophistication.

The technological environment

The environment of document supply is changing rapidly. Nowhere is this more apparent than in the area of technology. Information technology affects document supply not only because it offers enhanced and more rapid capabilities for bibliographic searching, verification and location, text and image storage, and for the transmission of orders and documents. It also drives change by raising clients' expectations and by altering the relationships between the various parties involved in the chain which links authors and readers. Many technologies are relevant to document supply (Hugenholtz, 1994; Kibirige, 1994). This section deals with selected technology applications, i.e. functional areas in which a number of technologies are typically brought to bear.

CD-ROM (compact disc read-only memory) is a popular technology, which is particularly attractive to end-users (Bartenbach, 1994; Griebel, 1994; Valauskas, 1994a). As a simple and robust technology which can be applied in relatively unsophisticated environments (Reng, 1994), it has been recognized and promoted as appropriate in developing countries (Fouché and Day, 1993; Keylard, 1993; Lippman, 1993; Abid and Péllisier, 1994; Khalil, 1994b; Levey, 1994; Priestley, 1994; Richer, 1994). CD-ROM first influenced document supply through the availability of bibliographic databases on CD-ROMs, particularly when end-users gained access to them (Cohn, 1993; Kanamugire, 1993; Pessah, 1993; Bartenbach, 1994). From indexing and abstracting databases the scope of CD-ROM has expanded to national bibliographies, books-in-print databases, library catalogues and union catalogues (*Canadian*, 1994; Gardner, 1994; Mauch, 1993; Richer, 1994). As high-capacity storage devices CD-ROMs have further potential to reshape document delivery (J. Barnes, 1994; Khalil, 1994a).

No other new application features more prominently in the current literature of document supply than the **Internet**, which is transforming the relationships between major stakeholders in scientific and scholarly communication, such as authors, publishers, libraries and readers (McLean, 1993; Bryant, 1994; Buckle, 1994; Cochrane, 1994; Gasson, 1994; Schauder, 1994; Swain and Cleveland, 1994; Van Brakel, 1994; Young, 1994). These developments also affect libraries

(Woodberry, 1993; Dunsire, 1994; Summerhill, 1994; Williamson, 1994). For developing countries the Internet holds great potential (Ferguson, 1994; Greene, 1994), but its use there is impeded by factors such as lack of expertise, unreliable electricity supply, lack of foreign currency and a national information policy vacuum (Abelsnes, 1994; Greeff, 1994; Hafkin, 1994; Morales Campos, 1994; Nyirenda, 1994; Santos-Labourdette, 1994; White, 1994; Zulu, 1994). If developing countries lack access to it, the electronic superhighway may actually 'widen the gap between rich and poor' (Cornish, 1994b).

The Internet has applications in three areas that are relevant to document supply. The first is the provision of access to the online public access catalogues (OPACs) of libraries (Cornish, 1994b; What's, 1994), union catalogues (Costers, 1994b; Meer, 1994; Tallim, 1994b), catalogues of booksellers and periodicals agents (Coleman, 1993), electronic table of contents (ETOC) databases (Andersen, 1994; Layland, 1994; Williams, 1994d) and other bibliographic databases (Elliott and Scott, 1994). The second is the ordering of documents (Boykin, 1994; Brandreth and MacKeigan, 1994; Summann, 1994; Tallim, 1994b). The third is the storage and transmission of a wide range of document types, including archival and heritage materials (American, 1994; What's, 1994), dissertations (S. Barnes, 1994), and instructional materials (Enssle, 1994).

It is becoming increasingly difficult to distinguish between **electronic publishing** and electronic document delivery. The impact of electronic publishing on the publication chain has been widely discussed (Marle, 1994; Mountifield and Van Brakel, 1994; Schauder, 1994; Van Brakel, 1994). Cochrane (1994) distinguishes between true electronic publishing, which amounts to 'the complete replacement of paper based publishing', and 'electronics in publishing', which consists of using information technology in publishing a product replicating 'something previously and concurrently published in its traditional paper format' (p.4). The latter is more common than the former.

Digitized material is easy to download and reassemble into a new compilation, making republication difficult to detect (Dorner, 1994). The copyright implications of electronic publishing are being studied in the European Community's CITED (Copyright In Transmitted Electronic Documents) project (Cornish, 1994a; Cornish 1994b; Cornish 1994f; Norman, 1994; Williams, 1994b). The complexity of electronic publications is also reflected in issues of bibliographic control (Byrum, 1994; Caplan, 1994; ISI, 1994) and standardization (Adams, 1994; Byrum, 1994).

The advent of electronic publishing has far-reaching long-term implications for libraries (Dunsire, 1994; Griebel, 1994; Line, 1994b; Nissley, 1994; Wooliscroft, 1994). Adams (1994) states that three basic assumptions of librarians concerning document delivery are being challenged:

- that bibliographic identification of desired items, location of holdings, and document delivery are three separate activities;

- that documents are delivered through an intermediary rather than directly; and
- that documents are delivered on paper in a form that is not easily manipulated.

Imaging is concerned with creating representations of documents that can be manipulated electronically. There are basically two sources of documents that can be stored, retrieved and delivered electronically. Either the document has been created electronically, or it has to be converted from written or printed format. For the conversion, other than rekeying the text, there are two main options: optical character recognition (OCR), to which intelligent character recognition (ICR) has more recently been added, and scanning. Rekeying, OCR and ICR yield ASCII text files which can be manipulated and searched down to the level of individual characters, but which cannot accommodate illustrations or other graphics. Scanning yields bit-mapped images of whole pages at a time, faithfully capturing the page layout, type fonts and graphics. However, text on a bit-mapped page image cannot be searched or manipulated and such images require a great deal of storage space (Bartenbach, 1994; Gibbs, 1994): in compressed form a page of text from a journal can require 90 kilobytes of storage; a photograph on that page would push it up to 300 kilobytes or more (Williams, 1994c).

Such of the imaging literature as is relevant to document supply comprises mainly accounts of experimentation, the main themes of which appear to be electronic document stores for electronic document delivery (Barden, 1994; S. Barnes, 1994; Grimshaw, 1994; Williams, 1994a); affordable generic (i.e. non-proprietary) imaging workstations (Brandreth and MacKeigan, 1994); means of compressing the large image files and transmitting document images over local area networks (LANs) (Gibbs, 1994) and over the Internet (Tallim, 1994b; Tehnzen, 1994); user workstations that can deal with both document images and the ASCII text required for searching image files (Geleijnse, 1994; Grimshaw, 1994); and copyright and legal issues arising from the use of imaging technology (Dixon, 1994; Rees, 1994; Roes and Dijkstra, 1994). Functioning applications fall into roughly two categories: (a) imaging of pictorial, archival and heritage materials for purposes of preservation and public access (S. Barnes, 1994; Giese, 1994; Lamolinara, 1994a; Lamolinara, 1994b; National, 1994; Rees, 1994; What's, 1994); (b) imaging for document storage and transmission in electronic document delivery systems (dealt with below).

Direct applications of **hypertext** (Milne, 1994) in document supply are quite meagre except in so far as it is utilized by the World Wide Web (WWW), which is used or proposed for certain document supply applications (Dallman *et al.*, 1994; Smith, 1994). Flanders (1994) describes a hypertext-based interlending directory for the state of Kansas. **Electronic table of contents (ETOC) databases** are dealt with below (pp. 277–279).

The business environment of document supply: changing roles in the publication chain

Social, political and economic factors (Hugenholtz, 1994; Schauder, 1994; Woodward, 1994) interact with technological capabilities to create the environment within which document supply functions. Generally speaking, the current business environment is characterized by a disturbance of traditional relationships between the major players: authors, publishers, periodicals subscription agents, bibliographic database producers, networks, bibliographic utilities and other service vendors, libraries and users. The causative factors that are described in the literature (Alexander, 1994; Bryant, 1994; Cochrane, 1994; Griebel, 1994; Line, 1994c; Poynder, 1994; Woodward, 1994) can be roughly grouped into push (constraining) and pull (opportunity) factors. Push factors include changes in academic institutions, rising demand for information sources, library budget constraints, continuing growth in the output of publications, rising prices of publications and services, and fluctuating exchange rates. They force the players to adapt. Pull factors seem to be mainly technological: spectacular advances in information technology generally, rapid growth in electronic networks on campus and worldwide, proliferation of electronic information sources, and internationalization of information and document supply. Pull factors provide opportunities to adapt. Of course, the factors interact and some factors can be read as presenting both constraints and opportunities. As the various factors act upon the players, the players respond, and their responses influence other players.

Libraries have responded to the push factors affecting them by cancelling journal subscriptions and relying more on resource sharing and commercial document delivery services as a substitute for the cancelled titles (Poynder, 1994). This shift from reliance on own collections toward ensuring access to material not held has been debated for at least two decades (cf. Gore, 1975). The terminology is evolving from 'access versus holdings' (or 'ownership') (Harloe and Budd, 1994) to 'just-in-time versus just-in-case' (Alexander, 1994). The new terminology may herald a real change in librarians' approach to acquisitions, in which the unit of acquisition becomes the journal article instead of the journal title (Luijendijk, 1994). This has given rise to the suggestion that acquisitions and interlending (document delivery) sections in libraries should be merged (Kent, 1993; Barwick, 1994c). At the macro-level this shift is reflected by the notion of the 'distributed national collection' (Henty, 1993; Shipp, 1993; Cochrane, 1994).

This does not obviate the threat that libraries will be bypassed by authors, publishers or document suppliers delivering directly to end-users. End-user searching and client-initiated ordering are growing (Costers, 1994a; Layland, 1994; Tenopir, 1994; UnCover begins, 1994). Librarians are likely to play a decreasing role in document supply and to lose some control of their acquisitions budgets (Line, 1994c). Although the electronic library is still some way off (Gils, 1994), librarians need to rethink their role in the future virtual library (Blagden and Ford 1994; Costers, 1994a; J.E. Cox, 1994a; Ellis and Rainford, 1994; Ellis *et al.*, 1994).

For journal publishers the result of journal cancellations by libraries is declining subscription sales. They respond *inter alia* by cutting discounts to subscriptions agents, who already have less business due to cancellations by libraries. Reduced discounts mean lower operating margins. Subscription agents face a shake-out in which many smaller companies will close or be acquired by larger companies (J.E. Cox, 1994b). Among the strategic options open to subscription agents is that of diversifying by, for example, moving into the ETOC and CAS-IAS market in response to shifts in library spending patterns (Alexander, 1994; Luijendijk, 1994). Periodical subscription agents that move into the CAS-IAS market in effect sell articles rather than journal subscriptions. They can take this a step further, and sell articles to end-users, eliminating libraries (Alexander 1994, J.E. Cox 1994a; Stephens 1994). Publishers too can eliminate intermediaries. Electronic publishing makes it possible for them to sell directly to end-users and charge for each instance of use (Boykin, 1994). Another response on the part of publishers is to clamp down aggressively on the use of copyrighted materials (Bunting, 1994). As traditional boundaries between sectors fade, publishers and periodicals subscription agents will have to share the document supply market with various other parties, including producers of indexing and abstracting databases, microform publishers and major libraries.

Interlending and pre-electronic document delivery

Many articles deal with both interlending and document delivery. Some compare interlending and commercial or other document delivery services in terms of cost, performance (fill rate and turnaround time), or user preferences (Kingma, 1994; Kinnucan, 1994, Kurosman and Durniak, 1994; Malamud and Levine, 1994; Van der Werff, 1994). Other articles purporting to deal with document delivery turn out to be concerned with quite conventional interlending. This section deals with interlending, as defined earlier, and with the less sophisticated forms of document delivery, meaning those systems and services in which limited and non-integrated use is made of electronic technology.

In the 1970s and 1980s it was customary for articles on interlending to start with an evocation of the frightening information explosion with which mankind was faced, and to set out the need for cooperation among libraries faced with an abundance of books and journals, rising prices, increasing user needs, and limited or declining budgets. In the meantime, the information explosion metaphor seems to have gone out of fashion. This does not mean that the output of books and journals is no longer growing (cf. Luijendijk, 1994). Even if the rate of publication has levelled off, the remaining three problems have become more acute (Cohn, 1993; Dolby, 1993; Griebel, 1994; Jackson, 1994a; Line, 1994c; Martin and Kendrick, 1994; Schwartz, 1994).

Another change is that the emphasis seems to have shifted somewhat, away from exhortations to cooperate and share resources towards support for the 'just-in-time' philosophy, which has already been referred to.

Currently the application of modern information technology appears to be the most prominent theme in the literature on interlending. Interlending is increasingly being conducted with the assistance of electronic systems, even if there are still some manual or human-mediated links in the chain that connects a client's bibliographic search with the arrival of the selected documents. Two forms of information technology that attracted much attention a decade ago have now matured and faded into the background: the application of computer software packages in interlending management (Pool, 1994; K.S. Thompson, 1994), and the use of fax in transmitting interlending requests (Barwick, 1994a; Barwick, 1994e).

The role of bibliographic networks and utilities in interlending was already a prominent theme in the literature a decade and more ago. The United States is particularly richly endowed with networks and utilities, which may operate at regional level (Yoo, 1994); nationally and internationally, for example the giant OCLC (Tenopir, 1994); or in a particular field, such as the health sciences (Prendergast, 1994). An issue of the *Bulletin of the Medical Library Association* featured several articles dealing with the linking of the US National Library of Medicine's personal computer-based GRATEFUL MED and LOANSOME DOC systems intended for the use of practising physicians to its DOCLINE interlending system for medical libraries (Lacroix, 1994; Lovas, 1994; Robishaw and Roth, 1994).

Powell and Burch (1994) discuss the changing role of regional networks in the United Kingdom. The Australian National Library's network of Australian bibliographic and directory databases, Ozline, is described by Layland (1994). Costers (1994a; 1994b; 1994c; 1994d) has described the role of networks generally and that of the Dutch Pica system system more particularly. An international dimension is added by the European Community-sponsored Project ION, which links interlending systems in three countries: France, the Netherlands and the United Kingdom (Deschamps 1994).

Compared with the situation ten years ago, users and libraries have a greater choice of networks to access, and of means of doing so. A major difference is made by the Internet, which is now a common theme. A listserv devoted to interlending and document delivery allows professionals to exchange information and ideas in this field (Rice, 1994a; Rice, 1994b). Tallim (1994b) describes the impact of the Internet on three areas of interlending and document delivery: bibliographic identification and location, requesting material and interlending management, and delivery of requested items.

Four threads run through the descriptions of networks in interlending:

- networks and utilities are no longer restricting themselves to databases of monographs and serials titles held in the collections of participating libraries, but are adding other bibliographic databases, in particular periodicals indexes based on table of contents information, for the use of their members or clients;
- end-user access is encouraged and facilitated by the more user-friendly screens and search procedures that have been made available by the networks;
- network databases, along with databases on CD-ROM, databases loaded on local file servers, and databases on the Internet (Miller, 1993) are often accessible via, or as an adjunct to, the library's OPAC, either on terminals in the library, or from the clients' offices and laboratories through the campus LAN. The impact of the availability of such databases via an OPAC is described by Pessah (1994);
- increasingly, bibliographic data and document ordering are linked. In many systems, users can see whether their own library holds the journals in which the articles appear that their bibliographic search has turned up. By pressing a few keys, they can place orders for the documents they want to see.

The terms 'interlending' and 'resource sharing' are often used as near-synonyms. Interlending is often the only form of resource sharing dealt with in articles purporting to deal with resource sharing in general. Nevertheless, resource sharing appears to be referred to less frequently than was the case a decade ago. It remains a current topic in Canada, where various factors affecting interlending have been analysed and a national strategy for interlending and document delivery has been proposed (*Canadian*, 1994), and in Australia, where the notion of a 'distributed national collection' is under discussion (Henty, 1993). In a paper on bibliographic control, Line (1994a) *inter alia* dealt with the bibliographic infrastructure needed for interlending and document delivery. At a more general level, Boissé (1994) has formulated eleven postulates on library cooperation. The first three postulates convey the flavour of the paper:

- 'Library cooperation is easy when money is plentiful';
- 'Library cooperation is easier to launch with someone else's money';
- 'The more meaningful it is, the more difficult it will be to implement.'

Another topic closely associated with interlending a decade ago that is much less prominent today is UAP (Cornish, 1994b; Cornish 1994d). Progress is reported annually in the *IFLA Yearbook* (Bradbury and Barwick, 1994), and in the *Newsletter* of the IFLA Section on Document Delivery and Interlending (Cornish, 1994f).

Costs, charges and payment systems constitute an important theme in current literature on interlending and document delivery (Dolby, 1993; Barwick, 1994b; Kingma, 1994). Economic and related pressures are forcing a break with a long tradition of *gratis* interlending in Denmark (Cotta-Schønberg and Winkel-Schwartz, 1994; Bjarnø, 1994) and Sweden (Nilsson, 1994a). In a survey of factors clients considered important in deciding how documents should be obtained, Kinnucan (1994) found that clients were concerned about costs even if they did not have to pay for the service themselves - which is somehow reassuring to know. Jackson (1994e) discusses reciprocal agreements, in terms of which libraries may waive or simplify payments due to one another, as a means of containing the costs of record-keeping and accounting. Another means of doing this is to use coupons or vouchers. IFLA's Office of International Lending has been developing a voucher scheme for international interlending transactions (Bradbury and Barwick, 1994; Cornish, 1994f; Gould, 1994; Mark and Fuchs, 1994).

A variety of other issues appears in the literature of interlending. In the area of human resources, team building (Raschke, 1994) and training (Cornish, 1994g; Cother, 1994; Jackson, 1994g) have received attention. In the US, two doctoral dissertations dealt with perceptions of interlending among high school media specialists (Mitchell, 1994) and academics' views of interlending policies, among other academic library policies (Withnell, 1994). The use of international standard book numbers (ISBNs) in interlending is the subject of an IFLA study (Cornish, 1994f; Mark and Fuchs, 1994), while Holm (1994) briefly refers to technical standards and protocols relating to interlending. The quality of interlending requests submitted by users has been evaluated by Good (1994), while Hébert (1994) has evaluated interlending performance in Canadian public libraries using unobtrusive measurement techniques. Practical matters dealt with include 'rush' (urgent) requests (Jackson, 1994d) and the physical delivery of requested material (N. Cox, 1994; Library book, 1994; *Library rate*, 1994; Smale, 1994).

Attention has been paid to interlending of various types of material. There have been two international surveys on the interlending of fiction (Barwick, 1994d; Barwick and Line, 1994; Cornish, 1994f). Other materials dealt with are braille and other material for the visually handicapped (Barwick, 1994b; Bays, 1994; Bradbury and Barwick,1994), and music (P. Thompson, 1994).

Most discussion on interlending and document delivery seems to be generated in the context of academic libraries, with national libraries in second place. In the United States, intercampus document delivery (Steffen and Deiss, 1994) as well as interlending in colleges (Kurosman and Durniak, 1994), community colleges (Miah, 1994), and school libraries (Anker, 1994; Mitchell, 1994) has received attention in the past year. The last are a vivid illustration of the cornucopia available to library users in the advanced industrial countries in comparison with the situation in some countries of the Third World where researchers would give their eye-teeth for the facilities available to American secondary school pupils.

A number of articles reflects more generally on activities in specific developed countries. In North America, the North American Interlibrary Loan and Document Delivery (NAILDD) Project has been launched by the Association of Research Libraries (ARL) (Jackson, 1994c; Jackson, 1994f; Machovec, 1994; New, 1994; Tallim, 1994a). Essentially it is aimed at improving the delivery of library materials to users at costs the libraries can sustain. Its programme of action heralds a radical rethink of interlending and document delivery, which assumes a distributed national collection and an electronic, user-initiated requesting environment. It places the user, rather than the library, at the centre of the system. Beaumont and Lunau (1994) give a general overview of challenges to interlending in Canada, while the situation in Nova Scotia has given rise to reflection (Bates, 1994) and brainstorming (People Development Ltd., 1994). Nishino (1994) reports the interlending impressions of a Japanese librarian visiting the United States and Canada.

Outside North America, Tehnzen (1994) describes the interlending and document supply activities of the University and Technical Information Library (UB/TIB), Hannover, already a well-known feature on the interlending landscape a decade ago. It is interesting to note that this institution's interest in microreprography has not waned. At least 23 of the articles cited in this review refer to the British Library Document Supply Centre (BLDSC), which so dominated the literature in our field ten years ago. Specific developments there are reflected in the appropriate contexts. Of more general interest are articles by Andersen (1994), Barwick (1994b; 1994c), Poynder (1994) and Williams (1994a). The BLDSC is still the world's foremost document supplier (Jackson, 1994a) and figures released by the BLDSC show that total demand rose in three consecutive years to reach a record of 3.69 million requests in 1993/94 (British Library. Document Supply Centre, 1994). The BLDSC has ambitious plans to double the total number of documents supplied in 1992 to over six million by 2002 (Carrigan, 1994). Friend (1994a) takes up an old theme by issuing a warning against excessive reliance on Boston Spa by the UK library community. The literature also reflects interlending issues and developments in the Netherlands (Hulsing-Ronteltap, 1994), Norway (Jackson, 1994b), Sweden and Scandinavia more generally (Nilsson, 1994b), and New Zealand (Broadbent, 1994).

Interlending and document delivery in Eastern Europe and the Third World

Recent political change in Eastern Europe continues to impinge upon resource sharing, interlending and document delivery. The change to a market economy in the countries of the former Soviet Union is affecting the operation of libraries in general, and has created new barriers to interlending, *inter alia* as a result of a lack of hard currency (Prosekova, 1993). Eronina and Komov (1994) discuss the current state of interlending and document delivery in the former Soviet Union and propose the development of a new system, while a proposed new Russian library network is described by Shraiberg and Goncharov (1994). A workshop run in Budapest during 1993 by the IFLA UAP Programme considered ways in which document supply services could be improved for those working in Eastern Europe (Cornish, 1993; Cornish, 1994c; Galuscova, 1994). In spite of the political *rapprochement*, a gap remains between libraries of Eastern and Western Europe. Because of the language factor, most Eastern European countries will always be net borrowers in international terms, as most of their languages are not read extensively outside their own borders. Libraries in former socialist countries relied on major collections in the former Soviet Union and each other for supply, but this is no longer possible for economic and political reasons. New approaches must be sought (Cornish, 1994d; Cornish, 1994e).

In developing countries, various factors, including lack of resources, inadequate official support and infrastructure, limited foreign currency, copyright restrictions, and poor bibliographic control, impede the availability of publications. Interlending is slow, costs are high, and international interlending involves transfers of foreign currency, which may be difficult. Publications are increasingly becoming available in digital format, but this could widen the gap between haves and have-nots (Cleveland, 1993; Keates, 1993). Information technology can play a role in improving the flow of information from North to South (Greene, 1993), but there are more fundamental factors, of an intellectual, ideological and economic nature, that inhibit the flow of information from South to North (Arunachalam, 1993).

The situation on the ground in the developing countries is vividly presented in the papers from the IFLA Pre-session Seminar on Interlending and Document Supply, held in Paris in August 1989, which were belatedly published in 1994 (*Interlending*, 1994). They fall into two groups, 'Roundtable discussions' and 'Country reports'. The 'Roundtable discussions' comprise six papers dealing with general aspects of interlending and document delivery: bibliographic access, resource collections, the organization of interlibrary loan and document supply, training, costs, and the role of the national library as a centre for document supply and interlibrary loan. The work on alternative national models, done by Line and others for the IFLA International Office for UAP and UNESCO's General Information Programme in the 1980s (cf. Line *et al.*, 1980) appears to have influenced several of these papers. There are 24 'country reports' ranging from half a page for Botswana to 13 pages for Morocco. They are somewhat uneven in content, but do throw some light on interlending and document supply in countries that are rarely mentioned in the professional literature of the developed countries.

The holding of the 1994 IFLA Conference in Havana prompted a number of conference papers dealing with interlending and document supply in the Caribbean (Ferguson, 1994; Richards, 1994) and Cuba (Núñes Fina *et al.*, 1994). A common thread running through these papers is that of very modest transaction volumes in spite of (or is it because of?) limited local resources. As far as international interlending is concerned, Ferguson reports that developed countries direct more requests to the Caribbean than they receive from there. Interlending between Mexico and the United States is on the increase, but the traffic remains small (Kahl, 1993; Morales Campos, 1994). In Chile a consortium of ten universities has set up a company named Knowledge Alert which provides a cooperative current awareness and document delivery service based on 3,000 journal titles held by the universities (Sol *et al.*, 1994).

Document delivery in the vast South Pacific region is touched on in articles on the Pacific Information Centre (PIC) (Simmons, 1993) and the Pacific Legal Information Network (Rannells, 1994).

Wijasuriya (1994) describes the history and activities of ASTINFO (Regional Network for the Exchange of Information Experience in Science and Technology in Asia and the Pacific) generally, and discusses a UNESCO-funded project to provide a document supply facility for the Asia-Pacific region, based at the National Library of Australia. The volume of requests reported seems to be disappointingly low. Suga and Urata (1993) describe the interlending and other cooperative activities of the Japanese Medical Library Association, which provides assistance to medical libraries in South-East Asia and Korea. Documentary information sources in China are discussed by Guangjun (1993) and Yitai (1993). The latter reports that resource sharing is still poorly developed in China and proposes that attention be paid to concrete measures such as interlending rules and standard request forms, as well as to a study of interlending demand. An office which will provide 'rigid supervision and high-ranking leadership' (p.285) should ensure the governance of the resource sharing system. Chand and Kumar (1993) describe the document delivery service of the Indian National Scientific Documentation Centre (INSDOC). The need for document supply in the Third World is illustrated by the fact that in 1980 India used to acquire about 50% of the 40,000 scientific journals published throughout the world, but now only 20% of the 60,000 being published. INSDOC is planning an electronic imaging network to enable it to satisfy 75% of Indian interlending demand.

The state of interlending in the Arabian Gulf in the aftermath of the Gulf War, in which most of Kuwait's library collections were destroyed, is described by Ibrahim (1993). On the basis of a survey of interlending requests at the King Fahd University of Petroleum and Minerals in Saudi Arabia, Kanamugire (1993) determined that the use of CD-ROM databases had led to a 14% increase in interlending requests. A workshop run by the IFLA UAP Programme in Cairo in January 1993 concentrated on the development of document delivery systems in the Arab-speaking regions. Participants concluded that there was a need to improve availability of publications in the region, and considered *inter alia* the development of a standard document delivery procedure in the region and the possibility of establishing an Arab document delivery centre (Cornish, 1993; Cornish, 1994h).

IFLA's Section on Document Delivery and Interlending, together with the UDT Core Programme, has launched a project to improve interlibrary loan communications and document delivery in Africa. The three objectives are to: (a) improve the competence of library personnel; (b) establish regional, national and global network links; and (c) support the negotiation of bulk treaties with major European document centres and libraries (Abelsnes, 1994; Mark and Fuchs, 1994; Project, 1994). With so much emphasis on transferring information from developed to developing countries, it is easy to overlook the value of information generated in Africa. The problems of access to indigenous Southern African information sources in Southern African countries are discussed by Lor (1993), while Sturges (1994) deals with grey literature in Africa. In a thought-provoking article on resource-sharing in Africa, Rosenberg (1993) states that innumerable meetings have been held on this topic, with little if any progress on the ground. She suggests that much of what has been said and written about resource sharing in Africa merely perpetuates the fallacy that 'resource sharing will somehow by itself remove the constraints ... preventing the successful implementation of resource sharing' (p.108). An account of factors, including lack of 'sharable resources', affecting library cooperation and resource sharing in Nigeria (Ozowa, 1993) appears to provide support for Rosenberg's views.

The problems impeding interlending and resource sharing in Africa are well illustrated by the situation of health sciences libraries in Zambia, where the high cost of photocopying, lack of photocopying facilities, lack of photocopying machine spare parts, high postal rates and lack of national union catalogues and serials holdings lists constitute significant barriers (Chisanga and Champo, 1993). Cooperation among Zambia's agricultural libraries is inhibited by similar factors (Chifwepa, 1993). Zimbabwe has a long history of interlending cooperation with South Africa. Ironically, just as South Africa rejoins the African family and the political barriers to cooperation are removed, the institution of interlending charges by South African libraries makes their resources less accessible to Zimbabweans (Doust, 1993). A number of Zimbabwean libraries are still members of the Southern African Interlending Scheme (SAIS), which now has 717 members in seven Southern African countries (Lor and De Beer, 1994; Membership, 1994). Traffic in the SAIS, surveyed by Lor and Hendrikz (1993), is increasingly being handled electronically with the use of the interlending module of SABINET, the South African Bibliographic and Information Network (Kemp, 1994). Recently there has been a resurgence of interest in local and sectoral cooperative schemes (Coetzee, 1994; Edwards, 1994; Els, 1994).

Electronic document supply systems

When can document delivery be described as electronic document delivery? Cawkell (1991) defined an electronic document delivery system (EDDS) as a system in which the kind of information usually provided in the form of print on paper is supplied and reproduced electronically. Roes and Dijkstra (1994) comment that this encompasses just about any form of document delivery provided something in the process is electronic, but overlooks the possibility that documents can be delivered without ever having been printed. Based on a broad understanding of electronic document delivery, they distinguish three generations of EDDS. The first generation comprises systems based on online ordering. The user generates a request by linking client data to a bibliographic record retrieved from an online database. The request is transmitted electronically and a list of requested items is generated. The rest is done manually: documents are taken from the shelf and photocopies are made after which copies are faxed or mailed to the requester. Some systems of this type are referred to in the literature that has been dealt with above (pp. 270–274); others are dealt with below (pp. 281–283).

Roes and Dijkstra's second generation comprises 'non-integrated supply-driven image-based systems' such as, by and large, ADONIS. The third generation comprises demand-driven 'integrated stand-alone image-based systems' or 'scaleable standalone systems'. The second and third generation systems both require human intervention which interrupts the electronic flow of processes, but at different points. They propose a fourth generation model, and they outline some characteristics of a fifth generation model. In the discussion that follows, the term 'electronic document *supply* system' (EDSSs) is used as the generic term in preference to 'electronic document delivery system' (EDDS) for systems in which a significant proportion of functions are carried out and linked by electronic means.

It is difficult to classify the various EDSSs as described in the literature in terms of the three to five generations proposed by Roes and Dijkstra (1994). Most systems cannot easily be pigeonholed because various characteristics need to be taken into account and a multidimensional classification is required. The terminology they use suggests that the following dichotomies may be relevant to such a multidimensional classification:

- integrated or non-integrated (i.e. whether or not the system is integrated with local reference databases);
- standalone or networked;
- image-based or text-based;
- supply-driven or demand-driven (whether the store of machine-readable documents is assembled in anticipation of, or in response to, demand).

It is suggested here that a simple, pragmatic classification of EDSSs can be constructed by taking two characteristics into account: (a) the functions that are performed and linked electronically, and (b) whether the system is open or closed.

To determine the first characteristic, one must consider the main functions of an EDSS. The following are suggested:

1. SEARCH: End-user bibliographic database searching.
2. REQUEST: Order generation by linking a bibliographic record to a user's particulars.
3. LOCATE: Location of a source for the required document.
4. ORDER: Order transmission.
5. COPY: Document reproduction (retrieving document from store and photocopying or scanning it).
6. DELIVER: Document transmission.
7. MANAGE: System management (verifying user's status and credit, transaction logging for purposes of copyright royalties, accounting and billing, redirection of unfilled orders, reporting to user and/or user's institution, etc.).

The second characteristic requires a distinction between open and closed EDSSs. A closed or self-contained EDSS limits the end-user's searches (SEARCH) to a given set selected from the universe of bibliographic references (as in a database on a CD-ROM). It also offers a limited range of sources from which documents may be ordered (LOCATE) and it limits the documents that can be supplied (COPY) to a given set of the universe of documents, for example to articles on a set of CD-ROMs covering a given range of journal titles. An open system does not impose the above-mentioned limitations. At least theoretically, it exposes the end-user to the whole universe of bibliographic references. Ideally the end-user of an open EDSS could also call upon an open EDSS to deliver any item from the universe of documents. A fully-integrated open EDSS is thus more complex than a fully-integrated closed EDSS.

In any EDSS there are a number of points where the electronic flow of processing may be interrupted. These discontinuities occur at the boundaries of the subsystems which carry out the seven basic functions. In a closed EDSS, subject to the constraints of the storage medium (e.g. CD-ROMs which may have to be physically swapped), it is at least theoretically possible to have seamless electronic interfaces between all the subsystems. In addition, the sets of bibliographic references and documents can be perfectly matched, so that the user is not referred to documents outside the system. However, this can be a disadvantage if the system's set of bibliographic references and documents does not match the user's needs. Furthermore, a closed EDSS could have a negative effect on intellectual work by reinforcing biases already existing in patterns of publishing and bibliographic control, for example biases in favour of mainstream scientific topics, English-language materials, and First World concerns. Thus in a closed EDSS the discontinuity occurs mainly at the boundary of the system as a whole.

276   *Document supply*

In an open EDSS discontinuities within the system, at the boundaries of the subsystems, are more likely. An extreme example is the conventional interlending system where the seven subsystems, even if some of them may be electronically assisted, are rarely electronically linked. The flow of information between them requires human, mostly manual, activity. As shown in the next section, in CAS-IAS systems subsystems 1 to 4 (SEARCH-REQUEST-LOCATE-ORDER), can be electronically linked. In the case of faxed documents or electronic transmission of scanned documents, subsystems 5 and 6 (COPY-DELIVER) are linked electronically. The Ariel system, often referred to as an EDSS, in fact merely comprises the COPY and DELIVER subsystems. Subsystem 7 (MANAGE) may be linked electronically to one or more of the other subsystems. The main discontinuity occurs at the boundaries of the COPY subsystem 5, the point at which, typically, journal volumes or issues have to be retrieved from the shelves and photocopied or scanned. Only a small set of the universe of documents can be stored in machine-readable form and it is difficult to anticipate which documents will be in demand. Copyright legislation may rule out altogether the storage of documents in electronic form.

On the basis of the above discussion, the following categories of document supply systems can be distinguished:

  a. Pre-electronic systems: loosely linked assemblages of the discrete SEARCH, REQUEST, LOCATE, ORDER, COPY, DELIVER, and MANAGE subsystems, comprising conventional interlending and non-electronic document delivery.
  b. CAS-IAS systems, open EDSSs in which subsystems 1 to 4, SEARCH-REQUEST-LOCATE-ORDER, are largely integrated electronically.
  c. Electronic document *delivery* systems in the narrow sense, open EDSSs in which subsystems 5 and 6, COPY-DELIVER, are electronically integrated.
  d. Closed EDSSs in which subsystems 1 to 7, SEARCH-REQUEST-LOCATE-ORDER-COPY-DELIVER-MANAGE, are largely integrated electronically or which are developing in this direction, but which are not seamlessly linked with the universe of bibliographic references and the universe of documents.
  e. More integrated open EDSSs (including hybrid open/closed systems), which are advancing towards the integration of the SEARCH-REQUEST-LOCATE-ORDER and the COPY-DELIVER chains.

The sections that follow deal with electronic document supply systems (EDSSs) of types (b), (c), (d) and (e). The term electronic document supply system (EDSS) is used here as the generic term, but when individual systems are referred to, the term electronic document delivery system (EDDS) is used if this is the way the systems are described in the relevant literature.

CAS-IAS systems

Traditionally it has been drummed into the heads of trainee librarians and information officers never to index or classify a document on the basis of its title. Considering how much time and effort library and information workers have expended on refining their intellectual technology for information storage and retrieval, the meteoric rise of electronic table of contents (ETOC) databases is quite remarkable. It is a fair guess that the emergence of these very large, multidisciplinary, machine-readable bibliographic databases is as much the result of technological capabilities and economic pressures as of new professional insights.

Two aspects of ETOC databases have implications for document supply. The first is the trend to integration of document delivery with bibliographic alerting services. This is not new and not unique to ETOC databases, but invariably their producers provide not only a bibliographic database but also commercial document ordering and delivery facilities. Copyright clearance charges are usually included in the document delivery fees (Boykin, 1994; Carrigan, 1994). These services are mainly limited to journal articles published in the journal titles that are most in demand - typically between 8,000 and 16,000 titles. The generic name given to these linked or integrated bibliographic databases and document delivery services is 'current awareness (or alerting) service-individual article supply' (CAS-IAS) (Luijendijk, 1994; Woodward, 1994).

The second aspect is the involvement in ETOC databases and CAS-IAS of companies and organizations that were not traditionally involved in the business of indexing the journal literature. Among those now involved in this field, either individually or in partnership with others, are bibliographic utilities or networks, national libraries and periodical subscription agents.

The first and most prominent entrant in this field seems to have been the Colorado Alliance of Research Libraries (CARL). Much has been written about its UnCover ETOC service which covers over 16,000 journal titles (UnCover begins, 1994). UnCover2 added a document delivery component (Barwick, 1994b; Tallim, 1994b; Whittaker and Malamud, 1994). UnCover is now a separate company jointly owned by CARL and the British bookseller and periodical subscription agent, Blackwell (Williams, 1994b). UnCover has been innovative in entering into partnerships with other organizations and by making the database available free of charge on the Internet (Carrigan, 1994; Valauskas, 1994b), where it serves to generate document delivery demand. Van der Werff (1994) compared the performance of UnCover2 with conventional interlending using OCLC, and found that interlending is usually adequate but that UnCover is very useful when material is wanted urgently and users are prepared to pay the average cost of $10–$12 per article. Bauwens (1994) compared the document delivery services of the BLDSC, INIST, UnCover and OCLC's FirstSearch, finding the first two relatively unresponsive while the latter two, which are more innovative, offered access to a more limited range of journal titles. For further descriptions and discussion of UnCover, see Jackson (1994a), Poynder (1994), Quint (1994) and Wooliscroft (1994).

Also in the first group is OCLC, with its ContentsFirst and ArticleFirst databases. OCLC offers the user the option to order articles identified in these databases through its electronic interlending subsystem (Leach and Tribble, 1993; Tallim, 1994b). In Europe the Dutch bibliographic network utility, Pica, commissioned periodical subscription agent Swets to produce its Online Contents database which is linked to Pica's RAPDOC document delivery service (Costers, 1994b; Eeden, 1994; Hulsing-Ronteltap, 1994; SDI, 1994; Williams, 1994d). Swets also markets the ETOC database under its own name, SwetScan, linked with its document delivery service, SwetsDoc. Swets has contracted BLDSC to provide the document delivery service. Users can access SwetScan and SwetsDoc through the Internet and pay for services rendered by credit card (Williams, 1994d).

Among national libraries, the British Library Document Supply Service was a logical entrant in the field, with its Inside Information database (Leach and Tribble, 1993; Woodward, 1994; Wooliscroft, 1994). The BLDSC has an agreement with UnCover in terms of which it serves as a backup supplier for articles UnCover is unable to supply. It also has an agreement with EBSCO, which markets BLDSC's services and provides ETOC and document delivery to its clients under the name CASIAS (Carrigan, 1994; Stephens, 1994). The National Library of Australia has entered into a partnership with the UnCover company for the inclusion of Australian material in the UnCover database and for document delivery to Australian libraries. UnCover Australia is also accessible on the Internet (Goodacre, 1994; Layland, 1994; UnCover Australia, 1994). In South Africa, SABINET, in collaboration with the Council for Scientific and Industrial Research, has mounted the Inside Information database on its network. Holdings information from the Southern African Cooperative Library Database is displayed with article records, so that articles can be obtained through domestic interlending if the journals are available in South Africa (Inside, 1994).

The entry into the field by periodicals subscription agents, while a quite logical development, is in some ways the most unsettling: the move of such firms from the supply of journals to the supply of individual articles calls into question *inter alia* the traditional roles of journal publishers and libraries. The involvement of Blackwell, EBSCO and Swets has already been referred to. Faxon entered the field with the Faxon Finder database, which covered over 10,000 journal titles, with full retrospective coverage going back to 1990, and the Faxon Xpress document delivery service, which offered 24–hour turnaround for delivery of articles by fax. Borsman (1994) reported on a beta test of this service in a medical library setting. During 1993/94 the Faxon company got into financial difficulties. Its European operations were sold to the Dutch firm of Swets and Zeitlinger (Eeden, 1994). The sale of its North American interests was something of a cliff-hanger, but they were eventually purchased by Dawson. Faxon's financial difficulties have been attributed to its entry into the CAS-IAS and electronic document delivery field, the start-up and development costs of which had been underestimated (Dawson, 1994). More generally, commentators have seen the fate of Faxon as evidence of instability in a rapidly evolving commercial document delivery market (Williams, 1994d).

Electronic document delivery systems (EDDS)

The pre-eminent system in this category is Ariel, developed by the (American) Research Libraries Group (RLG). The Ariel system comprises document transmission workstations linked by high-speed Internet data lines. The workstation consists of a microcomputer with a network interface card, a scanner, a printer, and the necessary software. After a requested document has been scanned at the Ariel workstation, the size of the image file is reduced using the RLG's data compression software. It is then transmitted over the network to another Ariel workstation, where the file is decompressed and printed out. By 1994 Ariel was a well-known system which no longer required detailed description, but a number of articles discussed its implementation in various settings: in a consortium of health sciences libraries in the United States (Bennett and Palmer, 1994), an experimental document delivery network linking seventeen research libraries in the five Nordic countries (Mickos, 1994), delivery of documents to a remote branch library of the Canada Institute of Scientific and Technical Information (CISTI) (Brandreth and MacKeigan, 1994), document transmission over the British academic network SuperJANET (Friend, 1994a; Friend, 1994b), the National Library of Canada (Murphy, 1994) and Pica's Netherlands Open Library Network (Costers, 1994c). In spite of the high technology, it appears to be used mainly in fairly conventional interlibrary settings. A number of disadvantages were mentioned in the literature, and these were being addressed in the development of a more advanced Windows-based version (Tallim, 1994b). At CISTI, on the other hand, a decision was taken to develop a new system called Intellidoc, which would be compatible with Ariel but which would not require dedicated workstations (Brandreth and MacKeigan, 1994; CISTI, 1994; Tallim, 1994b).

In the meantime, several other PC-based systems for scanning documents and transmitting them over the Internet are being developed. They include North Carolina State University's DDTP (Digitized Document Transmission Project) and the Ohio State network fax project (Fjällbrant, 1994; Mickos, 1994; Tallim, 1994b).

The EC's project EDIL (Electronic Document Interchange between Libraries) is concerned with the file transfer of scanned documents using the national scientific networks of France, Germany, the Netherlands and the United Kingdom, the main problem being the connection of these networks (Tehnzen, 1994).

Closed electronic document supply systems

The most striking example of systems in this category is ADONIS, developed in the 1980s by a consortium of major biomedical publishers who were concerned over loss of revenue due to photocopying. It is a CD-ROM-based service which provides full-text articles from over 600 biomedical journals. A subscription to ADONIS cost about US$15,000 in 1994. The subscribing institution receives one CD-ROM per week, containing the contents of over one hundred journal issues. Each CD-ROM contains page images and indexes. The latter are uploaded from the CD-ROM to the hard disk of the microcomputer to which the CD-ROM drive is linked, thereby building a database which can be searched for relevant articles. The articles themselves, being stored as bit-mapped images, are not searchable, but when they have been identified they can be called up for display on screen and printed out on a laser printer, which reproduces the original page layout complete with diagrams and illustrations. The ADONIS software includes an accounting and reporting subsystem which tallies up the number of copies made, and every quarter the subscriber is billed for the publishers' copyright charges, which are additional to the annual subscription and range from US$3.50 to US$10 (Grant, 1994; Woodward, 1994).

Morris (1994) describes an experiment in using ADONIS at the University of Wales College of Medicine, giving a detailed assessment of the appropriateness of ADONIS's journal coverage, usage and costs, and reasons for the College's decision not to implement the system. A key problem with a closed EDSS like ADONIS is that the selection of journal titles may not match the needs of the subscriber closely enough to justify the high subscription costs. In considering the appropriateness of ADONIS in developing countries, Grant (1994) pointed out that the CD-ROM technology is appropriate, but that the database has a Western bias.

Under the name of ProQuest PowerPages, UMI (University Microfilms International) offers a range of databases on CD-ROM, for example Business Periodicals, which covers more than 400 business journals. Libraries subscribe to these collections and use them as the basis for in-house document delivery. The system is similar to ADONIS, but the CD-ROMs are housed in specially designed high capacity CD-ROM jukeboxes at the subscribing institution. The jukeboxes can be linked to the institution's network, but the system is proprietary and cannot be used for material other than that supplied by ProQuest. It also differs from ADONIS in that royalties on copying are covered by a flat fee. UMI is also developing an online system called ADDS (Advanced Document Delivery System), which will be based on a client-server system at UMI's headquarters and will provide access to databases of abstracts, ASCII full text and bit-mapped images (Pack, 1994; Williams, 1994c).

Full-text online newspaper and newsletter databases offer a closed pool of documents, but differ from the preceding in providing only ASCII text (Glavash, 1994).

Many of the systems described in the literature do not yet fall within the category of an EDSS, but are developing in that direction. Tenopir (1994) describes the OCLC FirstSearch service, a user-friendly facility for online searching and document ordering. This does not currently meet the criteria for an EDSS, but a planned extension to the service will provide for the ASCII text of articles from 1500 periodical titles to be provided by UMI. The articles will not be searchable, but their availability will be indicated in the bibliographic database and will from there be requested for viewing, downloading and printing. This effectively takes FirstSearch in the direction of a hybrid open/closed system. Williams (1994d) describes the CD-ROM based Patents Express service of the Science Reference and Information Service (SRIS) of the British Library. Planned developments will allow orders to be placed electronically and faxes to be generated directly from the CD-ROMs.

Various research projects and development projects are reported. Geleijnse (1994) describes a cooperative project being undertaken by Tilburg University and Elsevier, in which the full text of 114 journals is made available on 2000 PCs linked to the University's LAN, with the aim, *inter alia*, of learning more about user behaviour, the use of the journal collection, and the nature of an electronic library. This is similar to the research aims of TULIP (The University LIcensing Project), which provides access to bit-mapped pages, ASCII text and bibliographic records, and is concerned with networked delivery of electronic journals (S. Barnes, 1994; Hunter, 1994; Hunter and Zijlstra, 1994) and of the Red Sage experiment, conducted by Springer Verlag and eleven universities (Butter, 1994; Kent, 1994; Nissley, 1994). Other projects that can be categorized here are Colorado State University's online reserve (short loan) system (Enssle, 1994), Georgetown University's prototype digital full-text system in the field of biotechnology (Broering, 1994), EURILIA (European Initiative in Library and Information in Aerospace) at Cranfield University (Blagden and Ford, 1994), and SAIL (System for Automated Interlibrary Loan), a pilot project involving the scanning and electronic storage of medical journals at the US National Library of Medicine (Lacroix, 1994).

Towards more integrated open electronic document supply systems

The experiments and development projects reported in the two preceding sections indicate the direction in which work on more advanced EDSSs is proceeding. Some important themes are greater integration of the document supply subsystems, the development of integrated document imaging workstations, connectivity between local and wide area networks, and more effective links between text and images.

The theme of integration is reflected by the German TIBQUICK project, which was aimed at completing the electronic chain between online searching in bibliographic databases and the ordering and delivering of literature held in the UB/

TIB by using modern information and communication technologies. It *inter alia* addressed a number of problems relating to boundaries between what I have termed the ORDER and COPY subsystems (Schroeder, 1994). In a similar vein, the Dutch academic/research network SURFNET undertook an electronic text project aimed at gaining experience at supplier, intermediary and end user levels (Andersen, 1994).

Half a century after Vannevar Bush (1945) conceptualized a scholar's workstation he called a memex, the literature reflects growing interest in the importance and needs of end-users. Increasingly the end-users, rather than the library or the document supplier, are placed at the centre of the document supply system; they are visualized (with little regard for their health) as more or less perpetually seated at a workstation from which they are able not only to access the OPAC of their institution's library, but also the OPACS of other libraries, union catalogues, and a variety of bibliographic databases. These searches are followed directly by online orders for documents that are speedily delivered to the same workstation, charged for by means of automatic accounting and cost-recovery procedures and paid for using a smart card (Costers, 1994c; Hulsing-Ronteltap; Martin and Kendrick, 1994). As already mentioned, the development of such workstations is being addressed by several research and development projects. Of interest in this connection are Engineering Information's Ei Reference Desk (Bartenbach, 1994), and project ELSA (European Libraries SGML Applications), which aims *inter alia* to develop a workstation for documents coded using SGML (Standard General Markup Language) an important source of machine-readable documents. The workstation would deliver such documents directly to end-users (Adams, 1994). Such systems empower users, but if end-users are able to use EDSSs without assistance, this will diminish the role of the library (Ellis *et al.*, 1994). However, a survey at two major Dutch research libraries showed that users still consider information supply to be the task of government-funded institutions rather than commercial organizations, and that a typical user still wants 'a not too expensive, legible photocopy of an article . . . on his desk within three or four days' (Gils, 1994). A market survey at Delft University of Technology yielded a similar finding (Waaijers, 1994).

A key problem in the development of an EDSS remains the timely provision of document images. On the one hand, research is proceeding on the technical feasibility of establishing electronic document stores for document delivery (Barden, 1994; Williams, 1994a). On the other hand, logistical problems must be addressed. If items are selected for scanning and storage in anticipation of demand, the chances are that at least a proportion of the material in the store will not be used sufficiently to recover scanning and storage costs. This is illustrated by the SAIL project (Lacroix, 1994) and by the reasons given for the decision of the University of Wales College of Medicine not to continue with ADONIS (Morris, 1994). If items are scanned as and when they are ordered, the electronic processing is interrupted by time-consuming manual procedures. There are various responses to this problem. One is to gain greater understanding of user needs and behaviour, as in projects such as TULIP and Red Sage, discussed above, and DIADEM (Digital Information Access Demonstration Centre) at Cranfield University (Blagden and Ford, 1994).

A second response is to build up a bank of articles scanned in response to demand, so that they are ready for second and later orders. Wooliscroft (1994) states that this is the practice of UnCover2. However, in many countries, including the United States, this could constitute a breach of copyright if not cleared with the publishers (Brandreth and MacKeigan, 1994; Gassaway, 1994; Hugenholtz, 1994; Tehnzen, 1994, Visser, 1994).

A third response is to develop hybrid electronic document supply systems consisting of a 'closed' component of documents scanned in anticipation of demand, and an 'open' component which provides access to on-demand scanning and transmission facilities. This is the approach adopted by large commercial document delivery organizations such as OCLC and UMI, which can back up their CD-ROM or online full-text services by a range of commercial document delivery options.

Roes and Dijkstra (1994) discuss what they term a fourth generation model of an EDDS. Such a model should *inter alia* comply with standards that are essential to communicate across systems, be integrated with existing library services including interlending and document delivery procedures, be able to accommodate future developments relating to the representation of documents, employ a demand-driven or a dual (demand and supply-driven) approach to the scanning of documents, store scanned documents when this does not conflict with copyright, output documents in various formats as required by users, communicate across wide area networks, and generate management information. This model forms the basis of the development of the Ariadne system at Tilburg University. They also outline some characteristics of a fifth generation model, which will support full multimedia document delivery and full integration of documents and reference databases, and which will be able to handle electronic publications (i.e. to import documents that are already in machine-readable format into the system) without the need for intensive preprocessing.

Conclusion

Ten years ago, the delivery of documents, whether commercially or through interlending, was typically the result of a number of discrete steps carried out, for the most part, by different parties. Users identified what they needed, using catalogues and other bibliographic tools, but after this had little to do with the procedures for borrowing or obtaining copies, which were largely carried out by the staff of the various agencies. Users only reappeared on the scene when they were notified that the requested items had arrived and had to be collected, or were unobtainable.

For many users of libraries in developed as well as developing countries, not much has changed - yet. In fact, many of the EDSSs mentioned above are being used to support interlending procedures. The literature of document supply nevertheless alerts us to changes that are taking place now and placing more control in the hands of the users. What are the main trends?

- As their options increase thanks to rapidly evolving information technology, end-users gain more control over the processes which lead to the supply of the documents they want. They are more knowledgeable about information systems and have higher expectations. Increasingly, they expect to receive service at their own workstations, potentially connected, through the organizational LAN, to a multitude of systems worldwide.
- Integration of literature searching, verification, location and placing of orders and the copying, dispatching, transmission and receipt of documents is proceeding apace. These steps are increasingly carried out electronically, within the same system, or through electronic links between systems.
- Work is proceeding on the integration of internal and external, closed and open systems, and on the integration of text and image delivery systems.
- More parties are involved in document delivery - moving beyond their conventional roles, forming partnerships and strategic alliances with others, and competing over what used to be libraries' business.
- Libraries are bypassed when users place orders directly with suppliers. They must expect to have less control over the acquisition of information materials from external sources as the distinctions between acquisitions and document delivery, and between publishing and document delivery, are blurred. Librarians are challenged to redefine their roles.

Ten years ago, the BLLD represented the dominant paradigm of document supply. Today no single organization dominates the field conceptually to the extent the BLLD did then. Perhaps the difficulty one has in weighing up and ranking the candidates indicates that a paradigm shift is taking place, one which is not confined to document supply, but which will affect all the links in the chain that connects authors and readers.

Acknowledgements

I thank the members of the Editorial Advising Board of *Librarianship and Information Work Worldwide* for alerting me to relevant literature published in their countries, and in many cases for providing copies of items that would have been difficult to obtain. I thank my colleagues at the State Library for their assistance and support while I was writing this chapter.

References

Abelsnes, K. (1994) The information super highway and the small country roads: smooth crossings, traffic jam or toll plazas? *Newsletter of the IFLA Section on Document Delivery and Interlending*, (December 1994), 85–96.

Abid, A. and Péllisier, D. (1994) CD-ROM in developing countries: a UNESCO perspective. *Inspel*, **28**(3), 366–376.

Adams, R. (1994) ELSA (European Libraries SGML Applications). *Library Technology News*, (13), 3–5.

Alexander, A.W. (1994) Access v. ownership: strategic implications for agents. *Serials Librarian*, **24**(3/4), 125–127.

American (1994) Memory goes on-line. *Library of Congress Information Bulletin*, **53**(20), 410–411.

Andersen, A. (1994) Det virtuelle bibliothek: DATALIB i Trondheim 26.28 oktober 1993. *DF Revy*, **17**(1), 10–11.

Anker, P.M. (1994) OCLC group access in high schools. *Computers in Libraries*, **14**(3), 18–20.

Arunachalam, S. (1993) Accessing information published in the Third World: should spreading the word from the Third World always be like swimming against the current? In: *Workshop on access to Third World journals and conference proceedings...; Barcelona, 1993*; ed. Michael Wise. Boston Spa: IFLA, Programme for Universal Availability of Publications, pp. 3–20.

Barden, P. (1994) The British Library Image Demonstrator Project. *Information Management and Technology*, **27**(5), 214–215.

Barnes, J. (1994) Networked images and document delivery. In: *Proceedings of the 15th national online meeting 1994, New York, 10–12 May 1994*, ed. Martha S. Williams. Metford, NJ: Learned Information, pp. 49–52.

Barnes, S. (1994) Selected digital library projects in the Cornell University Library system. *Library Hi Tech*, **12**(3), 33.

Bartenbach, B. (1994) CD-ROM challenges and opportunities: issues of concern to librarians - an introduction. *Inspel*, **28**(3), 298–306.

Barwick, M.M. (1994a) IFLA guidelines on the use of telefacsimile in interlending. *Newsletter of the IFLA Section on Document Delivery and Interlending*, (March 1994), 19–24.

Barwick, M.M. (1994b) Interlending and document supply - a review of recent literature:

XXV. *Interlending and Document Supply*, **22**(1), 25–35.
Barwick, M.M. (1994c) Interlending and document supply - a review of recent literature: XXVI. *Interlending and Document Supply*, **22**(3), 27–34.
Barwick, M.M. (1994d) Second survey on the interlending of fiction. *Newsletter of the IFLA Section on Interlending and Document Delivery*, (June 1994), 9–12.
Barwick, M.M. (1994e) The use of telefacsimile in interlending: guidelines from the International Federation of Library Associations and Institutions (IFLA). *Newsletter of the IFLA Section on Document Delivery and Interlending*, (December 1994), 43–49.
Barwick, M.M. and Line, M.B. (1994) The interlending of fiction. *Interlending and Document Supply*, **22**(3), 3–7.
Bates, I. (1994) *Improving document delivery in Nova Scotia*. [Unpublished keynote address given at a Conference on Document Delivery in Nova Scotia, April 21 & 22, (1994) Distributed with: People Development Limited (1994) *Report summarizing issues and solutions created during the "Building on Strengths" Conference on document delivery in Nova Scotia, April 21 & 22*.]
Bauwens, M. (1994) Document supply services: how well do they really deliver? *Information World Review*, (89), 14–16.
Bays, D. (1994) *Equalizing opportunity for disabled students: the contribution of the National Library of Canada and Canadian university libraries*. [Paper presented at the 60th IFLA General Conference, Havana (028–DISADV-1–E).]
Beaumont, J. and Lunau, C. (1994) Document supply: a challenge for Canadian libraries. *Interlending and Document Supply*, **22**(3), 15–21.
Behrens, S.J. (1993) Resource sharing and bibliographic access. *Mousaion*, **11**(2), 110–121.
Bennett, V.M. and Palmer, E.M. (1994) Electronic document delivery using the Internet. *Bulletin of the Medical Library Association*, **82**(2), 163–167.
Bibliography (1994a) of interlending and document supply: 31. *Interlending and Document Supply*, **22**(2), 24–31.
Bibliography (1994b) of interlending and document supply: 32. *Interlending and Document Supply*, **22**(4), 22–32.
Bjarnø, H. (1994) Cost finding and performance measures in ILL management. *Interlending and Document Supply*, **22**(2), 8–11.
Blagden, J. and Ford, J. (1994) The electronic library: a view from academia and the computer industry. *Managing Information*, **1**(6), 36–38.
Boissé, J.A. (1994) *Library cooperation: a remedy but not a panacea*. [Paper presented at the 60th IFLA General Conference, Havana (106–CONTR-2–E).]
Borsman, M.L. (1994) Faxon Finder/Faxon Xpress: report from a beta test site. *Bulletin of the Medical Library Association*, **82**(2), 168–170.
Boykin, J.F. (1994) Delivering information to users in the 1990's. In: *Technological university libraries in the nineties; proceedings of the 15th Biennial IATUL Conference Hamburg-Harburg, Germany, July 19–23, 1993*, ed. Dietmar Brandes and Elin Törnudd. Helsinki: Helsinki University of Technology Library, pp. 256–265.
Bradbury, D. and Barwick, M.M. (1994) UAP Core Programme and Office of International Lending: Annual report 1992. In: *IFLA annual 1993*. München: K.G. Saur, pp. 144–149.
Brandreth, M. and MacKeigan, C. (1994) Electronic document delivery - towards the virtual library. *Interlending and Document Supply*, **22**(1), 15–19.
British Library. Document Supply Centre (1994) *Facts and figures, April 1994*. Boston Spa:

The Centre.
Broadbent, V. (1994) A regional medical library service in New Zealand. *New Zealand Libraries*, **47**(12), 235–239.
Broering, N.C. (1994) A digital full-text biotechnology system at Georgetown University. *Library Hi Tech*, **12**(2), 85–91.
Bryant, E. (1994) Reinventing the university press. *Library Journal*, **119**(14), 147–149.
Buckle, D. (1994) Internet: strategic issues for libraries and librarians - a commercial perspective. *Aslib Proceedings*, **46**(11/12), 259–262.
Bunting, A. (1994) Legal considerations for document delivery services. *Bulletin of the Medical Library Association*, **82**(2), 183–187.
Bush, V. (1945) As we may think. *Atlantic Monthly*, **17**(4), 101–108.
Butter, K.A. (1994) Red Sage: the next step in delivery of electronic journals. *Medical Reference Services Quarterly*, **13**(3), 75–81.
Byrum, J.D. (1994) Text Encoding Initiative Guidelines published. *International Cataloguing and Bibliographic Control*, **23**(3), 60.
Canadian (1994) *information resource sharing strategy: discussion document*. Prepared by the Working Group to Review and Update the Canadian Resource Sharing Strategy for the National Library of Canada. [Unpublished document dated 10 May 1994.]
Caplan, P. (1994) Controlling e-journals: the Internet Resources Project, cataloging guidelines and USMARC. *Serials Librarian*, **24**(3/4), 103–111.
Carrigan, D.P. (1994) The emerging national periodicals system in the United States. *Scholarly Publishing*, **25**(2), 93–102.
Cawkell, A.E. (1994) Electronic document delivery systems. *Journal of Documentation*, **47**(1), 41–73.
Chand, P. and Kumar, S.R. (1993) Document delivery at the Indian National Scientific Documentation Centre. *Interlending and Document Supply*, **21**(2), 3–6.
Chifwepa, V. (1993) Agricultural library cooperation in Zambia. *Information Development*, **9**(1/2), 76–82.
Chisanga, C.J.J. and Champo, D. (1993) Factors affecting utility of keys to libraries' resources in Zambia. *Inspel*, **27**(4), 251–256.
CISTI (1994) awards contract to develop DD system. *Feliciter*, **40**(1),46.
Cleveland, G. (1993) *Packet radio: applications for libraries in developing countries*. Ottawa: IFLA International Office for Universal Dataflow and Telecommunications. (UDT Series on Data Communication Technologies and Standards for Libraries, report no. 5.)
Cochrane, T. (1994) Cooperation between publishers and university libraries. In: *Technological university libraries in the nineties; proceedings of the 15th Biennial IATUL Conference Hamburg-Harburg, Germany, July 19–23, 1993*, ed. Dietmar Brandes and Elin Törnudd. Helsinki: Helsinki University of Technology Library, pp. 1–8.
Coetzee, J.A. (1994) *'n Oorsig van die "Western Cape Library Cooperative Project"*. [Paper given at the Annual Conference, South African Institute for Librarianship and Information Science, 21 September 1994.]
Cohn, C. (1993) Document delivery of journal articles to Australasian libraries. *Australian and New Zealand Journal of Serials Librarianship*, **4**(2), 99–107.
Coleman, R. (1993) The Internet as pathway and provider: implications for acquisitions. In: *Creating our future in acquisitions: challenges in the 90s. ALIA/ACLIS Seminar, Broadbeach, Queensland, 23 August 1993*. Melbourne: Australian Library and Information

Association, Acquisitions Section, Victorian Group; Australian Council of Libraries and Information Services, Queensland State Committee, Acquisitions Subcommittee, pp. 76–81.

Cornish, G. (1993) UAP in the Arab world and Eastern Europe. *Focus on International and Comparative Librarianship*, **24**(2), 57–59.

Cornish, G.P. (1994a) Copyright issues related to electronic media. *Inspel*, **28**(3), 314–319.

Cornish, G.P. (1994b) The current state of UAP (Universal Availability of Publications): better, worse, or much the same? *Alexandria*, **6**(3), 215–225.

Cornish, G.P. (1994c) Document supply East and West. *Journal of Interlibrary Loan, Document Delivery and Information Supply*, **4**(3/4), 15–17.

Cornish, G.P. (1994d) Europe divided or united? Networking and document supply now and in the future. *Libri*, **44**(1), 63–76.

Cornish, G.P. (1994e) Mezinárodní spolupráce knihoven - sjednocuje nebo rozděluje Evropu? [International library cooperation - uniting or dividing Europe?] *I'94 Casopis* **36**(5), 116–121.

Cornish, G.P. (1994f) Progress report for the UAP Programme and Office for International Lending 1993/4. *Newsletter of the IFLA Section on Document Delivery and Interlending*, (December 1994), 53–59.

Cornish, G.P. (1994g) Training opportunities for interlibrary loan and document supply staff. *Journal of Education for Library and Information Sciences*, **35**(2), 138–146.

Cornish, G.P. (1994h) UAP in the Arab world and Eastern Europe. *Journal of Interlibrary Loan, Document Delivery and Information Supply* **4**(3/4), 13–14.

Costers, L. (1994a) Beheer en organisatie van de elektronische bibliotheek. *Pica Mededelingen*, **17**(1), 8–9.

Costers, L. (1994b) Developments in bibliographic control and networking in the Netherlands. In: *Proceedings of the Expert seminar on bibliographic control in South Africa, 19–20 May 1994, Pretoria*. Pretoria: State Library, pp.1–14. (Various pagings)

Costers, L. (1994c) OBN: nu en in de toekomst. *Pica Mededelingen*, **17**(1), 2–4.

Costers, L. (1994d) Strategieën voor het verder ontwikkelen van bibliotheeknetwerken. *Pica Mededelingen*, **17**(3), 4–8.

Cother, C. (1994) Interlibrary loans and document delivery: the 'tech knowlogy' connection. In: *The tech connection: proceedings of the 7th National Library Technicians Conference, Adelaide, 22–24 September 1993*, ed. E. Collins. Adelaide: Auslib Press, pp. 68–73.

Cotta-Schønberg, M. and Winkel-Schwartz, A. (1994) Gebyrer imellem bibliotekerne for interurbanlan. *DF-Revy*, **17**(2), 27–29.

Cox, J.E. (1994a) Can dinosaurs evolve? The future of publishers, vendors and librarians. *Learned Publishing*, **7**(2), 85–88.

Cox, J.E. (1994b) Mega vendor: threat or promise? *Serials Librarian*, **24**(3/4), 117–119.

Cox, N. (1994) A change of direction for books on the move. *Library Association Record*, **96**(10), 8,11.

Dallman, D. *et al.* (1994) Electronic pre-publishing for world-wide access: the case of high-energy physics. *Interlending and Document Supply*, **22**(2), 3–7.

Dawson (1994) gives Faxon Company a new beginning. *Library Journal*, **119**(19), 16.

Deschamps, C. (1993) Az ION program. [The ION project.] *Tudományos és Müszáki Tájekoztatás*, **41**(2), 57–62.

Dixon, R. (1994) Legal admissibility and probative value of document images. *Information Management and Technology*, 27(1), 38–40.
Dolby, E. (1993) What price acquisitions? In: *Creating our future in acquisitions: challenges in the 90s. ALIA/ACLIS Seminar, Broadbeach, Queensland, 23 August 1993*. Melbourne: Australian Library and Information Association, Acquisitions Section, Victorian Group; Australian Council of Libraries and Information Services, Queensland State Committee, Acquisitions Subcommittee, pp. 15–23.
Dorner, J. (1994) Whose text is it anyway? *Learned Publishing*, 7(1), 5–9.
Doust, R.W. (1993) Information resource sharing. *Zimbabwe librarian*, 25(1), 4,6–9.
Dunsire, G. (1994) The potential of the Internet and networks for library acquisitions. *Taking Stock* 3(2), 44–49.
Edwards, H.M. (1994) Library co-operation and resource sharing in South Africa: considerations for the future. *South African Journal of Library and Information Science*, 62(3), 113–116.
Eeden, E. van (1994) 'We zijn nu groter dan ooit'. *Boekblad*, 33 (19 Augustus), 10–11.
Elliott, J. and Scott, R.L. (1994) A World Wide Web/Mosaic home page for the US Department of Energy. *Managing Information*, 1(10), 39–41.
Ellis, A. and Rainford, A. (1994) The virtual library at the University of Western Australia. *IATUL News*, 3(1), 3–4.
Ellis, A. *et al.* (1994) Network document access: planning an electronic document delivery service; a case study. *Australian Library Review*, 11(1), 67–74.
Els, B. (1994) Dokumentlewering in die Wes-Kaap. *SAILIS Newsletter*, 14(11), 7.
Enssle, H.R. (1994) Reserve on-line: bringing reserve into the electronic age. *Information Technology and Libraries*, 13(3), 197–201.
Eronina, E.A. and Komov, V.V. (1994) ILL system in the network of research and sci-tech libraries of the FSU: problems and perspectives. *Inspel*, 28(8), 282–290.
Ferguson, S. (1994) Interlending and document delivery in the Caribbean: the perplexing reality. [Unnumbered paper presented at the 60th IFLA General Conference, Havana.]
Fjällbrant, N. (1994) IATUL and academic networks. In: *Technological university libraries in the nineties; proceedings of the 15th Biennial IATUL Conference Hamburg-Harburg, Germany, July 19–23, 1993*, ed. Dietmar Brandes and Elin Törnudd. Helsinki: Helsinki University of Technology Library, pp. 156–163.
Flanders, B. (1994) The Kansas Interlibrary Loan Directory and Manual (KILDM): A case study in applying hypertext technology to interlibrary loan information. *Journal of Interlibrary Loan, Document Delivery and Information Supply*, 5(1), 45–59.
Fouché, B. and Day, R. (1993) Problems of access to information in developing countries. [Unpublished paper presented at a meeting of the International Council for Scientific and Technical Information, Williamsburg, Virginia, 16–19 May 1993.]
Friend, F.J. (1994a) Electronic document delivery through library cooperation: a trial using SuperJANET, and future possibilities. *Interlending and Document Supply*, 22(4), 17–21.
Friend, F.J. (1994b) Spolupráce mezi východo- a západoevropskými knihovnami. [Cooperation between libraries of Eastern and Western Europe.] *I'94 Casopis*, 36(5), 122–124.
Galuscova, L. (1994) 3 mezinarodna konferencia o medzinarodnej medziknizničnej vypozicnej sluzbe a doplnovani fondov. [Third International Conference on International Interlending and Document Delivery.] *Knižnice a Informacie*, 26(6), 277–280.

Gardner, S. (1994) A descriptive study of statewide bibliographic databases. *Journal of Interlibrary Loan, Document Delivery and Information Supply* **4**(3/4), 169–221.

Gassaway, L.N. (1994) Document delivery. *Computers in Libraries*, **14**(5), 25–28,30–32.

Gasson, C. (1994) Fear and loathing in cyberspace, *Bookseller*, (4618), 20–21,24.

Geleijnse, H. (1994) Journal articles on the desktop. *Managing Information*, **1**(6), 34–35.

Gibbs, M. (1994) Imaging on networks: up close and in depth. *Inform*, **8**(1), 16–19,21–22.

Giese, D. (1994) The videodisk collection at the State Library of the Northern Territory. *National Library of Australia News*, **4**(10), 6–8.

Gils, W. van (1994) The paperless library: between myth and museum. *Information Services and Use*, **14**(1), 9–17.

Glavash, K. (1994) Full-text retrieval for document delivery: a viable option? *Online*, **18**(3), 81–84.

Good, H. (1994) Some observations on inter-library loans. In: *Technological university libraries in the nineties; proceedings of the 15th Biennial IATUL Conference Hamburg-Harburg, Germany, July 19–23, 1993*, ed. Dietmar Brandes and Elin Törnudd. Helsinki: Helsinki University of Technology Library, pp. 246–255.

Goodacre, C. (1994) Document delivery. *New Librarian*, **1**(3), 9–10.

Gore, D. (1975) (ed.) *Farewell to Alexandria: solutions to space, growth, and performance problems of libraries*. Westport, CT: Greenwood.

Gould, S. (1994) Voucher scheme to simplify payment for international interlibrary transactions: progress report to July 1994. *Newsletter of the IFLA Section on Document Delivery and Interlending*, (December 1994), 15–42.

Grant, S.L. (1994) *ADONIS: for developing countries?* [Paper presented at the 60th IFLA General Conference, Havana (011–BIOL-1-E).]

Greeff, R. (1994) *Southern Africa and the information superhighway*. [Unpublished paper delivered at the Powershift in South Africa Business Conference, Johannesburg, June 8, 1994.]

Greene, R. (1993) Au Nord et au Sud: même combat pour l'accès aux documents. *Documentation et bibliothèques*, **39**(3), 165–167.

Griebel, R. (1994) Electronic publishing and the acquisitions crisis in academic libraries. *Newsletter of the IFLA Section on Document Delivery and Interlending*, (March 1994), 45–59.

Grimshaw, A. (1994) ELINOR electronic library project. *Information Management and Technology*, **27**(1), 33–35.

Guangjun, M. (1993) Documentary resources of the Chinese Academy of Sciences and their rational distribution. *Library Acquisitions: Practice and Theory*, **17**(3), 287–294.

Hafkin, N.J. (1994) Capacity building for electronic communication in Africa: a project of the Pan-African Development Information System. *FID News Bulletin*, **44**(9), 175–178.

Harloe, B. and Budd, J.M. (1994) Collection development and scholarly communication in the era of electronic access. *Journal of Academic Librarianship*, **20**(2), 83–87.

Hébert, F. (1994) Service quality: an unobtrusive investigation of interlibrary loan in large public libraries in Canada. *Library and Information Science Research*, **16**(1), 3–21.

Henty, M. (1993) Resource sharing among Australian libraries: a distributed national collection. *Library Acquisitions: Practice and Theory*, **17**(3), 311–317.

Holm, L.A. (1994) Connectivity and protocols - the technical side: OSI and TCP/IP, FTP,

TELNET, SR, ILL, Update. *IFLA Journal*, **20**(2), 158–170.
Hugenholtz, P.B. (1994) Copyright and electronic document delivery services. *Interlending and Document Supply*, **22**(3), 8–14.
Hulsing-Ronteltap, R. (1994) NCC/IBL-systeem: verbreding en vernieuwing. *Open*, **26**(3), 76–79.
Hunter, K. (1994) Issues and experiments in electronic publishing and dissemination. *Information Technology and Libraries*, **13**(12), 127–132.
Hunter, K. and Zijlstra, J (1994) TULIP - the university licensing project. *Journal of Interlibrary Loan, Document Delivery and Information Supply*, **4**(3/4), 19–22.
Ibrahim, B.A. (1993) Interlibrary loans in the Arabian Gulf: issues and requisites. *Interlending and document supply*, **21**(2), 21–25.
Inside (1994) information on SABINET enhance [sic] document delivery. *SAILIS Newsletter*, **14**(11), 11.
Interlending (1994) *and document supply for developing countries; papers from the IFLA pre-session seminar on interlending and document supply, Paris, August 1989*, ed. Graham P Cornish and Sarah Gould. Boston Spa: IFLA, Programme for Universal Availability of Publications.
ISI (1994) to index electronic journals. *Managing Information*, **1**(11/12), 17.
Jackson, M.E. (1994a) Dissecting document delivery. *Information Today*, (November 1994), 44–45.
Jackson, M.E. (1994b) Interlibrary loan: Norwegian style. *Wilson Library Bulletin*, **68**(9), 67–68,118.
Jackson, M.E. (1994c) The North American Interlibrary Loan and Document Delivery Project: improving ILL for all types of libraries. *Public Libraries*, **33**(5), 273.
Jackson, M.E. (1994d) Please rush, need ASAP. *Wilson Library Bulletin*, **69**(1),68–69.
Jackson, M.E. (1994e) Reciprocal agreements. *Wilson Library Bulletin*, **68**(7), 67–68,134.
Jackson, M.E. (1994f) Redesigning access and delivery services. *Wilson Library Bulletin*, **69**(3), 73–74.
Jackson, M.E. (1994g) Training for ILL practitioners. *Wilson Library Bulletin*, **68**(5), 75–76.
Kahl, S.C. (1993) A first step: the U.S.-Mexico interlibrary loan project. *Journal of Interlibrary Loan, Document Delivery and Information Supply*, **4**(1), 17–24.
Kanamugire, A.B. (1993) Impact of CD-ROM database searching on interlibrary loans: the experience of a scientific and technological library in a developing country. *Journal of Interlibrary Loan, Document Delivery and Information Supply*, **4**(1), 25–34.
Keates, S. (1993) Universal availability of publications and the impact of new technology. *Asian Libraries* **3**(31), 66–71.
Kemp, G. (1994) SABINET se rol in die ontwikkeling van Suid-Afrika. *Meta-info Bulletin*, **3**(5), 6–8.
Kent, P.G. (1993) The acquisitions librarian and the electronic revolution. In: *Creating our future in acquisitions: challenges in the 90s. ALIA/ACLIS seminar, Broadbeach, Queensland, 23 August 1993*. Melbourne: Australian Library and Information Association, Acquisitions Section, Victorian Group; Australian Council of Libraries and Information Services, Queensland State Committee, Acquisitions Subcommittee, pp.82–88.
Keylard, M. (1993) CD-ROM implementation in developing countries: impacts and pitfalls. *IFLA Journal*, **19**(1), 35–47.
Khalil, M.A. (1994a) Creating a local journal database for electronic document delivery.

In: *Proceedings of the 15th National Online Meeting 1994, New York, 10–12 May 1994*, ed. M.S. Williams. Metford, NJ: Learned Information, pp. 263–273.

Khalil, M.A. (1994b) Document delivery and overcoming the barriers of cultural and technological gaps in developing countries. In: *Proceedings of the 15th National Online Meeting 1994, New York, 10–12 May 1994*, ed. Martha S. Williams. Metford, NJ: Learned Information, pp. 275–281.

Kibirige, H.M. (1994) Electronic full text information delivery: a study of the US infrastructure. In: *Proceedings of the 15th National Online Meeting 1994, New York, 10–12 May 1994*, ed. Martha S. Williams. Metford, NJ: Learned Information, pp. 283–290.

Kingma, B.R. (1994) Access to journal articles: a model of the cost efficiency of document delivery and library consortia. In: *ASIS '94; Proceedings of the 57th ASIS annual meeting, Alexandria, VA, 17–20 October 1994*. Medford, NJ: Learned Information, for the American Society for Information Science, pp. 8–16.

Kinnucan, M.T. (1994) Modeling user's [sic] preferences for document delivery. *OCLC Systems and Services*, **10**(2/3), 93–98.

Kurosman, K. and Durniak, B.A. (1994) Document delivery: a comparison of commercial document suppliers and interlibrary loan services. *College and Research Libraries*, **55**(2), 129–139.

Lacroix, E.M. (1994) SAIL: automating interlibrary loan. *Bulletin of the Medical Library Association*, **82**(2), 171–175.

Lamolinara, G. (1994a) Digital age: LC receives $13 million to put collections on-line. *Library of Congress Information Bulletin*, **53**(20), 407–409.

Lamolinara, G. (1994b) Getting on the information superhighway. *Library of Congress Information Bulletin* **53**(20), 409–410.

Layland, P. (1994) On-line with Ozline. *National Library of Australia News*, **5**(2), 6–8.

Leach, R.G. and Tribble, J.E. (1993) Electronic document delivery: new options for libraries. *Journal of Academic Librarianship*, **18**(6), 359–364.

Levey, L.A. (1994) (ed.) *CD-ROM for African research needs: some basic guidelines*. 3rd ed. Washington: Sub-Saharan Africa Program, American Association for the Advancement of Science.

Library book (1994) rate replacement proposals. *National Library [of Canada] News*, **26**(6), 12.

Library rate (1994) *(postal subsidy): results of a survey of Canadian libraries, November 1993 - February 1994*. Ottawa: Association pour l'avancement des sciences et des techniques de la documentation; Canadian Library Association; National Library of Canada.

Line, M.B. (1994a) How can bibliographic services be managed at a national level? In: *Proceedings of the Expert seminar on bibliographic control in South Africa, 19–20 May 1994, Pretoria*. Pretoria: State Library, pp. 1–9. (Various pagings.)

Line, M.B. (1994b) What to look for when planning national or regional document supply systems. In: *Interloading and document supply. Proceedings of the Third International Conference, held in Budapest, March 1993*. Ed. A.J. Swires. Boston Spa: IFLA Office for International Lending, pp. 66–73.

Line, M.B. (1994c) The implications of declining library resources and improving electronic technology for document access and supply. *Interlending and Document Supply*, **22**(2), 19–23.

Line, M.B. et al. (1980) *National interlending systems: a comparative study of existing systems and national models*. Paris: UNESCO General Information Programme.

Lippman, M.J. (1993) The library as information producer: the case of the Ministry of Health Library and Documentation Centre in Malawi. *Journal of Documentation*, **49**(1), 55–59.

Lor, P.J. (1993) Improving access to Southern African journals and conference proceedings: a view from down South. In: *Workshop on access to Third World journals and conference proceedings...; Barcelona, 1993*, ed. Michael Wise. Boston Spa: IFLA, Programme for Universal Availability of Publications, pp. 27–45.

Lor, P.J. and De Beer, J.F. (1994) The State Library in the service of South African science and scholarship. *South African Journal of Science*, **90**(8/9), 462–466.

Lor, P.J. and Hendrikz, F. (1993) Statistics of interlending traffic in the Southern African Interlending Scheme, 1985–1991. *South African Journal of Library and Information Science*, **61**(1), 11–18.

Lovas, I. (1994) A look at LOANSOME DOC service. *Bulletin of the Medical Library Association*, **82**(2), 176–180.

Luijendijk, W. (1994) Subscription agencies: fewer, tougher, more agile - and beleaguered. *Serials*, **7**(1), 79–82.

Machovec, G.S. (1994) Key elements in an advanced document delivery and ILL system. *Online Libraries and Microcomputers*, **12**(1), 1–5.

Malamud, J. and Levine, L. (1994) Introduction [to Symposium: Docushock: options for document delivery in the nineties.] *Bulletin of the Medical Library Association*, **82**(2), 161–187.

Mark, N. and Fuchs, H. (1994) Document delivery and interlending: annual report 1992/93. In: *IFLA annual 1993*. Munchen: K.G.Saur, 196–198.

Marle, G.A.J.S. van (1994) Electronic serial publishing and its effect on the traditional information chain. *Serials*, **7**(1), 17–28.

Martin, H.S. and Kendrick, C.L. (1994) A user-centered view of document delivery and interlibrary loan. *Library Administration and Management*, **8**(4), 223–227.

Mauch, J. (1993) We are all in this together. Electronic tools and their effect on our industry. In: *Creating our future in acquisitions: challenges in the 90s. ALIA/ACLIS Seminar, Broadbeach, Queensland, 23 August 1993*. Melbourne: Australian Library and Information Association, Acquisitions Section, Victorian Group; Australian Council of Libraries and Information Services, Queensland State Committee, Acquisitions Subcommittee, pp. 68–75.

McLean, N. (1993) Provision of scholarly information: the economics of supply and demand. *Australian Library Journal*, **42**(2), 94–97.

Meer, J.M. van der (1994) Met Z39.50 zoeken in Amerikaanse bestanden. *Pica Mededelingen*, **17**(3), 8–9.

Membership (1994) of the Southern African Interlending Scheme expands. *Journal of Interlibrary Loan, Document Delivery and Information Supply*, **4**(3/4), 5–6.

Miah, A.J. (1994) Automated library networking in American public community college learning resource centers. *Journal of Interlibrary Loan, Document Delivery and Information Supply*, **5**(1), 67–95.

Mickos, E. (1994) The use of the Internet in document delivery - a NORDINFO project. In: *Technological university libraries in the nineties; proceedings of the 15th Biennial IATUL Conference, Hamburg-Harburg, Germany, July 19–23, 1993*, ed. Dietmar Brandes and Elin Törnudd. Helsinki: Helsinki University of Technology Library, 266–275.

Miller, J. (1993) The electronic library information system as a source of interlibrary loan requests. *Journal of Interlibrary Loan, Document Delivery and Information Supply*, **4**(2), 17-28.

Milne, J.R. (1994) Hypertext and its implications for library services. *Library and Information Research News*, **18**(60), 24-29.

Mitchell, P.R. (1994) Perceptions of high school library media specialists toward interlibrary loan. *Journal of Interlibrary Loan, Document Delivery and Information Supply*, **4**(3/4), 81-154.

Model (1984) national interlibrary lending code. *Interlending and Document Supply*, **12**(1), 15-17.

Morales Campos, E. (1994) *Préstamo interbibliotecario entre México y los Estados Unidos.* [Paper presented at the 60th IFLA General Conference, Havana (125-DOCDEL-2-S).]

Morris, W. (1994) ADONIS: a document delivery solution? A case study. *Health Libraries Review*, **11**(1), 39-51.

Mountifield, H.M. and Van Brakel, P.A. (1994) Network-based electronic journals: a new source of information. *South African Journal of Library and Information Science*, **62**(1), 28-33.

Murphy, W. (1994) Update on ARIEL. *National Library News*, **26**(2/3), 11.

National (1994) digital library, The. *Information Retrieval and Library Automation*, **30**(5), 1-3.

New (1994) ILL project receives sponsors. *Feliciter*, **40**(2), 11-12.

Nilsson, K. (1994a) BIBSAM and its role in coordination and support of Swedish research libraries. *Alexandria*, 6(1), 63-71.

Nilsson, K. (1994b) Planning for document supply: Sweden and Scandinavia. *Interlending and Document Supply*, **22**(1), 3-6.

Nishino, K. (1994) Kazu's America/Canada training memo [in Japanese.] *Toshokan Zasshi/ Library journal*, 88(1), 42-43.

Nissley, M.J. (1994) Electronic publishing: implications for libraries and librarians part I: two views - the commercial STM publisher and the library educator: a report of ALCTS Electronic Publishing Discussion Group. [Conference report] *Library Acquisitions: Practice and Theory*, **18**(1), 108-110.

Norman, S. (1994) Electronic copyright: the issues. *IFLA Journal*, **20**(2), 171-175.

Núñes Fina, L. et al. (1994) *Préstamo interbibliotecario y suministro de documentos en Cuba.* [Paper presented at the 60th IFLA General Conference, Havana (050-DOCDEL-1-S).]

Nyirenda, B.T. (1994) Electronic mail and the UNIMA Fidonet network. *Project for African Research Libraries Notes*, **4**(1), 2-5.

Ozowa, V.N. (1993) Effective library co-operation in Nigeria: an El Dorado? *Journal of Interlibrary Loan, Document Delivery and Information Supply*, **4**(1), 35-44.

Pack, T. (1994) UMI - history in the making. *Library Hi Tech*, **12**(3), 91-100.

People Development Limited (1994) *Report summarizing issues and solutions created during the "Building on Strengths" Conference on document delivery in Nova Scotia, April 21 & 22, 1994.* [Unpublished report by People Development Ltd, Halifax, Nova Scotia.]

Pessah, R. (1994) Interlibrary loan service and the MPALS. *Journal of Interlibrary Loan, Document Delivery and Information Supply*, **5**(1), 19-22.

Pool, J.W. (1994) SAVEIT Version 2.0 offers time saving features. *Journal of Interlibrary Loan, Document Delivery and Information Supply*, **5**(1), 7-11.

Powell, B. and Burch, B. (1994) The changing role of the regional library systems. *Interlending and Document Supply*, **22**(3), 22–26.

Poynder, R. (1994) Getting virtual in Ulan Bator. *Information World Review*, (89), 12–13,19.

Prendergast, N.D. (1994) Trends in the use of the DOCLINE and the OCLC ILL Subsystem 1986–1992. *Bulletin of the Medical Library Association*, **82**(3), 271–276.

Priestley, C. (1994) Availability of publications in Africa: exchange of experience and future prospects. *FID News Bulletin*, **44**(4/5), 67–70.

Project (1994) to improve interlending and document delivery in developing countries. *UDT Newsletter*, (24), 3.

Prosekova, S.N. (1993) Interlending in new environments. *Resource Sharing and Information Networks*, **8**(2), 65–71.

Quint, B. (1994) Found money. *Information Today*, **11**(8), 7–9.

Rannells, E. (1994) The Pacific Legal Information Network. *Information Development*, **10**(1), 25–28.

Raschke, S.D. (1994) Team building in a university interlibrary services department: Part one - from mission statement to individual goals. *Journal of Interlibrary Loan, Document Delivery and Information Supply*, **5**(1), 33–44.

Rees, J. (1994) Information access versus document supply: the International Visual Arts Information Network project. *Interlending and Document Supply*, **22**(1), 20–24.

Reng, J. (1994) The technology knot: tying small libraries together through remote access. *Wilson Library Bulletin*, **68**(6), 38–40, 140.

Rice, S.S. (1994a) ILL-list conspectus. *Journal of Interlibrary Loan, Document Delivery and Information Supply*, **4**(3/4), 7–11.

Rice, S.S. (1994b) ILL-list conspectus. *Journal of Interlibrary Loan, Document Delivery and Information Supply*, **5**(1), 13–18.

Richards, A. (1994) *Library cooperation for social and cultural development within the Caribbean area*. [Paper presented at the 60th IFLA General Conference, Havana (081–LAC-5–EX).]

Richer, S. (1994) Le disque compact dans la Francophonie du sud. *Inspel*, **28**(3), 390–398.

Robishaw, S.M. and Roth, B.G. (1994) GRATEFUL MED - LOANSOME DOC outreach project in central Pennsylvania. *Bulletin of the Medical Library Association*, **82**(2), 206–213.

Roes, H. and Dijkstra, J. (1994) Ariadne: the next generation of electronic document delivery systems. *Electronic Library*, **12**(1), 13–20.

Rosenberg, D. (1993) Resource sharing - is it the answer for Africa? *African Journal of Library, Archives and Information Science*, **3**(2), 107–112.

Santos Labourdette, M.C. (1994) La comunicación Académica y la transferencia electrónica de documentos en la Red Universitaria en Cuba. [Paper delivered at the 60th IFLA General Conference, Havana (047–UN-1-5).]

Schauder, D. (1994) Electronic publishing of professional articles: attitudes of academics and implications for the scholarly communication industry. In: *Technological university libraries in the nineties; proceedings of the 15th Biennial IATUL Conference Hamburg-Harburg, Germany, July 19–23, 1993*, ed. Dietmar Brandes and Elin Törnudd. Helsinki: Helsinki University of Technology Library, pp. 31–35.

Schroeder, A. (1994) TIBQUICK - der schnellste Weg zur Fachliteratur. *Zeitschrift für Bibliothekswesen und Bibliographie*, **41**(1), 103–106.

Schwartz, C.A. (1994) Empirical analysis of literature loss. *Library Resources and Technical Services*, **38**(2), 133–138.

SDI (1994): online contents via e-mail. *Pica Mededelingen*, **17**(3), 11.

Section (1994) on Document Delivery and Interlending: a new name. *IFLA Journal*, **20**(1), 75–76.

Shipp, J. (1993) The way ahead: outcomes of the Changes in scholarly communication patterns conference, Canberra, 14–16 April 1993. *Australian Library Journal* **42**(2), 84–89.

Shraiberg, Y.L. and Goncharov, M.V. (1994) LIBNET - project of the major Russian libraries network. In: *Technological university libraries in the nineties; proceedings of the 15th Biennial IATUL Conference, Hamburg-Harburg, Germany, July 19–23, 1993*, ed. Dietmar Brandes and Elin Törnudd. Helsinki: Helsinki University of Technology Library, pp. 137–140.

Simmons, D. (1993) Bibliographic control in the South Pacific and the Pacific Information Centre (PIC). In: *Workshop on access to Third World journals and conference proceedings...; Barcelona, 1993*, ed. Michael Wise. Boston Spa: IFLA, Programme for Universal Availability of Publications, pp. 21–26.

Smale, C. (1994) Interlibrary loan bulk delivery service. *National Library [of Canada] News*, **26**(5), 6.

Smith, A. (1994) South Sea BUBL: an information service for the New Zealand library and information community. *New Zealand Libraries*, **47**(11), 210–212.

Sol, P. del *et al.* (1994) Knowledge Alert: management and technology for the co-operative acquisition and use of periodical publications in Chile. *Interlending and Document Supply*, **22**(2), 12–18.

Steffen, S.S. and Deiss, K. (1994) Document delivery to off-campus students: the Northwestern University experience. *Illinois Libraries*, **76**(1), 19–22.

Stephens, J.T. (1994) Future value-added services: remaining competitive in a new market. *Serials Librarian*, **24**(3/4), 121–123.

Sturges, P. (1994) Using grey literature in informal information services in Africa. *Journal of Documentation*, **50**(4), 273–290.

Suga, T. and Urata, K. (1993) Medical library cooperation: Asian countries and the Japanese Medical Library Association. *Journal of Interlibrary Loan and Information Supply*, **3**(4), 25–32.

Summann, F. (1994) Express-System für die Bestellung und Lieferung von Zeitschriftenaufsätzen JASON-NRW. *Zeitschrift für Bibliothekswesen und Bibliographie*, **41**(2), 222–229.

Summerhill, C.A. (1994) Connectivity and navigation: an overview of the global internetworked information infrastructure. *IFLA Journal*, **20**(2), 147–157.

Swain, L. and Cleveland, G. (1994) Overview of the Internet: origins, future, and issues. *IFLA journal*, **20**(1), 16–21.

Tallim, P. (1994a) National Library participation in the NAILDD project. *National Library [of Canada] News*, **26**(2), 5–6.

Tallim, P. (1994b) Using the Internet to support interlending and document delivery in North America. *Newsletter of the IFLA Section on Document Delivery and Interlending*, (December 1994), 65–84.

Tehnzen, J. (1994) Document supply and interlending at UB/TIB Hannover. In:

Technological university libraries in the nineties; proceedings of the 15th Biennial IATUL Conference, Hamburg-Harburg, Germany, July 19–23, 1993, ed. Dietmar Brandes and Elin Törnudd. Helsinki: Helsinki University of Technology Library, pp. 237–245.

Tenopir, C. (1994) A second look at FirstSearch. *Library Journal*, **119**(18), 30,32.

Thompson, K.S. (1994) The use of Q&A in interlibrary loan. *Journal of Interlibrary Loan, Document Delivery and Information Supply*, **5**(1), 61–66.

Thompson, P. (1994) Music and interlending in the United Kingdom: new perspectives. *Interlending and Document Supply*, **22**(4), 4–7.

UnCover Australia (1994) to begin. *ABN News with Ozline News*, (74), 7–8.

UnCover begins (1994) single-order service. *Library Journal*, **119**(18), 28.

Valauskas, E.J. (1994a) Alternatives to CD-ROM: issues and prospects. *Inspel*, **28**(3), 382–389.

Valauskas, E.J. (1994b) Using the Internet in libraries. *IFLA Journal*, **20**(1), 22–28.

Van Brakel, P.A. (1994) Veranderende kommunikasiewyses van wetenskaplikes: uitdagings vir die inligtingspesialis. *South African Journal of Library and Information Science*, **62**(1), 9–18.

Van der Werff, J. (1994) Which document delivery service best serves your patron: UnCover2 or ILL? *Journal of Interlibrary Loan, Document Delivery and Information Supply*, **5**(1), 23–31.

Visser, D. (1994) Reprografische capriolen van de wetgever: het nieuwe reprorecht en bibliotheken. *Open*, **26**(1), 7–10.

Waaijers, L. (1994) End-users' hopes and expectations. *Interlending and Document Supply*, **22**(1), 7–14.

What's (1994) in store at the Digital Library Visitors' Center. *Library of Congress Information Bulletin*, **53**(20), 411–412.

White, W.D. (1994) BOSTID's STI networking services. *FID News Bulletin*, **44**(4/5), 63–66.

Whittaker, M. and Malamud, J. (1994) UnCover: the article access solution. *Bulletin of the Medical Library Association*, **82**(8), 181–182.

Wijasuriya, D.E.K. (1994) ASTINFO - regionalis dokumentumellatas. [The ASTINFO regional approach to document support provisions.] *Tudományos és Műszáki Tájekoztatás*, **41**(2), 73–75.

Williams, B.J.S. (1994a) Automated document delivery at the British Library Document Supply Centre. *Information Management and Technology*, **27**(1), 36–37,40.

Williams, B.J.S. (1994b) Document delivery survey: April 1994. *FID News Bulletin*, **44**(4/5), 83–88.

Williams, B.J.S. (1994c) Document delivery survey: January 1994. *FID News Bulletin*, **44**(1), 16–20.

Williams, B.J.S. (1994d) Document delivery survey: September 1994. *FID News Bulletin*, **44**(9), 204–208.

Williamson, M. (1994) The National Library of Canada and the Internet. *Managing Information*, **1**(10):37–38.

Withnell, L.E. (1994) Faculty opinions of academic library service policies. *Journal of Interlibrary Loan, Document Delivery and Information Supply*, **4**(3/4), 23–79.

Woodberry, E. (1993) Keynote address. In: *Creating our future in acquisitions: challenges in the 90s. ALIA/ACLIS Seminar, Broadbeach, Queensland, 23 August 1993*. Melbourne: Australian Library and Information Association, Acquisitions Section, Victorian Group;

Australian Council of Libraries and Information Services, Queensland State Committee, Acquisitions Subcommittee, pp. 10–14.

Woodward, H. (1994) The impact of electronic information on serials collection development. *IFLA Journal*, **20**(1), 35–45.

Wooliscroft, M. (1994) Access and ownership: academic libraries' collecting and service responsibilities and the emerging benefits of electronic publishing and document supply. *New Zealand Libraries*, **47**(9), 170–180.

Yitai, G. (1993) Some issues in the development of documentary information resources in China. *Library Acquisitions: Practice and Theory*, **17**(3), 281–285.

Yoo, S. (1994) A structural analysis of interlibrary networks: a regional ILL network in the Western New York 3Rs region. *Journal of Interlibrary Loan, Document Delivery and Information Supply*, **4**(3/4), 155–167.

Young, P.R. (1994) Changing information access economics: new roles for libraries and librarians. *Information Technology and Libraries*, **13**(2), 103–114.

Zulu, S.F.C. (1994) Africa's survival plan for meeting the challenges of information technology in the 1990s and beyond. *Libri*, **44**(1), 77–94.

Information technology 11

Alan Poulter

Introduction

Twenty years ago, Daniel Bell, in a ground-breaking study (Bell, 1974), prophesied the coming of the information society, when information sector workers would outnumber those in manufacturing. This prophecy, as it turns out, has not yet been fulfilled completely. Information technology (IT), which for the purpose of this paper is defined as meaning devices which store, process and transmit data in digital form, was in its infancy in 1974. In 1994, it is revealing its true importance and power. El-Hadidy (1994) argues that there is universal acknowledgement that information is a resource vital for decision making, and that IT is now a powerful tool for economic development. IT can be used to transfer information from information-rich countries to information-poor countries.

As Burton (1994) points out, technology and society interact with each other in a complex way. A variety of reasons – some rational, like cost, and others not so rational, like custom – may explain why certain new technologies never become widespread and certain obsolete technologies persist. New technologies do not replace old technologies, rather they take their place alongside them, as Burton shows in his study of electronic mail.

As a consequence of this evolving patchwork of old and new technologies, it is difficult to point to a specific date on which 'things changed'. It is taken for granted now that on one disc can be stored text, images, sound and video. One device, the computer, can process all these media; one single computer network, whether spanning only a building or the entire globe, can transmit these media. In 1990, researchers at General Instruments changed the communications landscape when they were able to compress and send television signals in digital, rather than analogue, form. Griffith and Smith (1994) declare this as the 'technological equivalent of the fall of the Berlin Wall'. Brophy (1994) points to the release of the original IBM PC in 1982. Designed from off-the-shelf components, rather than from parts proprietary to IBM, it became the *de facto* market standard. The computer became a consumer item, rather than an expert's tool, following the appearance of the Apple Macintosh in 1984, which sported a graphical user interface (GUI) (Thompson, 1994). Selling a GUI for the IBM PC family contributed to making Bill Gates, chairperson of Microsoft, the richest man in America. Finally, Brophy remarks on the enormous impact of telecommunications networks, especially the Internet. The recent explosion of interest in the Internet can be explained by the appearance of a graphical Internet browser (Mosaic) in 1993.

Non-digital information technologies have fallen by the wayside, as Case (1994) makes clear in a paper on videotex; this technology was touted as the tool for the information society of fewer factories and natural resources. It promised an 'electronic cottage' that relied on analogue technology already in place (the television and the telephone) rather than equipment not then available (the digital computer). Videotex failed because of lack of impact, little interactivity and no agreed standards.

This chapter continues with a brief introduction to current developments in IT. The focus then narrows from an overview of its effects on the information industry in general, to concentrate on how it is changing the role of the library in that industry. Finally, the effects of IT on certain types of library and on the profession of librarianship will be examined.

Information technology developments

Nothing dates faster than the 'latest' in information technology. The company that used to lead the computer industry, IBM, had by 1994 fallen from first in the Fortune 500 listing of most admired corporations to 354th. The company achieved its past pre-eminent position through selling mainframe and mini-computers. Systems based on large IBM machines are being slowly replaced ('downsized' in the jargon) by networks of IBM PC-compatible microcomputers made by other companies. Relentless market pressure has, simultaneously, forced down prices and raised the performance specifications of such machines.

Apple has had similar problems to IBM (Thompson, 1994). Its proprietary Macintosh machines never achieved significant market share against technically inferior, but relatively open system, IBM PC compatibles. To compete, Apple has increased the power of its microcomputers by employing RISC (reduced-instruction-set computer) processors and tried to open new markets with PDAs (personal digital assistants), hand-held computers which function like a diary.

1994 also saw the popularity grow of multimedia IBM PC compatibles with CD-ROM drives (Bevan, 1994). Multimedia ('computing with sound and motion') blurs the boundary between entertainment and education. CD-ROM suppliers, like Microsoft, with their 'Microsoft Home' range, are focusing on the big educational and domestic markets. This will push prices down further, although it only costs one dollar to press a CD-ROM currently. The 'High Sierra' (ISO 9660) standard for CD-ROMs has ensured an open market. Small suppliers can compete by the use of cheap CD-R (compact-disc recordable) machines (Sengstack, 1994).

The requirement to work in multimedia pushes the storage and access capacities of optical discs to their limits, but these capacities are still increasing (Campbell and Proehl, 1994). Business is using optical discs as vast storage banks for document image processing (DIP) systems, which involve scanning paper documents to convert them into machine-readable images. Images of documents can be converted into text with optical character recognition (OCR) technology, which is becoming both cheap and powerful.

There is no one universal, open, image standard, although JPEG (Joint Photographic Experts Group) and GIF (Graphics Interchange Format) are contenders (Price, 1994). The latter was recently harmed by moves to enforce proprietary rights over its compression algorithm. As yet, there are no open standards for compound documents composed of both text and images, although there are proprietary offerings: for example, Adobe's PDF (Portable Document Format). Reinhardt (1994b) points out that some software suppliers are attempting to base their products around compound document handling, again by the use of proprietary standards like OpenDoc or OLE (Object Linking and Embedding).

The power of generic microcomputers using common data formats is greatly enhanced by networking them, to enable sharing of software and resources. The *de facto* market standard for operating LANs (local area networks) is currently Novell Netware. Hsu and Howard (1994) describe the usefulness of workflow systems for routing documents around the workplace LAN. Lotus has built a pre-eminent market position with Notes, a groupware package which helps people work and communicate over a LAN. Businesses can link via networks and use the EDI (electronic data interchange) standard to exchange records (Wayner, 1994).

Most networks operate on the client-server principle, which, in hardware terms, means that one central machine (the server) supports the other machines (the clients). For software, there is a corresponding split between functions carried out on the server machine and those on a client machine. Functions can thus be divided between two completely different software packages: one acting as server, the other as client. This has had a revolutionary effect for WANs (wide area networks) which have to connect all sorts of computers running various operating systems.

The exemplar here is the Internet, the global research and academic network. Machines on the Internet use a common, open protocol, TCP/IP, to communicate. Yet, prior to 1993, there was no one package which gave access to all Internet services and resources. J. Powell (1994) describes the development of the World

Wide Web (WWW), which originated as a network publishing project at CERN. A WWW server makes available information pages (computer files) in HTML (hypertext mark-up language) format. HTML is a derivative of the SGML (standard generalized mark-up language) standard. These pages can contain hypertext links to other such pages, creating a web of linked pages on a network. Multimedia information could also be linked from pages. Anyone with an understanding of HTML could publish on the Internet (R.E. Barry, 1994).

Mosaic, a WWW client, was released into the public domain in 1993. It ran on most common microcomputers and workstations. Morgan (1994) highlights its revolutionary feature as being the URL (universal resource locator), an open standard for identifying network resources. All Internet tools and services (gopher, WAIS, Telnet, USENET, FTP, archie), as well as WWW pages, could be addressed and accessed by URLs. Mosaic has been followed by a host of other WWW clients from commercial companies.

Nadeau (1994) estimates that between 15 and 20 million people use the Internet at present. At its current rate of growth, everyone on the planet will be connected by 2004! M.Williams (1994) focuses on government and commercial interest in the Internet, especially the explosive growth of commercial sites. Many companies (large and small) advertise and support their products using WWW pages. 1994 saw the first use of a URL in a radio commercial. The US government has made much legislative and statistical information available via the Internet. 1994 also saw details of the UK budget available on the Internet for the first time. Usage of commercial network services is also booming, aided by graphical client software being given to users: more than four million people subscribe to Compuserve, Prodigy, and America Online (Nadeau, 1994).

Reinhardt (1994a) uses the Internet as the prototype of the 'information superhighway', a phrase coined by US Vice-President Al Gore. The development of an information superhighway, seen as vital for US economic competitiveness, by a partnership of government and private industry, is enshrined in the NII (National Information Infrastructure). Henry (1994) sees the information superhighway as a seamless web of communications networks, databases and consumer electronics that will put vast amounts of information at users' finger tips.

There are a number of problems with the information superhighway concept, which are investigated by Griffith and Smith (1994). There is a fundamental conflict between the government objective of affordable, universal access, and the commercial imperative to make a profit. Some cable franchisees, for example, have been less than keen to wire less affluent or geographically spread communities.

Then there is the problem of how to give everyone the ability to find the information they want (if indeed they want information). Roesler and Hawkins (1994) describe the famous Apple 'Knowledge Navigator' video, which showed a voice-activated 'intelligent agent', a program which autonomously searches a network for information for its user. Agents like this are still hypothetical, but, in 1994,

General Magic unveiled Magic Cap, a GUI designed to simplify network searching, and Telescript, a scripting language for building network information retrieval agents (Reinhardt, 1994c).

Finally, there is the problem of security. How will access be authorized? How will individual privacy be safeguarded? How will information providers enforce copyright? The answer to these questions seems to be encryption. Public/private key encryption systems allow authentication routines, can hide private communications and enable 'digital signatures' to be added to digital data (Wayner, 1994). Commerce is keen to adopt this solution, as it would enable secure customer billing over a public network: credit card companies plan to offer such a service across the Internet. Government is less keen, as it makes private communications unreadable by law enforcement agencies. The US government is currently trying to encourage use of its 'clipper chip', an encryption device which would allow authorized monitoring of encrypted communications.

Implications for the information industry

Notwithstanding the information superhighway, the traditional infrastructure of the information industry is still very much alive. Authors write books and journal articles. Publishers publish them. Libraries acquire both these and the secondary sources (whether printed, online or CD-ROM) which list them. The first port of call of the information seeker is often the library.

Harloe and Budd (1994) remark that the end of the book has been predicted (repeatedly) for the last 25 years. Each year, 1994 being no exception, sees more books being published than in the previous year. Alston (1994) explains this by arguing that, since the population of the English-speaking world is 500 million plus, books on any topic can be published and find a market, as can multiple journals on popular topics and specialist academic journals. As a result, Green (1994) shows the book trade to be characterized by a large quantity of small orders and a large number of products and suppliers. It stands to benefit from EDI in terms of reducing order transmission costs, faster and cheaper invoicing, and better information on sales.

Barker (1994) is worried that paper is being consumed in enormous quantities to keep up with publication growth. He prefers electronic media as more economical and eco-friendly in the long term. Alston (1994) agrees about the conservation benefits, but points out that the problem is how to pay for access to texts in electronic form. His suggestion is for something like the Performing Rights Society. Cornish (1994) and Norman (1994) both state that library holdings cannot be legally digitized, as this would deprive the copyright holder of fees for multiple use. Wall (1994), in summarizing copyright issues, does mention cryptography and digital signatures, but neglects to go into detail.

The basic standard for the digital storage of text is ASCII (American Standard Code for Information Interchange). Popham (1994) argues that its disadvantage is that it represents the smallest elements (characters) only, and says nothing about the structure of the text. He recommends that electronic text be stored in SGML form, as the added mark-up codes do show structure. Being an independent standard, SGML makes electronic documents 'future proof', but there is a need to translate marked up text into a format which application software can use. In addition, this procedure might be highly labour-intensive, as SGML mark-up is a skilled task.

Rather than replacing books, IT has created alternatives. According to Lambert (1994), there are now 5,000 CD-ROM titles available, a tenfold increase over a four-year period. Bevan (1994) states their chief advantages over printed texts as being a reduction in storage costs and an increase in searchability. He gives as an example the Elsevier announcement that it will supply its annual books and periodicals catalogue on CD-ROM as it is 'more cost effective to send a disc than to produce a large paper catalogue with packaging and postage costs'. CD-ROMs have low error rates and high durability (although how long-term this is remains unknown). They are difficult to pirate, although CD-R machines may change this (Sengstack, 1994). Finally, Bevan (1994) considers their main drawback to be lack of currency: even monthly updates will not be frequent enough for some highly volatile information.

Many CD-ROMs are copies of printed sources or online databases, but this is changing, especially because of the added value of multimedia. Pountain (1994) describes a unique CD-ROM, which contains all the paintings on display in the National Gallery and supporting/explanatory text. Holzberg (1994) gives the history of Compton's *Multimedia Encyclopedia*, which started in 1986 containing nothing but text but now contains many multimedia items. CD-ROM is ideal for reference works like encyclopedias: they are cheaper than the printed version, they allow searching by keyword, and the information found is easily exported into a word processor. The market research firm PC-Data has had at least one encyclopedia on its top ten selling CD-ROM list since January 1993.

As well as complementing books, CD-ROMs complement online services by storing multimedia information which might be too slow and expensive to download. Nadeau (1944) gives an example of a hybrid online/CD-ROM product, the Microsoft Complete Baseball CD-ROM, which is supplemented by daily updates of match scores available online. Another beneficial effect of CD-ROMs, according to Bevan (1994), is that competition with CD-ROM search software interfaces has caused online services to improve their interfaces. There is still little commonality between the search interfaces of different online databases and CD-ROMs, or even between the CD-ROM and the database from which it was derived.

Traditional online databases are still thriving. Roesler and Hawkins (1994) state that there are at least 5,000 online databases. Most databases (like CD-ROMs) contain only references to information, not the information itself. These references are still overwhelmingly to journal articles and books. Although subject coverage is scattered and duplicated between databases in online and CD-ROM form, there is little likelihood of mergers between databases, according to Alston (1994). In fact, specialization in coverage is increasing, not decreasing.

Roesler and Hawkins (1994) are worried that users are overwhelmed by the huge amount of information available, the multiplicity of sources and the effort required to find the information they want. Help is at hand to filter and sort incoming information. For example, AppleSearch allows the creation of continuously running 'reporters', which search incoming e-mail, online feeds and networked CD-ROMs, then rank the items found before displaying them to the user. McCleary (1994) shows that filtered information services are particularly valuable for decision makers. There are specialized filters for a wide range of newsfeeds: for example, Sandpoint's Hoover. Even a basic service like Clarinet pipes live AP/Reuters newsfeeds into USENET groups (Everett, 1994). Such services tend to be marketed to end-users and not to library staff.

The IT developments mentioned previously – cheap, powerful microcomputers which are linked to global networks, and exchange digital information in standard forms – are most responsible for changing things (Ward, 1994). Brophy (1994) provides an excellent summary of how 'networked information' works. Information needed can be obtained from the most appropriate source, wherever that is. Information needed is obtained when it is wanted, 'just in time'. Information needed can be delivered to the users, wherever they are. Information searching and storage are both performed by users. Publishing can also be performed by users. Networked information, however, may not be *free* to the user. Cornish (1994) praises the possible effects of networking:

> If networking brings about a more efficient flow of information, greater contact between people, better understanding and greater knowledge then it will have succeeded.

However, networking promises great changes for the institution at the centre of the old information industry: the library.

Implications for libraries in general

Libraries have always appreciated the benefits of networking. Royan (1994) gives an exhaustive list of networking activities in libraries. He groups them into three categories: information (reference) access, document delivery and local information.

Barker (1994) notes that the earliest use of automation in libraries was to move from a card-based catalogue to an OPAC (online public access catalogue). Telecommunications made bibliographic networking possible, in which a group of libraries access a union database which contains records of their own materials, together with those for the holdings of other libraries. As a result, bibliographic standards developed through consensus, and were voluntary and technical, rather than qualitative (Simmons, 1994): UNIMARC is an example of a 'maxi' format from which a 'mini' local format would draw elements. Even so, Alston (1994) recognizes a need for greater detail in bibliographic records by including in them a listing of their contents, as very often a remote OPAC user does not know if a record is relevant or not.

Su (1994) agrees with the need to expand an OPAC's data content, but also raises ideas on how to enhance its functionality. Fieldhouse and Hancock-Beaulieu (1994) note that many features of their research system, OKAPI, are now appearing in OPACs from commercial suppliers. Tedd (1994) gives the features of what she calls 'third generation OPACs' as being natural language search statements, best match searching, relevance-ranked results and relevance-feedback options. Speculations on the next generation of OPACs involve not using textual search methods at all, but graphical browsing (Poulter, 1994).

Tedd (1994) notices a move away from proprietary library systems. Many products now run on a range of low-cost hardware and use-adapted generic software: for example, a relational database for bibliographic record storage. Library automation suppliers are beginning to offer client-server systems using the ISO Standard for Search and Retrieve, which is implemented in the USA as NISO (National Information Standards Organization) Z39.50 (Corey, 1994). This is a standard for a machine and software-independent search protocol: a user's search is translated into Z39.50 protocols by client, then translated back into whatever command language the target system needs by the server. This translation can be complicated in special cases, as, for example, when the requested search is not possible on the target system. Corey describes his work at the Florida Center for Library Automation in developing Z39.50 to make different library OPACs available via one menu, without different logon procedures, and searchable through one interface. Dempsey (1994) adds that Z39.50 is intended for MARC records, but it is possible to register other record types. It is potentially especially useful for connecting the plethora of machines and services on the Internet. Dempsey talks about the IRIS project, which offers access to OPACs of six Irish libraries running different library automation systems by using Z39.50.

Networking has also been applied to the multiplicity of CD-ROMs which libraries hold. As Lambert (1994) points out, CD-ROM was originally a single-user product, but it is more cost-effective to network, even allowing for technical and licensing costs. CD-ROMs are also useful in developing countries, which tend to lack a reliable telecommunications infrastructure, since they only require cheap microcomputers, as El Hadidy (1994) notes. However, not all databases are on CD-ROM yet. A single CD-ROM does not have enough storage capacity to hold some databases. Bevan (1994) cites Medline here: multi-disk searching by swapping is impractical, but CD-ROM jukeboxes, holding multiple CD-ROMs, can get around the problem. Competition between CD-ROM suppliers has prevented standards in user interfaces – Bevan says that there are 110 different varieties with different search software, but Z39.50 is a potential solution here. Rowley (1994) advises buyers of library systems to look out for those which run on a wide range of platforms, can be integrated with other systems, possess a GUI, offer advanced information retrieval features, and have support for multimedia and CD-ROMs.

Royan (1994) also mentions nationally-networked and funded services: for example, BIDS (Bath Information and Data Service), which, on behalf of UK academia, offers access to the ISI (Institute for Scientific Information) indexes and to EMBASE, among others. BIDS is accessed via JANET, the UK academic network and its usage is free to staff and students in higher education institutions in the UK.

The success of networking information resources can bring problems in the area of document delivery. Getting items on to library shelves quickly becomes more important. Royan gives the background to EDI usage in the UK. Book Industry Communications (BIC) was set up in 1991 to promote EDI standards for books. Since 1992, First Edition has offered an EDI gateway to fifteen or more book suppliers. Hendry and Johnson (1994) report from the University of Birmingham Library, which successfully uses EDI for two-thirds of its orders. Its specialist book suppliers, though, are unlikely to take up EDI.

Roes and Dijkstra (1994) discuss the variety of document delivery services, which supply documents to a library from outside. In electronic document delivery, documents may be sent by fax (as in the CARL UNCOVER service) or by e-mail, and they may be structured as ASCII, as graphic images or as combinations of these. At its most basic, document delivery details could be sent online to the document supplier. Either the document, or a photocopy, is returned by post. Some systems scan documents in advance of their being requested. In this sense, ADONIS, a CD-ROM containing the scanned full text of biomedical journals, updated every ten days, could be considered a document delivery system. ADONIS has raised fears that libraries may no longer be in a position to hold a collection of printed journals, should the project ever be terminated (B. Williams, 1944).

The latest type of document delivery systems also scan and read documents in advance of requests, but these documents come from local collections by agreement with publishers. Roes and Dijkstra (1994) mention the Mercury project at Carnegie Mellon, while Geleijnse (1994) describes the Elsevier and Tilburg experiment in the Netherlands. Elsevier is also involved in the TULIP project, with fifteen university libraries (Billings, 1994). Charges must be levied for these documents in order for libraries to stay within the copyright laws (Dixon, 1994). The ELINOR (Electronic Information Online Retrieval) project sought agreement with the publishers of 240 recommended textbooks and ten journals for the Business

Information Systems course at De Montfort University. These were scanned into PixTex/EFS and converted into ASCII text by OCR (Grimshaw, 1994). Smith (1994) recounts how the British Library, with its Initiatives for Access programme, is trying to develop the collection and preservation of digital material and the digitization of other vital material, like the Magna Carta. The British Library is also using PixTex/EFS for digitization.

Digitization raises the issue of ownership of information. In the traditional library, books and journals, once they are purchased, become owned property. With digital information from elsewhere, there is a need to pay a fee to use or access them, but there is no possibility of ownership. Brophy (1994), however, reminds us that there is another source of digital information: the authors themselves. Publishing via a network costs little except lost copyright revenues. Scholarly publishing by the invisible college could move online by means of e-journals, mailing lists, FTP sites and World Wide Web pages. While this seems to bypass libraries, as Morgan (1994) points out, someone like a librarian is still needed to organize network resources; the Internet being an example here of what happens to information on an unorganized network. Also, as Burton (1994) warns us when writing about e-mail, who is storing and preserving this material?

A library can preserve local material in digital form. Royan's (1994) third and final networking function is that of local information. A public library can set up a community information system. An academic library can run a campus-wide information service (CWIS).

Currently, we seem to be between the automated library, where collections are internal and paper-based, and procedures are computerized, and the virtual library, where collections are digital and external (Whitney and Glogoff, 1994). Cloyes (1994) adds that the virtual library should offer information delivery to the customer as well as search and retrieval opportunities for the customer's use. A. Powell (1994) describes three types of virtual library:

- a traditional library which disseminates some information electronically, so that some customers do not need to visit it;
- a library which has few or no physical resources, but which selectively disseminates information to its customers electronically;
- a nexus of information management activities within an organization, containing both centralized and dispersed elements.

The first type would include the EURILIA (European Initiative in Library and Information in Aerospace) project, in which five aerospace libraries, including Cranfield, provide a specialist information service to remote users (Blagden and Ford, 1994). The last two types are more likely to be business/corporate libraries, short on staff but able to afford technology to compensate, which can run an efficient, networked, current awareness and document management service for a parent organization.

Mori (1994) gives an excellent example of a virtual library in the Toshiba Business Information Center. It gathers and transmits information from videotapes, optical discs, CD-ROMs and online databases, but does not store it. It produces ICN (Information Center News), by searching databases, and scanning press releases and news faxes, which are then converted by OCR. Paying customers can register current awareness topics, on which they receive documents through the company LAN or fax. Raymond (1994), who terms herself the 'cybrarian' at Thinking Machines Corporation, has set up an e-mail redistribution of newswire stories. Ginsburg (1994) uses Lotus Notes and the packages Hoover and Newsedge at Bankers Trust Company, which automatically extract information from news feeds into Lotus Notes.

Virtual libraries can also manage an organization's documentation if it is in machine-readable form. As R.E. Barry (1994) argues, not only are modern organizations document-rich, but for many it would be no exaggeration to say that the document is the basis for most decisions. Bates and Allen (1994) also use Lotus Notes in the Central Information Resource Centre of MCI Communication, but this time to store and disseminate internal information resources (for example, press reports). Norbie (1994) is 'electronic librarian' at the Electronic Library at U S West and stores company documentation which is delivered exclusively through the company network.

Implications for academic libraries

How is the academic library affected by the transition to the virtual library? Harloe and Budd (1994) identify two trends: a move away from value being attributed to *size* of collection to *availability and deliverability* of collection, and a move from 'just in case' collection building to 'just in time' networked document delivery. Brophy (1994), looking more at the UK scene, highlights the development of the UK academic network JANET and latterly of SuperJANET, which has a data transfer rate of 140 megabytes per second, making network communications much faster. He goes on to note that this process is eased by three factors: most universities now have LANs of microcomputers through which library services can be delivered, library systems are becoming more standard, and users have become more computer-literate and sophisticated in their demands.

Some technology applications in academic libraries are maturing and recouping their installation costs. Blunden-Ellis and Graham (1994), in a recent survey, found the UK higher education market segment for library automation stable, with little change in the number of new installations. With 133 reported installations in a market of approximately 155, saturation was about 86%. Lambert (1994) states that users expect free CD-ROM services, so libraries cannot charge for them. Networked CD-ROMS have reduced the amounts of money required for online searching: between 1988–92, there was a 34% reduction in spending on mediated online searching in UK academic libraries. There is also a fixed cost advantage in networked online services like BIDS and its ISI databases, which have recently been joined by OCLC Firstsearch and EMBASE (Bevan, 1994).

The user wants these services and others to be integrated. On one level, this means access from a single interface. At another level, it implies some sort of convergence between library and computing services, either as a merged organizational unit or using the local computer network as a common carrier which service providers, like the library, use (Brophy, 1994).

There is plenty of activity in creating single interfaces. Mellendorf (1994) created a menu for Saginaw Valley State University Library for access to local OPACs, CARL UNCOVER, LC MARVEL, ERIC, the *Chronicle of Higher Education* Gopher, local census and map data, and weather forecasts. Friend (1994) used a Z39.50 client first to build an interface for Penn State University Library catalogue, and then added other databases. One search interface served for all. A similar feat was performed at the University of Ghent (Van De Sompel, 1994), where SilverPlatter's Electronic Reference Library (ERL) provided a common interface to all SilverPlatter CD-ROMs throughout campus. This used a proprietary protocol and not Z39.50.

Perhaps the most exciting tool for this type of task is a World Wide Web browser like Mosaic. J. Powell (1994) developed a gateway into a number of library services at Virginia Polytechnic Institute and State University, using World Wide Web browser software. This gateway leads to local documents, library user services, the local and other OPACs and Internet resources, grouped by subject. This was reasonably straightforward to do and had great potential for future development. Morgan (1994) reports on the Mr Serials project at North Carolina State University Libraries, which used World Wide Web to collect electronic serials. Entries were added to the OPAC for the e-journals *ALAWON* and *Public Access Computer Systems Review*. URLs for these journals were placed in the 856 MARC field, so that the OPAC user could read the text of the e-journals. J. Powell (1994) maintains that Gopher is inferior to World Wide Web for such tasks. It has restrictions on information presentation, e.g. a 70–character limit for menu items; there is also no equivalent of the URL. Bridges (1994), however, shows that Gopher is simple to use, easy to set up and perfectly adequate for handling ASCII documents.

A single interface to services has management implications. There is a feeling abroad that universities as organizations need a new approach to information strategies. Follett (Joint, 1993) is perhaps the clearest expression of this. The library must become involved in this change. Anderson (1994) is adamant that such strategies need to be driven by the user rather than the provider, and must be developed bottom-up, not top-down. Current institutional boundaries may not be conducive to such strategies, hence convergence. Because there is little involvement of 'professional' information managers here, then perhaps the professional librarian could play more of a role?

As well as being more proactive in designing its networked services, and in spreading good information practice, the library could change its role in the information industry. Whitney and Glogoff (1994) advocate that the library should integrate itself into scholarly communication. It should become a server, connecting users to a community of networked information like e-journals and World Wide Web pages. Rather than just delivery, the library could move into production (Schauder, 1994).

From their experience of the UMLibText Project at the University of Michigan Library, where digital texts were accessible via Mosaic, Warner and Barber (1994) argue that libraries should commit themselves to building up collections of digital texts, preferably marked up in SGML. In this task, academics might be the ally of the librarian, as they have little to lose by publishing papers electronically, and much to gain if their local library takes over management of such texts (Anderson 1994). Price-Wilkin (1994) believes that World Wide Web offers the creators of editions of literary or other works the ability to represent a vast, interconnected web of scholarly resources. The user can view resources as simply texts, as text with critical apparatus, or as digital image of text with editorial decisions. At the University of Virginia, a number of literature and history course materials were translated from SGML into HTML mark-up for browsing under the Web. Some structural elements were lost, however. A workable solution was to keep the texts in SGML and access them via a special SGML-aware retrieval tool, PAT, which itself was accessed via the World Wide Web.

Implications for public libraries

Academic libraries face some interesting challenges from the virtual library concept. Unfortunately, public libraries are not so lucky. They have had less to gain from networking in the past. Their users do not possess such tightly focused needs as those of academic libraries. In addition, public libraries (like every other type) have been facing continual financial pressures which have left them struggling to keep up with new technology.

The public library has not been completely bypassed by information technology. Blunden-Ellis (1994) found evidence of product switching as old library systems in public libraries came to the end of their life cycle. This was because the costs of a major upgrade or of a new system were equivalent. The Denver Public Library Booktech 200 project (McCune, 1994) shows an innovative way to select and order new materials, via online and CD-ROM sources. It was run by staff very much as a cooperative, in which some members teleworked. Reng (1994) describes the CLEAR (Coalition of Libraries to Expand Access to Resources) group of public and school libraries in eastern Washington State. They created a network of single user CD-ROM machines in member libraries, accessed by dial-up. Only a single user CD-ROM licence was needed per disc. The set-up was cheap, technically straightforward and secure, as dial-ins were accepted only from machines in the member libraries. The approach Teixeira (1994) adopted was even simpler. Her CISS (California Indian Subject Specialists) group formed over the network through e-mail. They now meet regularly and circulate a newsletter by e-mail.

On the positive side, Astbury (1994) argues that public libraries can exploit new technologies by providing remote access to library databases off-site, off-hours, from anywhere in a community, with librarians acting as technical advisors and guides to information sources. The public library's role in open learning could also be enhanced by networking. Doctor (1994) agrees that community-based information systems in public libraries should offer local information, increase educational opportunities and create links with local officials. There is also a role for the public library as a local gateway into a global network.

Astbury notes that public libraries are playing a role in Freenets, local community electronic networks, in parts of the USA and Canada and hopes that this could be a model for the future. One such example is the Charlotte's Web project at the Public Library of Charlotte and Mecklenburg County (S. Snow, 1995). In partnership with local schools and colleges, the Public Library was awarded a grant to set up a virtual library, for local access by dial in, or public terminals to the Internet. Local information was also to be carried as well as AIDS/HIV information, as part of another grant. Doctor (1994) gives a total of over 100 Freenets in 1993. They are mostly affiliated to the NPTN (National Public Telecomputing Network) and are all based on an 'electronic city' model. This means their menu choices are 'Main Street', 'Library', 'Schoolhouse', etc. Some of the newer Freenets are using World Wide Web as their software platform. Many of the Freenets have involvement from public libraries.

On a less optimistic note, Astbury is worried about the right of access to information, which is of paramount importance in modern societies. He sees the information superhighway stratifying individuals, classes and nations into information-rich or -poor, those that can pay and those that cannot. Buckle (1994) reports ominously that private-sector interests are lobbying the US government to establish a two-tier structure for the NII: the first tier for publicly funded R&D activities, and the second for commercial communications services. There is no mention of the non-profit information sector including public libraries. To Buckle, this reflects a failure by the library profession to influence the national debate on the NII.

Implications for the profession

Professional librarians seem to view the changes being wrought by information technology with a mixture of feelings, ranging from the distinctly adverse to the almost exultant. Perhaps the most trenchant criticism comes from Wisner (1994):

> The profession of librarianship is rooted in scholarly values, and can never – must never – be divided from them. We are neither managers nor administrators. And we are certainly not computer specialists.

Fine (1994) supports Wisner, saying: 'We have lost our sense of purpose and mission. We have succumbed to the technological imperative'. Quinn (1994) is worried that we are in danger of reducing knowledge to information. DeVinney (1994) remarks that bookstores now look like we think libraries ought to look, or used to look, while libraries now look like the Pentagon War Room.

A more hopeful approach is to recognize the value of the librarian as the mediator between the user and the machine. M. Snow (1994) believes 'that the more dehumanization caused by technology in libraries, the more critical becomes the presence of librarians, to provide a gracious human component'. Whitney and Glogoff (1994) stress that the focus must be on interconnecting systems, information resources, and users, rather than on the systems themselves. Shreeves (1994) concurs with this, saying that no-one denies the importance of human interaction between librarians and users, but warns that librarians cannot afford to ignore the inevitable transformation of scholarly communication into digital forms. Davies and Niessen (1994) see the network as just another tool in the reference librarian's armoury.

The value of the librarian is perhaps more clearly revealed now that users have experience of searching. Alston (1994) thinks that users need more instruction, not less, to cope with the sheer volume of available information. Astbury (1994) wants librarians to be able to help those users who do not have the technological literacy to search on their own. Bevan (1994) gives details of a survey carried out at Oakland University Library, which revealed that 36% of users regarded instruction in CD-ROM searching by a librarian as unnecessary. However, there was no evidence that these users were using the best search strategy. Lambert (1994), for example, complains of the extra burden on enquiry desks from helping users to search CD-ROMs. User searching of BIDS, OCLC Firstsearch and World Wide Web can be deceptively easy, so that users do not see the need for an expert intermediary. Librarians need to market themselves and their skills and to train users in these skills (Brophy, 1994). Librarians cannot simply point to a book any more. Vasi and LaGuardia (1994) write about setting up an electronic classroom, an Electronic Information Arcade, at University of California Santa Barbara Library, which had access to OPACs, CD-ROM and Internet sources for user training sessions. Finally, Wielhorski (1994) warns that remote users are no longer a small segment of library users. They access OPACs, CD-ROMs, the Internet and possibly online services. We must move to the idea that libraries are remote from users, rather than users being remote from libraries, and must provide training for the needs of remote users.

Users often complain about the disorganization of information on the Internet. Royan (1994) thinks that, although navigation on the Net this will take new technical skills, librarians already have other skills which will help to organize Internet resources and make them much more useful. J. Barry (1994) sees World Wide Web and HTML as increasing the librarian's ability to deliver value-added networked information. Rather than only provide printed materials at Internet training sessions, librarians can provide customized HTML pages for each group of users. As new Internet resources are discovered, they can be added to these pages, making them dynamic guides to network resources. Westerman (1994) gives an example of this in BSN (Business Sources on the Net), a guide to business information on the Internet, produced and managed by an *ad hoc* group of business librarians, who met through the mailing list BUSLIB-L. The process of gathering and compiling BSN expanded and developed the group's skills and knowledge. In turn, these augmented skills increased the usefulness of group members in their host libraries. The potential usefulness in applying library skills to organizing information on networks makes librarians vital members of organizations (Cronin, 1994).

Many library and information workers – the majority even – use information technology, but only a relatively small number, have come to regard information technology or library systems management as a full-time specialism. Muirhead (1994) performed a survey for the British Library Research and Development of 503 libraries, and only 55% said they had a systems librarian. Systems librarians were computer-trained librarians rather than the reverse. Norbie (1994) learned to work with the system developers at U S West, translating language of users into language of systems personnel. The main problem for systems librarians was in keeping up with technology. Jackson and Hoadley (1994) recommend the somewhat risky practice of acting as a test site as a good way to keep up with new technology.

Conclusion

Information technology poses a great challenge for librarians. On one hand, it offers incredible benefits. As Bevan (1994) says, one multimedia PC and a handful of CD-ROMs could make a data-poor school library data-rich. On the other hand it erodes the rationale for the very existence of libraries, since information which is provided (as it were, anonymously) through a network removes from users the need to know where or how any information they need is stored. To adapt, the librarian could change into a sort of network guru, who brings disparate sources together in a seamless presentation. It would be highly ironic if the oldest information profession were to become the first casualty of the information age.

References

Alston, R. (1994) The shape of libraries to come. *Library Review*, **43**(3), 24–31.
Anderson, M. (1994) Management, resources and IT in libraries. *ITs News*, (April), 14–21.
Astbury, R. (1994) The public library of the twenty-first century: the key information and learning centre of the community? *Libri*, **44**(20), 130–144.
Barker, P. (1994) Electronic libraries – vision of the future. *Electronic Library*, **12**(4), 221–229.
Barry, J. (1994) The hypertext markup language (HTML) and the World Wide Web: raising ASCII text to a new level of useability. *Public Access Computer Systems Review*, **5**(5), 5–62. [Also available via e-mail message GET BARRY PRV5N5 F=MAIL to LISTSERV@UHUPVM1.UH.EDU.]
Barry, R.E. (1994) Electronic document and records management systems: towards a methodology for requirements definition. *Information Management and Technology*, **27**(6), 251–260.
Bates, M.E and Allen, K. (1994) Lotus Notes in action: meeting corporate information needs. *Database*, (August), 27–38.
Bell, D. (1974) *The coming of the post-industrial society: a venture in social forecasting.* London: Heinemann.
Bevan, N. (1994) Transient technology? The future of CD-ROMs in libraries. *Program*, **28**(1), 1–14.
Billings, H. (1994) Supping with the devil: new library alliances in the information age. *Wilson Library Bulletin*, **69**(2), 33–37.
Blagden, J. and Ford, J. (1994) The electronic library: a view from academia and the computer industry. *Managing Information*, **1**(6), 36–38.
Blunden-Ellis, J. and Graham, M.E. (1994) A UK market survey of library automation system vendors (1992–1993). *Program*, **28**(2), 109–124.
Bridges, K. (1994) Gopher your library. *Wilson Library Bulletin*, **69**(3), 36–38.
Brophy, P. (1994) Networking in British academic libraries. *British Journal of Academic Librarianship*, **8**(1), 49–60.
Buckle, D. (1994) Internet: strategic issues for libraries and librarians – a commercial perspective. *Aslib Proceedings*, **46**(11/12), 259–262.
Burton, P.F. (1994) Electronic mail as an academic discussion forum. *Journal of Documentation*, **50**(2), 99–110.
Campbell, D.K. and Proehl, K. (1994) Optical advances. *Byte*, (March), 107–116.
Case, D.O. (1994) The social shaping of videotex: how information services for the public have evolved. *Journal of the American Society for Information Science*, **45**(7), 483–497.
Cloyes, K. (1994) The journey from vision to reality of a virtual library. *Special Libraries*,

84(4), 253–257.

Corey, J.F. (1994) A grant for Z39.50. *Library Hi-Tech*, **12**(1), 37–47.

Cornish, G.P. (1994) Europe divided or united? Networking and document supply, now and in the future. *Libri*, **44**(1), 63–76.

Cronin, M.J. (1994) *Doing business on the Internet: how the electronic highway is transforming American companies*. New York: Van Nostrand Reinhold.

Davies, D.G and Niessen, J.P. (1994) Negotiating the passage from user demands to needs. *Journal of Academic Librarianship*, **20**(3), 140–141.

Dempsey, L. (1994) Distributed library and information systems: the significance of Z39.50. *Managing Information*, **1**(6), 41–43.

DeVinney, G. (1994) Rushing toward the emerald city? *Journal of Academic Librarianship*, **20**(3), 91–92.

Dixon, R. (1994) Legal admissibility and probative value of document images. *Information Management and Technology*, **27**(1), 38–40.

Doctor, R. (1994) Justice and social equity in cyberspace. *Wilson Library Bulletin*, **68**(8), 35–39.

El Hadidy, B. (1994) The breakeven point for using CD-ROM versus online: a case study for database access in a developing country. *Journal of the American Society for Information Science*, **45**(4), 273–283.

Everett, V. (1994) US newspapers online. *Database*, (October/November), 14–25.

Fieldhouse, M. and Hancock-Beaulieu, M. (1994) The changing face of OKAPI. *Library Review*, **43**(4), 38–50.

Fine, S. (1994) A psychologist's response. *Journal of Academic Librarianship*, **20**(3), 138–139.

Friend, L. (1994) Databases by the dozen: the challenge of multiple interfaces at Penn State. *Wilson Library Bulletin*, **69**(1), 38–41.

Geleijnse, H. (1994) Journal articles on the desktop. *Managing Information*, **1**(6), 34–35.

Ginsburg, C.L. (1994) The realities of the virtual library. *Special Libraries*, **84**(4), 258–259.

Green, B. (1994) Towards international book trade EDI standards. *Vine*, (94), 5–10.

Griffith, J.B. and Smith, M.S. (1994) The information superhighway and the National Information Infrastructure (NII). *Journal of Academic Librarianship*, **20**(3), 93–95.

Grimshaw, A. (1994) ELINOR electronic library project. *Information Management and Technology*, **27**(1), 33–35.

Harloe, B. and Budd, J.M. (1994) Collection development and scholarly communication in the era of electronic access. *Journal of Academic Librarianship*, **20**(3), 83–95.

Hendry, I. and Johnson, R. (1994) BLCMP and EDI: EDI at the University of Birmingham: a case study. *Vine*, (94), 15–18.

Henry, C. (1994) New technology, more technologies: NREN metaphors. *Wilson Library Bulletin*, **69**(3), 30–32.

Holzberg, C.S. (1994) Multimedia encyclopedias get smart. *CD-ROM World*, (October), 62–65.

Hsu, M. and Howard, M. (1994) Work-flow and legacy systems. *Byte*, (July), 109–116.

Jackson, K.M. and Hoadley, I.B. (1994) To be or not to be: the test site dilemma. *Journal of Academic Librarianship*, **20**(3), 88–89.

Joint (1993) Funding Council's Libraries Review Group [chair: Sir Brian Follett]. *Report*. Bristol: HEFCE.

Lambert, J. (1994) Managing CD-ROM services in academic libraries. *Journal of Librarianship and Information Science,* **26**(1), 23–28.

McCleary, H. (1994) Filtered information services: a revolutionary new product or a new marketing strategy? *Online,* (July), 33–42.

McCune, B. (1994) Leading technology by the nose: Denver Public's Booktech 2000. *Wilson Library Bulletin,* **69**(3), 33–35.

Mellendorf, S.A. (1994) Automating access to Internet resources at the reference desk. *Online,* (September/October), 69–73.

Morgan, E.L. (1994) The World Wide Web and Mosaic: an overview for librarians. *Public Access Computer Systems Review,* **5**(6), 5–26. [Also available via e-mail message GET MORGAN PRV5N6 F=MAIL to LISTSERV@UHUPVM1.UH.EDU.]

Mori, A. (1994) The Toshiba Business Information Center moves toward the virtual library. *Special Libraries,* **84**(4), 277–280.

Muirhead, G.A. (1994) Current requirements and future prospects for systems librarians. *Electronic Library,* **12**(2), 97–107.

Nadeau, M. (1994) When worlds collide: hybrid CD-ROM and online services deliver today what high-speed links to the home promise tomorrow. *CD-ROM World,* (November), 48–52.

Norbie, D. (1994) The electronic library emerges at U S West. *Special Libraries,* **84**(4), 274–276.

Norman, S. (1994) The information bottleneck – electronic copyright issues. *Vine,* (96), 3–6.

Popham, M. (1994) An update on SGML: the standard generalised markup language. *Information Management and Technology,* **27**(6), 247–250.

Poulter, A. (1994) Building a browsable virtual reality library. *Aslib Proceedings,* **46**(6), 151–155.

Pountain, D. (1994) The fine art of CD-ROM publishing. *Byte,* (June), 47–54.

Powell, A. (1994) Management models and measurement in the virtual library. *Special Libraries,* **84**(4), 260–263.

Powell, J. (1994) Adventures with the World Wide Web: creating a hypertext library information system. *Database,* (February), 59–66.

Price, S.G. (1994) Image standards for document management. *Information Management and Technology,* **27**(1), 38–40.

Price-Wilkin, J. (1994) Using the World Wide Web to deliver complex electronic documents: implications for librarians. *Public Access Computer Systems Review,* **5**(3), 5–21. [Also available via e-mail message GET PRICEWIL PRV5N3 F=MAIL to LISTSERV@UHUPVM1.UH.EDU.]

Quinn, D. (1994) The information age: another giant step backward. *Journal of Academic Librarianship,* **20**(3), 134–135.

Raymond, S. (1994) NEWSFLASH! or one cybrarian's quest for electronic news delivery. *Special Libraries,* **84**(4), 270–273.

Reinhardt, A. (1994a) Building the data highway. *Byte,* (March), 46–74.

Reinhardt, A. (1994b) Managing the new document. *Byte,* (August), 90–104.

Reinhardt, A. (1994c) The network with smarts. *Byte,* (October), 50–64.

Reng, J. (1994) The technology knot: tying small libraries together through remote access. *Wilson Library Bulletin,* **68**(8), 38–40, 140.

Roes, H. and Dijkstra, J. (1994) Ariadne: the next generation of electronic document delivery systems. *Electronic Library*, **12**(1), 13–19.

Roesler, M. and Hawkins, D.T. (1994) Intelligent agents: software servants for an electronic information world (and more!). *Online*, (July), 19–32.

Rowley, J. (1994) Making the right choice: strategies and pointers for the selection of library and information systems. *Managing Information*, **1**(2), 26–31.

Royan, B. (1994) Libraries and networking: a briefing. *ITs News*, (April), 21–25.

Schauder, D. (1994) Electronic publishing of professional articles: attitudes of academics and implications for the scholarly communications industry. *Journal of the American Society for Information Science*, **45**(2), 73–100.

Sengstack, J. (1994) On a roll. *CD-ROM World*, (May), 42–47.

Shreeves, E. (1994) Embracing the inevitable. *Journal of Academic Librarianship*, **20**(3), 136–137.

Simmons, P. (1994) Preserving compatibility with standard data formats. *Program*, **28**(2), 109–124.

Smith, N. (1994) The British Library: initiatives for access. *Managing Information*, **1**(6), 39–40.

Snow, M. (1994) Forward with the people. *Journal of Academic Librarianship*, **20**(3), 142–143.

Snow, S. (1995) *Charlotte's Web shifts gears*. [Posting on USENET group comp.internet-happenings, 19 January.]

Su, S-F. (1994) Dialogue with an OPAC: how visionary was Swanson in 1964? *Library Quarterly*, **64**(2), 130–161.

Tedd, L.A. (1994) OPACs through the ages. *Library Review*, **43**(4), 27–37.

Teixeira, L. (1994) Magic of community: the telecommunications revolution and native American heritage. *Wilson Library Bulletin*, **69**(1), 34–37.

Thompson, T. (1994) The Macintosh at 10. *Byte*, (February), 47–54.

Van De Sompel, H. (1994) The Electronic Reference Library (ERL) at the University of Ghent. *Managing Information*, **1**(6), 44–46.

Vasi, J. and LaGuardia, C. (1994) Creating a library electronic classroom. *Online*, (September/October), 75–84.

Wall, R. (1994) Electrocopying and copyright plus copyright news items. *Managing Information*, **1**(4), 18–20.

Ward, S. (1994) Standards: their relevance to scientific and technical information. *Aslib Proceedings*, **46**(1), 3–14.

Warner, B.F and Barber, D. (1994) Building the digital library: the University of Michigan's UMLibText Project. *Information Technology and Libraries*, (March), 20–24.

Wayner, P. (1994) EDI moves the data. *Byte*, (October), 121–128.

Westerman, M. (1994) Business sources on the Net: a virtual library project. *Special Libraries*, **84**(4), 264–269.

Whitney, G. and Glogoff, S. (1994) Automation for the nineties: a review article. *Library Quarterly*, **64**(3), 319–331.

Wielhorski, K. (1994) Teaching remote users how to use electronic information resources. *Public Access Computer Systems Review*, **5**(4), 5–20. [Also available via e-mail message GET WIELHORS PRV5N4 F=MAIL to LISTSERV@UHUPVM1.UH.EDU.]

Williams, B. (1994) Automated document delivery at the British Library Document Supply

Centre: the technology and its merits. *Information Management and Technology*, 27(1), 36–40.

Williams, M. (1994) The Internet: implications for the information industry and database providers. *Online and CD ROM Review*, **18**(3), 149–156.

Wisner, W.H. (1994) Back toward people: a symposium. *Journal of Academic Librarianship*, **20**(3), 131–133.

Management

12

Patricia Layzell Ward

Introduction

During the preparation of this international review of management issues, a worrying question emerged. It has been difficult to find published accounts of changes known to be taking place in Eastern Europe and in South East Asia: it is not clear whether articles are being published locally and not being covered by the secondary services. There is a suspicion that managers may not be able to allocate time to write. Some interesting papers have appeared in conference proceedings, but this literature is not always well covered by the indexing and abstracting services.

However, if we look at the evidence that is to hand, it is clear that 'challenging' is an apt description for the role of a manager in 1994. It can be spoken with a lift in the tone of voice, or a downturn, depending on the events of the day. Financial cutbacks, changing organizational frameworks, developments in information technology, quality management, and performance measurement and accountability – all affect the Western manager, but this is not necessarily so elsewhere. In Eastern Europe, the impact of political change has been to create a situation similar to that of the period of reconstruction in the 1950s and 1960s in Western Europe. In South East Asia, there is economic growth in real terms, which has resulted, for example, in an impressive new building for the National Library of Malaysia (Perpustakaan Negara Malaysia, 1994).

Standing back from the reality of management today, in the Western world, to consider the past, is not an exercise which is promoted by today's blockbuster paperbacks on management. Management practices, however, follow a pattern determined by economic cycles. An examination of these cycles during the past 50 years suggests that library and information service managers are caught in what has been described as a vortex of conflicting philosophical, political and financial claims – claims, moreover, that can cause anguish, which may not be a helpful reaction. Rather, the causes should be examined and a different future projected (Sharr, 1994). A description of management theory from medieval times to the 1990s has been written for information workers. It focuses on ways of developing the skills required by the workforce of the future (Runge, 1994).

In order to plan for the future, the past must be considered if programmes of change are to be successfully implemented. Attention has been drawn to the need to be aware of public record retention laws (Wiegand, 1994): although the paper is written from a US perspective, the situation is nevertheless likely to be similar in other parts of the world, and it is perhaps ironic that librarians do not always perceive the value of their administrative records.

Aslib has introduced a 'Know How Series', which is a series of short guides to current management practices. Among the first subjects are strategic planning for library and information services (Corrall, 1994) and marketing a library service (Coote, 1994). The IFLA Round Table on Management decided in 1993 that there would be value in preparing a review of the general literature of management to assist in anticipating changes in philosophy and practice. The first review has been published (Layzell Ward, 1994). The use of consultants is increasing: a handbook reviews their value to library and information centre managers (Garten, 1993). Two accounts describe consultancies in planning automated systems in Switzerland and France (Pouillas, 1994; Wuest and Osswald, 1994).

The role of libraries

Economic rationalism and the advent of the electronic library have challenged the traditional role of the public library. In Australia, the need has been identified for legislation which would define the explicit role of public libraries so that quantifiable goals could be established to meet the demand for accountability (Catlin, 1994). Public library roles have been examined in the USA in order to evaluate their effectiveness: it was found that those with a greater variety of roles performed better than others, judged according to more than half the indicators used (House and Childers, 1994). An important text on the administration of public libraries in the USA is of wider value since it sets the service in a broader social context, stressing its history and importance to the community (Gertzog and Beckerman, 1994). Although absolute values (which may be unquantifiable in any direct manner) are fundamental to the profession, the rush to measure in an age of evaluation has resulted in their importance being recognized only implicitly, rather than being acknowledged explicitly. In the UK, the government has instituted a Public Library Review, and a final report is expected in 1995. A local councillor has criticized government policies regarding public libraries, and stated that they have a role as a centre for information, literature, learning, the community and culture (Heinitz, 1994). An exciting view of libraries in Singapore in the year 2000 has been described by a government committee. The new mission for the National Library is 'to expand continuously the nation's capacity to learn' (*Library*, 1994).

An editorial in the *Journal of Academic Librarianship* stresses that the current emphasis on technology has compromised the scholarly values of librarianship as scholarly communication has been transformed (Wisner, 1994). A survey of the opinions of chief librarians of Australian university libraries indicates that academic libraries may be too passive and reactive. The researchers consider that a proactive stance will need to be adopted if they are not to become marginalized (Oh and Woods, 1994). Two major reports concerning academic libraries in the UK were published towards the end of 1993, and action has been taken to implement their recommendations. One, known as the Follett Report (Joint, 1993), focuses on the future national needs, the impact of information technology and possibilities for further cooperation. The second considers the staffing implications of the proposed new models of service (John Fielden Consultancy, 1993).

An issue of *Library Trends* discusses the role of the library in corporate intelligence activities. It includes a review of the literature on corporate intelligence and how this is used in businesses, innovative uses of electronic sources, and the corporate intelligence profession (Walker, 1994). Bowker-Saur has introduced a new series on information services management which is setting the service in a broader management perspective, and relating information management to organizational management. Power, influence and advocacy in the information environment have been described in a stimulating text (StClair, 1994).

In Czechoslovakia a seminar for librarians and information scientists in the health care sector considered their changing role in a market economy – the transition in general, the adjustment of the health care sector and of libraries and information services, the change in their work and problems resulting from the economic changes (Transformace, 1994).

Planning and policy formulation

An introduction to strategic planning provides definitions drawn from the management literature and relates this to library management. The process is described, together with a case study of strategic planning in a UK academic library (Johnson, 1994). In the USA attention has been drawn to a model developed by Hensley and Schoppmajer for academic libraries. It operates on the assumption that people with similar motivations can agree on mutual goals to form beneficial partnerships for the advancement of shared interests (Birdsall and Hensley, 1994).

The application of long-range planning in public libraries produces a map which can yield a model giving that organization a shape or meaning which is difficult to determine in a complex social situation (Sutton, 1994). Programme budgeting can assist strategic planning by providing cost-finding methodologies to assist the decision as to which services should be retained, which should be cut back, and what can be eliminated from the budget (Robinson and Robinson, 1994).

A paper from Hungary reports the problems that can arise in planning when over-ambitious aims, set centrally, cannot be achieved at a local level. Impressive results were apparently achieved, but the situation of the smaller libraries changed very little. Given the central planning process being put in place in other parts of the world, such a cautious note of realism might be heeded (Ladosne Varju, 1994). Another cautionary comment is made from the Netherlands, where local government reorganization is taking place and the need is stressed for public libraries to maintain close links with related services such as education and services for the elderly (Pop, 1994). Reorganization of local government is also to occur in the UK: the outcome may be the emergence of integrated leisure directorates covering librarians, museums, arts, archeology, archives and records and bringing together leisure, heritage, and recreational facilities (Asser, 1994). In England, the move towards fewer and larger local authorities has been reversed, with proposals for more numerous and smaller services, and the question of whether they will have adequate resources is raised (Liddle, 1993). In Scotland, however, the trend seems to be in the opposite direction, and there will be fewer, but larger, authorities. It will be essential for senior managers to develop the political skills needed for the budget process (Midwinter, 1993). The effect of the reorganization in the UK has been discussed in a paper which focuses on questions of size and functional efficiency, arguing that large authorities have greater flexibility and scope for innovation, and are cost-effective (Midwinter and McVicar, 1994).

An interesting study in the Netherlands comes up with the suggestion that 'Librarians let themselves be managed, rather than exercize managerial influence'. A survey indicated that librarians leave policy decisions too often to library administrators (Schoen, 1994). In Turkey, planning is in progress to assist librarians to cope with the rapid growth of Istanbul and the migration of people from the rural areas to the cities, so that they may provide better access to information (Dokmeci and Korca, 1993).

A description of the planning and support role of central government in India indicates that, although committees and working groups have considered the problems of librarians in the 1985–90 five-year plan, no action has emerged, whereas in the field of science and technology the government has been more successful in linking a number of services into an effective information network, although major problems remain. These include the shortage and unreliability of power, the problem of developing a national cooperative system, and government support which develops long-range plans but which fails to provide adequate funds even for present needs (Navalani, 1994).

Finance

The literature concerning financial matters reports continuing concern about falling budgets, more positive attitudes towards increasing income from a range of external sources, and ways of stretching limited funding. An overview of the situation concerning US academic libraries appears in an issue of *Library Trends*. Attention is being focused on the costs involved in running libraries rather than the operating budget (Dunn and Martin, 1994). A new transitional budget model is proposed which emphasizes staff education, organizational flexibility, and experiment, in order to be able to create change (Campbell, 1994). The complexity of the financial transactions of a library has been described using a trend analysis in a college library (Hayes and Brown, 1993).

In India, economic recession is having an impact on library and information services (Abraham, 1993). The importance of information as a national resource and the role of public libraries are described (Ramaiah, 1993). At present growth rates, it will take a century to provide a minimum library service to all villages in India; various ways of speeding up this process are discussed. Japan's low economic growth has led to pressures on public libraries. Demand for better services grows and some new buildings have been erected, but no increase has taken place in the numbers of qualified staff (Sato, 1993). It has been recognized in France that information is a strategic resource which will allow businesses to conquer international markets, but the consequent growth in information needs occurs at a time of shrinking budgets (Bouthillier, 1994). The political changes taking place in Slovakia have resulted in closures of public libraries and the loss of funding for staff and acquisitions. A foundation has been established to try and arrange donations of books and funds (Kalinova, 1994). From the start of 1994, all Swedish state financial organizations will follow total budgeting and performance-oriented budgeting (Myllys, 1994).

One obvious consequence of the fall in budget allocations is that ways are being sought to reduce costs. Getting value for money from external training programmes has been examined in Australia (Novak, 1994). Brent Public Library in London was the first in the UK to go out to competitive tender for part of its branch network in 1994 (Tyerman, 1994). Franchising public library services is being piloted in UK public libraries and one trial has been described (Brown, 1994). Privatization and contracting out are also being considered in Germany, but further attention is being given to legal questions concerning the constitution, data protection, tax, and staffing (Beger, 1994). Staff cuts in US libraries are being examined as personnel cost projections become a major component in planning (Dewey, 1994). Rising information technology (IT) costs make a major impact in the electronic library and attention has been drawn to hidden costs (Pastine and Kacena, 1994). While the trend continues towards outsourcing specific functions in government and special libraries in the UK, social issues and their wide-ranging implications need to be addressed (Lawes, 1994).

The relationship between libraries and the book trade has been studied in the UK (Taking, 1994). The expanding range of suppliers, particularly of electronic services, has had an impact on budgets (Martin, 1994). Functional cost analysis has been examined in the UK National Health Service libraries, but it is felt that there is a need to consider the results in the light of the limitations experienced with the data collection and cost calculations (Jones and Nicholas, 1993). If the accounting concept of assets is applied to library materials, this can demonstrate that these are fixed information assets of the community and project a business-like approach to library management (McGinn, 1993). Life-cycle costing is another accounting concept, which has been applied to the acquisition and retention of materials at the British Library (Stephens, 1994). In the USA, a public library has set up a benefit assessment programme which boosts library property ratios in order to generate operating and maintenance funding (Cooper and Crouch, 1994). Activity-based costing, used in manufacturing, can be applied by information centres to provide better cost information (Danilenko, 1994).

Inevitably, services are having to introduce charges. A summary of the issues in relation to medical libraries in the UK has been prepared as a result of a survey (Webber, 1993). The British Broadcasting Corporation introduced producer choice, which has resulted in information and library services being charged to departments (Tait, 1994). In the Netherlands, a company, KEMA, bills users of the company library and has four important rules which it applies when operating its cost billing system – response time, reliability, competitiveness and value – but it finds the system is administratively cumbersome (Grotenhuis and Heijnekamp, 1994). Charging academic departments for services will commence in 1994 at a Finnish academic library (Nurminen, 1994). Charging policies and practices in London libraries and information services have been surveyed. The price mechanism cited by most respondents was 'what the market will bear', rather than cost-based prices (Tilson, 1994). The range of services has been extended at the State Library of Queensland, following a move to new premises. Community support has broadened and some of the services have been commercialized (Stephens and Hallam, 1994).

Fund-raising is also becoming more important. The Evans Library at Texas A & M University has described its successes and failures in this area (Hoadley, 1994b). Burlingame (1994) has written an overview of fund-raising activities designed to boost the acquisition budget in US academic libraries. A successful endowment campaign at the Chemistry Library at the University of Illinois coincided with centennial anniversary celebrations: over 1,100 alumni and faculty made donations (Chrzastowski, 1993). Endowments are also seen as an alternative source of income in South Africa, and a list of points to consider has been prepared; fund raising is also seen as an opportunity to market the library (Dyk, 1994). The university libraries of Africa suffer from poor financing, which affects their collections and hence their image. Additional sources of funding are needed, beyond the usual income from governments and overseas organizations, and so contributions from alumni and charges for some value-added services are being proposed (Alemna, 1994).

Resource sharing

The constraints of limited budgets make it imperative at least to consider the alternative strategy of *accessing* information itself – now that the requisite technology is in place – rather than *permanently acquiring* the mass of materials which may at some future date contain the exact item which is needed. These factors lie behind a description of resource sharing in the Caribbean (Richards, 1994). During the 1980s, cooperation grew among Japan's public libraries and extended to collection development and staff training, but the point is stressed that it must be 'based on libraries that have adequate financial support and staffing' (Takashima, 1993).

The 1993 Essen International Symposium took resource sharing as its theme and a series of interesting and informative papers discussed strategies and policies in a Canadian research library; a UK business information network; information networking in Scotland, the Nordic countries, north Texas, etc. The proceedings also contain a paper on both the dangers, and their solutions, involved in electronic resource-sharing (Helal and Weiss, 1994); this indicates that such a solution is not as simple as it may seem, for although it may be cost-effective and cost-beneficial, it will not be cheaper than earlier alternatives. A paper from Poland (Dudzinska and Wojciechowska, 1993) discusses the changing socio-economic situation, when describing cooperation in the network of the First Central Technological Library.

With falling budgets and the need for technological investment when creating new library services, it is not surprising that attention continues to be paid to the development of joint-use services. Combined public and school libraries may provide an attractive model to assist national development and meet educational and library goals in the less developed countries (Knuth, 1994). An up-beat article describes the development of a joint public and school library in Nevada, where the benefits are described as being 'numerous and exciting'. A checklist to determine whether local conditions are right for such a decision considers such factors as location, the management and administrative structures, planning, user needs, and who contributes what (Kinsey and Honig-Bear, 1994). The points to be considered when developing facilities in the academic library sector include the choice of partners, selecting a director, and operations management (Call, 1993). A study in a US academic library has found that significant cost savings can emerge from sharing facilities (Dedrick, 1994).

Staffing

Some new issues are apparent: they include health matters, the relative positions of women and men in the profession, and the inevitable need for flexibility in the workforce.

Several health and safety issues are emerging. In the Netherlands, employers have a legal obligation to list potential hazards; to ensure optimum results, staff should be involved in the process (Popma, 1994). Tensions in society are producing a situation in which public library staff may be harassed by users; although it has mainly been reported in the USA, this phenomenon may also be occurring in other countries (Smith, 1994).

The history of discrimination against women in librarianship in the Netherlands between 1900 and 1940 has painted a picture of the unsuitability of women for posts of responsibility in the profession, despite the large numbers entering in the early 1900s. Even though changes have taken place in society, the more senior posts are likely to be occupied by men (Nieboer, 1993). A survey of attitudes towards the employment of women in libraries in the UK between 1910 and 1970 indicates that discrimination acted against married women (Harrold, 1994). Demographic changes and the demand for skills have resulted in a change in the labour pool, and libraries need to adapt to cultural change and respond positively to acknowledge the aspirations and skills of women (McDermott, 1994). A management development programme for women has been successful in helping women to become more confident and assertive so that they can put forward their ideas, and take initiatives and additional responsibilities (Fawcett, 1994).

There is, however, writing which focuses on the role of men in society. In the USA a survey has been conducted among men concerning gender issues in the workplace (Carmichael, 1994). A study of men who attended US library schools between 1887 and 1921 describes how they set the context for the salary structures and gender stereotypes in a profession which quickly became dependent upon women (Passet, 1993).

In the USA there is concern that only a small percentage of new graduates from library schools is drawn from minority ethnic groups. Ways of increasing these numbers are discussed (McCook and Geist, 1993). The recruitment and retention of Afro-American librarians have been studied and ways have been described of providing an environment conducive to racial and ethnic inclusion within US academic librariies (Curry, 1994). Mentoring and networking are ways to provide a comfortable environment (Hernandez, 1994).

Flexibility in the workforce is emerging as a matter of concern to employees and management. In the Netherlands, attention has been given to the changing information requirements in society and its effect on staffing. The speed of change has accelerated as budget restrictions, decentralization, and market-oriented and customer care policies have been introduced. The process of change has been assisted by staff councils and the recognition that staff will need to be able to adapt to a range of duties (Broeren, 1994). At Tilburg Public Library, the administrative structure has been simplified, the personnel department disbanded, and the responsibility for staffing matters devolved to departmental heads (Schrader, 1994). The impact of change has created difficulties in UK public libraries: centralization has resulted in branch libraries being managed by non-professional staff, since new graduates have difficulty in gaining experience of staff management, a requirement for promotion to senior posts (Perry, 1994).

As economic conditions have changed, so the impact on career development has been felt by employees in all occupational groups, and librarians and information scientists have not been an exception. A rare study for the mid-1990s has been one which examined a sample of qualified librarians about their attitudes towards a career. The results indicated that there is a linear relationship between age and job satisfaction – as staff age, satisfaction increases. The study also illustrates the frustration encountered at later stages in a career if a person wishes to make a career change, since there is fierce competition for upper-level positions resulting from the flattening of hierarchies and cutbacks in higher education. Effective career development programmes are needed to overcome stagnation and dissatisfaction (Phillips *et al.*, 1994). The problem of a decreasing turnover in technical services has been exacerbated by the unwillingness of older staff to move house (Flowers, 1993). Age and a resulting lack of mobility are also of concern in the Netherlands: a programme of staff mobility has been set up in North Brabant, where more than half the staff are over 40 (Stein and Glaubitz, 1993). The situation has been made more difficult by budget cutbacks reducing the number of posts at middle-management level (Swarte, 1994). Job exchanges within Tilburg Public Libraries have been set up to provide wider experience (Aken, 1994). At Groningen, a staff exchange is operating between university and public libraries, but one participant, while welcoming the challenge of the change, feels that it is no solution to the larger issue of mobility (Veer, 1994). As a result of this lack of mobility, few new staff are being recruited and hence it becomes difficult to introduce new ideas. Ways of creating an atmosphere in which change is seen as an opportunity include staff training and job evaluation (Hulshoff and Klazen, 1993).

Japanese libraries are also experiencing problems in the labour market. Although the period since 1980 has seen growth for libraries, problems of the use of temporary contract staff, unqualified staff, and volunteers remain (Matsuik, 1993). The percentage of temporary staff in university libraries has risen from 28% in 1988 to 31% in 1992 (Tsuda and Tsuzuki, 1993).

There has been a noticeable growth in the number of employment agencies for the library and information service fields. In the Netherlands, the decentralization of public libraries in 1988 and a demand for temporary staff have resulted in the establishment of a number of agencies (Hoeks and Kuik, 1994). At Tilburg Public Library, where temporary staff are employed, it has been found necessary to concentrate permanent staff in the public service areas, with casual staff filling the behind-the-scenes services (Duijf, 1994). At Leicester University Library, success has been reported with the employment of professional auxiliaries as longer opening hours have been introduced at a time of declining budgets. A key factor in the success of this programme was organizing the auxiliaries to work alongside regular weekday staff for one afternoon a week (Bell et al., 1993). In the USA a survey of part-time librarians has indicated that their hourly salaries and benefits do not match those of their full-time counterparts. They have few opportunities for promotion and staff development, and their full-time colleagues do not see them as necessarily having a commitment to the profession (Hogue and Sisson, 1993). The good and the less good points of job sharing are reviewed, and the need to prepare specific job-sharing contracts is considered to be essential (Stennett, 1994). Developing career opportunities are emerging through teleworking, and a range of options for working outside library and information services has been described – including becoming a network guru (Lett, 1994).

Two other ways of providing library services have been described. One is circuit librarianship in US medical librarianship. The circuit riders provide information services to rural health professionals (Pifalo, 1994). Contract librarians who can manage company libraries need not mean that the library is being given less importance by an organization, but rather that they can revitalize the service (Hatfield, 1994).

Changing careers and making a move in a different direction feature in the literature, in spite of the problems noted above. Advice is given on how to choose the right time to make a move, assessing skills and knowledge, and the preparation of applications (Thompson, 1993). Opportunities for British library and information consultants to work overseas have been outlined (Cotton, 1993). Bagnall (1993) has described the experience of an academic librarian in becoming a counsellor and therapist.

As it becomes more difficult to maintain staff levels, then the question of the use of volunteers is raised. In the USA public library volunteers help with specialized services such as those to minority groups, the homebound, etc. (McCune, 1993). The practice is also emerging in Eastern Europe, but the need for guidance by professional staff is emphasized if enthusiasm is to be steered in the right direction (Janostikova, 1993).

In Russia, the personality requirements for a library manager have been studied, and a self-administration test for the reader indicates whether they may be managerial material (Suslova, 1993). One of the liveliest articles of the year is concerned with generating creativity among staff, and offers tools and techniques for this purpose (Kesselman, 1994).

Clearly, the question of training becomes more important, so it is timely that the UK Library Association has produced a set of training guides. A guide to induction describes a systematic approach to the preparation and delivery of programmes for new staff (Parry, 1993). Williamson (1993) analyses and considers how to identify the training needs of the individual and the organization. Phillips (1993) examines training in terms of setting objectives, ensuring quality and appropriateness, and the evaluation of outcomes. A short, clear guide to customer care provides practical advice for the development of good interpersonal skills, and strategies for coping with everyday situations (Lund and Patterson, 1994).

Organizational change

A guide to organizational development is a good starting point at which to consider organizational change (Raughley, 1994).

Academic libraries in the USA are changing their mission, becoming user-centred and empowering their staff to become more responsive. They are moving from providing a 'just-in-case' storehouse to a gateway to a 'just-in-time' service. A range of issues concerning scholarly publishing, technological innovation, empowerment, the new recruits needed for the profession, and the role of professional associations are among the topics discussed in an issue of the *Journal of Library Administration* (Butler, 1993). In Australia, a non-profit company has been established by senior library managers to raise the standard of management and bring about change through the provision of continuing education programmes. AIMA (the Australian Information Management Association) is located within the National Library of Australia and provides courses in Canberra and other parts of Australia (Trask, 1994).

Two papers provide case studies of organizational change in different parts of the world. At the Royal Library in Copenhagen, the concept of a service-oriented library was introduced in 1987. New standards of performance were set for staff and seven functional goals were formulated. Although the library has suffered financial cutbacks, funding was obtained for a building programme in 1993 (Krarup, 1993). The work of the Poznan University Library illustrates the nature and speed of the change process (Jazdon and Olszewski, 1994). The health services library at Columbia University has been reorganized to create a more flexible organization. The process and pitfalls have been described. An egg-shaped organizational chart has emerged, but staff were concerned that they did not know who was in charge. Electronic mail is used by all staff members to assist communication. As problems are identified, solutions are worked out (Jacobson, 1994).

Leadership and power

Sweeney (1994) has discussed leadership in a post-hierarchical library; by this, he means one which has a 'flattened' organization, is antibureaucratic, operates with fewer people, in cross-functional teams, and has a constant process of learning. In such an organizational setting, the aim is to focus on user satisfaction and greater staff empowerment. The leader has to adopt a user satisfaction mindset, develop a strategic plan and create the setting in which it can be implemented.

The role of the library director in a changing internal environment is one of the themes in an issue of *Library Trends* which is devoted to the library director (Hoadley, 1994a). A bright vision of the leadership role of librarians is that they will help to navigate society into the next century, which will result from the role of libraries and information in community empowerment (Schuman, 1994).

The question of gender and leadership, and whether they make a difference, has been discussed from a US viewpoint (Kaufman, 1993). A former President of the Australian Library and Information Association in 1993 has discussed power and the practice of librarianship, drawing attention to the idea that power comes from knowledge and to the Maori concept of *mana*, which recognizes that power is not related to position, but has to be earned by service to others (Cram, 1994).

Management information systems

Given the need for managers to make sound decisions, it was surprising that few references were found on the use of management information systems. An overview of management information and library management systems defines three levels of management – operational, tactical and strategic – with different management information needs at each level (Fisher and Rowley, 1994). A group decision support system is used at the University of Mississippi to support staff meetings (Aiken *et al.*, 1994).

Performance measurement and quality management

A guide to the literature on quality management for public librarians draws attention to the fact that there is little that is a new concept in management, for 'it was an issue for both leaders and consumers in Chinese writings from the fifth century BC'. While the review is intended for a UK audience, in that UK government documents are cited, it nevertheless ranges far more widely for the monograph and periodical literature (Milner *et al.*, 1994). A history of the quality movement in industry and the service sector stresses the need to determine customers needs and to put systems in place to measure customer satisfaction (Moores, 1994). A short introduction to performance measurement has been published in the Aslib 'Know How Series' (Abbott, 1994). The application of the ISO 9000 series standards to special libraries has been discussed in the light of a Nordic study. The standards were found to be of value, and the earlier objections seen to be based on myths, or on the way in which they had been implemented (Johannsen, 1994). A survey funded by the British Library Research and Development Department investigated the degree to which UK academic and public libraries considered quality measures as part of their performance measurement process (Porter, 1993).

Three reports examine specific initiatives on quality management. The Nordic Information Quality Project is described at a half-way stage. It is developing optimal procedures for well developed quality management standards (Clausen, 1994). The Nederlands Biblioteek en Lektuur Centrum has been studying the application of quality management in two public libraries which are acting as test sites: it is reported that there were some reservations about the project at the outset, but all staff are now convinced of its value and improvements to the services have been implemented (Bonsing-Wils, 1994). In Denmark, the Copenhagen Business School Library has approached the evolution of its service empirically, by taking a set of measures and testing them in order to establish a standard set of measures. This project aims to produce practical measures which can be easily applied and yield results, rather than work from a theoretical standpoint and then try to devise practical methods (Cotta-Schønberg and Line, 1994). In UK public libraries, quality management is being embedded into services. Brent Public Library adopted core values of quality, efficiency and customer service in 1991. Firm organizational guidelines have been set in place: a strong and committed leadership, a commissioning/contractor split, a belief in total quality, accountability, customer-led services, total ownership of change, simple and direct communication, maximum devolution and good staff development. Customer satisfaction has increased by a fifth, despite the fact that local taxation (hence income) has been reduced by nearly 50% (Tyerman, 1994). Within Westminster Public Libraries, there is now a contract culture; a report of a staff seminar outlines the guidelines and procedures (Lane, 1994). In France also, attention has been paid to ways of implementing a quality service. Dumont (1993) discusses the need to provide appropriate training for staff, setting in place ways of knowing clients' needs and evaluating their satisfaction. Critical factors for service excellence have been identified in South Africa: they include a commitment on the part of management and staff; stock; publicity and support systems; and service measurement and evaluation (Swart, 1994).

Some of the most interesting work in the field of library effectiveness is being carried out in New Zealand. The second stage of a study of public library effectiveness has been reported. This is identifying the broad dimensions of performance for which key measures can be established. The findings are similar to those identified in US research (Calvert and Cullen, 1994). A second paper, emerging from the same project, sets effectiveness in a social and political environment. It uses the example of the current political philosophy in New Zealand, and comments on the research to date and the relationship to the work of Van House and Childers (Calvert, 1994).

A different approach to academic library effectiveness is provided in an empirical study carried out in the USA. Rather than measuring output, it focuses on the user and argues that students learn in order to become information literate, instead of the more commonly accepted wisdom that they become information-literate in order to learn (McDonald and Micikas, 1994).

In the UK, work is in progress to develop a standardized national questionnaire to measure the views of users on quality (Fuegi, 1994). In the Netherlands, comment has been made on the way in which public libraries are overwhelmed by questionnaires, with little attention being paid to the use of the information collected. It is felt that sometimes they may have been used to delay management decisions (Prins, 1994).

Some attention is being paid to quantitative issues in performance measurement. A beginner's guide to efficiency measurement describes 'data envelopment analysis', which can be applied to libraries (Easun, 1994). Cost data and performance measurement are becoming of increasing value, when the intention is to supply documents as quickly as possible and at the lowest cost, as electronic document delivery supplements the traditional ways of obtaining documents on interlibrary loan. A model has been developed and tested which can be an application on a relational database (Bjarno, 1994). Research libraries in Finland have been working on their procedures for collecting statistical data; the number of questions has been halved and the process simplified. The result is that the data collected are now comparable, thus giving a clear picture of the operation of these libraries (Lind, 1994).

Information technology: management issues

Alongside the problems of falling budgets and market economies, there is the managerial headache – the what-when-how of computers and telecommunications in the library and information service. Decisions involve a major commitment of capital and recurrent funding, whatever the size of library. The difficulty is the same for the small school library as it is for the largest academic library – the only difference is that the rows of 000s are longer in the latter case. There is a range of systems, all of which the manager knows will be updated by a new and better product by the time decisions have been made and the system has been installed. The size of the problem also depends on which country you are in; recent experience indicates that it might be easier in some of the more remote parts of the globe than in the UK.

Keeping up to date with developments in IT is essential for all managers. The latest title in the Aslib Reader series brings together a collection of the best papers on the management of information and communications technology (Mansell, 1994). A review article (Roberts, 1994) discusses issues emerging from the use of IT, and makes the point that library managers:

> are given to uttering bold, if unsupportable generalizations, and employ punchy, if facile, slogans to obscure the reality of change . . . In this world of management, change is never for the worst.

A second conclusion is that, when confronted with information technology, many managers seem to lose the capacity for independent thought. They appear only too willing to sever links with the specialized forms of knowledge that invest their professionalism with credibility and utility; that is, an understanding of the information finding and using habits of their clientele.

There is a body of literature which promotes the virtual library – and another which questions how far we have moved in this direction. We look to the future and consider the possibilities of merging libraries, computer technology, and telecommunications: an interview with Eugenie Prime of Hewlett Packard offers her particular vision (Jajko, 1994). Another authority contends that it is still in its infancy and feels that there are three acceptable terms: 'the electronic library', 'the library without walls' and 'the networked library' (Oppenheim, 1994). If you need a definition of cyberspace, virtual reality and other mediaspace, then this has been provided, together with a view on the implications of these trends (Bauwens, 1994).

The steps that should be taken in planning, selecting, and purchasing a system have been described (Stocklova, 1994) The issues to be considered in taking the decision to automate and the constraints have been set down (Clyde, 1993). Reasons for automating systems and the benefits that may be obtained have been given from a Czech viewpoint. They centre on the value of eliminating clerical tasks and making operations more cost-effective (Krbec and Palka, 1994). Rowley (1994) discusses model strategies for the evaluation and selection of systems and software packages. A series of case studies of the way in which librarians solve problems relating to automation is particularly helpful, since it includes a bibliographic essay (Head, 1993). The systems on offer in the USA are not necessarily available in other parts of the world, but it is helpful to examine trends (Griffiths and Kertis, 1994). Once a system is installed, inevitably planning must start for its upgrading or replacement. The choice may be to stay with the original vendor or move to another (Warwick, 1994). Consideration of this question is given in a recent textbook (Cortez and Smorch, 1993). In developing a virtual library in an academic setting, collaboration between librarians and computer centres is essential (Creth, 1993).

In university libraries, networking has developed very speedily. The philosophy, strategy and implementation at Cornell University have been described (Garrison, 1994). At three US universities, surveys were carried out in 1987 and 1993 of staff reactions to automation. Most library employees welcomed it for the positive effects it could have on their jobs (Winstead, 1994).

A useful review of the ways in which IT can be used more effectively in special libraries indicates the range of applications now available (Dyer, 1994). One application that has revolutionized internal and external communication is electronic mail (Miller, 1994; O'Donaghue and Dickey, 1994).

A technical overview of networking CD-ROMs in the UK includes considerations of training and licensing (Simpson *et al.*, 1994). Difficulties can arise in other countries: the experience of a Saudi Arabian special library has been reported (Kanamugire, 1994). In Malaysia, there are few difficulties in implementing IT solutions, and the application of CD-ROM technology has been described (Yaacob, 1993). The experience of electronic document delivery in Canada has been discussed, together with problems of the incompatibility of some workstations (Brandreth and MacKeigan, 1994). The range of electronic serials currently available is described, with the factors which need to be considered in developing a collection management policy (Woodward, 1994). Two papers describe the setting up of networks: one of state-based electronic libraries in the USA, the other of public and school libraries in Washington State (Jerrey, 1994; Reg, 1994).

The experience of solving technological problems and keeping the machines running when computer manuals are inadequate indicates that only one per cent of cases could not be dealt with in-house, but had to be contracted out (Ballard, 1994).

The impact on users has yet to receive a great deal of attention. Sever (1994), borrowing from the field of anthropology, uses the concepts of culture shock and ethnocentricity to explain what the impact of the electronic library may be on users unfamiliar with computers.

Finally, consider an article which illustrates a point made at the start of this section: Cherry *et al.* (1994) include an evaluation checklist for online public access catalogues (OPACs), but they fail to consider user reaction, and focus upon the technical issues from the librarian's viewpoint rather than the user's. When will there be imaginative design of such interfaces, and the use of colour?

Housing the service

The use of information technology has created problems in providing the necessary cabling in a safe manner, and the environmental conditions in which users and the hardware can both be effective. Those who work in warmer climates quickly become aware that hardware has been designed for operating efficiently at lower temperatures. Heat generation becomes a problem. Indications in the office market are that many organizations will not consider older properties if they are expensive to adapt and result in high operating costs; such trends may also become evident in the housing of information and library services. In the UK, architects are aware of this problem when designing higher education libraries (Drake, 1994). Two new libraries have come into operation which have taken this into account: one is Croydon Public Library (Public, 1994), the other is Cranfield University (Blagden, 1994). The question of IT and special design considerations have been discussed in a paper from South Africa (Barraclough, 1993).

An Australian with lengthy experience of working with architects to produce attractive buildings from the viewpoint of visual impact, user and staff satisfaction has provided good advice on how to select a suitable architect and interior design team (Jones, 1994). The architectural and design planning process and the relationship between operating costs and designs have been discussed (Cohen, 1994). In recent years, attention has been paid to the way the building is presented; if defensibility dominates design, the building may have a closed-in feeling. Attention is being paid to the 'body language' of buildings in New Zealand, so that they can 'talk' to users (Melling, 1993).

Within the library, the importance of signage has been emphasized (Johnson, 1993). In the USA the need to provide facilities for disabled people is now mandatory and the experience is likely to be helpful to others (Lenn, 1993). Ergonomic issues arise from the use of IT and other equipment, but also affect the layout, design, and placing of furniture (Rooney, 1994). Questions of security are becoming of increasing importance. The theft of books, access to the building, and the safety of staff and users must be considered (Jones and Larkin, 1993).

Disaster planning is becoming a major management issue in all parts of the world. Australia's National Preservation Office provides practical advice, and indicates that there is more to disaster management than simply developing a plan (Archer, 1994). The impact of an earthquake in the Los Angeles area is described, together with the problems of funding the recovery efforts (Flagg, 1994). In Alabama, the aftermath of a flood is reported (Chadbourne, 1994).

Many special librarians have to move their libraries from time to time, and a list of factors to consider, and actions to be taken, has been prepared (Wells and Young, 1994). Perhaps it is a sign of the difficult times, but, when a new library was needed in Oregon, some government funding was made available to help with the move; this was supplemented by local fund-raising and volunteers carried out some of the work (Johnston, 1994).

Marketing and public relations

The application of marketing methods to libraries, and especially in the public sector, has received attention in recent years. The need to have a sophisticated understanding of the complex forces involved has emerged from research in Australia. Two major risks exist in applying a marketing model. It may be adapted to the needs of the organization in such a way that innovation can be claimed, yet the benefits to the user that it appears to offer may not be forthcoming. The claim to be a user-oriented organization must be substantiated by satisfied customers and motivated staff. Conversely, the model may be adopted uncritically, but the organization may not be able to cope with the demands placed on the system (Marks, 1994).

A study of UK public libraries and the way in which they view marketing has indicated that few understand the subject. The authors conclude that 'the need to provide a professional approach to marketing has become a pressing need' (Kinnell and MacDougall, 1994).

Making users aware of what the service can offer means increasing the visibility of the library. The need to build good relations with local media has been emphasized by East Brunswick Public Library (Karmazin, 1994). At Mastics-Moriches-Shirley Community Library, a programme has been established which invites local community leaders to the library to meet key staff for a buffet supper and tour (Verbesey and Catan, 1994).

The reality of management in 1994

The reality of management in the mid-1990s is that change is reshaping services as a result of a close scrutiny of funding and the need for accountability, and of changing approaches to accessing information through the use of computing and telecommunications. Greater demands are being placed upon all types of service – demands which must be met, for they come from an increasingly literate and information-conscious society. This results in an element of flexibility being part of a management strategy, and in changing philosophies, policies and practices which will draw funding and support from a wider range of sources. Flexibility is necessary in housing the service to meet changing community needs, and there has to be flexibility in the deployment of staff. Quality outcomes rely on sound administrative procedures which provide the information needed for managerial decision-making, and empathetic management to implement difficult decisions. Considerable responsibility also rests with those responsible for the recruitment, education and training of information and library staff to prepare them for the workplace of the later 1990s.

References

Abbott, C. (1994) *Performance measurement in library and information services* (Aslib Know How Series). London: Aslib.
Abraham, J. (1993) Economic recession and its impact on libraries and information centres. In: *Proceedings of the 19th All India Conference of IASLIC, Calcutta, India 26–29 December 1993*. Calcutta: IASLIC, pp. 1–4.
Aiken, M. et al. (1994) Group support systems in libraries. *Computers in Libraries*, **14**(2), 22–23.
Aken, G. van (1994) Op een veilige manier een andere baan verkennen: functieroulatie bij de OB Tilburg. *Bibliotheek en Samenleving*, **22**(7/8), 48–50.
Alemna, A. (1994) Alternative approaches to funding university libraries in Africa. *New Library World*, **95**(1112), 15–17.
Archer, E. (1994) Fires, floods and fallen paintings. *National Library of Australia News*, **5**(2), 9–11.
Asser, M. (1994) The integrated management of leisure directorates in UK public libraries. *Journal of Librarianship and Information Science*, **26**(2), 93–97.
Bagnall, C. (1993) On becoming an ex-librarian. *Librarian Career Development*, **1**(4), 19–20.
Ballard, T. (1994) Zen and the art of troubleshooting. *American Libraries*, **25**(1), 108–110.
Barraclough, C. (1993) Planning an automated library. *Cape Librarian*, **37**(10), 6–8.
Bauwens, M. (1994) What is cyberspace? *Computers in Libraries*, **14**(4), 42–48.
Beger, G. (1994) Outsourcing, privatisierung, bibliothek: Rechtliche Aspekte. *Bibliotheksdienst*, **28**(7), 1066–1073.
Bell, A. et al. (1993) Casual professional staff: contradictions in terms or a new paradigm? *Librarian Career Development*, **1**(4), 11–15.
Birdsall, D.G. and Hensley, O.D. (1994) A new strategic planning model for academic libraries. *College and Research Libraries*, **55**(2), 149–159.
Bjarno, H. [sic, for Bjarnø] (1994) Cost finding and performance measures in ILL management. *Interlending and Document Supply*, **22**(2), 8–11.
Blagden, J. (1994) Building for the future: Cranfield's new library. *New Library World*, **95**(1111), 15–24.
Bonsing-Wils, H. (1994) Kwaliteit wel meetbaar!: Maassluis maakt niveaus op de werkvloer zichtbaar. *Bibliotheek en Samenleving*, **22**(9), 26–29.
Bouthillier, F. (1994) La gestion financière des bibliothèques à l'heure de l'internationalization. *Argus*, **22**(3) 33–36.
Brandreth, M. and MacKeigan, C. (1994) Electronic document delivery – towards the virtual library. *Interlending and Document Supply*, **22**(1), 15–19.
Broeren, J. (1994) Het kernwoord luidt – flexibiliteit: personeelsbeleid in de openbare bibliotheek. *Bibliotheek en Samenleving*, **22**(7/8), 11–13.
Brown, S. (1994). Franchising public library services. *C and L Applications*, **7**(7), 8–9.
Burlingame, D.F. (1994) Fund-raising as a key to the library's future. *Library Trends*, **42**(3), 467–477.
Butler, M.A. (1993) (ed.) Libraries as user-centered organizations: imperatives for organizational change. *Journal of Library Administration*, **19**(3/4), 1–256.
Call, I.S.B. (1993) Joint-use libraries: just how good are they? *College and Research Libraries*, **54**(10), 551–552, 554–556.

Calvert, P.J. (1994) Library effectiveness: the search for a social context. *Journal of Librarianship and Information Science*, **26**(1), 15–21.

Calvert, P.J. and Cullen, R.J. (1994) Further dimensions of public library effectiveness, II: the second stage of the New Zealand study. *Library and Information Science Research*, **16**(2), 87–104.

Campbell, J.D. (1994) Getting comfortable with change: a new budget model for libraries in transition. *Library Trends*, **42**(3), 448–459.

Carmichael, J.V.(1994) Gender issues in the workplace: male librarians tell their side. *American Libraries*, **25**(3), 227–230.

Catlin, I. (1994) Redefining the role of the public library in legislation. *Australian Library Journal*, **43**(1), 49–55.

Chadbourne, R. (1994) A post-disaster primer: Elba on the rebound. *Wilson Library Bulletin*, **68**(9), 24–5.

Cherry, J.M. *et al.* (1994) OPACs in twelve Canadian academic libraries: an evaluation of functional capabilities and interface features. *Information Technology and Libraries*, **13**(3), 174–193.

Chrzastowski, E. (1993) A capital idea: a centennial celebration endowment campaign. *Bottom Line*, **7**(1), 13–16.

Clausen, H. (1994) The Nordic Information Quality Project: a halfway report. *New Library World* **95**(1114), 21–22.

Clyde, A. (1993) Automating the library? *Emergency Librarian*, **21**(2), 27–28.

Cohen, E. (1994) The architectural and interior design planning process. *Library Trends*, **42**(3), 547–563.

Cooper, J.M. and Crouch, M.C. (1994) Benefit assessment helps open doors of one cash-strapped California library. *American Libraries*, **25**(3), 232–234.

Coote, H. (1994) *How to market your library service effectively* (Aslib Know How Series). London: Aslib.

Corrall, S. (1994) *Strategic planning for library and information services* (Aslib Know How Series). London: Aslib.

Cortez, E. and Smorch, T. (1993) *Planning second generation automated library systems*. London: Greenwood Publishing Company.

Cotta-Schønberg, M. and Line, M.B. (1994) Evaluation of academic libraries with special reference to the Copenhagen Business School Library. *Journal of Librarianship and Information Science*, **26**(2), 55–69.

Cotton, R. (1993) Overseas opportunities for British library and information consultants – the way forward. *International Development*, **9**(4), 240–246.

Cram, J. (1994) Mana, manna, manner: power and the practice of librarianship. *Australian Library Journal*, **43**(2), 132–148.

Creth, S.D. (1993) Creating a virtual information organization: collaborative relationships between libraries and computing centres. *Journal of Library Administration*, **19**(3/4), 111–132.

Curry, D.A. (1994) Your worries ain't like mine: African American librarians and the pervasiveness of racism, prejudice and discrimination in academe. *Reference Librarian*, (45/46), 299–311.

Danilenko, G. (1994) Activity based costing for services: the corporate information center. *Special Libraries*, **85**(1), 24–29.

Dedrick, A.J. (1994) Shared academic library facilities: the unknown form of library cooperation. *College and Research Libraries*, **55**(5), 437–443.
Dewey, B.I. (1994) Personnel costs and patterns in libraries. *Library Trends*, **42**(3), 537–546.
Dokmeci, V. and Korca, P. (1993) Istanbul'da kutuphane sistemi planlasmasi. *Turk Kutuphaneciligi*, **7**(3), 174–180.
Drake, P. (1994) Higher education libraries. *Architects' Journal*, **199**(3), 38.
Dudzińska, E. and Wojciechowska, A. (1993) Wsplpraca bibliotek sieci I Centralnej Biblioteki Technicznej w nowych warunkach spoleczno-ekonomicznych. *Przegląd Biblioteczny*, **61**(3/4), 273–280.
Duijf, A. (1994) Kiezen voor de klant betekent beste medewerkers in de directe dienstverlening: werken met invallers. *Bibliotheek en Samenleving*, **22**(7/8), 24–25.
Dumont, M. (1993) Client et bibliothèque: à la recherche de l'équilibre. *Argus*, **22**(2), 7–11.
Dunn, J.A. and Martin, M.S. (1994) The whole cost of libraries. *Library Trends*, **42**(3), 564–578.
Dyer, H. (1994) Have you got what it takes ... and are you using all you could? *Electronic Library*, **12**(1), 37–48.
Dyk, F.van (1994) Fondsinsameling. *Cape Librarian*, **38**(2) 26–27.
Easun, S. (1994) Beginners' guide to efficiency measurement. *School Library Media Quarterly*, **22**(2), 103–106.
Fawcett, V. (1994) Springboard Women's Development Programme. *Library Management*, **15**(3), 21–23.
Fisher, S. and Rowley, J. (1994) Management information and library management systems: an overview. *Electronic Library*, **12**(2), 109–117.
Flagg, G. (1994) Libraries jolted by LA earthquake. *American Libraries*, **25**(3), 214–216, 219.
Flowers, K. (1993) The maturing worker in technical services. *Journal of Library Administration*, **18**(3/4), 145–158.
Fuegi, D. (1994) Towards a national standard for a public library survey. *Public Library Journal*, **9**(2), 49–51.
Garrison, W.V. (1994) Integrating networked information into library services: philosophy, strategy, and implementation at the Mann Library. In: *Proceedings of the Clinic on Library Applications of Data Proceedings, Illinois-University at Urbana-Champaign ... 1993*. Illinois: Illinois University at Urbana-Champaign, pp. 223–240.
Garten, E.D. (1993) *Using consultants in libraries and information centres: a management handbook*. London: Greenwood Publishing Group.
Gertzog, A. and Beckerman, E. (1994) *Administration and the public library*. Metuchen, NJ: Scarecrow Press.
Griffiths, J-M. and Kertis, K. (1994) Automated system marketplace 1994. *Library Journal*, **119**(6), 50–59.
Grotenhius, A.J.ter and Heijnekamp, S.J. (1994) The user pays: cost billing in a company library. *Library Management*, **15**(4), 17–21.
Harrold, A. (1994) 'Bright ribbons and thin shoes'. *Library Association Record*, **96**(2), 90.
Hatfield, D. (1994) Partnerships in information services: the contract library. *Special Libraries*, **85**(2), 77–80.
Hayes, S. and Brown, D. (1993) Accounting for your times! *Bottom Line*, **7**(2) 32–37.
Head, J.W. (1993) *Insider's guide to library automation: essays of practical experience*. London: Greenwood Publishing Group.

Heinitz, C. (1994) The Public Library Review: an elected member's view. *Public Library Journal*, **8**(6), 161–164.

Helal, A.H. and Weiss, J.W. (1994) (eds) *Resource sharing: new technologies as a must for the universal availability of information. Proceedings of the 16th International Essen Symposium.* Essen: Universitätsbibliothek Essen, pp. 1–311.

Hernandez, M.N.(1994) Mentoring, networking and supervision: parallelogram, vortex, or merging point? *Reference Librarian*, (45/46), 15–22.

Hoadley, I. B. (1994a) (ed.) The library director. *Library Trends*, **43**(1), 3–147.

Hoadley, I.B. (1994b) Future perfect: the library and its friends. *Library Administration and Management*, **8**(3) 161–165.

Hoeks, M. and Kuik, K. (1994) Een kans voor wie van afwisseling houdt: uitzenbureau voor bibliotheekmedewerkers in Gelderland en Noord-Holland. *Bibliotheek en Samenleving*, **22**(7/8), 43–47.

Hogue, E.M. and Sisson, L. (1993) Bargains of the century: part-time librarians. *Bottom Line*, **7**(2), 18–22.

House, N.A.V. and Childers, T.A. (1994) The use of public library roles for effectiveness evaluation. *Library and Information Science Research*, **16**(1), 41–58.

Hulshoff, M-A. and Klazen, M. (1993) Werk je daar nog steeds? Marktgerichte organisatie vereist flexibele medewerkers. *Bibliotheek en Samenleving*, **21**(9), 304–307.

Jacobson, S. (1994) Reorganization: premises, processes, and pitfalls. *Bulletin of the Medical Libraries Association*, **82**(4), 369–374.

Jajko, P. (1994) Visualizing the virtual library: an interview with Eugenie Prime. *Medical Reference Services Quarterly*, **13**(1), 97–109.

Janoštíková, B. (1993) Dobrovolna prace pro knihovny. *Knižnie a Informácie*, **25**(12), 515–517.

Jasdon, A. and Olszewski, T. (1994) Problems in the management and operation of academic libraries in Poland during the transition period. *Library Review*, **43**(8), 31–39.

Jerrey, R. (1994) Establishing a system of state-based electronic libraries. *Journal of Agricultural and Food Information*, **2**(1), 5–12.

Johannsen, C.G. (1994) Can the ISO standards on quality management be useful to libraries and how? *Inspel*, **28**(2), 227–239.

John Fielden Consultancy (1993). *Supporting expansion: a report on human resource management in academic libraries* . . . Bristol: HEFCE.

Johnson, C. (1993) Signs of the times: signage in the library. *Wilson Library Bulletin*, **68**(3), 40–42.

Johnson, H. (1994) Strategic planning for modern libraries. *Library Management*, **15**(1), 7–18.

Johnston, R. (1994) Helping hands: volunteers build a new library. *Wilson Library Bulletin*, **68**(5), 25–28.

Joint (1993) Funding Councils' Libraries Review Group [chair: Sir Brian Follett]. *Report*. Bristol: HEFCE.

Jones, D. (1994) Picking a winner: the selection of a design team for a library project. *Australian Library Journal*, **43**(1), 28–34.

Jones, D. and Larkin, G. (1993) Securing a good design: a library building consultant and an architect consider library security. *Australasian Public Libraries and Information Services*, **6**(4), 164–170.

Jones, L. and Nicholas, D. (1993) Costing medical libraries: the feasibility of functional cost analysis. *Health Libraries Review,* **10**(4) 169–201.
Kalinova, V. (1994) Nadacia J.C. Hronskeho. *I'94 Casopis,* **36**(4), 105–107.
Kanamugire, A.B. (1994) Developing a CD-ROM service in Saudi Arabia: some lessons for developing countries. *Journal of Information Science,* **20**(2), 99–107.
Karmazin, S. (1994) Library success through visibility. *New Jersey Libraries,* **27**(3), 12–14.
Kaufman, P.T. (1993) Library leadership: does gender make a difference? *Journal of Library Administration,* **18**(3/4), 109–128.
Kesselman, M. (1994) Ideas come from everywhere: generating creativity for your library. *Wilson Library Bulletin,* **68**(9), 42–44.
Kinnell, M. and MacDougall, J. (1994). *Meeting the marketing challenge: strategies for public libraries and leisure services.* London: Taylor Graham.
Kinsey, S. and Honig-Bear, S. (1994) Joint-use libraries: more bang for your bucks. *Wilson Library Bulletin,* **69**(4), 37–39, 132.
Knuth, R. (1994) Libraries, literacy and development: combined libraries as an option for developing countries: a brief communication. *International Information and Library Review,* **26**(2), 77–89.
Krarup, K. (1993) The process of modernisation and organisational change: a case study of the Royal Library from the viewpoint of applied sociology. *Nordinfo-Nytt,* (4), 12–24.
Krbec, P. and Palka, P. (1994) Duvody a prinosy automatizace knihovnickych praci. *I'94 Casopis,* **36**(2), 40, 45–46.
Ladosne Varju, I.L. (1994) Célok a tanácsi könyvtárügyben szervezetszociológiai elemzés. *Könyvtári Figyelö,* **40**(1), 49–60.
Lane, G. (1994) Quality inspection in Westminster. *Public Library Journal,* **9**(2), 39–40.
Lawes, A. (1994) Contracting out. *New Library World,* **95**(1114), 8–12.
Layzell Ward, P. (1994) Review of the general literature on management. *IFLA Journal,* **20**(4), 449–458
Lenn, K. (1993) Climbing the mountain: the Americans with Disabilities Act. *Wilson Library Bulletin,* **68**(4), 36–39.
Lett, B. (1994) Teleworking and the library of the future. *Managing Information,* **1**(4), 27–29.
Library (1994) *2000: investing in a learning nation: report of the Library 2000 Review Committee.* Singapore: SNP Publications.
Liddle, D. (1993) Back to the future. *Public Library Journal,* **8**(6), 177–180.
Lind, A.L. (1994) Tieteellisten kirjastojen yhteistilaston uudistaminen 1993. *Signum,* **27**(4), 103–105.
Lund, K. and Patterson, H. (1994) *Customer care.* London: AAL Publishing.
McCook, K. de la P. and Geist, P. (1993) Diversity deferred: where are the minority librarians? *Library Journal,* **118**(18), 35–38.
McCune, B.F. (1993) The new volunteerism: making it pay off for your library. *American Libraries,* **24**(9), 822–824.
McDermott, E. (1994) Who needs equal opportunities? Libraries do! *New Library World,* **95**(1112), 9–14.
McDonald, J.A. and Micikas, L.B. (1994) *Academic libraries: the dimensions of their effectiveness.* Westport, CT: Greenwood.

McGinn, H.F. (1993) Information assets. *Bottom Line*, 7(2), 40–41.
Mansell, R. (1994) (ed.) *Management of information and communications technology* (Aslib Reader Series, no. 9.). London: Aslib.
Marks, L. (1994) Marketing and the public sector library: some unresolved issues. *Australian Library Journal*, 43(1), 17–27.
Martin, M.S. (1994) (ed.) Library finance: new needs, new models. *Library Trends*, 42(3), 369–582.
Matsuik, I. (1993). Librarianship and employment in 1980–92. *Toshokan-Kai*, 45(1), 170–176.
Melling, G. (1993) The body language of library buildings. *New Zealand Libraries*, 47(8), 150–156.
Midwinter, A. (1993) Reorganising Scotland's public library authorities. *Scottish Libraries*, (41), 6–7.
Midwinter, A. and McVicar, M. (1994) Reconstructing public library authorities in the Celtic fringe. *Public Library Journal*, 9(1), 21–22.
Miller, J.P. (1994) Should you get wired? *Library Journal*, 119(2), 47–49.
Milner, E. *et al.* (1994) Quality management: the public library debate. *Public Library Journal*, 9(6), 151–157.
Moores, B. (1994) Concepts of quality management in industry and the service sector. *Inspel*, 28(2), 211–218.
Myllys, H. (1994) Ruotsistako mallia korkeakoulun kirjaston roolin kohottamiseen? *Signum*, 27(1), 1–4.
Navalani, K. (1994) The third wave and Third World libraries. *Third World Libraries*, 4(2), 33–35.
Nieboer, M. (1993) Juffrouw Bits: denkbeelden in Nederland over de (on)geschiktheid van vrouwen voor het bibliotheekberoep 1900–1940. *Open*, 25(9), 319–323.
Novak, J. (1994) Value for money: getting the most out of external training programs. *Australian Academic and Research Libraries*, 25(1), 1–8.
Nurminen, T. (1994) Kirjastopalvelut sisaiseen veloitukseen. *Signum*, 27(4), 106–107.
O'Donaghue, M. and Dickey, W. (1994) Electronic mail in academic libraries: is it worth the investment? *New Library World*, 95(1112), 4–8.
Oh, D. and Woods, G. (1994) The future of Australian academic libraries. *Australian Academic and Research Libraries*, 25(3) 149–158.
Oppenheim, C. (1994) The virtual library: some common sense please. *Managing Information*, 1(1), 26–27.
Parry, J. (1993) *Induction* (Library Training Guides). London: Library Association.
Passet, J.E. (1993) Men in a feminized profession: the male librarian, 1887–1921. *Libraries and Culture*, 28(4), 385–402.
Pastine, M. and Kacena, C. (1994) Library automation, networking, and other online and new technology costs in academic libraries. *Library Trends*, 42(1), 524–536.
Perpustakaan Negara Malaysia (1994) *Warisan ilmu*. Kuala Lumpur: PNM.
Perry, R. (1994) My wonderful career! *Assistant Librarian*, 87(4), 58–59.
Phillips, J.S. *et al.* (1994) Evolution of affective career outcomes: a field study of academic librarians. *College and Research Libraries*, 55(6), 541–549.
Phillips, S. (1993) *Evaluation* (Library Training Guides). London: Library Association.
Pifalo, V. (1994) Circuit librarianship: a twentieth anniversary appraisal. *Medical Reference*

Services Quarterly, **13**(1), 19–33.

Pop, J.J.H. (1994) 'Bibliotheken moeten sterke band met het openbaar bestuur houden': bestuurlijke reorganisatie van Nederland komt er aan. *Bibliotheek en Samenleving*, **22**(1), 17–20.

Popma, J. (1994) Bibliotheken moeten welzijnsrisico's opsporen: risicoinventarisatie arbeidsomstandigheden niet zonder betrokkenheid van werknemers. *Bibliotheek en Samenleving*, **22**(7/8), 14–16.

Porter, L. (1993) *Quality initiatives in British library and information services*. London: British Library. (British Library Research and Development Report no. 6105).

Pouillas, M-T. (1994) Consultants, mode d'emploi. *Bulletin des Bibliothèques de France*, **39**(3), 46–49.

Prins, H. (1994) De waarde van het getal: onderzoeksdrift bibliotheken gebaseerd op drogredenen. *Bibliotheek en Samenleving*, **22**(5), 22–24.

Public (1994) library revitalises Croydon. *Architects' Journal*, **199**(1), 29–39.

Ramaiah, L.S. (1993) Public libraries and public finances in India: a critical perspective. *Herald of Library Science*, **32**(3–4), 171–180.

Raughley, C.S. (1994) A librarian's guide to organization development. Part 1. Understanding the basics. *Medical Reference Services Quarterly*, **13**(3), 83–92.

Reg, J. (1994) The technology knot: tying small libraries together through remote access. *Wilson Library Bulletin*, **68**(8), 38–40, 140.

Richards, T. (1994) Resource sharing in the Caribbean, with special reference to the University of the West Indies. *Third World Libraries*, **4**(2), 31–32.

Roberts, N. (1994) Management and IT: a review article. *Journal of Librarianship and Information Science*, **26**(3), 165–167.

Robinson, B.M. and Robinson, S. (1994) Strategic planning and program budgeting for libraries. *Library Trends*, **42**(3), 420–427.

Rooney, J. (1994) Ergonomics in academic libraries. *Library Management*, **15**(1), 26–35.

Rowley, J. (1994) Making the right choice: strategies and pointers for the selection of library and information systems. *Managing Information*, **1**(2), 26–29, 31.

Runge, L.D. (1994) The manager and information worker of the 1990s. *Information Strategy*, **10**(4), 7–14.

Sato, M. (1993) The financial affairs of local government and public libraries. *Toshokan-Kai*, **45**(1), 55–61.

Schoen, A. (1994) 'Bibliothecarissen laten zich makkelijker sturen, dan dat ze een sturende invloed hebben': interview met Wenda Flier. *Bibliotheek en Samenleving*, **22**(2), 11–14.

Schrader, J.M. (1994) Hoe minder schakels, hoe minder ruis: het personeelsbeleid van de OB Tilburg. *Bibliotheek en Samenleving*, **22**(7/8), 17–18.

Schuman, P.G. (1994) Leaders manage the dream. *Wilson Library Bulletin*, **68**(7), 41–44, 139.

Sever, I. (1994) Electronic information retrieval as culture shock: an anthropological exploration. *RQ*, **33**(3), 336–341.

Sharr, F.A. (1994) Economic cycles and the health of libraries. *Australasian Public Libraries and Information Services*, **7**(2), 81–83.

Simpson, E. *et al.* (1994) Networking CD-ROMs: technical overview and the view from the Manchester Business School. *Journal of Information Science*, **20**(1), 146–154.

Smith, N.M. (1994) Staff harassment by patrons: why administrators flinch. *American*

Libraries, 25(4), 316.

StClair, G. (1994) *Power and influence: enhancing information services within an organization.* East Grinstead: Bowker-Saur.

Stein, F. and Glaubitz, M. (1993) 'Als je ziet dat de helft van je personeel boven de veertig is, dan moet je nu jets doen': Noordbrabantse bibliothekn gaan werken aan mobiliteit. *Bibliotheek en Samenleving*, 21(12), 414–418.

Stennett, R. (1994) Job sharing in librarianship. *Librarian Career Development*, 2(1), 23–29.

Stephens, A. (1994) The application of life cycle costing in libraries: a case study based on acquisition and retention of library materials in the British Library. *IFLA Journal*, 20(2), 130–140.

Stephens, D. and Hallam, M. (1994) Commercialising the State Library of Queensland. *Australian Library Journal*, 43(1), 3–8.

Stocklova, A. (1994) Chystate se automatizovat provoz khihovny? *I'94 Casopis*, 36(4), 91–94.

Suslova, I.M. (1993) Bibliotechnyi menedzher: trebovaniya k lichnosti. *Nauchnye-Tekhnicheskie Biblioteki*, (7), 32–43.

Sutton, B. (1994) The modeling function of range planning in public libraries. *Library Administration and Management*, 8(3), 151–160.

Swart, I. (1994) Service excellence in libraries. *Cape Librarian*, 38(1), 56.

Swarte, J.L. (1994) 'Er zijn weinig mogelijkheden de Romario's in de bibliotheek hoger te belonen dan de spitsen die voortduren naast schieten': lonen in de openbare bibliotheken. *Bibliotheek en Samenleving*, 22(3), 16–22.

Sweeney, R.T. (1994) Leadership in the post-hierarchical library. *Library Trends*, 43(1), 62–94.

Tait, F. (1994) Producer choice: selling information at the BBC. *Managing Information*, 1(3), 31, 33–34.

Takashima, A. (1993) A review of library cooperation in the 1980s. [in Japanese] *Toshokan-Kai [Library World]*, 45(5), 404–407.

Taking (1994) stock *Libraries and the Book Trade: Journal of the National Acquisitions Group*, 3(2).

Thompson, V. (1993) Time for a change. *Librarian Career Development*, 1(4), 16–18.

Tilson, Y. (1994) Income generation and pricing in libraries. *Library Management*, 15(2), 5–17.

Transformace (1994) zdravotnictvi a informatacni sluzby. *I'94 Casopis*, 36(3), 77–78.

Trask, M. (1994) Meeting the challenge of organisational change: an Australian continuing education initiative for libraries. *Australian Academic and Research Libraries*, 25(3), 182–196.

Tsuda, M. and Tsuzuki, H. (1993) Temporary staff in private university libraries [in Japanese]. *Toshokan Zasshi [Library Journal]*, 87(11), 801–804.

Tyerman, K. (1994) Brent's pilot project goes live. *New Library World*, 95(1115), 27.

Veer, L. der (1994) 'In de openbare bibliotheek vind ik het werk veel leuker': uitwisselingsplan personeel OB-UB. *Bibliotheek en Samenleving*, 22(7/8), 50–52.

Verbesey, J.R. and Catan, R. (1994) The leaders' tour. *American Libraries*, 25(10), 917–918.

Walker, T.D. (1994) (ed.) The library in corporate intelligence activities. *Library Trends*, 43(2), 149–287.

Warwick, R.T. (1994) Moving to a new automated system: some issues. *New Jersey Libraries*, 27(2), 11–14.

Webber, S. (1993) Charging for library and information services in medical libraries: a review of the literature and a survey of current practice. *Health Libraries Review*, **10**(4), 202–223.

Wells, M. and Young, R. (1994) Making your move and getting it right. *Special Libraries*, **85**(3), 145–153.

Wiegand, S.A. (1994) Lawmakers, lawbreakers: the problem of library record destruction. *American Libraries*, **25**(1), 102–103, 106.

Williamson, M. (1993) *Training needs analysis* (Library Training Guides). London: Library Association.

Winstead, E.B. (1994) Staff reactions to automation. *Computers in Libraries*, **14**(4), 18–21.

Wisner, W.H. (1994) Back toward people: a symposium. *Journal of Academic Librarianship*, **20**(3), 131–132.

Woodward, H. (1994) The impact of electronic information on serials collection management. *Serials*, **7**(1), 29–36.

Wuest, R. and Osswald, A. (1994) Interaction between the consultant and the client: a two-sided view from the National Library of Switzerland. *Information Services and Use*, **14**(1), 51–57.

Yaacob, R.A. (1993) Application of CD-ROM technology in Malaysian libraries and information centres: its growing importance. In: *Online Information 93. Proceedings of the 17th International Online Information Meeting. London . . . 1993.* Oxford: Learned Information (Europe) Ltd, pp. 625–638.

Epilogue

Graham Mackenzie

Each year one of the editors takes on the task of writing an Epilogue to the volume just completed, picking out, as it were, the plums from the pie and giving a personal reaction to the whole. Each year it becomes more difficult to epitomize (in the original literal sense) what has come to the fore in the interval since the previous volume was compiled. Often this difficulty arises from, or is compounded by, a perception that the developments described in the text are merely that – developments rather than new departures. This is certainly the case this year; as one editor stressed previously, our profession tends to proceed by evolution rather than revolution, however difficult some of the workers at the coal face may find it to believe this.

There are, however, some pointers to the future: one which struck home sharply this year was the comment by Wainwright and Bátonyi in their chapter on national libraries:

> In passing, we note that the 1994 review may well be the last in which it would be wise to rely only on printed sources. As discussed later, many of the national libraries in countries with an advanced level of computing and networking now have information servers, usually based on the World Wide Web, which contain the latest information relating to their collections and services. While some of this information is available in printed sources such as annual reports, newsletters and guides, increasingly the servers include internal working documents, press releases, organizational information and information for the public which is not generally accessible in any other way, and is adding significantly to our knowledge of the institutions concerned.

To those of us who started our careers 30 or more years ago, in the pre-computer age, this is a daunting thought: however, we have studied to adapt to the new electronic world – some, perhaps, with more enthusiasm than others – there is still an underlying prejudice (deep-seated and perhaps unreasonable, sometimes unadmitted, but nowadays more often consciously resisted) that print is best, that a document read on a transient screen can never provide *quite* the same experience, can still never be as *totally* trusted, as a 'real' book or periodical.

A second point of interest is the manner in which several chapters carry on previous debates on 'just-in-case' versus 'just-in-time', the two contrasting philosophies of meeting readers' needs by stock-holding or by a different form of document provision which exploits external sources at the point of need. It seems that the proponents of the former are gradually losing the argument, this is partly because of increasing restrictions on acquisitions budgets (although, as some authors point out, resource sharing does not so much cut overall costs as give a more acceptable service at a similar cost). The major reason for the change in attitudes is that the technology of networking (which is enabling, rather than an actual agent for change) is making it quicker and easier, as well as cheaper than ever before, to share resources among libraries of all types.

There is, however, an obverse to this coin: the strategy of sharing, of cooperation, may work reasonably well in the developed world, where library budgets are restricted, but still not too skimped, where the technology actually works, and the money can usually be found to replace systems when they become obsolescent, where the databases are mounted and publicly accessible, where the staff are reasonably competent to operate the systems in place. In the Third World, however, few of these preconditions for success may apply: acquisitions budgets may be almost non-existent (hence there are very few resources which *can* be shared); bibliographic control is rudimentary; power supplies are erratic; spares and servicing for even simple electrical equipment, let alone computers, may involve delays of weeks or months, and staff are still near the bottom of the learning curve. In such conditions to talk of the Internet as the answer to information problems is not reasonable; even the bibliographic CD may not be more than a palliative.

This gap between the information-rich and information-poor parts of the world is not going to close easily or rapidly; yet we cannot ignore or put aside the benefits of technology simply because we cannot make them available immediately to every scholar worldwide. When trying to put the year's work in context, Arms writes in his introductory chapter that he 'concentrates almost exclusively on technology and its impact on libraries', which he believes to be the most significant development. The technical barriers are falling rapidly. Storing information on disc is probably cheaper nowadays than storing paper publications on shelves in a library, and this has transformed the whole basis of the profession. The economics of library computing have also been turned upside down, so that where the question 25 years ago was how a computer system might be funded – and significant numbers, both in the UK and abroad, owed their existence to external research funding – nowadays they and the networks which depend on them are viewed as totally integral to mainstream librarianship, to the extent that they have become a normal operational expense, and many managers would rather sacrifice large portions of their acquisitions budget than try to do without them. One chapter after another repeats this theme: the future lies with the computer and the network.

Acting as devil's advocate, I searched for a contrary view. Once or twice I found hints of mental reservations, or statements of real difficulties still to be overcome: problems of copyright and how the role of publishers might be reconciled with the wish of governments to have a seamless, profit-free world of information available to all. One sceptic is cited, saying with bitter irony, 'In this world of [library] management change is never for the worse'. Yet, overall, none of the chapter authors is willing to deny that – for good or ill, but mainly for good – technology has permanently changed the way in which we may best serve our readers' needs: to quote the Iron Lady, the previous Prime Minister of the UK, now Lady Thatcher, 'There *is* no alternative!'

There is also a trend towards a change in the control of systems as end-users grow more familiar with them: if the user, whether academic or member of the public, can acquire hands-on experience of OPACs, the Internet and other search tools he will quickly become as expert in their use as the average librarian, who will be forced to redefine his function. Although the most forceful statement of this argument is found in Lor's chapter on document supply, it appears elsewhere too. But perhaps we do not need to adopt a Luddite attitude here: there are plenty of other areas where scarce staffing resources can be redeployed, and have we not been trying for many years to educate users in exactly such skills and make them more self-sufficient?

A new departure for *LIWW* this year is the inclusion of a group of three chapters on specific geographical areas; there is much here to interest the profession as a whole and to widen its horizons. The particular value of these chapters is that they cover a period of several years, and make available material which would otherwise remain behind a barrier of unfamiliar languages. Szántó, for example, recounts the changes arising in the USSR and Eastern European nations from the break up of their communist regimes: many of these have taken the form of scaling down previous generous library provision, but he concludes that this is not altogether a bad thing, since much of it was misapplied, being geared largely to social and political engineering. The fundamental philosophy of the profession in these countries has moved dramatically towards a position more akin to that of the West, and the present weakened structure of libraries in many of these countries will gradually grow stronger.

Hepworth and Cheng cover developments in Southeast Asia, a large and diverse area which is largely *terra incognita* in the West. It is a pleasant surprise to learn how much of interest and value has been achieved there, with (for example) networks and convergence between computing and librarianship following a rapidly-growing economic prosperity.

Finally, Vitiello provides a detached 'bird's-eye' view of the overall position of libraries in Western Europe: again there is discussion of the ownership access question, but the cultural divide (in library terms) between the northern and southern states is given some prominence. He sees this as the major obstacle facing those who wish to introduce 'harmonization' of libraries across the European Union.

Subject index

Note: Entries appear under separate countries and regions with the exception of the United Kingdom and the United States, for both of which the references are too numerous for page numbers.

AACR 160
ABINIA 38
academic libraries 99–120, 196–198, 242–244
  converged services 106–107
  implications of IT for 309–311
  in the UK 5, 100, 103, 106, 108, 109, 115, 196, 197, 323
  in the USA 6, 109–110, 114, 324, 331, 334, 336
  networking in 335–336
  see also Follett Report
access versus ownership 107–108, 111, 116, 265, 308
acquisition policies 22, 119, 144–145, 158, 265
ADONIS 280, 307
African countries 38, 60–61, 79–80, 86, 91, 110, 148, 273, 326–327
aid programmes 39–41, 148
Albania 80
Arab-speaking regions 272–273
Argentina 138
Ariel workstations 279
Asian countries 38–39, 46, 52–57, 233–252, 272
  see also Pacific region
Association for Computing Machinery (ACM) 8–9
audiovisual materials 27–28, 193
Australia 22, 32, 39, 40–41, 42, 46, 59, 77, 83, 84, 85, 87, 88–89, 90, 100, 105, 107, 108, 111–112, 116, 119, 135, 142, 148, 158, 161, 162, 164, 166, 169, 249, 267, 268, 272, 278, 322, 323, 325, 326, 331, 332, 337, 338
  see also distributed national collection
Austria 20–21, 29, 47
authority control 158–159, 170–171
automation, *see* information technology
Bahamas 140
Belgium 46, 47, 61, 196
bibliographic access projects 35–38
bibliographic control and access 157–177
bibliographic databases 167–168
blind persons, services for 48
book world:
  cooperation across 23, 112, 188, 236–237, 326
Bosnia-Herzegovina 39
Botswana 79, 271
Brazil 105
Brunei Darussalam 243, 244, 245, 246
buildings 31, 32–33, 83–84, 191–192, 242
  and design 336–337
  Bibliothèque Nationale de France 50–52, 192
  British Library 5, 48–50
Bulgaria 45, 205, 212
business information services 314
Cambodia 53

354 *Subject index*

campus-wide information service (CWIS) 107
Canada 22, 38, 42, 43, 46, 48, 61, 77, 83, 85, 86, 88, 89, 105, 110, 114, 116, 145; 158, 160, 164, 170, 268, 269, 270, 279, 312, 336
career development 329–330
Caribbean countries 271–272, 327
CARL systems 173, 277
CAS-IAS systems 266, 276–279
CASLIN project 221
catalogues and cataloguing 35–38, 145–146, 157–177
  authority control 158–159, 170–171
  automation of the process 169–170
  changes in practice 166–168
  retrospective conversion 47
  rules and rule interpretations 160–162
  special materials 162
  use of transaction logs 173
Catalonia 30, 165, 197
CD-ROMs 36, 44–45, 112, 219, 240, 262, 280–281, 300–301, 304–305, 306–307
  networking of 336
Central and Eastern Europe 24–26, 30, 34, 37, 45, 80–81, 134, 142, 145, 148, 167, 203–224, 330
  decline of libraries in 204–207
  interlending and document delivery in 270–271
  needs of minorities 215–217
  professional press in 223–224
charging for services 34, 82–83, 188–189, 195–196, 269, 326
Chile 110, 141, 272
China 39, 46, 56, 82, 88, 167, 236, 272
classification 163
collection development 144–145
collection evaluation 119
Commonwealth of Independent States (CIS) 205, 212
compact disc recordable (CD-R) 301
Computerized Bibliographic Record Actions group (CoBRA) 36–37
computing centres:
  relationship with libraries 3, 106–107, 310, 335
conservation, *see* preservation and conservation
consultants 322, 330
contracting out 87–88, 168, 325–326
convergence 3, 106–107, 310, 335

cooperation and resource sharing 20–23, 35–41, 35–37, 44, 109–111, 145, 158–159, 198–199, 235, 251, 279, 282, 327
  see also distributed national collection
copyright 9, 11, 34, 116, 198, 263, 283, 303–304
corporate intelligence 323
Croatia 47, 81
Cuba 81, 138, 272
cyberspace 335
cybrarian' 309
Czech Republic 25, 37, 44, 45, 47, 205, 207–208, 212–213, 218, 219, 220, 221, 335
Czechoslovakia 138, 323
Denmark 29, 32, 89, 119, 188, 190, 194, 199, 269, 331, 333
developing countries 7, 233–252, 324, 327
  access to information in 240–241, 263
  interlending and document delivery in 271–273, 280
  national libraries in 23–24
digitization of collections 42–44, 308
Directorate-General XIII 187, 198–199
disabled persons, services for 48
disaster planning 337
distributed national collection 22, 158, 265
document delivery, *see* document supply
document image processing 115, 264
document supply 35, 42, 113–114, 259–285
  definition 260–262
  electronic 274–283
  impact of information technology 262–264
  in the UK 267, 270, 277–278, 279, 281, 283, 284
  in the USA 267, 269, 270, 277–282
  pre-electronic 266–273, 276
Eastern Europe, *see* Central and Eastern Europe
education and training 4–5, 91, 118, 249–250, 330–331
  in the USA 5
  library schools 220
Egypt 86, 119
electronic document delivery systems 276, 279
  see also document supply
electronic journals 104, 175
Electronic Libraries, Impact on People of 105

Subject index 355

Electronic Library Project (ELINOR) 115
electronic publishing 8–10, 27–28, 111–112, 113, 174–175, 263–264, 311
electronic table of contents (ETOCs) 277
ELINOR project 307–308
Elsevier 9–10
encryption 303
Estonia 25, 33, 45, 80
ETOCs 277
European Union:
access to information about 82
European-wide cooperation 35–37, 44, 145, 198–199, 279, 282, 308
expert systems 169
Experts, International Commission of 40
fiction, subject access to 162
Fiji 58
filtered information services 305
financial planning and management 325–327
Finland 21, 45, 89, 141, 334
Follett Report 11–12, 100, 109, 115, 323
France 27, 28, 34, 43, 50–52, 101, 109, 118, 119, 188, 190, 192, 193, 194, 197, 199, 267, 322, 325, 333
Freenets 312
fund-raising 34, 326
Georgia 212
Germany 32, 86, 87, 101–102, 105, 118, 137, 138, 139, 141, 145, 147, 159, 188, 190, 194, 199, 270, 281–282, 325
Ghana 102, 110
Gopher 176, 310
government publications 168
Greece 46, 165, 199
grey literature 37
Gypsies 217
Hong Kong 56, 140
humanities:
machine-readable texts in 175
use of networks 7
Hungarian minorities 215–216
Hungary 25, 28, 30–31, 45, 80, 119, 138, 141, 206, 208–209, 214, 218, 219–220, 221, 223, 271, 324
hypertext 176–177, 219, 264, 302
imaging 115, 264
IMPEL project 105
India 21, 55, 78, 139, 141, 272, 324, 325
Indonesia 53, 239, 243, 244, 245, 247, 249–250

information superhighway 302
information technology 1–2, 41–47, 88–90, 147–148, 169–170, 217–220, 246–249, 299–315
and the information industry 303–305
effect on design of buildings 336–337
impact on document supply 262–264
implications for libraries 305–314
in Eastern Europe 45
in the UK 302, 307, 308, 309–310, 311, 312
in the USA 302, 303, 305, 306, 307, 309, 310, 311–312
management issues 334–336
'infornomics' 222–223
intellectual property rights 84
see also copyright
interlending 266–270
see also document supply
Interlending Open Systems Network (Project ION) 115
Internet 42, 44, 89, 105–106, 113, 118, 173–174, 249, 262–264, 301–303
addresses 41
billing service 11
impact on cataloguers 157
ION, see Project ION
Ireland 194
Italy 194, 199
JANET 197, 309
Japan 20, 33, 39, 48, 78, 142, 167, 272, 309, 325, 327, 329
job-sharing 330
joint-use services 19–21, 141–142, 327
journal articles 266, 276–279
journal articles, online 10
journals 107–108, 223–224
jukebox systems 42
'just in case' or 'just in time', see access versus ownership
Kiribati 23
Korea 57, 272
language and terminology 164–166
handling of scripts 46, 164–165
Laos 53–54, 239
Latin American countries 44, 134, 135, 138, 167
Latvia 45, 80, 84, 142, 165
LCRIs 161
LCSH 162
leadership qualities 331–332

legal deposit 26–29, 31, 212, 213
legislation 24–26, 84–85, 209–210
Lenin Library 211
librarians, changing role of 103–105, 117–118, 311, 313–315, 322–323
Library of Congress rule interpretations (LCRIs) 161
Library of Congress subject headings (LCSH) 163
Lithuania 25, 80, 142
Malawi 80
Malaysia 54, 120, 235, 238–239, 241, 242, 243–244, 245, 247, 248, 250, 336
Maldives, The 55
management 29–30, 86–88, 251, 321–338
management information systems 332
maps 47
MARC conversion procedures 36–37
mark-up language 8
marketing 87, 322, 338
medical information services 280, 281, 307
Memory of the World programme 37, 44
Mexico 138, 272
Minnauki concept 211–212
minorities, needs of 215–217, 238, 241
Miquel Report 101
Morocco 271
Mosaic 2, 300, 302, 310
Myanmar 239–240, 244, 249, 250
nation states, decline of 18
national bibliographies 23, 168, 192
national information policies 187–189, 237–240
national libraries 15–62, 211–212, 237–240, 242
  in the USA 20, 43
  joint-use services 19–21
  link with parliamentary libraries 142–143
  regional groupings 38–39
  role of 16–24, 191–193
  use of information technology 41–47
Netherlands 20, 30, 32, 44, 79, 85, 103, 115, 191, 194, 196, 199, 267, 270, 278, 279, 281, 282, 283, 307, 310, 324, 328, 329, 333, 334
networking 21–24, 103, 189–191, 197–198, 267–268, 301–303, 335–336
  and document supply 42
  benefits for libraries 305–309
  in public libraries 311–312
New Zealand 22, 23, 24, 32, 39, 46, 59, 79, 87, 90, 114, 142, 158, 161, 165, 270, 333–334, 337
Nicaragua 40
Nigeria 23, 24, 81, 112, 119, 273
Niue 23
Nordic countries 84, 102, 110, 119, 270, 279, 333
Norway 20, 27, 30, 32, 89, 119
OCLC FirstSearch service 281
online databases 304–305
online information, citing of 3–4
OPACs 157, 159–160, 171–173, 305–306, 336
optical discs 301
outsourcing 87–88, 168, 325–326
ownership, see access versus ownership
Pacific region 23, 38–39, 57–59, 148, 272
Pakistan 55
Papua New Guinea 23
para-national libraries 211
parliamentary libraries 133–149
  categories of 139–143
  clientele 143
  in the UK 135, 137, 139, 140–141, 148
  in the USA 136, 139, 141–142, 145
  joint-use services 141–142
  oversight committees 136–137
  research services in 140–141, 142
performance measurement and evaluation 87, 118–119, 332–334
PHARE project 220
Philippines 241, 243, 248, 250, 251
PICA (Project for Integrated Catalogue Automation) 191, 267, 278
Poland 45, 80, 88, 102, 108, 138, 141, 206, 208, 213, 221, 327
Polish minorities 215, 216
Portugal 139, 188
preprints 9
preservation and conservation 6–7, 39, 251–252
Project ION 197–198, 267
ProQuest Power Pages 280
protocols, see standards and protocols
Public Lending Right (UK) 84
public libraries 77–92, 193–196, 212, 241–242, 322–323
  implications of IT for 311–312
  in the UK 322–323, 325, 333, 338
  in the USA 322, 338
  strategic planning and programme budgeting 324

Subject index 357

UNESCO Public Library Manifesto 78, 195
public relations 338
publishing industry 113, 266
 in Central and Eastern Europe 223–224
 relationship with libraries 107–108, 236–237
 see also electronic publishing
quality management 87, 118–120, 332–334
 see also total quality management
quasi-national libraries 19–21
Quebec 61
Red Sage project 281, 283
reference services 117–118, 146–147
remote users 313–314
research (LIS) 3, 10, 12, 50
research and development 10–12
 role of national libraries 19
research services
 in parliamentary libraries 140–141, 142
resource sharing, *see* cooperation and resource sharing
retrospective conversion 47
Romania 40, 217
Russia 17, 25–26, 33, 39, 40, 45, 46, 61, 90, 138, 148, 204–205, 209, 210–212, 217, 218–219, 220, 222–223, 271, 330
Russian State Library 211, 212
Ruthenians 215
Saudi Arabia 61, 78, 272, 336
Scandinavia, *see* Nordic countries
scholarly communication, changes in 107–108, 113, 174–175, 265–266, 311
school libraries 244–245
schools of librarianship 220
Scotland 79, 190, 324
scripts, handling of 46, 164–165
Senegal 119
serials 107–108, 223–224
Singapore 45, 46, 54, 234, 235, 237–238, 242, 243, 245, 246, 247, 248, 250, 251, 323
Slovak minorities 216
Slovakia 45, 47, 84–85, 206–208, 214–215, 218, 220, 221, 325
Slovenia 34
'socionomics' 222
SOD (search, order and deliver) 261
Solomon Islands 58, 140
South Africa 32, 60–61, 79, 81, 110, 119, 273, 278, 326, 333, 337

Southeast Asia, *see* Asian countries
Soviet Union 138
Spain 28, 30, 43, 61, 139, 141, 146, 148, 165, 188, 190, 197
special collections 47
special libraries 245–246, 336
 see also parliamentary libraries
special needs, services for 48
staff organization and structure 328–332
standards and protocols 176–177, 306
strategic planning 31–32, 49–50, 322, 323–324
Subject access 162–163
subscription agents 266, 278
Swaziland 84
Sweden 21, 28, 40, 61, 84, 110, 114, 269, 325
Switzerland 21, 26, 30, 46, 190, 322
systems librarians 314
Taiwan 39, 57
TEMPUS programme 220–221
Thailand 54–55, 241–242, 244, 245, 248, 250, 251
thesauri 145–146, 158, 162–163, 171
Third World, *see* developing countries
total quality management 91, 119
training, *see* education and training
transaction logs 173
TULIP project 9, 281, 283
Turkey 324
Tuvalu 23
UAP (Universal Availability of Publications) 268
Ukraine 212
UnCover 277–278, 283, 307
UNESCO Public Library Manifesto 78, 195
Unicode 164
UNIMARC 36–37
Universal Availability of Publications (UAP) 268
universal resource locators (URLs) 4
university libraries, *see* academic libraries
Uralica database 166
user education 240
user needs and evaluation 78–80, 90, 172, 240–241, 313–314
Venezuela 81–82
videotex 300
Vietnam 38, 55, 234, 251
virtual library 21, 42–44, 102–103, 116, 175, 308–309, 335
 cataloguing tools 176–177

volunteer workers 330
Wales 32, 46, 47, 282
WebCrawler 177
women, discrimination against 328
women in development 241
workstations 282

World Wide Web 2–3, 10, 41, 176–177, 301–302, 310, 311
Yugoslavia 81
Z39.50 176, 306
Zambia 273
Zimbabwe 61, 273

Author index

Abbas, H.A. 78
Abbott, C. 333
Abdullah Yaacob 250
Abelsnes, K. 263, 273
Abid, A. 78, 262
Abraham, A. 55
Abraham, J. 325
Adamiec, W. 208
Adams, R. 263, 282
Adeniran, O.R. 112
Agenjo, X. 45
Ahmad Sarji Abdul Hamid 239
Aho, M. 166
Aiken, M. 332
Aken, G. van 329
Akeroyd, J. 100
Akhtar, A.H. 56
Alan, R. 169
Alderson, K. 77
Alemna, A. 327
Alexander, A.W. 265, 266
Alexanderson, B. 134
Ali bin Haji Kayum 244
Aliprand, J.M. 164
Allen, K. 309
Allen, L. 159, 172
Alley, B. 168
Alston, R. 303, 305, 306, 313
Altuna, B. 165
Amanah Ahmad 250
Anaprayot, P. 246
Ancillani, G. 189
Andersen, A. 263, 270, 282
Anderson, M. 310, 311

Andrassy, L. 216
André, P.Q.J. 40, 43
Andreeva, I. 138, 148
Angeles, B.B. 243
Anker, P.M. 269
Antonsson, B. 16, 40, 62
Antopol'skiĭ, A.B. 218
Anuar, H. 236
Anyanwu, V. 23
Archer, E. 337
Arlante, S.M. 251
Armarego, J. 169
Arms, W.Y. 8, 10
Arnold, K. 103, 115
Arnóth, K. 221
Arnoult, J.-M. 37
Árosy, A.L. 220
Artamonov, G.T. 222
Arunachalam, S. 271
Ashcroft, M.A. 77
Ashley, C. 105
Asser, M. 324
Astbury, R. 312, 313
Attia, R. 60
Audunson, R. 78, 86
Azhari bin Haji Suhaimi 246
Azizah Sidek 241
Bagnall, C. 330
Baker, D. 115
Bakonyi, P. 214
Balaam, A. 172
Balik, V. 37
Ballance, V. 46
Ballard, T. 173, 336

Bandyopadhyay, R. 162
Bannenberg, N. 137
Barber, D. 311
Barbier-Wiesser, F.-G. 134, 148
Barbuto, B.M. 117
Barden, P. 264, 282
Barker, P. 305
Barnes, J. 262
Barnes, S. 263, 264, 281
Barnes, S.J. 175
Baron, D. 79, 90
Barraclough, C. 337
Barral, S. 101
Barreau, J.-C. 188
Barrie, A. 165
Barry, A. 107
Barry, J. 176, 314
Barry, R.E. 302, 309
Bartenbach, B. 262, 264, 282
Barua, B.P. 21, 55
Barwick, M. 114
Barwick, M.M. 260, 265, 267, 268, 269, 270, 277
Bates, I. 270
Bates, M.E. 309
Bátonyi, V. 349
Batt, C. 89, 90
Bauermeister, O. 31
Bauwens, M. 114, 277, 335
Bays, D. 48, 269
Beall, J. 162
Bearman, D. 7
Beaudiquez, M. 52

Author index

Beaumont, J. 22, 270
Beckerman, E. 88, 322
Beger, G. 325
Begum, R. 247
Behrens, S.J. 261
Bell, A. 330
Bell, D. 222, 299
Bell, H.K. 103
Bennett, V.M. 279
Bennion, B.C. 108
Beriault, J.-E. 38
Berners-Lee, T.J. 2
Berry, J.N. 34
Bertrand, A.-M. 188
Best, J.J. 158
Betancourt Valverde, V. 38
Bevan, N. 112, 300, 304, 306, 310, 313, 314
Bicknell, T. 118
Biddiscombe, R. 107
Bierbaum, E.G. 160
Biliński, L. 213
Billings, H. 307
Birdsall, D.G. 323
Bisbrouck, M.-F. 101
Biszak, S. 219
Bjarnø, H. 269, 334
Bjornshauge, L. 103
Blagden, J. 104, 266, 281, 283, 308, 337
Blake, P. 42
Błońska, L. 221
Blumendorf, P. 221
Blunden-Ellis, J. 109, 309, 311
Boissé, J.A. 268
Bokos, G. 46
Bolos, A.M. 17, 241
Bonsing-Wils, H. 333
Booker, D. 83
Boonyakanchana, C. 241
Born, K. 108
Borodin, O.R. 17, 26
Borsman, M.L. 278
Boss, R.W. 159
Boudet, I. 52
Bouri, E.N. 86
Bourke, L. 162
Bourne, R. 23, 168
Bouthillier, F. 325
Bowker, R.R. 20

Boykin, J.F. 261, 263, 266, 277
Bradbury, D. 32, 268, 269
Braid, A. 114
Braid, J.A. 42
Brandreth, M. 114, 115, 263, 264, 279, 283, 336
Branin, J.J. 107
Brault, J.-R. 17, 18–19
Bridges, K. 310
Brindley, L.J. 100
Bringedal, T. 89
Broadbent, V. 270
Broady, J. 101
Broeren, J. 329
Broering, N.C. 281
Brooks, R. 88
Brophy, P. 87, 104, 106, 111, 300, 308, 309, 310, 313
Brown, C.C. 119
Brown, D. 325
Brown, J.D. 118
Brown, J.M. 174
Brown, S. 325
Brożek, A. 219
Bryant, E. 262, 265
Bryant, M.N. 138
Buckland, M.K. 172
Buckle, D. 262, 312
Budd, J.M. 108, 109, 111, 265, 303, 309
Bulavas, V. 25
Bundy, A. 77, 83, 88
Bunting, A. 266
Burakowski, J. 206
Burch, B. 267
Burgetová, J. 205, 213
Burlingame, D.F. 326
Burrow, D. 6
Burrows, T. 174
Burton, P.A. 172
Burton, P.F. 299, 308
Butcher, R. 46, 49
Butler, M.A. 331
Butrimenko, A. 218
Butter, K.A. 104, 281
Butterworth, M. 240, 250, 251
Byrum, J.D. 263
Cabral, A. 147
Cain, J. 164

Callahan, D. 166
Calvert, P.J. 87, 333, 334
Camden, B.P. 166
Campbell, D.K. 301
Campbell, J.D. 325
Campbell, R. 100
Caplan, P. 172, 174, 263
Carbone, P. 101, 109
Carlin, J. 86
Carmichael, J.V. 328
Caro, C. 38
Carrigan, D.P. 270, 277, 278
Casale, M. 88, 112
Case, D.O. 300
Catan, R. 338
Cathro, W. 158
Catlin, I. 84, 322
Cavanagh, A.K. 100
Cawkell, A.E. 274
Čejpek, J. 221, 222
Çelik, H. 137, 146, 148
Cevallos, E.E. 117
Chadbourne, R. 337
Champo, D. 273
Chan, D.F.C. 240, 246
Chan, Y.-S. 24
Chand, P. 272
Chandler, G. 187
Chauveinc, M. 101
Cherhal, E. 105
Chernyĭ, A.I. 212
Cherry, J.M. 160, 336
Chevallier, A. 28
Chifwepa, V. 273
Childers, T.A. 87, 322
Chintawong, W. 244
Chisanga, C.J.J. 273
Chkhenkeli, T.I. 212
Chollampe, K. 246
Chong, K.Y. 236
Chrzastowski, E. 326
Chu, J. 88
Chudá, S. 221
Clausen, H. 333
Clayden, J. 166
Clayton, C. 87
Cleese, J. 85, 92
Clements, R. 135
Cleveland, G. 262, 271
Cloyes, K. 308
Clyde, A. 335

Author index

Cochrane, T. 107, 262, 263, 265
Cockrill, A. 101
Cockshaw, P. 62
Coetzee, J.A. 273
Cohen, E. 337
Cohn, C. 262, 267
Coleman, R. 263
Conkling, T.W. 112
Connor, D. 82
Cook, B. 107
Cooper, J.L. 166
Cooper, J.M. 326
Cooper, W. 103
Coote, H. 322
Corey, J.F. 176, 306
Corn, M. 42
Cornish, G. 19, 22, 28, 193, 218, 261, 263, 268, 269, 271, 273, 303, 305
Corrall, S. 322
Cortez, E. 335
Costers, L. 263, 265, 266, 267, 278, 279, 282
Cother, C. 269
Cotta-Schønberg, M. 102, 119, 269, 333
Cottam, K.M. 86
Cotton, R. 330
Courage, M.A. 218
Cousins, S.A. 164
Cox, J.E. 266
Cox, N. 269
Craig, J. 49
Cram, J. 332
Crawford, G.A. 119
Crawford, W. 160, 174
Cressent, J.-P. 119
Creth, S.D. 104, 105, 106, 335
Cromer, D.E. 118
Cronin, M.J. 314
Crook, A. 22
Cross, N. 234
Crouch, M.C. 326
Cullen, R.J. 333
Curry, A. 83, 86, 89
Curry, D.A. 328
Czajka, S. 80
Czajkowski, Fr. 221
Czene, G. 215

Dahlø, R. 27, 30
Daines, G. 79, 85
Dallman, D. 264
Danilenko, G. 326
Dan'shina, I.V. 215
Davies, D.G. 313
Davis, R. 81
Day, A. 48
Day, R. 262
De Beer, J. 15, 16
De Beer, J.F. 273
Debnath, S. 139
Dedrick, A.J. 110, 327
Deiss, K. 269
de Jager, K. 119
del Sol, P. 110
Delano, M. 137, 141
Demeshko, L. 215
Dempsey, L. 306
Denehy, C.C. 162
Denise, O.H. 100
Deschamps, C. 267
DeVinney, G. 313
Dewey, B.I. 325
Dianskaya, G.P. 221
Diaz, K.R. 118
Dickey, W. 336
Dickson, L.K. 119
Dijkstra, J. 115, 264, 274, 307
Ditzler, C. 43
Dixon, R. 264, 307
Dobrowolski, Z. 219
Doctor, R. 312
Dokmeci, V. 324
Dolan, M. 82
Dolby, E. 267, 269
Dommen, A.J. 234
Donaldson, E. 86
Donovan, B. 111
Dorner, J. 263
Dorsch, J.L. 42
Doust, R.W. 273
Drabenstott, K.M. 172
Drake, P. 337
Du Prez, I. 38
Duchemin, P.-Y. 51
Duckett, B. 172
Dudik, J. 218
Dudzińska, E. 221, 327
Duijf, A. 330

Duke, J.K. 160
Dumont, M. 333
Dunn, J.A. 325
Dunsire, G. 117, 169, 263
Durniak, B.A. 116, 266, 269
Dusoulier, N. 104
Dworaczek, M. 104
Dyer, H. 336
Dyk, F. van 326
Dzherelievskaya, I.K. 220
Easun, S. 334
Ede, S. 49
Edwards, C. 105, 110
Edwards, H.M. 273
Eeden, E. van 278
Eenmaa, I. 25, 142
Eichert, C. 86
Eide, E. 20
Ekoja, I.I. 119
El Hadidy, B. 299, 306
Elliot, J. 168
Elliott, J. 263
Elliott, V. 111, 114
Ellis, A. 116, 266, 282
Els, B. 273
Emerek, L. 78
England, L. 79
Englefield, D. 134, 135, 139
Ensor, P. 171
Enssle, H.R. 263, 281
Eronina, E.A. 271
Ershova, T.V. 28
Ertel, M. 164
Esin, J.O. 107
Etheredge, L.S. 21
Everest, A. 42
Everett, V. 305
Eversberg, B. 159
Fagerli, H.M. 27
Fakudze, Q.N. 84
Farrell, J.M. 20
Fawcett, V. 328
Feather, J. 91
Feistner, J. 218
Feliu, X. 137, 141
Ferguson, S. 263, 272
Ferl, T. 173
Fernández de Zamora, R.M. 138
Fernández Mera, M.V. 146
Ferreira, S.M.S.P. 105

Fialkoff, F. 20, 83
Fieldhouse, M. 306
Filippov, I.S. 62
Fine, S. 313
Fisher, S. 332
Fisher, S.R. 104, 105
Fjällbrant, N. 279
Flagg, G. 77, 337
Flanders, B. 264
Fleet, C. 47
Floistad, B. 146
Flowers, K. 329
Fonotov, G. 220
Ford, J. 104, 266, 281, 283, 308
Forget, L. 38
Fouché, B. 262
Fourie, J.A. 79
Fox, B.L. 83
Fraisse, E. 118
Frank, R. 220
Franz, L. 163
Freedland, J. 86
Friend, F.J. 115, 270, 279
Friend, L. 310
Fry, H. 110
Fuchs, H. 260, 269, 273
Fuegi, D. 90, 334
Fülöp, G. 221
Fülöp, M. 216
Fuseler, E.A. 114
Gajtkó, É. 214
Gallimore, A. 82
Gani, F. 53, 239
García de la Oliva, A. 139
Gardner, N. 104, 106
Gardner, S. 262
Garnes, K. 119
Garrison, W.V. 336
Garten, E.D. 322
Gartner, R. 106
Gassaway, L.N. 261, 283
Gasson, C. 113, 262
Gattégno, J. 195
Gavrilenko, N. 138
Geist, P. 328
Geleijnse, H. 103, 264, 281, 307
Gertzog, A. 88, 322
Gibbs, M. 264
Giese, D. 32, 264

Gil i Albert, T. 139
Gils, W. van 265, 282
Gilyarevskii, R.S. 219
Ginsburg, C.L. 309
Girón, A. 30
Glaubitz, M. 329
Glavash, K. 280
Glogoff, S. 308, 311, 313
Glover, H. 104, 105
Gobel, R. 244
Goldsmid, I. 218
Gomba, Sz. 220
Goncharov, M.V. 271
González Dubon de Pazos, I. 139
Gonzalo, M. 141
Gonzalo, M.A. 145
Goodacre, C. 105, 261, 278
Goossens, P. 44
Gore, D. 265
Gorfunkel, A. 46
Gorman, M. 160, 175
Gould, S. 269
Goulding, A. 90, 91
Grachev, V.I. 222
Graham, G. 107
Graham, M.E. 309
Granheim, E. 84
Grant, S.L. 280
Grau, R.M. 145
Greeff, R. 263
Green, B. 30
Green, D. 21
Greene, R. 263, 271
Greenwood, D. 49
Greig, E. 165
Grenier, J. 91
Griebel, R. 102, 262, 263, 265, 267
Griffith, J.B. 299, 302
Griffiths, J.-M. 21, 335
Grimshaw, A. 264, 308
Grootaers, C. 103
Grotenhuis, A.J. ter 326
Guangjun, M. 272
Guaysuwan, P. 251
Gudauskas, R. 80
Guilhaud, D. 80
Gunton, D. 81
Gupta, C.P. 139
Habeeb, H.H. 56

Hafkin, N.J. 263
Hafner, A.W. 88
Hagenbruch, H. 42
Hahn, G. 137, 138, 139, 141, 146, 147
Hall, C. 85
Hallam, M. 83, 326
Hanakova, J. 224
Hancock-Beaulieu, M. 306
Hanfman, D.T. 31
Hanson, T. 112
Hardjoprakoso, M. 53, 239, 241
Hariyadi, U. 53, 239
Harloe, B. 108, 109, 111, 265, 303, 309
Harnesk, J. 102
Harris, C. 100
Harrold, A. 328
Harry, V. 112
Hartley, R.J. 164
Hatfield, D. 330
Hawkins, A.M. 172
Hawkins, B.L. 103
Hawkins, D.T. 302, 304
Hawks, C.P. 169
Hay, S. 176
Hayes, S. 325
Haynes, K.J.M. 168
Head, J.W. 335
Heavner, P.F. 144
Hébert, H.F. 269
Heijnekamp, S.J. 326
Heinitz, C. 85, 323
Helal, A.H. 327
Hemola, H. 213, 221
Henchy, J. 234, 251
Hendrikz, F. 15, 16, 273
Hendry, I. 307
Henry, C. 302
Hensley, O.D. 323
Henty, M. 22, 265, 268
Hepworth, M. 251
Hernández, F. 45
Hernandez, M.N. 328
Heseltine, R. 103, 104, 114
Hicks, J. 84
Hildenbrand, S. 80
Hildreth, C. 189
Hoadley, I.B. 314, 326, 332
Hodossy, D. 215

Author index

Hoeks, M. 329
Hoffmann, H. 161
Hogue, E.M. 330
Hojsgaard, U. 190
Holley, R.P. 162
Holm, L.A. 269
Holt, L. 146
Holzberg, C.S. 304
Honig-Bear, S. 327
Hoogcarspel, A. 175
Hopkins, L. 85
Horton, W. 39
Horvát, Á. 220
Horváth, T. 220, 221
House, N.A.V. 322
Howard, M. 301
Howley, L. 168
Howorka, B. 210, 213
Hrabinska, T. 221
Hsu, M. 301
Hugenholtz, B. 198
Hugenholtz, P.B. 114, 261, 262, 265, 283
Hughill, B. 77, 79
Hulshoff, M.-A. 329
Hulsing-Ronteltap, R. 270, 278, 282
Hunt, C.J. 99, 100, 119
Hunter, K. 9, 113, 281
Huszár, E. 219, 221
Huthwaite, A. 161, 173
Ibrahim, B.A. 272
Ifidon, B.I. 119
Intner, S.S. 166, 168
Ishizuka, E. 20
Iwasawa, S. 39
Jackson, K.M. 314
Jackson, M.E. 261, 267, 269, 270, 278
Jacobson, S. 331
Jacquesson, A. 189, 190
Jajko, P. 335
Jamaiah Osman 245
James, S. 172
Jamet, D. 50
Janes, J.W. 173
Janostikova, B. 330
Jarvis, H. 53, 55, 234
Jasdon, A. 331
Jaudenes Casaubon, M. 166
Jauslin, J.F. 26, 30, 31

Jazdon, A. 102, 108
Jeng, L.H. 169
Jeremiah, D. 46
Jerrey, R. 336
Johannsen, C.G. 333
John, N. 148
Johnson, C. 337
Johnson, F.E. 42
Johnson, H. 323
Johnson, P. 175
Johnson, R. 307
Johnston, R. 337
Jones, D. 337
Jones, L. 326
Jordan, T. 89
Judge, P. 119
Kacena, C. 108, 325
Kadir, M.A. 38
Kahin, B. 175
Kahl, S.C. 272
Kalinová, V. 207, 215, 221, 325
Kan, L.-B. 57
Kanakamani, T. 242
Kanamugire, A.B. 262, 272, 336
Kaneko, H. 165
Karbach, E. 206
Karmazin, S. 338
Kartus, E. 169
Karvalics, L. 210
Katuščák, D. 215
Kaufman, P.T. 332
Keates, S. 271
Kedrovskiĭ, G.V. 204, 210
Kelly, P. 111
Kemp, G. 273
Kemp, I. 119
Kendrick, C.L. 267, 282
Kenjo, T. 33
Kent, P.G. 265, 281
Kertész, A. 220
Kertis, K. 335
Kesselman, M. 330
Kessler, J. 52
Ketcham, L. 108
Keylard, M. 262
Khalil, M.A. 262
Khoo, C.S.C. 169
Khoo, S.M. 241
Kiang-Koh, L.L. 240

Kibirige, H.M. 262
Kiegel, J. 169
Kinder, R. 89
Kingma, B.R. 266, 269
Kinnell, M. 87, 119, 338
Kinnucan, M.T. 116, 266, 269
Kinsey, S. 327
Kirkus-Lamont, J. 22
Kisiedu, C.O. 110
Kiss, J. 216
Kitt, S. 104, 106
Klazen, M. 329
Klinec, P. 84
Klyuev, V.K. 220
Knoll, A. 37
Knuth, R. 327
Kock, T. 105
Koepp, D. 103
Kofoed, P. 104
Koh, B.S. 242
Kohl, D.F. 158
Kohl, E. 133, 134, 135, 136, 139, 140, 143, 144, 145, 146, 148
Kokas, K. 219
Kolodziejska, J. 79, 88
Koltay, T. 219
Komov, V.V. 271
Koopman, A. 176
Korca, P. 324
Kordon, D. 148
Korsah, J.E. 102
Kovač, M.A. 16
Kovács, D.K. 221
Krarup, K. 29, 32, 331
Krbec, P. 335
Kreslins, K. 165
Kronenfeld, M. 168
Krotyuk, N. 215
Kruger, J.A. 79
Ku, K.M. 147
Kuik, K. 329
Kulikovski, L. 216
Kulisiewicz, W. 141
Kumar, S.R. 272
Kurosman, K. 116, 266, 269
Kuz'min, E. 90, 204, 209
Kuzmińska, Kr. 206, 213
Lacroix, E.-M. 40, 42, 267, 281, 282

Ladizesky, K. 49
Ladosné Varjú, I. 208, 324
LaGuardia, C. 313
Lai, Y.P. 247
Lamadrid Sauza, J.L. 135
Lamaro, E. 146
Lambert, J. 112, 304, 306, 309, 313
lamolinara, G. 264
Lancaster, F.W. 172
Landwirth, T.K. 42
Lane, G. 333
Lang, B. 37, 49
Langenberg, D.N. 106
Lanier, D. 106, 174
Lapelerie, F. 118
Larkin, G. 337
Larsen, R.L. 103, 109
Larson, C.A. 119
Lary, M. 174
Launo, R. 21
Law, D. 100, 109, 112, 113, 197
Lawes, A. 326
Layland, P. 46, 263, 265, 267, 278
Layzell Ward, P. 322
Leach, A. 79
Leach, R.G. 278
LeBlanc, J.D. 166
Lee, C.-F. 57
Lee, C.C. 24
Lee, P. 57
Lehmann, K.-D. 32, 34, 37
Lengyel, M. 219
Lenn, K. 337
Leonard, B.G. 108
Leonard, W.P. 104, 116
Lesher, M. 108
Lesk, M.E. 10
Lester, D. 173, 176
Lett, B. 330
Levey, L.A. 262
Levine, L. 266
Lewis, D. 6
Lewis, D.W. 117
Liahut Baldomar, D.M. 138
Liddle, D. 324
Lim, A.E. 247
Lim, K.C. 247
Lim, L.U.W. 236

Lim, P. 236
Lind, A.L. 334
Lindley, J.A. 144, 146, 147
Line, M.B. 16, 17, 18, 24, 31, 41, 99, 100, 115, 119, 193, 261, 263, 265, 267, 268, 269, 271, 333
Lipow, A.G. 117
Lippman, M.J. 262
Little, K. 162
Liu, E.F. 58
Lloyd, K. 167
Lock, G. 136, 141
López Alsina, M. 141
Lor, P.J. 61, 273
Lovas, I. 42, 267
Lovecy, I. 106
Luckham, B. 79
Luijendijk, W. 265, 266, 277
Lukáts, J. 215
Lunau, C. 22, 270
Lund, K. 331
Lyall, J. 251
Lyon, J. 99, 100, 107
Maben, M. 162
McCallum, S. 164
McCarthy, P. 108
McCleary, H. 305
McClellan, D. 172
McClure, C.R. 89
McCombs, G.M. 174
McCook, K. de la P. 328
McCoy, P.S. 173
McCune, B. 311
McCune, B.F. 330
McCurley, H.H. 171
McDermott, E. 328
MacDonald, A.H. 104
McDonald, D.R. 109
McDonald, J.A. 334
McDonald, T. 90
MacDougall, J. 87, 338
McGinn, H.F. 326
McGowan, I.D. 37
Machovec, G.S. 114, 270
Macia, M. 148
MacKeigan, C. 114, 115, 263, 264, 279, 283, 336
McLaughlin, P.W. 118
MacLean, H. 148
McLean, N. 262

MacLeod, J. 166, 167
McMillan, G. 104
McNulty, T. 48
McPherson, M. 111
McRobbie, S. 113
McSean, A. 112
McVey, E.M. 31
McVicar, M. 85, 324
Mah, C.K. 245
Maj, J. 80
Malamud, J. 266, 277
Malhotra, G.C. 139, 141
Malley, I. 49
Mamah, Z. 60
Mansell, R. 335
Marchant, M. 79
Mariah Haji Kamis 245
Mariam Abdul Kadir 251
Mark, N. 260, 269, 273
Marker, R.J. 160
Marks, L. 87
Marle, G.A.J.S. van 263
Marte, H. 21
Martin, H.S. 267, 282
Martin, M.S. 325, 326
Martín González, A. 141
Martos, B. 221
Mascapac, G.A. 248
Mason, M.G. 20
Mason, T. 34
Massisimo, A. 190
Massuard, A. 34
Matheson, A. 22
Matoušová, M. 207, 218
Matsuik, I. 329
Mauch, J. 262
Mayol, C. 190
Meadows, A.J. 50
Meer, J.M. van der 263
Mellendorf, S.A. 310
Melling, G. 337
Melot, M. 51
Mendes, H.R. 102
Metcalfe, M. 105
Mezynski, A. 141
Miah, A.J. 269
Micco, M. 163, 169
Michaels Valderrama, D. 139
Michalowski, J. 137, 141
Michold, U. 105

Micikas, L.B. 334
Mickos, E. 279
Midwinter, A. 85, 324
Miller, J. 268
Miller, J.P. 336
Millsap, L. 173
Milne, J.R. 264
Milner, E. 87, 332
Minns, A. 81
Miquel, A. 101
Mitchell, E.S. 119
Mitchell, P.R. 269
Mittermeyer, D. 86
Miyashiro, N. 48
Moahi, K.H. 79
Mohd Sharif Mohd Saad 250, 251
Mohor, J. 220
Mohr, D.A. 167
Molchanova, O.P. 219
Moline, S. 114
Molinelli, N.G. 134, 138
Monau, R.M. 79
Montero, C.L. 62
Mood, T.A. 117
Mookerjee, B.P. 162
Moores, B. 332
Morales Campos, E. 263, 272
Morgan, E.L. 176, 302, 308, 310
Mori, A. 309
Morris, W. 280, 282
Motais de Narbonne, A.-M. 109
Mountifield, H.M. 263
Mowat, I. 39
Mowat, I.R.M. 113
Muffett, D.J.M. 85
Muirhead, G.A. 314
Mulliner, K. 249
Munasque, N.V. 38
Munkoe, L. 86
Muns, R.C. 176
Muranivskiĭ, T.V. 222
Murtomaa, E. 164, 165
Myers, J. 77
Myers, J.E. 175
Mylik, M. 221
Myllys, H. 325
Nadeau, M. 302, 304

Nassimbeni, M. 61
Naun, C.C. 158
Navalani, K. 324
Nawrocka, E. 141
Naylor, B. 111
Neelameghan, A. 163
Nellie Dato Paduka Haji Sunny 244, 245
Nelson, C.O. 83
Nelson, M. 34
Neo, B.S. 234, 237
Nera, C.M. 242
Ng, K.K. 240
Ngian, L.C. 240, 251
Nguyen, P.T. 234, 237, 239
Nicholas, D. 326
Nicholas, M. 161
Nicklin, J.L. 110
Nieboer, M. 328
Niegaard, H. 78
Nielsen, E.K. 17
Niessen, J.P. 313
Nilsson, K. 21, 114, 269, 270
Nishino, K. 270
Nisonger, T.E. 119
Nissley, M.J. 263, 281
Nofsinger, M.M. 117
Norbie, D. 309, 314
Norgard, B.A. 159
Norma Abu Seman 250, 251
Norman, S. 263, 303
Notess, G.R. 41
Novak, J. 325
Nováková, M. 220
Nugent, A. 41
Nuhu, A. 81
Núñes-Fina, L. 272
Nurminen, T. 326
Nyirenda, B.T. 263
Obenaus, G. 105
Obra Sierra, S. 139
O'Brien, L. 105
Oda, M. 87
Oddy, P. 160, 175
O'Donoghue, M. 336
O'Donovan, K. 106
Oh, D. 322
Okàlová, M. 215
Okerson, A. 175

Olsen, J. 113
Olszewski, L.J. 170
Olszewski, T. 102, 108, 331
Omar, L. 81
Omar Samsuri 245
Ong, K. 243
Oppenheim, C. 103, 112, 335
Orum, A. 103
Osif, B.A. 112
Osipova, I.P. 223
Osswald, A. 46, 105, 322
Owen, T. 104
Ozowa, V.N. 273
Pack, T. 280
Paesa, M. 141
Pagés Hernández, R. 138
Painter, J.D. 8
Palka, P. 335
Pallet, F. 81
Pallier, D. 101
Palmer, E.M. 279
Panyella, V. 30
Paoli Bolio, F.J. 135
Papp, I. 80, 82, 214
Parker, J. 84
Parr, E. 135
Parry, J. 330
Parusi, G. 217
Pasquignon, A. 51
Passet, J.E. 328
Pastine, M. 108, 325
Pateman, J. 80
Patterson, H. 331
Pearce, J. 161
Pelle, F. 101
Pelling, B.-M. 40
Pellisier, D. 262
Pelzer, N.L. 163
Perrault, A.H. 107
Perry, R. 329
Pessah, R. 262, 268
Phillips, A. 49
Phillips, J.S. 329
Phillips, S. 330
Piaczynska, M. 221
Pienaar, R.E. 81
Pifalo, V. 25, 213
Pilling, S. 107
Pingaud, B. 188
Pinion, C.F. 27

Pinkerton, B. 177
Pinson, J. 100
Pisa, M.G. 40, 43
Pita, M. 139
Pitkin, G.M. 107
Plaister, J. 80
Poll, R. 118
Poo, D.C.C. 169
Pool, J.W. 267
Pop, J.J.H. 85, 324
Popham, M. 304
Popma, J. 328
Popp, R. 163, 169
Poprady, G. 28, 31
Porter, L. 333
Pouillas, M.-T. 322
Poulain, M. 193, 194
Pountain, D. 304
Powell, A. 308
Powell, B. 267
Powell, J. 107, 301, 310
Powell, T. 165
Powledge, T. 89
Poynder, R. 265, 270, 278
Premsmit, P. 250
Prendergast, N.D. 267
Preston, B. 77
Price, S.G. 301
Price-Wilkin, J. 177, 311
Priestley, C. 262
Prins, H. 334
Proehl, K. 301
Pröhle, E. 141
Prokop, I. 220
Prosekova, S.N. 271
Przybyszewski, W. 206, 220
Quinn, D. 313
Quinn, D.B. 104
Quint, B. 114, 278
Raed, E. 138
Rainford, A. 266
Raitt, D. 104
Rajamani, S. 139
Ramachandran, R. 237, 238
Ramaiah, L.S. 325
Rannells, E. 272
Ransome, A. 135
Raptis, P. 165
Raschke, S.D. 269
Raseroka, H.K. 79, 86
Rast, E. 166

Raughley, C.S. 331
Raymond, S. 309
Reagor, M.A. 160
Redmond, M. 112
Rees, F. 116
Rees, J. 264
Reg, J. 336
Rehman, S.U. 120
Reid, E.O.F. 240, 244, 249
Reinhardt, A. 301, 302, 303
Reng, J. 262, 311
Renoult, D. 118, 190, 192, 197, 198
Rexa, D. 215
Rice, S.S. 261, 267
Richard, M. 52
Richards, A. 272
Richards, D.H. 85
Richards, P.S. 223
Richards, T. 327
Richer, S. 262
Ridley, M. 177
Roberts, B. 19
Roberts, J.K. 100
Roberts, N. 335
Robinson, B.M. 324
Robinson, S. 324
Robinson, W.H. 134, 136, 138, 139, 140, 142, 147
Robishaw, S.M. 267
Roboz, P. 219
Roda, J.-C. 118
Rodgers, D.L. 104
Roes, H. 115, 264, 274, 283, 307
Roesler, M. 302, 304
Rompas, J.P. 245
Ronai, I. 138
Rooks, D. 175
Rooney, J. 337
Rosca, E. 216
Rosenberg, D. 273
Rosenberg, V. 116
Rosenfeld, L.B. 173
Ross, R.E. 167
Roth, B.G. 267
Rothnie, L. 107
Rowley, J. 90, 114, 307, 332, 335
Royan, B. 305, 307, 308, 314

Rugaas, B. 32, 38
Runge, L.D. 322
Rupešová, M. 205
Russell, R. 135
Ryle, M. 137
Sa'ati, Y.M. 62
Sabaratnam, S. 250
Sadowska, J. 45
Sajjad ur Rehman 245
Salaba, A. 165
Salisbury, L. 117
Salmond, R. 162
Salomonsen, A. 36
Sanson, J. 51
Santos-Labourdette, M.C. 263
Sarria, A.M. 139
Sasse, M. 174
Sato, M. 325
Saunders, L.M. 103
Saunders, R. 168
Sauvageau, P. 62
Savige, D. 77
Schauder, D. 107, 111, 113, 262, 263, 265, 311
Scheppke, J. 79
Schick, R. 139, 141, 146, 147
Schiller, N. 118
Schimizzi, A.J. 161
Schlabach, M.L. 175
Schoen, A. 324
Schrader, J.M. 329
Schroeder, A. 282
Schulte-Nolke, P. 87
Schuman, P.G. 332
Schuneman, A. 167
Schwartz, C.A. 267
Scott, M. 62
Scott, P. 39
Scott, R.L. 118, 263
Segešová, L. 207
Seiden, P. 107
Sengstack, J. 301, 304
September, P.E. 81
Sercan, C.S. 167
Serov, V. 208
Sersikova, A. 209
Setiarso, B. 247
Sever, I. 336
Sexton, M. 38
Seymour, V.S. 167

Sha, V.T. 157
Shahar Banun Jaafar 239, 243, 248
Shahrozat Ibrahim 250
Shaikha Zakaria 243
Sharifah Naema Syed Mansor Al-Idrus 243
Sharr, F.A. 322
Shatberashvili, O.B. 205
Shaw, D. 175
Shawyer, J. 49
Shepherd, C. 135
Shepherd, M.A. 172
Sherayko, C.C. 168
Shipp, J. 265
Shongwe, N.F. 80
Shraiberg, Y. 45, 138, 142, 148
Shraiberg, Y.L. 271
Shreeves, E. 313
Silk, P. 135
Siman, P. 221
Simmons, D. 23, 58, 59, 272
Simmons, M. 85
Simmons, P. 306
Simon, N. 51
Simpson, E. 336
Singleton, A. 113
Sinnott, E. 172
Sirbu, M. 11
Siriwongworawat, S. 248
Sisson, L. 330
Siti Rodziah Othman 251
Skaliczki, J. 206
Skandera, B. 221
Skaradziński, B. 216
Skogmar, G. 110
Skuodyte, E. 80
Skvortsov, V.V. 221
Sližová, D. 220
Sloan, E. 175
Smale, C. 269
Smethurst, B. 114
Smita, D. 80, 84
Smith, A. 264
Smith, A.E. 24
Smith, A.W. 37
Smith, M.S. 299, 302
Smith, N.M. 308, 328
Smith, P. 115
Smith, R. 36, 168

Smith, S.J. 167
Smorch, T. 335
Snow, M. 104, 313
Snow, S. 312
Sojka, J. 206
Sol, P. del 272
Solyanik, A. 212
Sonnevend, P. 214
Sordylowa, B. 206, 208
Sosna, K. 138
Stäglich, D. 119
Stanton, D. 107
StClair, G. 323
Steffen, S.S. 269
Stein, F. 329
Stennett, R. 330
Stephens, A. 326
Stephens, D. 83, 326
Stephens, J.T. 266, 278
Sterling Folker, J. 88
Stiller, L. 53
Stocklova, A. 335
Stoker, D. 100
Stokes, R. 164
Stopforth, C. 119
Strandvik, T. 119
Stroud, G. 87
Studwell, W.E. 165, 166, 174
Stueart, R.D. 249
Sturges, P. 91, 273
Su, S.-F. 306
Subbotin, M.M. 219
Suchańková, A. 213
Sudarsono, B. 247
Suga, T. 272
Sulaiman, F. 242
Sulistyo-Basuki 250
Summann, F. 263
Summerhill, C.A. 263
Sumsion, J. 91, 100
Suslova, I.M. 220, 330
Sutton, B. 324
Svoboda, M. 45, 220, 221
Swain, L. 105, 262
Swart, I. 333
Swarte, J.L. 329
Sweeney, R.T. 331
Syliva, M. 108
Szántó, P. 210, 214
Szelle, B. 220

Szocki, J. 221
Szymanowski, W. 220, 221
Tait, F. 326
Takashima, A. 327
Tallim, P. 263, 264, 267, 270, 277, 278, 279
Tallin, P. 43
Tammekann, E.-M. 141
Tan, D. 242
Tan, M. 245
Tanfield, J. 139, 141
Tang, S. 56
Tarlit, R.Y. 251
Taylor, A.G. 104, 105, 174
Taylor, R. 80
Tedd, L. 107
Tedd, L.A. 306
Tehnzen, J. 264, 270, 279, 283
Teixeira, L. 312
Tenopir, C. 265, 267, 281
Teo, P. 236
Tereshchenko, S.S. 211, 217
Tereshin, V.I. 221
Thomas, B. 84
Thompson, K.S. 267
Thompson, P. 269
Thompson, T. 300
Thompson, V. 330
Tilson, Y. 326
Todd, O. 194
Todd, R.J. 162
Tolnai, G. 220
Tomlinson, J. 104
Tontyaporn, B. 245
Törnudd, E. 102
Torréns Valdés, R. 138
Torres Santo Domingo, N. 166
Tószegi, Zs. 219, 220, 221, 223
Trainor, J. 161
Trancygier, T. 220
Trask, M. 331
Tribble, J.E. 278
Trotter, J.E. 278
Trotter, R. 163
Truesdell, C.B. 116
Tsao, J.H. 167
Tseng, C.-C. 57, 58
Tsuda, M. 329

Tsuzuki, H. 329
Tuimoala, S. 58
Turner, F. 43
Turock, B. 86
Tuten, J.H. 110
Tyagi, K.G. 21
Tyerman, K. 325, 333
Tygar, J.D. 11
Tyulina, N.I. 221
Um, Y.A. 57
Ungár, T. 216
Urata, K. 272
Usherwood, R. 78, 86, 87
Vadász, Á. 219
Vajda, E. 219, 221
Vajda, K. 220
Vajda, M. 220
Valauskas, E.J. 262, 277
Vallejo, R.M. 250
Valm, T. 80
Van Brakel, P.A. 262, 263
Van Cuyck, A. 118
Van De Sompel, H. 310
Van der Werf, T. 44
Van der Werff, J. 266, 277
Van Dooren, B. 101
Van Drimmelen, W. 30, 32
Van House, N.A. 87
Van Trier, G. 30, 32
Varga, S. 220
Varlamova, S.F. 26
Vásárhelyi, P. 219
Vasi, J. 313
Vasilenko, G.I. 221
Veer, L. der 329
Verbeek, J. 79
Verbesey, J.R. 338
Verstraete, J. 88
Verwer, R. 78
Vestheim, G. 78
Vickers, S. 115
Vickers, S.C.J. 49
Vigurskiř, K.V. 218
Vintro i Castells, J. 139
Visser, D. 283
Vitiello, G. 27, 192, 193
Vontorčik, E. 208
Vroomans, M. 53
Waaijers, L. 282
Waddell, C. 100, 108
Wainwright, E. 17, 22, 349

Wainwright, J. 148
Wali, M.H. 60
Walker, A. 146, 162
Walker, G. 88
Walker, T.D. 323
Wall, R. 303
Wallace, P.M. 173
Wan, W. 17
Ward, M. 176
Wardaya, S.S. 244
Warlock, D.R. 113
Warner, B.F. 311
Warrick, Y.S. 160
Warwick, R.T. 335
Washington, N. 110
Waters, R.L. 79
Watjen, H.-J. 119
Watson, M. 107
Watt, I. 87
Wattananusitt, P. 55
Watters, C. 172
Wayner, P. 301, 303
Webber, S. 326
Weimer, K.H. 162
Weinberg, B.H. 163
Weiss, J.W. 327
Weiss, K.B. 169
Weller, M.S. 172
Wellhoff, M.-C. 51
Wells, A. 161, 164
Wells, M. 337
Westbrook, L. 90
Westell, M. 107
Westerman, M. 314
Westra, P.E. 60, 61
White, H.S. 109
White, W.D. 263
Whitney, G. 308, 311, 313
Whittaker, M. 114, 277
Widdiscombe, R.P. 114
Wiebe, V.G. 104
Wiegand, S.A. 322
Wielhorski, K. 313
Wiggins, R. 176
Wijasuriya, D.E.K. 272
Wilkins, W. 106, 174
Wille, N.E. 188
Williams, B. 115, 307
Williams, B.J.S. 263, 264, 270, 277, 278, 279, 280, 281, 282

Williams, E.B. 24
Williams, M. 302
Williams, P. 59
Williamson, M. 263, 330
Williamson, N.J. 46
Winkel-Schwartz, A. 102, 269
Winkler, B.J. 174
Winkworth, I.R. 119
Winstead, E.B. 336
Wisner, W.H. 104, 313, 323
Wisser, D. 198
Withnell, L.E. 269
Wojciechowska, A. 221, 327
Wolpert, A.J. 100
Wood, A. 115
Wood, D.N. 37, 42
Woodberry, E. 263
Woodhouse, S. 163
Woods, G. 100, 323
Woodward, H. 107, 265, 277, 278, 280, 336
Wool, G.J. 171
Woolfrey, L. 81
Wooliscroft, M. 116, 263, 278, 283
Wu, A.H. 165
Wu, J.Y.-T. 20
Wuest, R. 19, 46, 322
Xiao, Y. 163
Yaacob, R.A. 336
Yamaguchi, G. 78
Yanakieva, T. 205, 212
Yap, S.S.B. 243
Yastrebova, E. 220
Yee 161
Yitai, G. 272
Yoo, S. 267
Young, P.R. 262
Young, R. 337
Young, W.L. 27
Zainab Ibrahim 245
Zaiton Osman 239, 243
Zaitsev, V.G. 223
Zaitsev, V.N. 25, 26, 33, 45
Zalainé Kovács, É. 223
Zaluzhshaya, M. 45
Zarzębski, T. 221
Zeng, L. 167
Zijlstra, J. 9, 115, 281, 283
Zulu, S.F.C. 263